Mark L. Kleinman was an associate professor of history at the University of Wisconsin at Oshkosh. He is now living and working in Sacramento, California.

A World of Hope,
a World of Fear

A World of Hope, a World of Fear

Henry A. Wallace, Reinhold Niebuhr,
and American Liberalism

Mark L. Kleinman

Ohio State University Press
Columbus

Some material from chapter 2 was orginally published in "Searching for the 'Inner Light': The Development of Henry A. Wallace's Experimental Spiritualism," by Mark L. Kleinman, *The Annals of Iowa* 53 (Summer 1994): 195–218. Copyright © 1994 State Historical Society of Iowa. Used with the permission of the publisher.

Library of Congress Cataloging-in-Publication Data

Kleinman, Mark L.
  A world of hope, a world of fear : Henry A. Wallace, Reinhold Niebuhr, and American liberalism / Mark L. Kleinman.
     p. cm.
  Includes bibliographical references (p.   ) and index.
  ISBN 0-8142-0844-4 (alk. paper)
  1. Wallace, Henry Agard, 1888–1965—Political and social views.
2. Niebuhr, Reinhold, 1892–1971—Political and social views.
3. Liberalism—United States—History—20th century.   4. United States—Politics and government—20th century.   5. United States—Foreign relations—1945–1989.   6. Cold War.   I. Title.
E748.W23 K58   2000
320.51′3′097309045—dc21   99-050990

Text and jacket design by Daniel R. O'Dair Graphic Design.
Type set in Adobe Galliard by G & S Typesetters, Inc.
Printed by Thomson-Shore, Inc.

9 8 7 6 5 4 3 2 1

In this world there are only two tragedies. One is not getting what one wants, and the other is getting it.

—Oscar Wilde, *Lady Windermere's Fan*

Another such victory over the Romans, and we are undone.

—Plutarch, *Life of Pyrrhus*

Contents

Preface

In May 1952, at the height of the McCarthy era, playwright Lillian Hellman was called to testify before the House Committee on Un-American Activities (HUAC) regarding her alleged involvement with New York and Hollywood communists during the 1930s. Hellman, who may or may not have been an actual party member, was without question an ardent, longtime supporter of progressive social and political causes. She had cultivated an elegantly radical public persona. Before and during her testimony she was skillfully counseled by a young liberal lawyer named Joseph Rauh, who would go on to have a distinguished career as a civil liberties and civil rights attorney. It was an ironic pairing, Hellman with her chic fellow traveler's image defended by Rauh, who was an influential member and eventually national chairman of the well-known and staunchly anticommunist liberal organization, Americans for Democratic Action. The pairing symbolized the complex dynamic between those American liberals who were willing to consider cooperation with communists and those who opposed it categorically. In her 1976 memoir of the events surrounding her HUAC testimony, Hellman suggested a tragic outcome of that dynamic. She was writing of a familiar cohort of liberal journalists and commentators, among whom she might have included her lawyer, Rauh. Hellman reckoned that of those many "thoughtful and distinguished" individuals, none had even by the mid-1970s "yet found it a part of conscience to admit that their Cold War anti-Communism was perverted, possibly against their wishes," into much that they eventually came to oppose, ranging from the Vietnam war to the presidency of Richard Nixon.[1]

Hellman was touching on a larger cold war truth: the connection between what could be termed an unconscious "surrender" by American liberals in years immediately following World War II and the subsequent course of U.S. politics and foreign policy.

The effects of that surrender were evident more than a generation later, in the 1988 U.S. presidential campaign, when Republican presidential candidate George Bush invoked the phrase "card carrying member" regarding Democratic candidate Michael Dukakis's membership in the mainstream American Civil Liberties Union, knowing that those words would evoke in older voters' minds memories of the days when the phrase was followed by the words "of the Communist Party." Remarkably, Dukakis failed to respond to Bush's tactic. During the campaign even the word *liberal* came under fire, as if liberalism were not a major component of the modern American political tradition but instead a marginal and vaguely subversive extreme. This suspicion of liberalism has persisted into the 1990s, with liberal leaders rarely willing to defend progressive policies on their own merits, instead attempting to dilute or transmogrify them into conservative ones. Yet as the Hellman anecdote implies, this inability of American liberalism to stand its ground is not a recent development. It did not issue from the Republican revolution of the 1980s and 1990s and it actually predated Hellman's experience before HUAC in 1952. In fact it emerged in the late 1940s during the first years of the cold war, arising out of liberal debates over international affairs.

Five and a half years before Hellman's congressional testimony, in fall 1946, the Protestant theologian and liberal political commentator Reinhold Niebuhr wrote an article that Henry Luce published in the October 21 issue of *Life* magazine. Probably the most widely read article of Niebuhr's hugely prolific career, "The Fight for Germany" was a watershed in American cold war culture.[2] By 1946 Niebuhr was already one of the nation's foremost commentators on international affairs. His widely published analyses were highly regarded by much of the "attentive public" as well as by individuals within policy-making circles.[3] A central theme of Niebuhr's article was a vehement attack on another American liberal prominent in the ongoing national discussion of foreign relations, Henry Agard Wallace, who had recently and controversially been compelled to resign from his post as secretary of commerce in the administration of President Harry S. Truman. Niebuhr made clear that it was not Wallace's outlook on domestic policy he opposed. Indeed, Niebuhr insisted, he actually belonged to Wallace's "school of thought in domestic politics."[4] This remark expressed Niebuhr's own well-known advocacy of the progressive social and economic reforms embodied in the New Deal. Wallace—first as secretary of agriculture, then as vice president, and finally as secretary of commerce—had become second in the public mind only to Franklin D. Roosevelt as champion of the New Deal's policies.[5] What Niebuhr assailed Wallace for was his perspective on international relations, specifically those between the Soviet Union and the United States, as expressed in a speech Wallace had given in September at a progressive political rally at Madison Square Garden in New York City. The speech engendered great controversy, within both the administration and the national press. The position that Wallace took—critical of the United States as well as Russia and calling for a greater degree of tolerance and cooperation in U.S. policy toward the Soviets—clearly opposed the hard line that Secretary of State James Byrnes was repeatedly articulating while in Europe for a meeting of foreign ministers. Following Byrnes's irate protest, Truman demanded Wallace's resignation from the cabinet.[6]

Invoking the already assimilated gospel of the "Munich analog," Niebuhr declared that Wallace's line of reasoning regarding Russia was "dangerous because it is based upon illusions similar to those . . . of another decade in regard to Nazism" and could initiate the same "fateful procedure" that led to world war in 1939.[7] In constructing his attack on Wallace as he did, Niebuhr articulated the fundamental tenets of "cold war liberalism": strong support for progressive domestic reform in combination with vehement opposition to communism both at home and abroad, with that opposition justified in great part by the logic of Munich. Moreover, because of its focus on Wallace, Niebuhr's article marked a decisive split—or the culmination of a split—in liberal ranks in the United States, what Walter LaFeber has termed the "Wallace-Niebuhr division."[8] On one side of the division stood cold war liberals like Niebuhr and his associates in organizations such as the Union for Democratic Action (and, later, Americans for Democratic Action). On the other side stood figures like Wallace and the members of the various liberal political action committees that eventually formed the Progressive Party in 1948. I have termed such individuals "popular front" liberals, intentionally invoking the tradition of the European "Popular Front" of the interwar era. It seems an apt invocation, since Wallace and his associates, in their advocacy of the same sort of domestic reform championed by the cold war liberals, were, like the liberals of the original Popular Front, willing to cooperate with communists or at least were not immediately troubled by the possibility of such cooperation.[9] This division in the liberal community proved crucial both to the development of the American contribution to the cold war as well as to American domestic politics during the latter half of the twentieth century.

When Wallace resigned from Truman's cabinet in 1946, the liberal point of view advocating a search for common ground with the Soviet Union was already moribund. Wallace's crushing defeat in 1948 as the Progressive Party's presidential candidate marked its death. From that time on there was no longer any influential political position from which to criticize the nation's unyielding stance toward the Soviet Union.[10] To do so was to risk being regarded as a naïf at best, certainly a fool and unwitting accomplice or, more likely as time went on, a subversive and traitor. Liberals with such critical inclinations buried them, perhaps even forgot them, and in the process contributed to the advent of the "cold war consensus." It is possible, however, that what has been viewed as a consensus, implying full and open debate over alternatives, was in reality the death-knell of debate and, ultimately, of reflection.

By the late 1940s discussion of international relations in the United States was already quite constrained conceptually. That constraint led not all that indirectly by 1950 to Senator Joseph McCarthy's infamous national debut in Wheeling, West Virginia, as well as to Korea and, eventually, to Vietnam.[11] The longer American liberals accepted this constraint, the more difficult it became for them to transcend it, until the tragedy of the nation's experience in Vietnam unfolded on the domestic stage in the 1960s. During the mid-1960s, as the war in Vietnam became a dominant influence in American culture, some Americans felt compelled for the first time in twenty years to examine the assumptions underlying their nation's foreign policy, assumptions that had driven the global pursuit of U.S. aims and assertion of American values.

Yet even Vietnam's impact on American thinking seems to have been only transitory. As the Hellman anecdote implies, the choices made by anticommunist liberals in the 1940s unintentionally contributed to the evolution of policies that controverted the very values such individuals championed. Those choices also helped develop a political habit, as it were, of reflexive submission by liberals to conservative imperatives.[12] It is a habit that persists into the present in American political culture, beyond the end of the cold war that engendered it, as the Bush-Dukakis case suggests. During the cold war it appeared in liberal acceptance, and often creation, of U.S. foreign policies that supported oppressive regimes from Southeast Asia to Latin America to the Middle East, all justified by the logic of opposing communism. Even the Persian Gulf War, coming after the cold war's end, attested to the persistent power of the Munich analog.

As communist regimes around the world fell in the recent past— one is quite tempted to say "like dominoes"—many Americans assumed that such collapses resulted only from the policies pursued by American administrations throughout the postwar years rather than from the profound and inherent weaknesses of the regimes themselves. Such assumptions are a product of the same narrow conceptualization of the world that evolved in America during the first years after World War II. That worldview was predicated on the belief that with communism and the Soviet Union there could be no arenas of cooperation, only absolute opposition. Indeed, the metaphors of American cold war foreign policy—George Kennan's "containment," the Truman Doctrine's "rotten apples," and Dwight Eisenhower's "dominoes"—all implied that the Soviet Union was not another nation to be negotiated with but rather a manifestation of a kind of global plague requiring the quarantine of its victims to protect the "free world" until the infection was eradicated. This was less diplomacy than an ideological variation on bacterial warfare. Yet its implications were accepted with little reflection and even less criticism by cold war liberals. In other words, part of what

America lost was the vitality of any genuine opposition in its politics and foreign policy. At the very least this has meant the profound impoverishment of American political culture; it has doubtless contributed as well to the amplification of a towering insensitivity—as well as inefficiency—in foreign policy. In the context of the atomic age, it has also put the nation and the world at tremendous risk.[13]

Saying this does not imply the belief that the United States should have "surrendered" to communism or the Soviet Union, as some seem to think it does. In 1993, for instance, John Lewis Gaddis, a renowned historian of U.S. foreign relations, asserted that the "revisionist" analysis of American cold war foreign policy, effectively beginning with William Appleman Williams's 1959 book, *The Tragedy of American Diplomacy,* failed to take due account of the actual brutality of Stalin and the Soviet regime in its extensive critique of U.S. policy. The irony of Gaddis's attack on revisionism lay in its implicit replication of the Manichaean worldview of cold war era American political culture, in its complete acceptance of the Munich analog—including that principle's confusion of compromise with capitulation—and its suggestion that one had no business criticizing the policies of the United States if one did not also focus explicitly on the cruel realities of the Soviet state. The ultimate implication of Gaddis's perspective was of intellectual surrender: that writing critically of American foreign policy somehow validated the politics and foreign policy of the Soviet Union.[14]

In a related sense much recent scholarship, in some instances based upon newly opened Eastern bloc archives, attempts to shed light on various aspects of the question of communist subversion within the United States. Several books, for example, argue for the existence of a much wider communist effort at espionage and subversion than previously acknowledged. The overarching thesis of this historiography seems to be that since Soviet activities within America are now "proven," then revisionist critiques of domestic anticommunism have been rendered illegitimate. In fact, all of these studies have received extensive and detailed criticism, generally concluding that these authors have read much more into the new documents than is really there. In other words, while there is no question of the existence of Soviet espionage, as well as subversion on the part of American communists, it still is in no way clear that the extent of either ever constituted a serious threat to the nation's security, the only imaginable basis for renouncing a critical analysis of U.S. politics and policy making. In any case, none of these works succeeds in justifying their implied resurrection of the "either/or" construction of 1940s and 1950s American political culture, which stipulated that one was either altogether anticommunist and anti-Soviet or one was a subversive or dupe.[15]

The threat that the legacies of cold war thinking present the United States has changed little over time. The threat is not primarily or even necessarily that, by precluding the possibility of moderation toward the Soviet Union, such thinking actually may have postponed the events which occurred in communist countries since the late 1980s— although that might indeed be the case. The greater danger is that the self-imposed critical constraint of the cold war liberals made it possible for Americans and their leaders to go on believing that America really did control world events during the postwar era, that this actually was, as Henry Luce boldly declared, the "American Century." If individuals like Henry A. Wallace, who called for moderation and sought to widen the terms of debate, were wrong in hoping that any degree of international harmony was attainable after 1945, then they should have had the chance to be proven so. In the end we are left with the very real possibility that the Soviets were going to remain intransigent despite American efforts and ultimately would pick their own moment for transforming their society. If this is true, then the United States may have wasted many lives—American and non-American—and much treasure in self-delusion. Perhaps America's greatest loss in the cold war was in depriving itself of the freedom to find out if its worst fears were valid. The ultimate effect of that self-deprivation was the erosion of the very intellectual and political freedoms that American politics and policy ostensibly sought to preserve. This truly was a perversion of liberal intentions. In the long run it prevented many Americans from apprehending even the "lessons" of their history, leaving them only with its illusions.

Finishing this book took far longer than I ever anticipated. Indeed, I sometimes wonder if I would have begun the process had I known how long it would last. Yet despite the years and the difficulty of bringing it to completion, this project at times gave me great pleasure as well. Above all it brought me into contact with many remarkable, insightful, and decent people. Together they influenced this process profoundly, although I suppose the usual disclaimer applies: the final decisions regarding what to include or exclude were mine. Where I got it right I owe tremendous debts; the mistakes I must claim alone. My gratitude stands in any case.

Joyce Appleby and Bart Bernstein helped me conceptualize this project from the beginning and followed its course closely, reading everything and giving helpful and encouraging counsel throughout. Paul Boyer became interested in the book during the last several years I was working on it and has read and criticized at least one draft of every chapter, and in several cases more. Beyond their astute scholarly input, I have treasured my friendship with these three individuals.

Barbara Hanrahan, former director of the Ohio State University Press, deserves special thanks for her wonderfully enthusiastic reception of the manuscript (and its author) as well as for the remarkably efficient manner in which she moved it from the status of prospect to that of forthcoming publication. I am also grateful to Ruth Melville, managing editor at OSU Press, for her professionalism and good humor. Copy editor Tonia Payne rescued me from numerous syntactical miscues (among other things).

Many people have read parts of this manuscript (in various forms) or have discussed its ideas with me at length. Their insights and criticisms have only improved the final product. They include Steve Haber, Bill Deverell, Michael Bernstein, Robert Marc Friedman, Michael Parrish, David Gutierrez, Sandy Lakoff, Larry Simon, Richard Kirkendell, Susie Porter, Geoff Smith, J. Samuel Walker, Chuck Nathanson, Marvin Bergman, Noel Carroll, Howard Brick, John Pettegrew, Kate Boyer, Mark Hineline, Jerry Shenk, Gordon Hutner, Mary Yeager, Ed Linenthal, Andrew O'Shaughnessy, Virginia Crane, Werner Braatz, Franca Baricelli, Lane Earns, Kim Rivers, and Sally McKee. (My apologies to anyone I have forgotten.) I also want to express my gratitude to the thousands of students I have taught—both at the University of California, San Diego, and at the University of Wisconsin, Oshkosh—who have always compelled me to clarify my ideas.

I wish to acknowledge the University of California's Institute on Global Conflict and Cooperation for its generous support of this study in its earliest stages, as well as the Faculty Development Board of the University of Wisconsin, Oshkosh, for several years of research grants that were crucial to the book's completion. Paul Boyer gets a second round of thanks as director of the Institute for Research in the Humanities at the University of Wisconsin, Madison, where I was fortunate enough to spend a superb year—in a wonderfully stimulating and collegial atmosphere—while completing the writing and revision of the manuscript.

In the selfless manner that characterizes their profession, many archivists and librarians gave freely and extensively of their expertise over the years, contributing enormously to this project's completion. I particularly want to thank those at the Franklin Delano Roosevelt Library, the Library of Congress, the National Archives, the State Historical Society of Wisconsin, and, especially, Earl Rogers and his staff in Special Collections at the University of Iowa Libraries. Thanks also to Erin Czech of UW Oshkosh's Polk Library.

Ivan McGuire, Dirk Hansen, Kathie Nirschl, and Tom Smith have given me the gift of their friendship in so many ways and for so many years that something of their souls must have made its way into the words I have written. I hope I have done well by them.

Finally, I dedicate this book to my parents, Abram and Freda Kleinman, whose constancy and love have helped sustain me over the years. Their pride and pleasure in the successful conclusion of this endeavor remain a source of great joy to me.

PART 1

1

Introduction

———◆———

THE "WALLACE-NIEBUHR division" did not arise instantaneously
in 1946. It emerged out of inchoate differences evolving within the
American liberal community throughout World War II, primarily regarding international affairs. Less than a year after the United States'
entry into the war, Wallace and Niebuhr themselves had already articulated somewhat conflicting positions in the nascent liberal dispute over
the nature of the postwar world and America's role in it, that is, over
American "internationalism." [1] On one side of this dispute stood those
liberals, like Wallace, whose vision included hopes for continued cooperation between the Soviet Union and the United States, an end
to international aggression, and perhaps even the attainment of world
government. Opposed to, or rather critical of, this position were individuals, such as Niebuhr, who clearly favored an internationalist foreign
policy but questioned the likelihood of the immediate or near-term
global cooperation that their more optimistic fellow liberals expected.
They called instead for a thoroughly skeptical, tough outlook in the
formulation of American foreign policy, particularly toward the Soviet
Union. During the first year and a half after the war's end these groups
hardened into two distinct factions: "cold war" and "popular front"
liberals.

By late 1946 Niebuhr and Wallace personified, respectively, the cold
war (or anticommunist) liberal and popular front liberal camps within
the larger universe of American liberalism. There is no evidence that the
two men knew each other at all prior to World War II, although it is
likely that they knew of each other. Yet both men wielded a great deal

3

of influence in various sectors of the attentive public before, during, and after World War II, and both sought to lead the debate on postwar foreign policy. Niebuhr, a second-generation German-American, was America's preeminent Protestant theologian and an internationally respected commentator on U.S. politics and foreign relations. In addition, he is also numbered among the founders—along with Hans Morgenthau, George Kennan, and Walter Lippmann—of the so-called realist analysis of international relations that developed in the United States.[2] Wallace was the heir of an Iowa agrarian dynasty, many generations American, and powerful in both farm publishing and farm-bloc politics. FDR's secretary of agriculture from 1933 until he became vice president in 1940, Wallace was closely identified with the New Deal. His crusade for the "Century of the Common Man" culminated in a failed third-party run at the presidency in 1948, leaving him tainted as an apparent dupe of the Communist Party. Well before that, however, Wallace personified the ideal of international cooperation that eventually provided the target for Niebuhr's critique of global affairs.

If the opposition of cold war and popular front liberals, personified by Niebuhr and Wallace, influenced the course of postwar American politics and foreign policy, and so the course of the cold war, then understanding the emergence of that opposition is of fundamental importance. Illuminating the roots—common and divergent, complementary and conflicting—of the outlooks that these two men held by 1946 is the first task of this book. They were roots that reached back to the first decades of the twentieth century. By the 1910s the United States was completing the rapid, dislocating transformation into a modern industrial nation that began during the previous half century. This transition induced in many Americans an alienation that the ravages of the Great Depression only magnified. Historians from Richard Hofstadter to Jackson Lears have described how the rise of modern civilization created profound existential anxieties in many Americans around the turn of the century.[3] The repercussions of this era of cultural metamorphosis continued to exert a powerful influence on the outlook of Americans who, like Wallace and Niebuhr, were in their middle or late years by the 1940s. Connected to, as well as concurrent with, this social transition was the rise of the United States to world power. America stepped onto the world stage for the first time in a significant way in World War I. World War II only amplified, albeit hugely, this change in national stature. For many Americans this development was just as disturbing as the advent of industrialization. American responses, in both foreign and domestic realms, to this sort of disorientation were to a great extent attempts to reassert old values in new forms, and sometimes in not such new forms.

That the transformation from an agrarian to an industrial culture was of signal importance to the course of modern American history has not gone unnoticed. It very much informs the literature on domestic social, cultural, and political history. With few exceptions, however, the impact of this transition on the way Americans thought about international relations, especially in later decades of the twentieth century, has not been examined.[4] Both Wallace and Niebuhr were of the generation of Americans that came to maturity in the midst of this turbulent era, and both were fundamentally shaped by it. They were part of a wider public discussion, at times becoming topics in themselves. For this reason a study juxtaposing their respective intellectual and personal odysseys is quite valuable. It will enable us to understand how the development of modern urban-industrial culture contributed both to American liberal thinking about post–World War II foreign affairs and, by implication, to the formulation of foreign policy. More specifically, such an inquiry will illuminate the origins of the division that emerged in American liberal ranks during the 1940s, which affected not only the genesis of the U.S. foreign policy that informed the cold war but also the history of American domestic politics during subsequent decades.

In addition, this analysis will demonstrate that aspects of American culture that do not at first consideration—or even second—appear clearly connected to world affairs were often the ones that exerted the greatest influence on the formation of perceptions of those affairs. Thinking about international relations was, and is, far more than just a product of prior thinking about international relations. It derives from the entire cultural experience and is as much an artifact of that experience as, say, literature or art. The respective assessments made of global matters by Wallace and Niebuhr were grounded in the very terms in which each man conceptualized both America's transformation into a modern industrial society and the profound dilemmas issuing from that transformation. Niebuhr's cold war liberalism and Wallace's popular front liberalism were products of their individual backgrounds, of their own histories in the context of American history. Even when considering their temperamental differences, the division between them can be rendered in terms of cultural history: roughly as an opposition between Wallace's progressivist optimism and Niebuhr's proto-postmodernist skepticism.

Not surprisingly, since the outlooks of these two men were grounded in their individual pasts, their commentaries remained tied to those pasts. This meant, among other things, that Niebuhr and Wallace often were not writing about the same issues and events, and that even when they were, each might weigh a particular topic quite differently. This was especially true prior to World War II. If one runs through a list of the "major" international events before December 1941, one often will find quite a disparity between the respective levels of attention devoted by Niebuhr and Wallace to any particular episode. Niebuhr commented at some length on virtually all the occurrences that come to mind. In marked contrast, Wallace tended to focus on those questions and developments directly related to international economic relations and especially the aspects of those relations that bore in some manner on the well-being of American agriculture. Nevertheless, part 1 of this study, covering the years 1915 to 1942, portrays the evolution of two parallel and rather complementary liberal commentaries on society, politics, economics, and foreign policy. Until the mid-1940s these two men thought very much alike. Although after those years they came into opposition, it would be an exaggeration to stress too much a foreshadowing of that conflict early on.

In the first decades of their careers both Wallace and Niebuhr partook in what was arguably the main project of many American culture critics of the early twentieth century, liberal or otherwise. As Richard Pells has shown, during the Progressive Era, the interwar era, and the Depression numerous social thinkers in the United States were trying to determine the values by which men and women should direct their lives in the modern urban-industrial civilization in which they found themselves.[5] Often these commentators made use of traditional ideals, in some cases attempting to apply them directly, as if to draw American society back in time. In other cases they attempted to transform these ideals into new, modernized guides for existence in a high-speed technological world. Notions like "cooperation," which Wallace so staunchly championed, were advocated during the first two decades of the century by writers such as Herbert Croly of the *New Republic,* who called for the establishment of an "organic" society that would transcend the political and economic, a society in which "individuals and groups harmoniously interacted." During the 1920s other writers, including Lewis Mumford, Van Wyck Brooks, and Harold Stearns put forth similar perspectives. In the 1930s these commentators were joined by groups like the Agrarians, who articulated several visions for reforming American society by grounding it in southern rural values.[6]

In this context Wallace watched with despair the decline of American rural culture in the face of the rapid industrialization of the early twentieth century. During the 1920s he crusaded for the preservation of rural communities and the values associated with them because he saw them threatened by the changes taking place in American society. A great part of his crusade fixed upon what he viewed as a necessity: the establishment of a cooperative farm culture in the United States. He championed ideas and programs that he believed would foster a sense of community. In the late 1920s he began to apply this central principle to new visions of, first, a cooperative national civilization and, ultimately, a cooperative international community. By the early 1930s his commentary on foreign affairs revolved around concepts of community, sharing, and above all an internationalized version of the old agrarian ethic of "cooperation." To the extent that in the 1930s and early 1940s Wallace extrapolated his vision for the preservation of Midwestern American rural life as a model for global affairs, it could be said that his thinking about those affairs was not so much American liberalism writ internationally as international relations writ locally.

In analogous fashion Niebuhr's social and political criticism in the 1920s focused on the individual's growing sense of dislocation in the midst of modern urban-industrial civilization. Because of this, Niebuhr's evaluation of international relations from the late twenties onward maintained a persistent concern with the potential for different social systems to mitigate such alienation. Despite the flaws that he noted in American culture, Niebuhr ultimately came to believe it still had greater potential than any alternative for ministering to the spiritual needs of men and women adrift in a technological world. This view was integral to much of his commentary, eventually becoming a central component of his criticism of the Soviet Union. Although Marxism explicitly addressed questions of social equality that were crucial in Niebuhr's mind, its solutions—at least as they evolved in Russia—were philosophically mechanistic in his view, and thus impersonal. By 1942 Niebuhr believed that American society, despite its inherent inequities, held greater promise for alleviating the disaffection created by modern industrial civilization than did Soviet Russia's enforced social equality, which by that time he considered both artificial and alienating.

Niebuhr's commentary during the 1920s and 1930s insisted, in a manner untypical of most American political discourse, on the complexity of the human condition. This insight was manifested in Niebuhr's judgment that no value system could relieve completely the dilemmas of modern life. No single vision could ever be a panacea. Indeed, instead of a sometimes overly simplistic vision for the future such as Wallace put forth, Niebuhr's attack on unsophisticated, mechanistic thinking effectively became something of an anti-vision. All prescriptions for social, economic, and political salvation, Niebuhr repeatedly argued, fell short of their goals, so expectations for reform should always be limited. He made this point even regarding philosophies he shared and institutions he was part of. Niebuhr criticized the ideas he adhered to as well as those he rejected. He was at his most incisive, and most characteristically ironic, as a critic working from the inside out: a liberal criticizing liberalism, a Protestant criticizing Protestantism, an American criticizing America.

In the 1920s, for instance, while the minister of a Protestant church in the thoroughly industrialized city of Detroit, Niebuhr suggested that Protestantism might do well to examine the mystery-laden rituals and liturgies of Catholicism as models of spiritual means for helping to ease the widespread social disaffection he perceived all around. This sort of logic was mirrored in Niebuhr's social and political analyses and in his tendency to draw on strains of political thought other than liberalism, including Marxism, as grounding for his liberal critique of liberal think-ing. His style of argumentation, including the real insight of his de-mand for the recognition of the complex nature of human affairs, gave Niebuhr's commentaries a powerful ring of truth, especially since they were often effectively self-criticisms. This construction was crucial to Niebuhr's commentary in that it underscored his contention that no particular social system could be entirely successful in alleviating the existential pain borne by the individual in modern civilization.

One might say, then, that Wallace most represented those culture critics who aimed to revise the old values of small-town, rural America in such a manner as to render them valid in the modern world (a manner that included, eventually and ironically, Wallace's wholehearted accep-tance of technology and "progress"). Niebuhr, not quite conversely, rejected all liberal panaceas, even as he argued for progressive and Chris-tian values. It was a rejection that can even seem postmodern in its criti-cal self-reflection, and I argue that it had the effect of undermining much that Niebuhr himself would have termed valuable in perspectives such as Wallace's.

Henry A. Wallace is usually remembered for his greatest failure, as a third-party candidate for the presidency in 1948 on the communism-tainted Progressive Party ticket. Yet during the three decades prior to the 1948 campaign, Wallace had several highly successful public careers. In the 1910s and 1920s he was a nationally respected agricultural sci-entist, farm editor, and Midwestern agrarian spokesman. During the 1930s, as Franklin Roosevelt's innovative and effective secretary of agriculture, Wallace was identified more in the public mind with the reforms of the New Deal than anyone save Roosevelt himself. During World War II, as vice president, Wallace was internationally renowned as the great American champion of the "Century of the Common Man." As late as June 1946 he was ranked in polls as one of the "most admired" men in the United States.[7] One suspects that had he not ended his public career as the Progressive Party's presidential candidate in 1948, Wallace's historical reputation would be far more laudatory.

Part 2 of this study is concerned specifically with the emergent split in the liberal community during the mid-1940s, ultimately issuing in the battle over Wallace's 1948 presidential candidacy. That candidacy issued from Wallace's notorious opposition to Harry S. Truman's hard-line foreign policy toward the Soviet Union, for which he was forced to resign the office of secretary of commerce in 1946. Wallace's disillusionment with both the domestic and foreign policies of the Truman administration only increased during the following year, leading him to his quixotic political crusade of 1948. During the 1948 campaign Wallace was perceived by many, including Niebuhr, as little more than a naive figurehead for the communists who allegedly ran the Progressive Party. Yet, as this study makes clear, in 1948 Wallace continued to advocate virtually all of the same issues and ideals he had stood for throughout the years of depression and war, issues and ideals for which American liberals had long respected him. The impact upon his reputation of the dismal failure of his presidential campaign in 1948 was in this sense a terrifically unwarranted, even tragic ending to a productive and honorable public career that had spanned well over a generation of American history.

This turn of events in Wallace's life—a career dominated by effectiveness and accolades but ending in ignominy—has two immediate and connected implications for this study, beyond the possibility of righting a historical (and historiographical) wrong. The first is a need to explain why it was, and has to a great extent remained, so easy to denigrate Wallace's reputation. There are several likely reasons. A central one was Wallace's personality, which did not readily inspire either enthusiasm or loyalty, certainly not in the manner of a Franklin Roosevelt. Individuals who knew him and commentators who wrote about him during his career often characterized him in terms such as "awkward" or "distant." His colleagues in government in the 1930s and 1940s often described him in mixed terms. Secretary of State Cordell Hull thus could compliment Wallace as "extremely energetic" and yet criticize his inclination to "explore new theories" with such abandon as to create embarrassment and political difficulties for the Roosevelt administration. Similarly, Treasury Secretary Henry Morgenthau could characterize Wallace positively as a "Yankee businessman with . . . horse sense" in one context, yet in another as "stubborn, often disingenuous, . . . something of a dreamer, even a mystic." Harold Ickes, another

Wallace colleague in the New Deal administration, with whom Wallace had a frequently contentious relationship, at one time described Wallace as "too aloof," insisting that people felt "they could not get close to him," that he "talked to them from afar." Even closer associates, subordinates within the Department of Agriculture for example, felt that they never got to know the real Wallace, "never met his mind," that there was "always something about him that you [didn't] quite understand."[8] At times, at least in his correspondence, Wallace could even appear emotionally distant from members of his immediate family.[9]

Such remarks lend themselves to speculation that Wallace ultimately failed at politics because he never was a politician by nature. It is a speculation that, while not altogether true, is again borne out by the assessments of familiar contemporaries. Certainly Wallace learned many of the techniques of politics. During both the 1940 and 1944 presidential campaigns he proved himself a fairly canny and tenacious campaigner. Yet he entered public office in 1933 as an appointed expert and only ran for office twice, in 1940 and 1948 (in 1944 he campaigned for the Roosevelt-Truman ticket). Wallace never seemed to become a politician in his essence, particularly in terms of interpersonal skills and public relations. Thus one close associate could comment on Wallace's inclination against politicking for his own advancement, his lack of political expertise generally, his unconcern with his own image, and his fundamentally nonpolitical nature.[10]

Mixed or outright negative recollections of Wallace were augmented, as we will see, by his relatively poor relations with the press throughout his career. Journalists frequently misrepresented, often with great sarcasm, Wallace's eccentricities as well as his admittedly oversimplified and sometimes obscure references and metaphors. Such negative journalistic portraits were even perpetuated in some cases by historians. For example, in his multivolume history of the Great Depression and the New Deal, Arthur Schlesinger Jr.—a founding member of Americans for Democratic Action and a central figure in that organization's attack on Wallace in 1948—borrowed from right-wing columnist Westbrook Pegler in describing Wallace as a "spiritual window-shopper" who sought the means for joining "together the two halves of his own personality." Even sympathetic historians have characterized Wallace as "introverted and self-defensive" in his personal relationships, an individual difficult to know and, by implication, to feel sympathy toward.[11]

As several of the above examples suggest, derogatory images of Wallace were often grounded in rumors of his actual spiritualistic endeavors, which I examine at length in chapter 2. These images were exacerbated during the 1948 presidential campaign by widespread assertions that Wallace was a starry-eyed dupe of the Communist Party and later by the general cultural climate of the early cold war and McCarthy eras. Such assessments of Wallace were often taken as evidence of his intellectual inconsistency and helped undermine the credibility of policies he advocated. By the late 1960s and 1970s, in the context of wide-ranging criticisms of American society and culture, evaluations of Wallace improved. Various writers noted his contributions to American political culture; some insisted that Wallace was a political thinker far ahead of his time.[12] Yet in many of these works the question of Wallace's spiritualism, so damning in the minds of earlier critics, was either sidestepped or not explored to its fullest.[13] For example, although Norman D. Markowitz clearly sensed the influence of Wallace's spiritualism on his social and political philosophy, he limited his discussion primarily to an extensive and illuminating appendix on Wallace's connection with the émigré Russian mystic, Nicholas Roerich.[14] Such lacunae rendered even these more favorable treatments of Wallace incomplete, presenting as they did only a truncated view of the spiritualistic pursuits that formed an important part of the framework of his early social, political, and internationalist commentaries. It has only been in the last several years that historians have finally engaged this problematic aspect of Wallace's personality directly, making clear its influence upon his political philosophy and perhaps, by so doing, making it possible to finally and fully examine his political and cultural commentary.[15]

Addressing the question of why Wallace was so easily dismissed, politically and historically, after 1948 leads us to consider the second implication for this book of what I have termed the tragic culmination of Wallace's career. It is the implicit critical inclination of this study in favor of Wallace and the popular front liberals. In part I suspect this is an unavoidable trait in a work explicitly seeking to rescue a subject from relative historical and historiographical obscurity. Yet I am categorically not engaged in an attempt to beatify Wallace and his associates, nor even to suggest, as have others, that he was a man ahead of his time, whatever that might mean. Indeed, I would argue that both Wallace and Niebuhr, however exceptional they may have been, were Americans altogether of their historical era. They both exhibited, for example, a powerful, often unconscious American nationalism that, particularly in Wallace's case, could shade into a sort of cultural imperialism. And if Niebuhr could be too critical, too skeptical at times, Wallace was perfectly capable of projecting an overly simplistic, romanticized vision of his nation's and the world's futures. Both men had blinders on, obscuring aspects of reality. The conventional view of Niebuhr as the realist and Wallace as the dewy-eyed idealist misses this point. If I present a more critical view of Niebuhr and the cold war liberals, particularly in part 2, I do not mean to imply agreement with the positions of the popular fronters in any given case.

I am interested, rather, in demonstrating, among other things, how the actions taken by the anticommunist liberals contributed, often inadvertently and thus ironically, to a momentum of ideas and events that tended to degrade the very values they championed. There was much to criticize about Wallace and the popular fronters' positions, both in content and presentation. In this sense it is clear that both sides of the liberal split had serious failings. Nevertheless, it is my contention that there were many valid aspects to the popular front liberal commentary that deserved a much fuller and longer discussion than they ultimately received. Since that did not occur, and since this book is attempting to explain why, and since I also argue that the actions of the cold war liberals contributed mightily to that outcome, this study cannot help but be more critical of the cold war liberals, even though I find much of transcendent value in their outlook. In the end, if this study contributes to our understanding of American cold war political culture, it will do so not by insisting that the thought and actions of some American liberals were wrong but rather by asking how American liberals thought, period: by asking what constituted reality for these two groups and how, in a broader sense, they could perceive situations in such different ways despite so many shared assumptions.

Wallace's early background was characterized by continuities, several of which not only foreshadowed his later public career but eventually informed his social and political commentary as well. His grandfather, "Uncle Henry" Wallace, the patriarch of the "dynasty," had gone to Iowa from Pennsylvania in 1877 as a progressive minister in the United Presbyterian Church. Although he left the ministry for reasons of health, taking up farming as well as, eventually, journalism, his religious beliefs continued to have a profound effect upon his life. In later years Henry A. Wallace spoke of his mother's great influence in his life. It was from her he claimed to have gained much of his great love for plants. Wallace's most recent biographers also suggest that it was from May Brodhead Wallace that he absorbed a rather "austere moral code" that probably informed his personal awkwardness and distance.[16] Yet it is also clear that Wallace absorbed much from Uncle Henry as well. Because of the extraordinary closeness between grandfather and grandson, the former's well developed and frequently articulated religious beliefs deeply affected the younger Wallace.[17] During the 1920s and early 1930s, throughout his tenure as editor of the family's farm newspaper, *Wallaces' Farmer,* Wallace featured one of his grandfather's thousands of religious "Sayings"—aphoristic guides to the conduct of one's life in the style of the Social Gospel—on each weekly editorial page. He also ran reprints of Uncle Henry's weekly "Our Sabbath School Lesson," originally published when the elder Wallace's name topped the paper's masthead.

Yet a proclivity toward a non-mainstream, mystical religiosity was apparent early on in the younger Wallace. As a young man he rejected what he characterized as the "severely logical" sermons of the Presbyterians, for a time in favor of scientific skepticism. When he returned to the Protestant fold as an Episcopalian in his adulthood, it was after being drawn back to Christianity in general by the "spiritual beauty" of the Catholic mass.[18] By the late 1920s Wallace's spiritual explorations led him to Hinduism, Bahaism, astrology, and Native American religion. Through the early 1930s, right up until the time he took national office, Wallace spent a great deal of time studying the then-popular Western religion-philosophy Theosophy, which drew heavily on Hinduism. With the support of several individuals who shared his spiritual propensity, Wallace intertwined his science and his spiritual studies into what I have termed an "experimental spiritualism" that became a philosophical foundation for his social and political critiques. His wide-ranging spiritual beliefs were generally only implicit in his editorials, although they still had a powerful impact on his thought. After Wallace entered national politics in 1933, his spiritualism mixed subtly with the Judeo-Christian tradition of his youth, shaping his expectations regarding human capacities while also forming an important moral underpinning of his cooperative vision for America and the world.

Uncle Henry's establishment of the Wallaces in Iowa in the late nineteenth century did not mark the family's start in America. By the time Henry A. Wallace was born, in 1888, some of his ancestors, themselves descended from three centuries of Scottish husbandmen, had been farming in this country for over 150 years.[19] Having left the ministry, Uncle Henry began his agricultural career in 1877 and quickly proved himself adept at "scientific farming," making use of "all the latest techniques of husbandry." His son, Henry C. Wallace (Henry A.'s father), carried this interest in experimental farming further, for a short time as a professor of agriculture at Iowa State College at Ames (now Iowa State University).[20] Henry A. Wallace was thus brought up in both an agricultural and academic environment. This being the case, it is not surprising that one of his careers was in agricultural science, specifically corn genetics. Probing the mysteries of agricultural breeding in both plants and animals remained Wallace's great passion throughout his life, while an experimental, scientific perspective informed his thinking more generally.

The men of the Wallace family in each generation were among the most influential supporters of agrarian and progressive political causes in the United States. Uncle Henry's appointment, for instance, to Theodore Roosevelt's Country Life Commission, established for the purpose of investigating the conditions of rural life in America, reflected the elder Wallace's stature as "one of the paramount agrarian spokesmen of his day."[21] Over a decade later Henry A. Wallace's editorials took up many of the problems with which the commission concerned itself as well as many of its suggested solutions. That Wallace found himself early in 1921 writing those editorials resulted from his father's acceptance of the portfolio of the secretary of agriculture, a position that Uncle Henry had declined in 1896, and that Henry A. accepted in 1933. Other than the platform of national office, the primary channel for the Wallaces' advocacy of agrarian goals was their newspaper, *Wallaces' Farmer,* which they first published in 1895. As we will see, in many ways it stands as the best example of the continuity in values and endeavors that Wallace grew up with. The editorship of *Wallaces' Farmer* remained within the purview of each Henry in succession, until Henry A. left for Washington, D.C., in 1933 to attempt to build the world he envisioned upon a foundation made up of equal parts science, spiritualism, and agrarian philosophy.

Also a product of the Midwest, Niebuhr went on to become the foremost American Protestant theologian of this century. He was most widely known, however, as a political philosopher who developed a far-reaching critique of liberal thought. Niebuhr began his career as a preacher in the German Evangelical Synod of North America but spent most of his life as a professor at Union Theological Seminary in New York City. Early in his career he established a reputation for himself outside of his ministry, primarily through his journalistic efforts in liberal as well as liberal Christian periodicals. A strong supporter of Woodrow Wilson's post–World War I plans for global security, Niebuhr, like many liberals, became disillusioned with them after Versailles and the rejection of the peace treaty by the U.S. Senate. A pacifist briefly during the 1920s, he began during that decade to develop his attack on liberal political thought, domestic and international. Significantly, this critique was deeply intertwined, though not always explicitly so, with his theological critique of liberal Christianity, which has been called "Christian realism." By the beginning of World War II Niebuhr had become one of the leading American commentators on foreign affairs.

Yet although Niebuhr, like Wallace, was a native of the Midwest, he did not grow up with the same unquestioning sense of place and purpose with which Wallace reached adulthood. The continuities in Niebuhr's background were of a different sort. Wallace's grandfather had been the last somewhat itinerant member of the family, but Gustav Niebuhr, Reinhold's father, "was used to pulling up stakes." In fact, Niebuhr's family had been in Wright City, Missouri, for only a few months when he was born in June 1892. And Wright City was just the latest of the several parishes Gustav had been assigned to since his ordination as a minister of the German Evangelical Synod of North America, in 1885.[22]

Gustav Niebuhr's itinerancy predated his entry into the ministry. Born the son of a "large farmer" in central Germany, Gustav emigrated to the United States in 1881 at the age of eighteen to get away from both a dictatorial father and service in the German army. He lived at first with cousins outside of Freeport, Illinois, working as a hand on their farm. After a short time there he left for Chicago, where he worked in a sewing machine factory. In Chicago Gustav lived the worldly life of a somewhat " 'wild' young man."[23] After less than two years in the big city, when his health collapsed, he returned to his cousins' farm.

It was there in 1883 that Gustav underwent a conversion experience. It apparently resulted, in the most immediate sense, from his profound reaction to a sermon he had listened to at the Evangelical Synod's church in Freeport. Soon after, he decided to study for the Synod's ministry at Eden Theological Seminary, the institution at which Reinhold also trained twenty-seven years later. Gustav finished Eden's program in two years, being ordained in 1885. Following a brief stint in a church in New Orleans, he left for San Francisco to take over the Synod's church there. Gustav's next move took place when he, his wife, and their two eldest children moved to Missouri, just prior to Reinhold's birth.[24]

Although the Niebuhr family resided in Missouri for a decade, Richard Fox writes that the "young children [numbering four, after the 1894 birth of H. Richard] did not see much of their father during" those years. Gustav spent most of his time traveling from church to church—much as Reinhold would do throughout his career—on important administrative assignments for the Synod. In 1899 he resigned the parish he then held in St. Charles, Missouri, to take on the full-time role of "traveling representative" for a Synod program that established residences "for the epileptic and feebleminded." With his family in St. Charles, Gustav was often absent for months, sometimes making treks to serve as temporary pastor in parishes as far away as Utah. It was not until 1902, when he accepted the position of pastor of St. John's

Church in Lincoln, Illinois, that Gustav settled down. Even then it took the offer of a prestigious parish, complete with a newly built parsonage, as well as the directorship of the parochial school and the superintendency of an associated hospital, to make him stay put. In his ambition as well as his outgoing, peripatetic nature Gustav Niebuhr foreshadowed his middle son's character.[25]

The denomination that Gustav Niebuhr elected to minister in, and that Reinhold was raised in, had a large impact on the latter's development. The Evangelical Synod, centered in the Midwest, was an American version of the Prussian Union Church, the church that Gustav had been baptized in as a child. It was created in 1817 by the command of King Friedrich Wilhelm III, when he decided that there were political benefits to ending the theological disputes between the Lutheran and Reformed churches. The ecumenism resulting from this theological fusion was reflected in the Evangelical Synod. Characterizing itself as neither Lutheran nor Calvinist, the Synod "was typical of much nineteenth-century German and American Protestantism" in that it tended to eschew rationalism in favor of a "pietistic stress on the heart." The Synod's theology was nondoctrinaire, however, even utilitarian, encouraging "a fundamentally open, accommodating, pragmatic attitude toward other denominations," as well as toward American culture in general.[26] This open, pragmatic attitude was apparent in Reinhold Niebuhr's theology, such as when he invoked Catholicism, Anglicanism, or Judaism as positive examples in his criticism of liberal Protestantism. This pragmatism, integral to his theology, underpinned his political philosophy as well.

Like his father—indeed, very much because of him—Niebuhr chose to become a preacher in the German Evangelical Synod. Fox argues, however, that the younger Niebuhr selected his career without a great deal of reflection. He became a preacher partly out of admiration for a father who in certain respects doted on him and whom he idolized in return and partly out of the pressure created by Gustav's death in 1913. At that time twenty-one-year-old Reinhold was just finishing what were effectively his college studies at Eden Seminary and was pressed into immediate, if temporary, service as his own father's replacement. When Gustav died, his son "came to see his own life as the completion of his father's." Any opportunity to question whether this was the future he really wanted was precluded, at least for the moment, by Reinhold's shouldering of what had been his father's responsibilities.[27] But unlike his father, and his own disclaimers notwithstanding, Reinhold entered the ministry with an unsureness about his choice of professions that influenced his entire career.

This self-doubt was manifested early on, beginning during Niebuhr's years as a student at the Yale Divinity School. Both a sense of inadequate intellectual preparation and his own ethnic background made him feel himself to be little more than "a young German-American from the provinces."[28] While Niebuhr for the most part overcame his feelings of intellectual inferiority, his ambivalence regarding his German-American ethnicity persisted, becoming particularly apparent during World War I. In some ways it too never completely disappeared. Throughout his career his commentary, both religious and political, often focused on Germany, either as a topic in and of itself or as an illustration of some point within his analysis. During the 1920s and 1930s, for instance, Niebuhr frequently invoked developments in Germany as the clearest examples of the social and spiritual ravages wrought by the advent of modern industrial civilization. In Germany of the interwar era Niebuhr detected most clearly the crushing impact that the industrial world had on people's lives as well as examples of the many ways in which he felt the Protestant church failed in lessening that impact. In addition, his post–World War II return to Germany—in fact and in his commentary—was crucial in the crystallization of his cold war liberalism.

Niebuhr's doubts, which formed a subtle foundation for his persistently skeptical interpretation of events, were unquestionably part of the motivation behind his prolific and successful efforts to reach out into other areas of endeavor, including academia, journalism, and political commentary. Doing so enabled him to attain a sense of self-validation, perhaps even of legitimacy, relative to mainstream American culture.[29] In effect Niebuhr single-handedly resurrected religion's viability as a basis for political and social analysis, although it should be noted that many who accepted his political philosophy disregarded its theological underpinnings. Throughout his life Niebuhr characterized himself as a preacher, not a theologian, and in fact became a mainstay of the eastern collegiate preaching circuit that existed during the first half of this century. Yet his self-description was at best incomplete. The areas of his greatest influence on American culture belied his modest claims. Niebuhr's reputation resulted primarily from his theologically based political commentary, as it was promulgated in his widely read books that were published by major houses, as well as in such prestigious journals as the *Nation, The Christian Century, The New Republic, Atlantic Monthly,* and *Life.* Indeed, considering the tremendous volume of his journalism during the years 1920–48—somewhere around sixteen hundred articles, columns, and book reviews—it could be argued that he was more than anything else a journalist.

It may finally be helpful to assess Wallace and Niebuhr—particularly Niebuhr—within a framework loosely delineated by terms such as "insider" and "outsider" relative to the American cultural mainstream. Both men can be characterized as twentieth-century American liberals. Yet they were products of equally common but dissimilar American experiences, a fact often reflected in the very different foci of their commentaries. Wallace, a product of the heartland, was a farmer from a farming family as well as a public champion of rural America. His vision arose from his initial desire to perpetuate the type of community and the associated values he felt so thoroughly a part of and that he saw threatened by the culture of the urban, industrial world. For Wallace, being what I call an "insider," culturally speaking, was subtle. It consisted in an essentially unconscious sense of relationship between kin and place. Nevertheless, and with great irony, by the late 1940s he had become the cultural outsider.

Whereas during the 1930s Wallace nurtured what he believed to be innate social desires for community and cooperation, Niebuhr stressed what he viewed as ultimately, or at least effectively, irreconcilable differences between the morality of individuals and groups as well as the individual's fundamental need to feel connected to community. While Wallace's outlook was that of an Anglo-American Midwesterner, centrally concerned with sense of place, Niebuhr's was that of a second-generation ethnic immigrant—if not eastern European, still without Anglo roots. Without an organic cultural link to Anglo-American life, such individuals often were aware of great differences between their own ethnic cultures and the mainstream of American culture, even as they tried to assimilate to it.

It is even possible to speculate that a youthful experience of perceiving oneself as an outsider may have been a common formative influence in the development of the realist perspective with which Niebuhr is so often associated. George Kennan, for example, poignantly recounted in his memoirs his own sense of being a Midwestern "oddball on campus" at Princeton, of being shy and on the margins of college social life. Similarly, Ronald Steel's portrayal of Walter Lippmann depicts an individual who struggled to deny his Jewish ethnicity and whose seeming aloofness was a cover for shyness and emotional hypersensitivity.[30] Niebuhr's experience was similar to these other aspirants to the American mainstream. He struggled, not untypically for a second-generation American, with his own ethnic background and, though born in a relatively small Midwestern town, he became most comfortable within the urban intellectual community of the eastern United States. His commentaries reflected these orientations, and his version of the outsider experience helps explain why, as we shall see, the 1938 Munich crisis so profoundly influenced his view of western, and particularly American, culture. For Niebuhr, Munich crystallized his perception that, for all of its flaws, in America an outsider at least could survive and ultimately even thrive.

If Niebuhr felt himself, at least early in his career, to be outside of the American mainstream in terms of both profession and ethnicity, in the course of his career he fashioned the means for overcoming such feelings. By the beginning of World War II he had returned liberal Christianity to a position of political and social influence in American life while concurrently making his own commentary into required reading for several generations of American intellectuals, students, and statesmen. Yet his perspective remained that of an individual who continued to experience himself on the outside looking in, critical of all visions, religious or political, social or economic. Like Wallace, Niebuhr saw a threat in modern urban-industrial culture, but for him there could never be a complete resolution of the dilemmas posed by life in the twentieth century. He tried to explain this to his fellow citizens, to make them more aware of their circumstances and, in the case of their nation, more cognizant of what he considered the viable choices available in the global arena. By the late 1940s, however, Niebuhr's efforts resulted in an irony that perhaps he himself would have appreciated better than anyone, had he sensed it. His skepticism fundamentally shaped American liberal political discourse and by so doing helped create an atmosphere that eventually foreclosed consideration of the ideas of individuals such as Wallace. Whatever vision finally remained to the American people was narrow indeed.

A final note on two aspects of this study: first, I should point out that although this book clearly partakes of intellectual biography, it is not intellectual biography per se. I am specifically interested in the evolution of Wallace's and Niebuhr's commentaries on certain topics over time, an evolution consistently evident in their journalism and speeches and of which their books were often culminating restatements rather than new intellectual breakthroughs. This was particularly the case with Niebuhr. Thus I do not extensively analyze all of the two men's "big books." Those I do discuss at length I examine because their content or format stood as especially significant examples of the development of one or the other's thinking. Second, there is a large chronological asymmetry between the two parts of this book. Part 1 covers nearly three decades of history, from around 1915 to 1942. It is primarily devoted to analyzing the evolution of Wallace's and Niebuhr's respective cultural critiques. Part 2, however, has a rather telescoped chronology, covering only some six years (1942–48, with an epilogue set in 1952). Overarching themes that were decades in developing are less likely to be obvious in such a relatively brief passage of time. Instead, they form a context or basis for illuminating—and adding ironic resonance to—the events of 1942–48. Indeed, Part 1 should be viewed as a prologue to Part 2. It establishes at great length and in great detail the development of the outlooks that led these two men, and the groups with which they became involved, to opposition. Part 2 shows in comparable detail the characteristics and implications of that opposition as it unfolded during and immediately after World War II.

2

"Key Note for a 'New Age'"

The Foundations of Wallace's Vision of a Cooperative Civilization

I N MARCH 1921 Henry Cantwell Wallace, father of Henry Agard Wallace, left Des Moines for Washington, D.C., to begin his tenure as secretary of agriculture in the Harding administration. From then until Henry A. followed his father's path to the Department of Agriculture twelve years later, the editorship of *Wallaces' Farmer* and its attendant responsibilities belonged to the younger Wallace. Above all, this included writing each edition's two full pages of editorials, more than four thousand words per week. Wallace managed such an output through the use of a Dictaphone onto whose cylinders he could dictate upward of two hundred words per minute on a familiar topic.[1]

Wallace actually began writing for his family's journal as early as 1907, when he published the results of some of his first corn-yield tests. In 1909, just prior to his senior year at Iowa State College, he toured the western United States, sending back columns on irrigation methods used in the various states he visited. From that time on he wrote regularly for *Wallaces' Farmer,* most often as an anonymous staff writer but occasionally under his own byline.[2] Nevertheless, it was during the 1920s and early 1930s, in his editorials and in frequent longer articles under his byline, that Wallace sketched out a multifaceted vision of an American civilization grounded in the values of rural America. It was a vision informed by his eclectic interests, reflecting his science, his spiritualistic religiosity, and his insider's sense of connection to Midwestern farm culture.

23

Early Influences

In his early-1950s Columbia University Oral History Project interview, Wallace asserted at length that one of the greatest intellectual influences of his young adulthood had been Pragmatist psychologist and philosopher William James.[3] James's influence on Niebuhr's early thought is quite clear, as we shall see. Such is not the case with Wallace, however, beyond his own assertion of it much later in his life. Nevertheless, with that assertion in mind, it is possible to suggest the outlines of James's impact on Wallace's thinking.

In his interview Wallace attested to reading "five or six volumes" of James's work, beginning while he was in college, and of being affected particularly by James's book *The Varieties of Religious Experience,* first published in 1902. Wallace explained that James's writing directly contributed to his decision, around 1916, to leave the United Presbyterian Church, in part because the church's minister was uncomfortable with Wallace's use of James in the Sunday school class he taught in Des Moines. Wallace downplayed his departure from the church, noting that he joined the Episcopal Church some years later, around 1930, but failed to mention at all his extensive studies in spiritualistic belief systems, particularly Theosophy, during the intervening years.[4] It was an unsurprising lacuna in 1951, in light of the public grief Wallace was subjected to at various points in his career—most recently in the Progressive Party campaign of 1948—over mere rumors of his spiritualistic endeavors. Yet knowing that Wallace's reading of James not only impelled his departure from mainstream Protestantism but also occurred at the outset of the most intensely mystical/spiritualistic period of his life suggests that James influenced Wallace profoundly.

What James did for Wallace was fortify already existent inclinations, in two ways. In response to a gentle question from the interviewer regarding his rumored mysticism, Wallace, once more evading the question of his extensive non-mainstream religious experiences, acknowledged that James enabled him to become what he termed a "*practical* mystic." James's writings had done this by awakening within Wallace a transcendent desire to discover "what is worthwhile" in life, no matter where the path of discovery might lead.[5] It was an outlook that jibed well with the other great influences in Wallace's life, personal and professional. In addition, in his books James made a multifaceted argument for the validity of religious knowledge of all sorts in the modern, science-oriented world, an argument that profoundly affected the young Niebuhr and probably Wallace as well. It was an effect that was likely augmented for Wallace by James's willingness to discuss quite seriously—"to countenance," as Wallace's most recent biographers put it—both Eastern beliefs in reincarnation and karma, and the qualities and substance of mystical experience more generally.[6] James, in other words, gave an essentially scientific validation to interests of Wallace's that were burgeoning just at the time that Wallace happened to be exposed to James's writing.

Wallace's outlook was also informed by two other important influences in his life. One was his professional background as a scientist, essentially an agricultural geneticist. The discipline of the scientific method's extension of knowledge by experimentation underpinned Wallace's approach to all questions, scientific in nature or not. This inclination in turn had an impact on the other crucial factor underlying Wallace's vision, which was his absorption with religion, specifically with various forms of spiritualism. In his assessment, strengthened by James's logic, religion in general and spiritualism in particular were, like science, simply methods, subject to experimental validation, of gaining a better understanding of both nature and the human condition. By the early 1930s, with the support of several individuals who shared his spiritual propensity, Wallace intertwined his science and his spiritual studies into a philosophical foundation for his social and political critiques.

Even had he chosen to, Wallace could not have ignored the changes that had occurred in America during the half century before he took over sole editorship of *Wallaces' Farmer*. These changes touched him too closely, in too many ways. Indeed, in a sense his own life was a microcosm of a dilemma he tried to resolve in his writings. As both an agricultural scientist and farmer, Wallace embodied the paradox that was characteristic of American agriculture in the early twentieth century. On the one hand, farmers felt compelled to partake in the advances in scientific and mechanical knowledge that could increase their production. On the other hand, they still were bound up in an intensely individualistic enterprise that was quite traditional, drawing powerfully on the American veneration of self-help and isolated independence. In the first two decades of the twentieth century, farming in the United States remained predominantly a small-scale, family enterprise. Despite the advent of corporate farming and agricultural cooperatives in many parts of the nation, the average farmer shifted for himself.

In addition, even as agriculture utilized new techniques and technologies, it remained powerfully constrained by the vagaries of the weather. And knowledge about the weather continued to be a mixture of fledgling science with long-held beliefs that now seem most comparable to fortune-telling. While farmers utilized much of the new meteorological research available during the early years of the century, many of them still held to their own systems of weather prediction, usually an intermingling of experienced observation of seasons, sky, and animal activity along with the questionable insights of farmers' almanacs.

A similar dualism of science and tradition formed a powerful amalgam in Wallace, one that was apparent in his understanding of issues and events. His was an essentially scientific perspective, informed by his training and interests. Understanding Wallace as a scientist helps explain his penchant for applying his conception of the scientific method—essentially a disciplined open-mindedness—to a whole range of issues outside of science. He was willing to examine any theory of knowledge, including those that others might view as eccentric. Wallace refused to reject any creed or hypothesis a priori. No matter how superficially repugnant a particular proposition's conceptual basis might seem to some, Wallace treated it as worthy of consideration until examination and trial proved otherwise.

Agricultural experimentation itself remained a primary pursuit of Wallace's during the 1920s and early 1930s. Some of the results of his ongoing experimental efforts appeared in editorial columns and articles he wrote for *Wallaces' Farmer*. He covered diverse topics, ranging from innovative methods of corn cultivation to the care and breeding of hogs and poultry.[7] During these same years Wallace established a successful seed-corn company, Hi-Bred Corn (still in existence), to market the results of his years of highly innovative work in corn hybridization.[8] During this time, while *Wallaces' Farmer* was the central focus of his activities, Wallace also corresponded with more than a score of individuals throughout the United States who undertook various corn-strain interbreeding trials at his behest.[9] By the end of the decade this correspondence extended to other parts of the world, contributing to Wallace's growing awareness of international interdependence.[10]

Wallace's scientific background and the experimental perspective it created conditioned his approach to many areas of inquiry, professional and otherwise, ranging from statistical methodologies associated with both plant and animal breeding to the compilation of genealogical records. In the latter case he believed that such records could help establish an individual's sense of identity. This sort of self-knowledge, Wallace believed, led to a sense of responsibility and "place in the world." It was a conclusion that suggests once again the importance that Wallace put upon experiencing oneself in terms of kinship and place, a sense of belonging that for him must have been reinforced by his own genealogical studies.[11]

Wallace's statistical penchant occasionally was evident in his social commentary. For example, during the early 1920s he became concerned with the gradual shift in Iowa's population from countryside to city. This population movement, which Wallace "discovered" in several statistical analyses he made during the 1920s, was part of the nationwide shift begun during the decades after the Civil War. Wallace's interest in it was amplified by his growing fear that the culture of rural America might disappear, overwhelmed by an ascendant urban industrial civilization. He worried that individuals "more than a generation away from the farm . . . lose all sympathy with the farmer and all knowledge of his situation," ultimately undermining the rural sector's political power. When that happened there would be nothing to prevent the United States from transforming into a dominantly urban society.[12]

Wallace's Experimental Spiritualism

Wallace's scientific-experimentalist approach appeared in other pursuits, including his profound curiosity about the spiritual world. Wallace's spiritual explorations led him to Hinduism, Bahaism, astrology, and Native American religion. Wallace was most captivated during the 1920s and early 1930s, however, by the "wisdom religion" of Theosophy, a religious system eminently suited to his philosophical intertwining of science and spiritualism.[13] Established in New York in 1875 and attracting predominantly middle-class professionals already "active in nontraditional forms of religion and spirituality," the Theosophical Society grew fairly quickly to international proportions, ultimately developing many offshoots and experiencing several schisms.[14]

Attempting to transcend the "cleavage between science and religion" by returning to an "ancient wisdom-tradition" of the Far East, Theosophists asserted that supernatural revelation, imparted to spiritually sensitive individuals by semidivine beings, could inform rational, deductive reasoning about the nature of the physical world. Influenced by East Indian religious traditions, Theosophists called these near-divinities "masters" or "mahatmas." Also derived from Eastern spiritualism was Theosophy's acknowledgment of the existence of an eternal process of reincarnation, driven by the principle of karma.[15]

One of Wallace's earliest Theosophical associations was with George W. "Æ" Russell, whom he first met on a trip to Dublin, Ireland, in 1912 and became reacquainted with when Russell visited the United States in 1930 and 1931. Russell was an Irish poet and mystic, a central figure in the Irish literary renaissance of the late nineteenth century, which itself was strongly influenced by Theosophy. By the time Wallace met him Russell had spent years studying religion, mysticism, and Theosophy. His writings were heavily laden with his sense of a supernatural realm that one could connect with only outside the city, only by getting back to the land, to the primitive earth. Foreshadowing a strain of environmental philosophy that developed later in the century, Russell wrote of the earth as a living, breathing being, at times even as a mystical, seductive woman.[16]

Recalling Russell in the Columbia interview years later, Wallace suggested a connection between Russell's thinking and the manner in which he had been motivated by the writings of William James. Although he did not mention Russell's mysticism per se, Wallace claimed, in virtually the same language he had used regarding James, that Russell shared his own central concern with "what was worthwhile in life." Russell's mysticism always came back to the earth, which he also described as a sort of living temple, "the floor of a cathedral where altar and Presence are everywhere." To partake in the cathedral's holiness,

Russell contended, required staying close to the ways and values of rural life. Indeed, in his writing Russell placed much of the blame for society's problems, as Wallace did later, on the modern world's thoughts being "too much with the cities." It was only by getting back to the land—reentering the cathedral, as it were—that civilization could save itself. If people would "grow intimate with earth" they would lose their desire for power and possessions and return to what was worthwhile.[17]

This fundamental idea, that a return to the earth as a spiritual fountainhead could lead to a new era of human existence, supported the other major facet of Russell's life, his activities as a leader in the Irish agricultural cooperative movement. His cooperative philosophy and his endeavors to implement it paralleled Wallace's own strong advocacy of cooperation and heightened Wallace's interest in Russell's land-oriented spiritualism. Impressed at the time by what he viewed as Russell's "practical" mysticism, Wallace lamented his own lack of Russell's apparent degree of "facility of mental movement in the spiritual world." Yet in defending Russell's spiritual abilities to a close but skeptical friend, Wallace implied that he himself had had some psychic experiences. Manifesting his experimentalist demeanor, Wallace insisted that "it is a mistake for scientific and the common sense people to shut the door to some of these things which they cannot understand."[18]

By the early 1930s Wallace's attraction to Russell's spiritualism and to Theosophy led to his involvement in something of a network of spiritualists.[19] For Wallace the primary focus of this fellowship was Charles Roos, a Scandinavian-American poet and lyricist as well as an aficionado of Native American culture. From childhood Roos had lived with "Indians, woodsmen, [and] hunters" and had worked as a miner, a cowboy, and a woodsman. He was clearly at home in the outdoors. In the 1930s and 1940s Roos and his wife, Juanita—also a lyricist and a newspaper editor—served as U.S. government inspectors for all Indian reservations west of Michigan. Their lyrical and poetic work focused largely on nature, the wilderness, and Native American life and knowledge.[20]

Roos's spirituality, grounded in Native American religion, was, like Russell's, based on an affinity for the land, for nature, for the earth itself. As Wallace put it, "Charley . . . laid particular emphasis on the necessity for the American religion finding its roots in our own earth."

To Wallace this seemed similar to Russell's assertion that the absence of a "mystical feeling about the American soil" was the "great lack in American culture." Wallace agreed. He believed that he and Roos shared Russell's conviction about what was required to change such a deplorable spiritual situation.[21]

For Wallace, concerned as he was with the decline of the rural culture of his Iowa youth, it went without saying that involvement with the land, especially farming, was as much a spiritual endeavor as a practical one. It was a feeling that dated back to his childhood tutoring by the great botanist George Washington Carver, a student of Wallace's father at Iowa State College. As a child Wallace accompanied Carver on botanical field trips. From Carver Wallace gained a sense that "God was in every plant and rock and tree" and that the farmer was "obligated . . . to call on the God in whom he so deeply believed and felt as a creative force all around him."[22] If God or some spiritual essence was present in plants and in the land, then those closest to the land must be best suited to nurturing such powers, and Roos appeared to be just such an individual. Roos's affinity for the earth was strong and clear. And, like Wallace's, his spiritualism was also tied to Theosophy. By the time Wallace met them, both Charles and Juanita had been associated with a Theosophical group known as the Society of the Temple of the People for thirty-one years.[23]

Led by Dr. William H. Dower and Francia A. La Due, the temple was an offshoot of an early Theosophical Society lodge. In 1903 Dower, a licensed physician, and La Due led their followers to California and settled near the coast north of Santa Barbara, hoping to create a sanitarium nearby and intending to teach "love and harmony in order to conquer all abnormality and disease." Dower and La Due's community, Halcyon, was incorporated in 1905 as the Temple Home Association, a cooperative colony, a feature that probably attracted Wallace.[24]

In November 1931 Wallace sent his six dollars annual dues to the temple and began correspondence lessons in its brand of Theosophy. Dower characterized him as a "very fine student" whose answers to the course questions indicated "a splendid knowledge" of Theosophy's fundamentals.[25] Dower also answered Wallace's questions about issues outside the immediate realm of Theosophy. When Wallace queried him, for instance, about the causes of the Great Depression, Dower responded in a manner that touched the very core of the issues that had been troubling Wallace for more than a decade. The Depression, Dower wrote, made clear that the commercial, technological civilization of the West was fundamentally flawed and could only be salvaged by basic social, economic, and political change. The conclusion was not lost on Wallace.[26]

Dower's Indian connection—specifically his having been "adopted" by the Syracuse, New York, Onondaga tribe—also attracted Wallace, who had come to place high value on Native American culture. For example, when he first described Charles Roos to George Russell, he stressed Roos's belief "that there is a great need of some of the fundamental spirituality of the old Indian religions being introduced into our modern American attitude." Such observations reflected Wallace's perception, articulated as early as 1925, of a "spiritual hunger abroad in the land." By the early 1930s Wallace worried that in a spiritual and moral sense American society was falling apart in a rather passive manner, as he put it, "without much struggling."[27] He believed that the nation's spiritual void, while in great part a result of the rapid and haphazard process of industrialization, had been vastly amplified by the material and psychological devastation of the Great Depression. Moreover, by this time Wallace had been watching for more than a decade the effects on rural society of both the cultural transition and what can be considered foreshocks of the Depression. Because of all these factors, Wallace found himself thinking a lot about how he might help to fill the emptiness in American culture just as he pondered means to lessen America's social and economic ills. It was clear to him that as the world was collapsing economically in global depression, it was time for a "new religious longing" to appear if a "new order" were to issue from the "chaos."[28] Just as he proved willing to experiment with social and economic policy as a member of Roosevelt's New Deal administration, Wallace was ready to experiment with possible remedies for the spiritual ailments of civilization.

Wallace and Nicholas Roerich

Such concerns help explain the best-known and most controversial of Wallace's spiritual associations: that with Russian émigré artist, poet, essayist, and theosophical spiritualist Nicholas Roerich.[29] It was the relationship that perhaps best demonstrates how far Wallace's freely commingled interests could lead him down the path of the unconventional. Wallace apparently came into contact with Roerich around 1929–30, at the time he was renewing his acquaintance with George Russell. Considering Wallace's interest in both Russell and Charles Roos, his attraction to Roerich's mystical writings makes sense. Perhaps better than any of Wallace's other spiritualist associates, Roerich wove together the different threads of Wallace's vision.

Roerich passionately advocated an eclectic pursuit of knowledge, writing of science and mysticism in similar terms, according each its due as a source of life-enhancing wisdom. Roerich not only saw value in various forms of wisdom; he presented them in metaphors that would strongly attract an individual of Wallace's agricultural inclinations. Roerich wrote of the open-minded pursuit of knowledge—approaching the "realm of light"—as nurturing "the garden of Light." Creative thought, he insisted, like the "most delicate flowers . . . must be cultivated." [30]

In the 1920s and 1930s Roerich promoted an international treaty providing for the protection of the cultural treasures of all nations during wartime. The "Roerich Pact" became a reality in 1935 as a Pan-American treaty protecting "artistic, religious and scientific institutions and historic monuments." As a champion of the pact and a member of Franklin Roosevelt's cabinet, Wallace was the signatory for the United States.[31] At about the same time Wallace, as secretary of agriculture, commissioned Roerich to head up a Department of Agriculture expedition to Asia in search of drought-resistant grasses that might benefit the drought-ravaged American Midwest. Roerich was something of an expert in Asian culture, so he was at least an arguably valid choice to lead a scientific foray into that part of the world. Nevertheless, Roerich's dubious political activities while in China ultimately led to the collapse of the expedition in an embarrassing international relations controversy. Wallace contributed to the controversy by first defending Roerich unquestioningly against various accusations of misconduct and then completely disengaging from him when it became apparent that the accusations were accurate.[32]

Wallace's relationship with Roerich, especially its spiritual aspects, became an issue more than a decade later, during the political campaign of 1948. Then their association was brought to light by the conservative columnist Westbrook Pegler, who smeared Wallace by publishing and critically interpreting several letters Wallace had written to Roerich and Roerich's secretary. Pegler harped on aspects of the correspondence, some of which may have been faked, in such a way as to make it seem that Wallace had been under the mystical sway of Roerich, with Roerich portrayed as Wallace's "guru." [33]

The vast majority of the more than 150 letters consisted of Wallace's comments, couched in spiritualistic language, on various policy issues in which he and Roerich shared an interest. Topics included U.S.-Japanese and U.S.-Soviet relations, the Roerich Pact, Roerich's museum in New York City, and the Department of Agriculture expedition that Roerich led to China. Wallace brought a theosophical perspective to the descriptions he made to Roerich of his daily struggles in government. [34] Even though the substance of most of the letters was essentially political, they also reveal the nature of Wallace's spiritualism as well as the way in which it informed his social and political visions. In one instance, for example, Wallace exhibited his affinity for Native American spiritualism, stating that the "earth beat, the Indian rythm [*sic*] of Ancient America haunts me like a faint fragrance from the past while I strive to center my complete forces on the pressing problems of the day." On another occasion Wallace articulated his strong sense of the spiritual as well as his belief that he was somehow excluded from it by his duties in public life. He pointed out that he had long been aware of the "occasional fragrance from that other world which is the real world," yet he believed that for the time being he "must live in the outer world" while preparing himself for a more spiritual future. Wallace also suggested the spirit in which he viewed coming political struggles when he wrote Roerich, claiming the "seat perilous—in letters of fire—for the one who has won the right to come by using the inner principles to conquer in the outer world." "What challenge!" he exulted. "What adventure! What patience and grief!" [35]

Ever since Pegler called attention to the letters in 1948, discussion of the Wallace-Roerich connection has focused largely on whether or not Wallace actually wrote the letters, the subtext being that if he had written them it would be proof of his alleged "fuzzy-mindedness."

In fact, it is almost certain that Wallace did write many if not all of the more than 150 items that make up the collection. Names familiar from Wallace's other correspondence—including those of Dower and Roos—appear in several of the so-called Guru Letters. Those names probably would not have been collectively known to any of Wallace's contemporaries, save those few with an extremely intimate knowledge of his affairs. Many of the other terms Wallace used in the letters, such as the "masters," the "land of the masters," and the "light," as well as various sobriquets—the "One" and the "Flaming One," for FDR, or the "Sour One," for Secretary of State Cordell Hull—are similar to terms found in the writings of Russell, Dower, and Roerich.[36] Even in his occasional use of the word "guru" it seems likely that Wallace was simply minding his jargon, as any careful scientist would. Roerich himself defined *guru* as nothing more than an "experienced preceptor."[37] Considering Roerich's experience in spiritual and theosophical matters, characterizing him as "guru" would have been for Wallace, the diligent student, an appropriate choice for a term of endearment.

In the end, debating the authenticity of the Guru Letters makes sense only if the letters are considered aberrant. But in the context of Wallace's mystical explorations of the 1920s and 1930s the content of the Guru Letters hardly appears extraordinary. Wallace's involvement with Roerich arose out of his ongoing spiritual studies; it was just one more manifestation of his openness to any form of knowledge that might fill the spiritual vacuum he perceived in modern society. As Norman Markowitz has written, Wallace's controversial letters to Roerich were simply "another expression of his lifelong search to find a grand mechanism" to "reconcile order with freedom and science with religion."[38]

Considering Politics

In 1932 the Wallace family lost *Wallaces' Farmer* to the vicissitudes of the Great Depression. A year earlier Wallace had written a friend that if such an event were to occur, he might run for the United States Senate from Iowa as a Democrat. Charles Roos was all for Wallace's entry into

American politics. He believed that Wallace should become senator and then return to Iowa as its governor. Even if defeat was likely, Roos still thought that Wallace should opt for the senatorial campaign. Although Wallace might lose the election, Roos argued, the " 'publicity' will be Big Medicine for other things the Gods have in store for you." A loss, if it did occur, would not hurt Wallace and would in fact garner him much notoriety and support.[39]

Yet Wallace hesitated to embark on a career in national politics. He pointed out to Roos that he was considering staying with *Wallaces' Farmer* as editor for a few more years and then pursuing his corn studies full time. That course would allow Wallace to devote much of his time to endeavors in which he and Roos could collaborate. Wallace told Roos that he feared that a successful run for the Senate might prevent a "peaceful exit" from his current life to one that he hoped for, centered on their friendship and the "Inner Life."[40]

For Wallace a political career was only one possible means to a much more important end: to find an appropriate way to address the spiritual weakness he discerned in an economically and socially afflicted modern America. Wallace continually wondered how he might work for this "cause." Because Charles Roos's spiritualism combined many of the features he deemed vital, Wallace believed that both he and Roos were inclined toward working out the "spiritual foundations" for a "true creative . . . expression for the American people." At one point Wallace insisted to a correspondent that he was at heart "neither a corn breeder nor an editor," but rather a "searcher for methods of bringing the 'Inner light' to outward manifestation and raising outward manifestation to the Inner light." "*Most important,*" Wallace insisted, was the need to discover the "key note of the new age."[41] His concurrent pursuit of scientific and spiritual knowledge convinced Wallace that there were many paths to its discovery. Scientific studies, he concluded, ultimately were no more valid as paths to knowledge than the work he undertook with his various spiritualist colleagues and mentors.

Above all, Wallace hoped that in some combination these diverse ways of seeking knowledge would yield solutions to the overwhelming problems now facing civilization. Even as his family was losing ownership of the newspaper that had been at the center of its collective life for almost four decades, Wallace did not lose his passion for this search. In April 1932, as he reflected on the loss of *Wallaces' Farmer,* he wrote to Roos that the "zest of life is with me." Wallace suggested that modern civilization would most likely deteriorate before it improved, yet he still insisted that it was "an honor to be alive in these days."[42]

After the summer of 1932 Wallace did not press the perspective he had gained from his theosophical and related spiritual studies, either in his last editorials while still in Iowa or—with the implicit exception of his choice of Roerich for the Asian grass expedition of 1934—in his public activities after becoming secretary of agriculture. Once he was in office his theosophical spiritualism receded into the deep background of his public thought, replaced in his official writings and utterances, such as his 1934 book *Statesmanship and Religion,* by an Old Testament, Judeo-Christian spiritualism in a more publicly acceptable style similar to that of his grandfather.

It is not clear to what extent Wallace continued his private spiritual studies during his years of public service from 1933 to 1948. As we shall see, the perspective he gained from them certainly informed his thinking and policy making, even if he did not express it in anything approaching an explicit sense. By the time Wallace left Iowa to take up national office in 1933, his spiritual experimentation had covered a wide range of philosophies and attained a fairly high level of sophistication. Decades before the spiritual renaissance of the 1960s and the advent of the "New Age" movement of the 1980s, Wallace addressed the spiritual disaffection that he and many others saw as the great dilemma of urban-industrial civilization. Wallace searched for the means that would enable him and other Americans to adjust emotionally and psychically to the disorienting changes of the previous seventy-five years, and he did so in a manner that uniquely combined the two sides of his intellect. From a modern perspective science and spiritualism seemed wholly incompatible. Indeed, the distinctions between them formed a rough analog for the tensions existent in early twentieth-century American culture between the traditions of the preindustrial past and the scientific outlook of industrial civilization. But whether or not the spiritualistic component of Wallace's outlook appears incongruent with his science, it is clear that Wallace did not come by it lightly. It arose rather from the disciplined explorations of a scientist into the circumstances of the modern human condition.

Corporate Farming and the Evils of the City

During the 1920s and early 1930s, as Wallace pursued his scientific and spiritual endeavors, he also developed an extensive critique of modern industrial culture. In his editorials in *Wallaces' Farmer* Wallace touched on numerous aspects of American society, in the process constructing a vision of a civilization worth living in. He attempted to reconcile the remembered American traditions of family farming and small-town rural life with the imposing changes brought about by industrialization and urbanization. In doing so Wallace wove together various threads of American culture, ranging from aspects of nineteenth-century agrarian protest to the more modern themes of the Progressive Era.

Reflecting his own sense of place, much of Wallace's outlook derived from his belief in the superiority of agrarian values and rural life. Indeed, at times this belief was so powerful as to imply an ambivalence on Wallace's part toward the culture of science and technology that he otherwise championed. Yet despite such a valuation of American rural culture as well as his explicit desire to rescue it from apparent decline, by the time he left Iowa to join Roosevelt's cabinet, Wallace fashioned a social perspective that looked beyond the countryside. That perspective served as the basis of his larger national and ultimately international vision.

Wallace perceived evidence of the decline of rural America in various processes, including one that was for him ambiguously troubling: the advent of corporate farming. Appearing with increasing frequency in the American Midwest throughout the late 1920s and early 1930s, corporate farms exemplified the dynamic tension in farm culture between traditional techniques and modern technology, a tension that Wallace himself in some aspects personified. In Wallace's view the crucial stimulus to corporate farming was increasingly efficient machinery rather than the actual consolidation of acreage. New technology provided the catalyst for large acreage farming, whether or not such farms were established by an actual corporation. Wallace predicted that large-scale farming would win out because the agricultural "mechanics" on such farms, supervised by corporate-type managers and receiving a wage for their labor, would produce agricultural commodities more economically than could be done with the system of family labor.[43]

Against the grain of long-established Western liberal beliefs about the inevitable social benefits of science and technology, Wallace foresaw in the advent of corporate farming great inequities as well as the potential demise of the rural culture he held dear. By the early 1930s, in fact, as the Great Depression reached its nadir, he began to accept as inevitable the transformation of rural life. Although some would "gravely question the new order of things," such questioning would not prevent the changes. Moreover, he feared that in some agriculturally marginal areas, where the land could not be efficiently worked by the new methods, the effects of the new order would be devastating. Along with the "glories of the new age," Wallace wrote, there might also be a great deal of "ghastly human suffering."[44]

Wallace's perspective on corporate farming was grounded in part in a harsh view of "the city" that he shared with agrarian leaders of earlier eras. His assessment of city life formed a prominent and at times almost shrill aspect of his social philosophy. Exhibiting the influence of Progressive Era drives for urban health reform and articulating an anti-urban aspect of what Richard Hofstadter characterized as the "agrarian myth," Wallace contended that the city held dangers even for human physiology. He believed the product of an urban existence was an individual of weak vitality, a poor basis for the generations of Americans to come. In this sense to speak of the nation's future as primarily revolving around city life effectively was to speak of the "merits of national suicide."[45]

In Wallace's version of the agrarian myth, the city meant cultural suicide as well, as it destroyed any semblance of the individuality that many believed to be one of the farmer's best traits. Urban-industrial life furthered both social and economic standardization, a threat "creeping into the realm of ideas, manners and beliefs." Contending that the rise of mass culture had gone too far, Wallace pointed out that Americans more and more "read the same sort of newspapers, with the same syndicated features" and listened to "the same talks over the radio." As time passed, Americans even lived in what Wallace perceived as duplicate communities. And the individuals living in these duplicate towns were appearing and acting like duplicate humans, "as much alike as a row of mechanical dolls in a toy store window."[46]

Ultimately, Wallace was convinced, the ascendancy of the city threatened American democracy itself. In the mid-twenties, before the Great Depression, many American farmers were already in difficult financial straits. Yet Wallace continued to hope that change would eventually favor the rural population, that agricultural prices would rise as the urban population grew, regaining for farmers their historic prosperity and prestige. Nevertheless, even in this hypothetical agrarian renaissance Wallace foresaw grave danger for American society. In his imagined future rising food prices would provoke urban workers to protest, striking for higher wages, but to no avail. In the face of the farmers' relative prosperity, the "town and city workers will loudly proclaim that something is wrong," finally turning to violence to attain their desires. At that time, Wallace warned, circumstances in America would be similar to those existing in Italy just prior to the rise of Mussolini and the Fascists.[47] The unbridled growth of the cities would lead to the end—in one sense or another—of the United States.

Much of the problem, according to Wallace's critique, arose from the obsession of the eastern U.S. urban population with the development of commerce and industry. Easterners were blind to the needs of the farmer, caring only that "he will continue to produce large crops cheaply." Not concerned with rural life, eastern urbanites were wholly absorbed in the expansion of their urban commercial civilization. They did not seem to care if that expansion resulted in social upheaval and perhaps even international warfare.[48]

Industrialization and Imperialism

The idea that urban-industrial civilization by its nature tended toward war was a theme that Wallace's commentary of the 1920s shared with a diverse group of culture critics. In elaborating upon it Wallace frequently cited England as an example of what the United States could expect if it became an entirely urban civilization, concerned only with commerce and industry while its rural culture withered. By deciding at the outset of the industrial revolution to found their economic existence on manufacturing and overseas trade, Wallace believed that the English had committed their nation to colonial imperialism. He viewed the American Revolution as the first sign of the risk that inhered in such a policy. Yet even when the policy was successful, Wallace contended, it was only temporary. Closely echoing the logic V. I. Lenin so infamously articulated at the outset of the Russian Revolution, Wallace claimed that "imperialism defeats itself." He argued that colonies became disillusioned with their unfair lot and revolted, economically or militarily, in either manner crippling the empire's commerce. Contemporary economic revolts in English colonies such as India only seemed to bear out his logic.[49]

It was in the short term, however, that Wallace foresaw the most disastrous results of imperialism. Maintenance of empire meant "wars, big armies, big navies, and the expenses that go with them," both in matériel and humanity. Sticking to his British example, Wallace noted that by 1927 Great Britain had fought wars in "Egypt, India, South Africa, China and a dozen other places" for the protection of its trade.[50] Yet such behavior on the part of modern nations, Wallace suggested, was hardly restricted to the British. It was common to them all, potentially even the United States.

In asserting this Wallace was contributing to the rise of what some historians have called the "devil theory" of war, which arose in America during the 1920s out of revisionist critiques of U.S. involvement in World War I. Its central contention was that financiers and munitions makers had manipulated American foreign policy toward intervention in order to reap the profits of war production.[51] Wallace's version of the devil theory was strengthened not only by his use of a pseudo-Marxist critique of industrial capitalism but also the critique made by the disenchanted Progressive historian Charles Beard. A leading proponent of the devil theory during the 1920s, Beard was part of a group of intellectuals writing in journals such as the *Nation* and the *New Republic* who were disillusioned by the outcome of U.S. participation in World

War I.[52] Such disillusionment on Beard's part was reflected in his portrayal of a belligerent American foreign policy, driven since the late nineteenth century by concerns over "investments and trade." Beard's critique was manifested not only in his journalistic output but in a multivolume history of the United States cowritten with his wife, the historian Mary Beard. The first two volumes of *The Rise of American Civilization* were published in 1927, and Wallace read them closely.[53] In their light Wallace concluded that modern war arose out of the competition between the "industrialized nations" over exploitable "underdeveloped countries." Even the Great War, he insisted, had been largely the result of commercial rivalry between England and Germany.[54]

By the early 1920s Wallace feared that the United States appeared to be taking the same course as had Great Britain. Wallace warned that America was quickly becoming an empire despite itself. That this was the case seemed evident to him by 1922, in the light of U.S. policy regarding Allied debts from the World War. Wallace argued that American insistence on the repayment of the debts—an aspect of American foreign policy that he criticized extensively during the next decade and a half—was undermining both the European and American economies. It forced the Europeans to stop buying U.S. farm produce while simultaneously compelling them to flood America with manufactured goods to finance their debt. Wallace posited that eventually Americans would turn to foreign investment, to the actual buying of "European factories and European real estate," when other methods of repayment proved ineffective. That was when Wallace expected serious trouble to begin.[55]

On this point Wallace was again in agreement with the Beards, who insisted that as American foreign investment increased the United States government would increasingly support such investment with force. "The flag," the Beards declared, indeed "followed trade."[56] To Wallace this already seemed the case in Latin America, where by the mid-1920s there were U.S. troops in several nations and American naval squadrons anchored off the coasts of quite a few more. In light of such developments he worried that the United States could easily be drawn into a "serious war" simply by protecting its citizens' foreign financial ventures.[57]

By the latter half of the decade it was apparent to Wallace that critiques of American foreign policy such as the Beards' remained cogent, that the United States was prepared to go quite a distance down the path of imperialism. For instance, in both Cuba and the Philippines Wallace noted that American assurances of liberty following the Spanish-American war had gone unfulfilled. While Cuba was "nominally independent," Wallace insisted that the U.S. government in fact kept close control over Cuban affairs, even maintaining a contingent of marines there to protect the "big investments of wealthy Americans." And the Filipinos, promised independence after the Spanish were defeated in 1898, never actually attained it, even after fighting a second war of liberation against their American liberators.[58]

It is important to remember that Wallace's elaboration of the devil theory had a purpose that transcended its condemnation of those whose greed threatened to draw America into war. He believed that such behavior only existed because of the United States' transformation. In Wallace's interpretation a crucial choice faced Americans in the 1920s between a wholly urban-industrial civilization or a society that maintained a significant place for agrarian life with what he believed to be its more humane, community-oriented values. Wallace was persuaded that rural culture could stand as a bulwark against the chaos that characterized city life, compelling Americans to rethink the nature of the society they were creating.

The Origins of Wallace's Cooperative Ethic

If the vilification of the city was a central theme in Wallace's commentary of the 1920s, it represented more than just the persistence of nineteenth-century populist fears of eastern urban conspiracies. As Wallace articulated his critique of the modern world, he also developed a quintessentially American communal philosophy—an analog, as it were, to the European constructions of socialism and communism. Implying once more his sense of place, Wallace's philosophy was grounded in Midwestern American agrarian values, above all in the ethic of "cooperation," a touchstone of nineteenth-century agrarian politics in the

United States. It was on this foundation that Wallace built his assessment of the weaknesses of urban-industrial society. More important, around the concept of cooperation Wallace fashioned a vision of a different and, in his view, better American civilization. It was a vision based upon ideals that he saw embodied by an increasingly threatened rural culture.

In 1904 Uncle Henry had written that "the natural development of industry is: first, competition; second, combination; third, cooperation."[59] Twenty years later his grandson still championed this American dialectic. In contrast to Marxism's prophecy of proletarian revolution and socialism's desire for increased government control of industry, "cooperative commonwealth," Wallace declared, was "the distant end toward which we are working."[60] He envisioned a society made up of a variety of cooperative organizations and communities, all held together by a shared cooperative ethic.

More than anything else, Wallace's expectation of a cooperative society implied a definition of self-interest quite different from that usually associated with the free enterprise capitalism of the 1920s. It suggested a social basis for the calculation of interests. This was not simply a concern with guaranteeing security and prosperity for all the individual members of the community but rather a belief that there was no individual well-being outside the context of a wholly vital society. Profit did not equal self-interest. Indeed, Wallace's vision of a cooperative culture rejected the evaluation of interests solely from the point of view of the individual bent on self-aggrandizement.

In arguing for such a position Wallace was exhibiting, as did other social critics of the era, the influence of cultural economist Thorstein Veblen. Wallace had first read Veblen's works—the seminal *Theory of the Leisure Class* as well as *The Theory of Business Enterprise*—around 1916 and had been strongly persuaded by Veblen's assessment of modern industrial civilization, above all his argument that modern technological society had come too much under the damaging sway of the businessman and his "business principles."[61] Energized by Veblen's critique, Wallace contended that the interconnectedness of the modern technological world meant that the general welfare was best served by actions that kept the entire social economy running smoothly. He insisted that the "profit motive" had to be done away with, since it was not a basis "on which can be built any lasting and desirable civilization." Neither competition nor combination had turned out to be solutions to the injustice of a "society that overpays the speculator and the business trickster, and underpays the producer." The act of working no longer received respect for its own sake but was judged only in terms of the profit it might create. People had little respect for those individuals who forwent opportunities for greater profit in favor of doing work that they enjoyed and that they believed benefited the community. The "American ideal," as Wallace termed it, had become one that valued only taking advantage of all opportunities with no reflection on social ramifications.[62]

Something else was needed, a new ethic to anchor modern industrial society, so that reward would go to those who most fulfilled their responsibilities to their fellow citizens. Wallace reckoned that people worked for two reasons only: for security, which included clothing, shelter, and food, and for what Veblen had called "the instinct of workmanship," meaning a natural "propensity" to pursue work in the most effective manner possible, avoiding "futile effort."[63] In Wallace's vision the complement to the instinct of workmanship was a social conscience and, derived from that, a concept of social service. Like Uncle Henry he suggested that cooperation arose from a communal impulse inherent in men and women. It came from an "instinctive desire" in people to create something useful to their fellow humans. Wallace wanted to combine the individual's social conscience with an appeal to Veblen's instinct of workmanship. Unlike industrial corporations, cooperatives would not aim at creating a dividend for stockholders living in some far-off place with no personal connection to the cooperative's endeavor. Instead, cooperatives would work to attain increased returns—and not only financial ones—for their members.[64]

More than a focus on social service, however, differentiated cooperation from the various forms of combination that existed in the industrial world. A final, crucial distinction in Wallace's mind was the expectation that all cooperative associations must be truly democratic in nature.[65] Since one of what Wallace termed the "intangible sources" of income from cooperation was the feeling of shared responsibility, any cooperative that was not wholly democratic in its operations would fail in its function.[66] Wallace recognized that this principle could become problematic when cooperation was practiced on a large scale. But he believed that the increased efficiencies that could be attained by larger enterprises, highlighted by the rise of corporate farming, made it worth the risk.

In the 1920s Wallace perceived America at a watershed. He wondered whether Americans were capable of creating democratic mechanisms of social regulation that could restrain the profit-hunting businessman while improving the life of the average citizen. Was it possible, he asked, to have "social efficiency and individual liberty in its best sense at the same time?"[67] With these questions, Wallace found himself confronting the old American conundrum, dating back to the nation's colonial origins, of how to balance the ideal of individual liberty with that of social responsibility. In the early decades of the twentieth century Wallace believed that the time had arrived to give greater weight to the latter principle.

Wallace was ambivalent as to what this meant for American culture. He hedged, for instance, as to whether the people of the United States would have to accept some degree of socialism. This was evident, for example, in his 1925 defense of the perennial McNary-Haugen bill for dealing with agricultural surpluses. Repeatedly put forth by representatives of agriculture during the 1920s (and repeatedly rejected by the Harding and Coolidge administrations), McNary-Haugen proposed to create a federal government export corporation for agricultural produce. Proponents of the plan, like Wallace, expected to raise farm prices by using the export corporation to dump agricultural surpluses abroad.[68] While its likely efficacy was admittedly arguable, Wallace insisted that McNary-Haugen should have its experimental trial and vehemently defended it against attacks labeling it socialist and even "bolshevist." Yet in his defense of the bill Wallace contended that to avoid "pure anarchy" there had to be some tinkering done with the so-called natural laws of economics. He pointed out, furthermore, that there were already many forms of regulation codified in the United States and that they were not decried as socialist. Wallace asked whether those who raged against the McNary-Haugen bill on this basis were ready to characterize tariff and immigration law, as well as the Federal Reserve Act, as "socialism" and "bolshevism." He wondered why it was that only laws proposing analogous regulation to the benefit of farmers were attacked in such terms.[69]

As the situation during the 1920s worsened for farmers, Wallace lost his fear of the word "socialism," actually insisting that "every man is at once a socialist and an anarchist." He effectively reconstituted the American conundrum in these terms, contending that the "urge for regulation" waged a continual battle with the "urge for perfect freedom," a construction he returned to repeatedly during the next two decades. "Anarchy" became Wallace's metaphor for unfettered, free enterprise capitalism. He buttressed this construct with another metaphor, drawn from his background in agricultural science and implying his essential faith in the necessity of experimentation. Wallace posited that the "old definition of a weed as a plant in the wrong place" was helpful in thinking about concepts such as regulation and freedom, socialism and capitalism. Just as sweet clover could be a weed in a corn field but "highly valuable" as a hay or pasture crop, so could either socialism or economic anarchy be both dangerous and valuable. In and of themselves they were meaningless, Wallace insisted—concepts without a context. With an experimenter's logic he suggested that the task for Americans was not to eliminate either principle but to understand both and discover by trial their proper balance within the bounds of shifting social contingencies.[70]

Cooperation in National and International Society

Wallace's thinking about cooperation began with an assessment of rural society for two reasons. First, it was what he knew best and, at the start, was most concerned with. Sharing the sensibilities of both Charles Roos and George Russell, while expressing another central tenet of the agrarian myth, Wallace suggested that farm and small-town life made up the only facet of American culture that at this early juncture in the twentieth century still contained the potential for satisfying the nation's desperate spiritual needs. Farm life was the very source, Wallace insisted, of "our virtues, our religious habits of thought, . . . [of] our very being."[71] The second and perhaps more practical reason for Wallace to commence his discussion of cooperation in the realm of agriculture was simply because it was there that the greatest efforts in cooperation had been undertaken by the 1920s. He frequently wrote of the already numerous examples of agricultural cooperation in the production, storage, shipping, and marketing of various crops.[72]

Yet Wallace also believed that at some point the ideal of cooperation had to extend beyond farming communities, to the rest of the nation. He understood that if his vision was to be realized it would require cooperation to develop not only within the national rural community but between the rural and urban worlds as well. At some point the same city dwellers that he criticized for their insensitivity to farmers' needs had to accept that their own futures depended on the survival of the rural culture.

As Wallace saw it, prior to the Great War urban laborers and farmers were in analogous situations. But immediately after the war it appeared that labor had profited at the farmer's expense; union efforts raised workers' wages, forcing up the prices of tariff-protected manufactured goods, while farmers' income decreased owing to the falling prices of generally unprotected agricultural produce. By the mid-1920s, however, Wallace discerned a change in organized labor's attitude, which gave him some hope. Some labor leaders seemed to exhibit "both sympathy and knowledge" of the farm situation. American Federation of Labor (AFL) support for an important agricultural bill under consideration by Congress in 1927 suggested to Wallace that workers and their representatives might be developing the sort of "broad outlook" that could give impetus to real cooperation between farmers and workers.[73]

Toward the end of the decade Wallace thought that businessmen also were coming around. He suggested optimistically that they were finally beginning to understand the relationship between the well-being of agriculture and the vitality of the larger economic community.[74] The Great Depression augmented this tendency, Wallace sensed, helping change the attitude of businessmen as never before. Indeed, he believed that the Depression was compelling everyone—businessmen, urban workers, and farmers—to come to terms with their respective biases, as centralization would require "both intelligence and openness of mind" if it were to be cooperative and thus humane.[75] Only the development of a tolerant spirit of community could set the stage for a truly cooperative national culture.

A similar temperament, Wallace implied, was required for a cooperative international order. As early as 1921 he articulated something like an international cooperative ethic, calling for a compassionate "morality" in world affairs, especially regarding the issue of war debts and their impact on the international economy. By the early 1920s, as the ramifications of the reparations problem became clear, it was apparent to Wallace that supposedly "impractical moral precepts," such as "forgive those who despitefully use you," held real economic significance. An international economy existed, created by the technological artifacts of the industrial age, whether national leaders recognized it or not. In light of this interdependent global community, Wallace believed it obvious that vengeance taken by one nation on another inevitably backfired.[76]

The truth of this conclusion seemed clear by the early 1930s. The United States and its former allies had failed to resolve the war debts and reparations quandary, which Wallace and other commentators—including Niebuhr—viewed as the major problem in global affairs. The failure on the part of the Western nations to temper their policy with leniency, if not with Wallace's hoped-for morality, greatly contributed to the chaotic state of the world economy, which undermined international relations in general. Wallace found it extraordinary that a civilization possessed of "wonderful inventions for producing the good things of life" could collectively destroy it all simply because its members refused to trust each other.[77]

Wallace was convinced that global cooperation, like the cooperation he longed for in American society, was greatly impeded by "ignorance and prejudice," which divided in this case not farmers from workers and businessmen but "nation from nation." In the same sense Wallace expected that the international situation would only improve when there developed "understanding, charity and confidence" among nations, that is, when nations adopted among themselves an ethic of cooperation. This meant that the peoples of all lands had to comprehend their mutual interdependence. Americans, Wallace insisted, must realize that "the welfare of Jones in Detroit, or Jones in England, or Shultz in Germany, not only touches our instinct to be helpful to other members of the great human family; it bears directly on our own welfare." Such an understanding was obvious to Wallace, believing as he did in a cooperative human instinct. He insisted to his readers that "as kindly human beings"—as well as financially astute ones—they should commit themselves to the betterment of their urban countrymen and -women as well as to that of other peoples around the world. In the end, Wallace was certain that issues such as the tariff, war debts and the distribution of wealth intimately affected all people, "as citizens of the world, as neighbors of the farmers and workers of every land."[78] That knowledge motivated him throughout the 1930s, after he left the Midwest to take up his duties in the nation's capital.

3

The "Transcendent Value of Personality"

Niebuhr's Critique of Modern Civilization

In the 1920s, primarily in his editorials in *Wallaces' Farmer,* Wallace laid out a vision of a civilization based on an American communal ethic. He presented this vision from the point of view of a man firmly entrenched in place and time, a Midwestern American whose family reached back several generations. Niebuhr did not have such a sense of place. Instead he had a complex of personal tensions and doubts concerning his ethnic background, his religious denomination, and his profession that were apparent in his writing during these years and that help explain the nature of the cultural critique he developed.

Niebuhr's self-doubt was apparent from the time he arrived at Yale Divinity School in 1913, when he sensed that he had entered an "elite bastion" in which his background made him feel, at least initially, as little more than a provincial outsider: as he described himself at the time, "a mongrel among thoroughbreds."[1] This uncertainty about self and career persisted in Niebuhr at least through his first professional decade. During his years as pastor of Bethel Church in Detroit, from 1916 until he left for New York in 1928 to join the faculty of the Union Theological Seminary, Niebuhr often questioned his choice of profession. The diary he kept during these early years—published in 1929 as *Leaves from the Notebook of a Tamed Cynic*—frequently exhibited this unsureness.[2] In it Niebuhr wondered if he was fit to minister to his parishioners and, if so, whether his ministrations gave any real succor to men and women ground down by a technological society that, in his

50

view, increasingly worshiped only at the dual altars of science and emotionless rationalism.

Such doubts help explain Niebuhr's central concern with the wide-ranging effects of industrial civilization on the life of the individual. This concern in turn led Niebuhr to his early interpretation of international relations, which for him was another aspect of the modern industrial world. Unlike Wallace, Niebuhr did not present a portrait or vision of the society he wanted to see. Rather his writings of the 1920s present us with the beginnings of a system of ironic social and political criticism combined with an obliquely introspective self-analysis that leave the historian a rather difficult task. Whereas Wallace placed his vision in plain sight, Niebuhr's antivision must be determined by inference and implication. His commentary was that of the Old Testament prophet; at times he perhaps intended no less. His message was an ironic confluence of warnings and judgments instead of specific prescriptions.

Niebuhr and William James

Connected to Niebuhr's introspection, and important to comprehending the origins of his commentary on American culture, was his understanding of the nature of human knowledge and its connection to reality. An excellent starting place for examining the epistemological underpinnings of Niebuhr's early thought is his bachelor in divinity thesis, written at Yale in 1914 and titled "The Validity and Certainty of Religious Knowledge." It exhibited Niebuhr's powerful need, as an aspiring young minister, to define a Christianity relevant to the modern scientific world, a concern that remained central in his thinking during the next decade and a half.

In his thesis Niebuhr drew on William James's notion of "realism" as a means of validating religious supernaturalism in "rational" terms. This enabled him to justify belief in religious revelation and faith within the intellectual bounds of the modern scientific outlook. By attacking absolutist idealism, an important philosophical basis of Western liberalism, in Niebuhr's view James became part of the "revolt of a growing moral consciousness" taking place in modern society. Individuals possessed of such consciousness, Niebuhr contended, were tired of engaging in life's struggle and coming away with a sense of powerlessness. They wanted to know that their efforts might have some real effect on the world.[3] Wallace was motivated by James to a "practical" mysticism and a search for the "worthwhile." For Niebuhr, James's philosophy offered a chance to know that such engagement might have real social impact.

What James did for Niebuhr was to attack effectively the rigid positivism that framed idealist philosophical thought. James condemned it in its most extreme form as "vicious intellectualism," arguing that mathematical or positivistic reasoning about human behavior was too mechanical and simplistic to adequately describe reality. James argued for the need to encounter life in order to know it. Further, and perhaps most important to the young Niebuhr, James made an explicit connection between the philosophy he was proposing and knowledge gained through religious experience, implying that a religious life could be a life of action. He disdained the absolute idealist insistence on an all-encompassing deity, arguing that God was not necessarily omnipotent or omniscient, which implied that experiential knowledge—religious or otherwise—could face the rationalism of the positivists as an equally valid explanation of the world. The two forms of knowledge, James speculated, might even come together harmoniously.[4]

With empiricist philosophy, James legitimized religious wisdom gained through experience along with experiential knowledge in general. By doing so he extended to Niebuhr an intellectual validation of religion that was comparable in its sophistication to scientific reasoning, during an era when all else seemed bent on undermining religion's credibility. At the same time James's critique enabled Niebuhr to form a crucial component of his developing logic. The philosophical idealism that James assailed was an important foundation of liberal thought, religious and secular, whose most important effect, Niebuhr asserted, was the perpetuation of a "complacent hope" that humanity's struggle was destined to work out well in the end. Such a hope, with its implication that people could have all at once the "glory of responsibility" and the expectation of "ultimate victory" in their struggle, made no sense to Niebuhr. By arguing this Niebuhr split asunder the immediate connection between moral idealism and action. He did not reject the former altogether; he simply argued that it had been overstressed by liberal idealists, reformers of various stripes who for too long had assumed that their own efforts were actually the irresistible machinations of a divine providence bent on human progress.[5] In asserting this Niebuhr began to establish the logic that one day would bring him into conflict with Wallace.

In his bachelor's thesis Niebuhr began to move moral idealism to a realm outside human action, that is, outside of history. Although he allowed that it could serve as a sort of transcendent norm, he did not believe it should be part of the calculus of action. Niebuhr's separation of moral idealism from human action had great significance in his thinking as he developed his critiques of various ameliorative ideologies ranging from liberalism to Marxism, from Pragmatism to pacifism, in realms both domestic and international. What started in 1914 as an explanation of why people should not expect too much of allegedly moral endeavors eventually formed a large part of the basis for Niebuhr's "realist" argument for removing moral idealism from immediate consideration in political and foreign policy making.

A Multifaceted Sense of Inadequacy

A year after completing his bachelor's thesis, Niebuhr completed his master's degree and began what turned out to be his only pastorate, at the Bethel Church of the German Evangelical Synod in Detroit. During his years at Bethel, and despite James's validation of religious knowledge, Niebuhr often felt himself something of an anachronism, not always sure if the ministry was an appropriate pursuit in the modern industrial world. In this sense the doubts he experienced at Yale persisted, remaining very much a part of his self-perception after arriving in Detroit.[6]

Such doubts were manifested on numerous occasions. On a ministerial visit to a hospital, for instance, Niebuhr felt antiquated in the presence of the doctors and nurses. Next to these agents of modern science, he perceived himself as being like an "ancient medicine man" suddenly transported into the twentieth century, and he suspected that the medical personnel saw him in the same way. On such occasions Niebuhr might continue to believe that "Jesus healed people," but he could not prevent himself from remembering that a large part of that healing took place "among the demented," whose testimony to its effectiveness might not be so credible.[7]

Niebuhr's misgivings grew stronger when he compared himself with another archetype of the modern era, the "businessman." In one instance at least this comparison took on a tacitly personal tone, suggesting that Niebuhr envied businessmen for more than just their connection to the instrumentalities of industrial civilization. Observing the dynamic young businessmen in his church, Niebuhr seemed jealous of their spontaneity. They seemed to lack the self-consciousness of the "more studious people," among whom he implicitly included himself. While they put thought and planning into their endeavors, they never stopped the "adventure of life"; they did not get caught up, as he so obviously did, in stultifying reflection on life's "difficulties and inadequacies." The thirty-four-year-old nondating bachelor went on to add that extroverted individuals in general seemed "happier and more wholesome" than introverts, pursuing their activities with "more robust energy" than did the "moody intellectuals."[8] One cannot help but assume that Niebuhr was once more referring to himself in the latter category, feeling very much the outsider looking in.

Niebuhr's biographer Richard Fox writes that one of Niebuhr's greatest disappointments upon his arrival at Bethel was in the "Germanness" of his congregation. Fox argues that this letdown stemmed primarily from Niebuhr's desire to seek his own self-improvement through "Americanization," which included the difficult mastery of English writing skills. Upon his arrival at Bethel Niebuhr feared that his efforts at mastering English—crucial to his mainstream journalistic aspirations—would be impeded by the demands of the synod's Germanic traditions, particularly that of German-language services. Yet Niebuhr's intention to Americanize himself did not arise solely from a desire for personal and professional improvement. It arose as well from a sense of exclusion engendered by his own and his parishioners' ethnicity.[9]

Some of this self-consciousness was tied specifically to the relative obscurity of his denomination, as is evident in a 1916 diary entry. In it he suggested that if he were a doctor, people would come to him for help on the basis of his medical skills. Instead, he felt that he could approach professionally only those who were "labeled" as he was religiously (and thus ethnically). He finally concluded, perhaps with a degree of unconscious denial, that what he considered his own "inferiority complex" stemmed from the numerically small membership of the German synod (rather than from the synod's cultural marginalization). If only he were part of a larger church, he speculated, he might "strut about and claim its glory" for himself. Implying his uncertainty as to whether he would remain in the profession he had now fully, if unreflectively, entered into, Niebuhr presciently suggested that if he did, he would have to discover an interdenominational means for occasionally stepping beyond his sect.[10]

German-Americans and the War

Niebuhr's concern with his German-American roots, apart from his church, was amplified by the start of World War I and the dilemma it posed all Americans of German origin. In the summer of 1916 he published an article in the *Atlantic Monthly* that was notable for a couple of reasons. The article effectively marked the beginning of Niebuhr's lifelong career in mainstream American intellectual journalism. Yet in its rather convoluted critique of German-American behavior during the first two years of the war, it also reflected the tension inside Niebuhr regarding his ethnic background. The frustration Niebuhr exhibited in the article arose in part from his perception that his fellow German ministers in Detroit were too accepting of German propaganda. They lacked "real interest in the welfare" of the United States and demonstrated "no genuine American patriotism." In the article Niebuhr argued that German-Americans "failed" America in two ways: by not exhibiting loyalty to American ideals and by not placing their specifically German traits in the service of those ideals.[11] In effect he was asserting, rather contradictorily, that Americans of German origin had not become culturally American and at the same time had not used their "Germanness" to strengthen American culture.

As his argument developed it grew stranger and harsher. German-Americans made contributions only to the economic side of American society, not to its "soul-life." He contended that the typical German-American demonstrated characteristic "thrift and industry" but only participated socially where personal interests overlapped general interests. In particular, the virtues of German-Americans seemed to Niebuhr to be too individualistic. They failed to show any real concern with what he considered the "great moral, political, or religious questions" of the Progressive Era. As proof of this failure Niebuhr argued that German-Americans consistently demonstrated indifference to American political problems, unlike, he suggested oddly, the Irish.[12] Ultimately Niebuhr made a very strained argument whose inadvertent thrust was a condemnation of German-Americans for acting more or less like average Anglo-Americans: looking out for their individual interests and not participating to any extraordinary extent in political affairs. In effect Niebuhr reproached those who shared his ethnic background not for failing to act like the average American but for not collectively becoming liberal reformers. He created a relatively simplistic model of German-Americanism, criticized it in a contradictory manner for not supporting American cultural values with its own cultural inheritance, and finally buttressed the critique with an attack on behavior that was at worst conservative but typically American nonetheless.

America's entry into the war only increased the contradictory feelings Niebuhr held concerning his ethnic background, which in turn led him to some further instances of tortured reasoning. For example, while reflecting on the war after ministerial visits to army training camps in 1918, he was filled with a sense of his own hypocrisy for not being able to side with the pacifists. The main reason for these feelings, he believed, was his "German blood." Nevertheless, he felt that his support for the war was a valid position, since a nation had a "right to be pretty sensitive about its unity." If one were to disavow one's nation's cause in such a time of crisis, Niebuhr insisted that it should be done only because of an unquestionably "higher loyalty." For himself, he worried that even a partial disavowal of America's war effort, however valid, would lead others to assume he had some latent loyalty to Germany.[13] Niebuhr's sense of his own ethnicity precluded the possibility of a neutral pacifism on his part, although he in no way accused all pacifists of supporting the German empire.

The underlying issue for Niebuhr was the demonstration of loyalty. He felt that it was absolutely necessary, especially during this war, that German-Americans actively prove their patriotism to the United States and, most essentially, their loyalty to American beliefs. Perhaps reaching for his own sense of spiritual connection to the United States, in lieu of an ethnic one, Niebuhr asserted that an American's love of country should derive from more than the fervency of blood ties. It should come from a sense of "kinship" grounded in "ideals and principles," what Niebuhr characterized as "spiritual kinship" and implied was even justified by the gospel. For Niebuhr a fundamentally important feature of American culture was this idea of loyalty to principle instead of "race," the focus of patriotism in Europe. American patriotism, he insisted, was founded on loyalty to the "institutions and ideals of democracy." To be American above all meant accepting America ideals.[14] In asserting this Niebuhr began to fashion an intellectual way out of his ethnicity. He was not Anglo-Saxon and never would be, but he believed he could be American by adhering to American values, by privileging American ideals above his German heritage.

This trend in Niebuhr's wartime thought culminated in an article he wrote in spring 1918 for the *Evangelical Herald,* his church's journal. In his role as general secretary of the War Welfare Commission of the Evangelical Synod he made what strikes a reader now as a rather excessively patriotic call for "Love of Country." Acknowledging that on occasion nations have abused their citizens' loyalty, Niebuhr still insisted that patriotism in the individual was "sublime and noble." Continuing with an illuminating choice of words, he declared that one had to be "dead of soul" to be unable to love the "land of his birth *or adoption.*" And one crucial proof of one's love of country was tolerance of its faults. Faintly foreshadowing the logic that would allow him to defend American culture in the 1940s and 1950s, Niebuhr contended that despite the nation's faults, if one loved it, one had to be "as tolerant as possible" in criticizing those faults. One need not be blind to the nation's failings to be patriotic, but it was necessary to demonstrate that criticisms were "criticisms of love." [15]

One test of one's love of country drew upon Niebuhr's argument that loyalty to America required the acceptance of American ideals. He asked his ethnic German readers if they appreciated "the individuality, the qualities of soul" that made America "great." If one had no appreciation for these values, if one could not see the worth of American "idealism," one did not truly love America, Niebuhr declared. In concluding he insisted almost rapturously that America was more than the sum of its material wealth. It was in fact "an ideal not yet fully realized but in the process of realization." [16] For Niebuhr, who usually spent his words stressing the need to beware of too strong a reliance on moralistic ideals, this construction was revealing. While upholding the validity of social criticism, he nevertheless defined Americanism as an appreciation of American ideals. He thus maintained the separation between morality and action that he had first delineated at Yale while simultaneously building a bridge into the culture he longed so much to feel a part of.

Personality and the Industrial Life

Not surprisingly, Niebuhr's longing to enter the mainstream of American life influenced his thinking tremendously. It made him highly sensitive to issues that touched on the question of the individual's sense of place in the world. In Niebuhr's philosophy this was exhibited in his use of the term "personality." In theology questions of personality were those concerned with an individual's experience of connection to the divine, of one's grounding in an ultimate "person," that is, God. [17] Niebuhr extended the word's use into his social and political discussions in a manner analogous to Wallace's argument in defense of cooperation, on the grounds that there was no individual well-being outside the context of a wholly vital society. For Niebuhr the concept of personality was a way to focus on the overwhelming alienation he saw in modern industrial society. Concern for personality was in part Niebuhr's way of coming to grips with his own sense of alienation.

Niebuhr's interest in personality was woven into much of his writing during the 1920s. It underlay, for example, his assessment of urban life, in which he shared much with Wallace. Like Wallace, Niebuhr saw a great deal of the spiritual damage of the modern world manifested in city life. Cities embodied overcrowding, corruption, crime, and poverty. Niebuhr believed that city life, built to support a factory-oriented economy, separated people from their natural environment and relationships, rendering them "morbid, self-conscious and artificial." Although he did not exhibit Wallace's enthusiasm for rural life, Niebuhr's acceptance of aspects of the agrarian myth supported his explanation of the spiritual isolation he saw all around him in Detroit during the 1920s.[18]

If cities had appeared as a result of the growth of industrial civilization, then it made sense that their immediate cause—the factory—stood at the center of Niebuhr's assessment of the damage done to personality. While in Detroit Niebuhr had close exposure to the dehumanizing nature of factory labor. Tours through factories demonstrated to him that life on the assembly line was "artificial . . . like a strange world." He noted that workers always seemed exhausted from their demanding labors and found no pleasure in their work. They worked only to survive.[19] Niebuhr, again like Wallace, evoked an imagined earlier time, a time when men and women supposedly felt close to their work, gaining satisfaction from it. He recalled an era when manual labor was neither drudgery nor slavery.

The problem, in Niebuhr's interpretation, was that modern industry, like the modern city and the modern nation, had become a "tyrant servant" to humanity. Technology should have provided people with higher levels of comfort and leisure, but instead it depersonalized production, taking away the worker's "creative joy." As Wallace argued regarding technology's impact on agriculture, Niebuhr declared that in creating our new industrial world all had been sacrificed for mechanical efficiency. No one gave any consideration to the tendency of modern technology to destroy the social connections that the right sort of labor could provide. In place of craftsmanship people had substituted materialism: a lifeless concern with simply "owning things."[20]

In the 1920s Detroit exemplified the modern industrial city. Its industrial plant revolved around one of the most modern of industries, automobile production. And in the early twentieth century there was one man whose name was synonymous with the automobile industry: Henry Ford, whom the public associated above all with the development of the "assembly line." Not surprisingly, it was the assembly line and its creator that became, for Niebuhr, dual symbols of much that was wrong with the factory worker's life.

In Niebuhr's commentary Ford personified the dilemma of modern industrial society in both his public position and his methods of production. Niebuhr conceded that the high level of efficiency found in the American automobile industry was due at least in part to its correspondingly high level of managerial "despotism." It was the pretensions of morality on the part of industrial despots that Niebuhr found preposterous. Yet it was the social acceptance of just such pretensions that allowed Ford and others like him to create a productive process that was physically brutal as well as degrading of personality. For example, when Ford announced in 1926 that he was cutting his workers' week down to five days, his advertising executives made it sound as if Ford was benevolently giving his employees an extra day off each week. Niebuhr, however, pointed out that in reality Ford just sped up the already high assembly-line speed so as to more than make up for any decrease in production. In truth, Niebuhr concluded, Ford simply saved the salary he would have paid for a sixth day of work.[21] Not only was Ford pushing his workers at a mind-numbing pace on the line, he was doing so while paying them less than ever for their efforts.

Personality, War, and Nationalism

If Henry Ford personified, for Niebuhr, one major aspect of the damage done the individual by the modern world, there was another significant, related theme in his commentary of the 1920s. Extending his analysis outward from industrial Detroit, Niebuhr utilized modern technological warfare as another lens through which to observe the depersonalizing effects of industrial civilization generally. In Niebuhr's analysis World War I offered more proof of how the advent of industrial civilization robbed men and women of any feeling of personal connection to the forces that governed their lives.

One thing was clear to Niebuhr: the process of making war in the modern world epitomized technological standardization and depersonalization. In a powerful essay published in the November 1916 *Atlantic Monthly,* Niebuhr argued that one of the greatest tragedies of the European war was its demonstration, despite liberal hopes to the contrary, that history had not especially favored "individual life." Ironically, although the rise of democracy in the West stressed the value of the individual, the concurrent rise of modern warfare demanded "an unprecedented suppression of individuality." Modern warfare's character was manifested not only in developments such as the newest forms and uses of artillery but in the "machine-like" nature of the military itself.[22] The modern West may have come to value the ideal of the individual above all else, but the way its wars were fought forced thousands of individuals into an amorphous, destructive mass, effectively overwhelming the uniqueness of any of its human components.

Niebuhr's writings suggest that he also saw modern war as a product of modern nationalism, which in his analysis contributed as much to the sublimation of the individual as did the high-technology industrial process. Niebuhr first addressed this issue specifically in his 1916 article in *Atlantic Monthly.* He considered the sacrifice of the "individual life" to the nation to be, as the article's title said, "The Nation's Crime against the Individual." This was not an entirely new phenomenon, he allowed, as the individual's needs had always been to a large degree subordinated to those of society. World War I, however, was a culmination of this historical unfairness. Yet the war had come about because of two additional developments that combined with nascent nationalisms. The first was the rise of "racial solidarity," which, in Niebuhr's view, partly accounted for the development of the modern German nation. Arguing in a manner that foreshadowed the tortuous logic of the articles he wrote after America's entrance into the war, Niebuhr insisted that Germany was a nation made up of various peoples, in implicit comparison to the United States. Yet Germany's nationalism derived from the "intense self-consciousness of a single race." Allowing that this was to some extent true of all nations, Niebuhr still contended that Germany was the best example of racially grounded national solidarity.[23] His implicit opposition of America and Germany on this fundamental issue is illuminating, for it reinforces the conclusion that the war heightened Niebuhr's personal dilemma over his ethnic roots, which in turn strengthened his concern with the erosion of personality.

The other historical development augmenting nationalism's effect, according to Niebuhr, was the rise of democracy. Democracy's impact was also ironic. Niebuhr of course acknowledged the validity of the belief that democracy was beneficial to the individual. Yet that belief's greatest impact, he argued, nullified its intent; evil issued from good. Certainly democracy had done much to free humans from tyranny, especially by supporting the rise of "constitutionalism" and thereby stable nation-states. But Niebuhr also posited that democracy increased the ability of the state to exploit the individual, as he believed the current war so clearly demonstrated.[24]

Niebuhr's overarching point here was that even if nationalism per se was not inevitably oppressive, it had definitely been rendered so by concurrent cultural developments such as racial solidarity and the rise of democracy. The problem that Niebuhr saw growing out of this confluence was that it prevented nations from recognizing a fundamental change in the world. Nationalism's mistake lay not in the size of its demands upon the individual but in the fact that it asked "so much to so little purpose." In the modern technological world the nation was no longer the individual's "ultimate community"; now, Niebuhr insisted, citizens of the world's nations were also citizens of the world. As Wallace might have asserted, Niebuhr insisted that the interconnectedness of twentieth-century civilization obligated each individual to all others. Nationalism, however, tragically compelled individuals to place national interests above the interests of the human community.[25]

Without quite realizing it Niebuhr was extending his division between morality and action to his analysis of the roots of the policies of nations. He was beginning to articulate an argument that was a central feature of his political commentary by the early 1930s, culminating in his book *Moral Man and Immoral Society*. Individual citizens might be capable of altruistic—that is, morally idealistic—behavior, such as sacrificing their lives in war for comrades and country. But those sacrifices were made, Niebuhr contended, because the leaders of modern nations understood the great level of support their citizens gave to transcendent principles. Yet such principles had not in any real sense dictated the international alliances that had formed. They could not have done so, Niebuhr declared, because by the early twentieth century no single nation could any longer validly lay claim to the "sole championship" of moral principles that transcended the powers and boundaries of individual nations.[26]

In arguing this Niebuhr implied that the basic values of Western liberalism, the ones that he considered quintessentially American principles binding the land of his birth together, were generally accepted by the peoples of the world. In other words, an international community of a transcendent, or rather an immanent, nature existed. By grounding this immanent international community in American principles, Niebuhr foreshadowed his post-1938 advocacy of Western culture. In 1916, however, he was about to commence more than two decades of rather harsh criticism of that same culture. In an assumption close to, but not quite the same as, one made by many Americans during the era of Wilsonian diplomacy, Niebuhr laid the fault for evil digressions from a moral internationalism not as much with the actions of leaders as with the almost mindless predilections of personlike nations unable to adjust to the vast changes of the modern world. Individual human beings could act altruistically, from what they felt were "universal values." Nations as of yet could still only act reflexively, on the basis of their perceived self-interests. In asserting this Niebuhr implicitly rejected Wallace's expectations regarding the extension of cooperative behavior from individuals to nations.

Economic Nationalism and International Affairs

In the case of the Great War, "interests," to Niebuhr, meant "commercial rivalry" resulting from "economic ambitions." Agreeing with interpretations like Wallace's that argued that nations went to war to secure imperialistic commercial goals, Niebuhr in 1916 remarked almost glibly that it was not even necessary to establish that the root cause of modern war was commercial rivalry; it was a given. Articulating his own version of the devil theory, he insisted that virtually all international conflicts arose from struggles for commercial supremacy. For Niebuhr, as for Wallace, it was tragic that citizens, with all their "idealism and sensitive moral instincts," gave up their lives in conflicts that only determined which states gained economic power. Niebuhr expanded this assessment throughout the 1920s, continually refining his version of the devil theory, reasoning that industrial concerns aggravated international tensions and ultimately concluding that humans could no longer control the technological monster they had created.[27]

In developing his interpretation of the causes of modern war Niebuhr began to describe the role he saw for America in the world. In an argument similar to one made frequently by Wallace in *Wallaces' Farmer* he insisted that the war made clear the reality of international interdependence. Americans might believe they could preserve their nation's prosperity while Europe's was wrecked, but eventually that belief would be proven wrong. Sooner or later, Niebuhr was certain, the citizens of the United States would learn that "no nation liveth of itself alone." And if global interdependence was indeed a fact, then the U.S. was, willy-nilly, a dominant participant. Americans had to accept this situation and the responsibilities that attended their country's new position. Thus in 1923 Niebuhr, too, supported the idea of an American policy of easing war debts, especially for France, in order to get that nation to lighten reparations demands on the Germans. Doing so would aid the recovery of the German economy, weakening the influence of the nationalists in German politics. Niebuhr believed this to be an important aim, since German nationalism aggravated French militarism.[28] In Niebuhr's construction the United States was clearly caught up in the causal circle of European wars, which themselves resulted from the mindless compulsions of modern industrialism.

Much depended on American actions, yet as far as Niebuhr could tell in the 1920s, the United States was constrained by its own economically based nationalism. This perception was augmented by his interpretation of developments at the London Conference of 1924, which issued in the so-called Dawes Plan. The plan was intended to settle the war debts-reparations conundrum—opening the door for German and general European economic recovery—by decreasing both Germany's overall reparations debt and its near-term reparations payments. Additionally, the German economy would be given an initial boost from international loans. The conference and its outcome gave Niebuhr some cause for optimism, especially since it seemed to him that the pact was made by liberal governments that had taken control of their respective countries from nationalists. Niebuhr suggested, however, that any agreement was vulnerable to American actions. He noted that both the conference and the Dawes Plan were dominated by "American bankers" and "American money," which did not make him optimistic. In Niebuhr's view the participation of the United States most likely resulted from the compelling American belief in the need to market the nation's prodigious industrial output. For the moment the United States appeared too economically self-interested, and Niebuhr doubted that policies based on such motivations could create enduring peace.[29]

Although Niebuhr was concerned during the 1920s with what he construed as a dichotomy between the possibility of individual and national altruism, he still believed at times that this state of affairs could change. Eventually, however, this contrast between persons and nations became more distinct for Niebuhr, leading him to argue that moral behavior ought never to be expected from nations. This implied that nations acting on the basis of their self-calculated national interests, economic or otherwise, were only being "realistic." The separation Niebuhr created between the ability of an individual to act on a self-sacrificing moral basis as opposed to the inability of a nation (or other collective) to do so was a constant and evolving theme in his writing from the early 1920s through the late 1930s.[30] It was central to Niebuhr's thought, and it contributed greatly to the impact he had on the thinking of Americans concerned with international relations during the 1930s and 1940s.

While Niebuhr did suggest in the 1920s that there might be a way out of the dilemma of selfish nationalism, he also acknowledged that the international community, to understate the case, was rather weak. Strengthening it, Niebuhr contended, required some transcendent ideal or cause that most, if not all, the people of the world believed in, an ideal that could not be co-opted by any national government. Both during and after the Great War many liberals placed their hopes for international transcendence in the League of Nations. While the peace conference was underway at Versailles Niebuhr was skeptical, but he did retain some optimism for the treaty. He was afraid above all that Woodrow Wilson, in face-to-face confrontations with supremely nationalistic French and British leaders, would compromise American ideals. Yet although he felt that the Europeans would ultimately beguile Wilson into acceding to a harsh peace, Niebuhr hoped that ideas would eventually "create reality." Even if at first the League might be no more than an association of victors, he believed that the "redemptive idea" at the League's heart would persist. Once again manifesting his valuation of idealism as an important transcendent norm, he insisted that while the realities of life often defeated ideals, the latter had a tendency of proving themselves valid in the end, of "taking vengeance upon the facts which momentarily imprison them."[31] Nevertheless, whatever encouragement Niebuhr may have felt concerning the League of Nations did not last long into the 1920s. By the middle of the decade he viewed institutions like the League as failed "mechanisms" for forcing peace into existence, little more than window dressing—essentially the same view he would hold of the United Nations two decades later.[32]

The Example of Germany

Niebuhr's pessimism regarding the League led him to look elsewhere for a transcendent motivation for international cooperation. Interestingly, though not surprisingly, one of the places that seemed to render Niebuhr quietly hopeful was Germany, the nation that for him best exemplified the damaging influence of nationalism in the industrialized twentieth century. Throughout the early 1920s Niebuhr exhibited a fascination with postwar Germany, which probably reflected the push and pull within himself as much as it did his concern with international affairs. Generally speaking, when he wrote on conditions in Europe—social, economic, or political—his focus was Germany, though he often extrapolated his conclusions. During these years Niebuhr published upward of a dozen feature magazine articles dealing with different facets of life in postwar Germany. The fact that most of them were published in journals not aimed at particularly German-American audiences (e.g., *The Christian Century, Atlantic Monthly, The Nation*) suggests the importance that Germany continued to hold in Niebuhr's thoughts as he developed his commentary on contemporary events. In the end he was convinced that anyone who wanted to understand the problems facing the postwar world would find Germany an especially "fruitful and rewarding study" because one could observe there in microcosm all the tensions of modern industrial civilization.[33]

Niebuhr believed that, of all the European nations, Germany was most devastated by World War I. This meant that, more than any other nation, Germany lacked the wealth and luxury that otherwise would paper over a modern nation's "moral limitations." Instead, in Germany those limitations were highlighted by the effects of the war, making the nation a clear example for Niebuhr of the damage done by industrial civilization. It allowed him to point out the social and economic dangers threatening the United States, which he reckoned was only superficially better off.[34]

It is illuminating that in Germany Niebuhr also found reason for optimism regarding international relations. Then again, in view of his penchant for irony as well as his internal tension over his ethnicity, it perhaps is not so surprising that Niebuhr saw promise in a situation that to others could hardly seem auspicious. One of the sources of the optimism Niebuhr felt was the existence of two strains of religiously based internationalism persisting in German domestic politics in the 1920s. Niebuhr believed the German Democrats, including a large contingent of "Jewish intellectuals," to be "sincere republicans" devoted to the goal of peace, in part because of the "Semitic genius for internationalism." At the same time the German Catholic Party was the only political party that had moved outside the interclass struggle in Germany. It too was staunchly republican and worked just as hard as the Democrats for Continental peace.[35]

The sad irony for Niebuhr was that it was these two "medieval" religions and not his own "modern" Protestantism that were tackling the dilemmas created by modern civilization. Nevertheless, this circumstance fit well with Niebuhr's overall critique of modern Protestantism. Drawing on his understanding of Max Weber's writings, Niebuhr declared that it was Protestantism whose "penchant for independence" not only contributed to the immoral character of modern industrialism but also gave rise to the concept of a morally autonomous nation. Catholicism, Niebuhr suggested, actually proved better at keeping faith with the struggles of the common people, who, as workers, bore the greatest burdens in contemporary civilization. This being the case, Niebuhr concluded that a political grouping grounded in Catholicism lent at least some promise of success to the cause of internationalism.[36]

The persistence of the republican Weimar government in Germany was another factor informing Niebuhr's hopes for world affairs. In Germany at the end of summer 1924 Niebuhr witnessed the celebration of the fifth anniversary of the Weimar constitution. As bad as things were in Germany in the early 1920s, Niebuhr felt justified in writing back to the readers of the *Evangelical Herald* that it was likely that the republic had already survived the "worst storms." He felt that the foes of the government were disorganized, while those who stood with the republic were staunch in their determination and seemed to hold a majority.[37]

This assessment was supported by the apparent weakness of what Niebuhr described in an earlier article as the German "klan," made up of "nationalist and monarchist extremists." These were of course the original Nazis, already headed by the two best-known party leaders, Adolf Hitler and Erich von Ludendorff. Noting the intense racism of the National Socialists, focusing primarily on the Jews, Niebuhr still concluded that the German klan was not very strong, certainly not as powerful as its American counterpart (at peak strength in 1924). Above all he was convinced that an organization made up of monarchists and extremists had little hope of success, primarily because German workers, the target of the National Socialists' enlistment campaigns, were in his estimation strongly supportive of the republic, extremely anti-militarist, and not especially race prejudiced. In fact, Niebuhr believed that the National Socialists would very soon disappear from German politics, although he did expect that their rather vicious strain of anti-Semitism would persist in German society for quite a while to come.[38] He was half right.

Niebuhr's assessment of the predilections of German labor was part of what led him to such inaccurate prophesies regarding German and, ultimately, European affairs. He perceived an almost heroic perseverance on the part of German workers in the face of the severe economic dislocations of the postwar years. Labor was the cause, while resurrection of personality was the ideal, that could lead the men and women of his time to surmount the ravages of nationalistic competition. As we have already seen, a large portion of his writing on domestic affairs focused on the human degradation caused by industrial labor, and it was in championing the struggle of the working class that Niebuhr came politically to socialism in the 1920s. Even his religious commentary during this period, which will be discussed shortly, dealt with creating a Protestantism that would be less a "tool" of the middle class and more a true advocate of working people, whose sense of self-worth was so damaged by industrial society. It is not surprising, then, to find that Niebuhr saw hope for better international relations in an inherently internationalist working class, epitomized by German labor.

The conditions under which German workers struggled during the 1920s were, in Niebuhr's view, the worst in Europe. He wrote at length about the ravages of German inflation, ultimately insisting—with a metaphor that invoked the plight of American workers—that Germany had become the "sweatshop" of the world. Yet not only did the German workers persevere through such a horrendous existence, they continued, if barely, to stand as a bulwark against the extremisms of the nationalists and the communists. In Niebuhr's interpretation German labor was another potential bridge to European peace, along with that of the Catholic and German Democratic parties. Meetings he witnessed between German, French, and English workers in which agreement was reached on the reparations question convinced Niebuhr as well as the workers themselves that if only they held more political power in their respective countries, they could solve Europe's problems and bring peace to the continent.[39]

Protestantism, Personality, and Reform

Niebuhr was certainly not the first to see labor as an internationalizing force. This of course was a basic assumption of Marxism, with which Niebuhr was developing a complicated and ambivalent intellectual relationship by the mid-1920s. But Niebuhr was not suggesting a collectivist social policy. Rather he was bringing closure to his critique of modern industrial civilization. Nationalism, to Niebuhr, was one of the most dangerous forces in the modern industrial world. It both amplified and was amplified by contemporary economic and productive processes. The working class, whether in Detroit under the thumb of Henry Ford or in Berlin oppressed by impending economic collapse, suffered the most, in war and peace, from the effects of this evil combination. Thus, as Marxism insisted, Niebuhr realized that laborers had the most to gain if humanity succeeded in controlling these forces. Niebuhr, however, did not usually propose to attain such goals through violent revolution, nor even, necessarily, by an equalitarian improvement of material life.

Niebuhr was not ultimately concerned with the material life of the individual, worker or otherwise. It was not Ford's or American industry's lack of real benevolence that was most significant in Niebuhr's criticism. Unlike many other social reformers of this era, Niebuhr believed that even an industry that surrendered all that labor demanded in terms of wages and hours but did not give workers any chance for the "exercise of personal initiative" remained a peril to society. What was most damaging about the modern factory was its destruction of personality. Its automated production processes had taken away, Niebuhr wrote, "most of the creative and personal satisfactions which make human life tolerable." Since this was the case, he believed it was of paramount importance that the worker's role be altered in a manner that indicated "he is recognized as a *personality* in the industrial society."[40]

Niebuhr believed that a sense of connection to the social productive process had to be restored to all individuals. This was where religion's role was crucial. Yet for Niebuhr the nature of that role differed in degree and character from the proposals of other social reformers of this era. This included advocates of the Social Gospel, with whom he shared many immediate goals. One area where Niebuhr disagreed with many of his contemporaries was over the stress they placed on individual morality. In 1920 he was fairly optimistic, asserting that American politics and society were heading in the direction of "some kind of democratization of industry and some degree of socialization of property." The churches could well contribute to this process by appealing to the consciences of the capitalists, but Niebuhr did not think this sufficient. American churches needed to be less concerned with "personal salvation" and "individual sin" and more with the evils of interclass oppression. It was not enough to simply have more benevolent individual businessmen. Like Wallace, Niebuhr believed it was necessary for the basic values of society to change.[41]

Unlike Wallace, however, Niebuhr soon realized there were great obstacles preventing this sort of transformation from taking place, one of which was American Protestantism itself. Showing once again the influence of Weber's thesis, Niebuhr explained that Protestantism was by its nature individualistic, which in the economic realm was expressed in the principle of laissez-faire. Thus Niebuhr believed that much of Protestantism combined a well-developed moral sensitivity with a "complete indifference" to social problems.[42] This argument was similar to his suggestion that Protestantism contributed to the rise of the idea of a morally autonomous nation. The only difference was in the field of human affairs under observation. In one case it was international relations, in the other, intrasocial. In both situations he further developed the morality split he first outlined at Yale: the individual was capable of moral altruism, the social group was not (or, at best, was less so). Just as Niebuhr's evolving analysis of foreign affairs hung on this construction, so did his criticism of American social reform.[43]

One of Niebuhr's primary objections regarding the Social Gospel was its advocates' assumption that individual morality was somehow directly transferable to the various social groupings that an individual might belong to. He complained in his diary that far too many sermons were grounded in the assumption that churchgoers were "committed to the ethical ideals of Jesus" and that they were thus the primary source of "energy" for social reform. Yet Niebuhr hardly found this a valid conclusion. He contended that it was actually very difficult to move individuals who subscribed to a "general ideal" to apply that ideal specifically. Amplifying this difficulty was the fact that the church itself continually was willing to rouse moral emotions but generally did little to connect those emotions to specific actions.[44]

While it would be inaccurate to portray Wallace as an outright champion of the Social Gospel, particularly during the years of his rejection of Protestantism, in Niebuhr's critique of the Social Gospel we can still observe the early outlines of the critique he later brought to bear against Wallace's liberalism. By 1907 Walter Rauschenbusch, the predominant figure of the Social Gospel movement, had asserted the primacy of individual salvation on the road leading to social reconstruction. The salvation of individuals, he argued, ultimately would evolve into a saved society.[45] Niebuhr of course did not foresee any such process. Indeed, what was clear to him was that many of the ills of modern society resulted from the lack of transference of individual morality to the social group. Once again drawing upon Weber, Niebuhr argued that Protestantism's exaggeration of individual righteousness actually had given moral authority to the rise of capitalist business practices. The incredible wealth produced by the latter eventually gutted the underlying morality.[46] In other words, individual religious morality had very much contributed to social evil instead of social morality.

Niebuhr also disagreed with Rauschenbusch and his adherents' belief that social scientific knowledge could empower Christianity in its quest for social reconstruction, a position one could imagine Wallace holding. Niebuhr had no such faith in the social sciences. Foreshadowing his vehement 1932 attack on John Dewey, Niebuhr called instead for an "ultra-rationality," an intelligence beyond the limits of scientifically oriented knowledge. He believed that social morality derived from a "reverence for personality" that was not necessarily rational. Rather, it resulted from experiential religious knowledge, the sort that William James's work had first helped Niebuhr understand. One of the great mistakes Niebuhr felt social reformers made was in assuming that group conflicts could be settled by rationality alone. Manifesting the nature of his evolving socialism, he insisted that what was required was moral restraint upon the overlapping needs of individuals and groups, and the moral restraint Niebuhr envisioned could only come from the knowledge gained by experience and faith. As he had first done in his bachelor's thesis, Niebuhr again insisted that while scientific intelligence had great value, it could also render a person or a society too sophisticatedly impersonal. It could create powerful technical capacities ungoverned by any humane sensitivity. It was crucial, Niebuhr contended, to "preserve . . . naivete" and the wisdom inherent in it to maintain what he termed a "poetic outlook."[47]

Re-creating Protestantism for an Industrial Society

Such reasoning led Niebuhr to praise Catholicism and its symbolic ritualism during these years, another point of divergence from Rauschenbusch and the Social Gospel. While Rauschenbusch had written that it was the turning of early Christianity to sacramental ritual that had "paralyzed its power of moral transformation," Niebuhr, conversely, saw much value in the ceremonialism of the Catholic Church.[48] Part of this arose from his doubts about his own denomination and the value of its services as well as those of liberal Protestantism in general. For Niebuhr religion at its best was like poetry, and poetry's truth inhered in its symbols. This meant, in a way that James (and probably Wallace) would understand, that symbolic religious ritual was frequently more meaningful than the drab prose with which Niebuhr believed most Protestant preachers tried to "grasp the ineffable."[49] For Niebuhr ritual had the advantage of the dramatic tension inherent in its presentation.

Niebuhr's doubts about the effectiveness of Protestant nonritual in reconnecting the individual to the divine informed his overall critique of the modern world. Although he did suggest that the authoritarianism of the medieval Church diluted its sense of social responsibility, he still believed the Catholic Church of the Middle Ages had something of a "social conscience" that present-day Protestantism could learn from. Of greater import to Niebuhr, the Catholic Church retained some of this social conscience in the modern era, certainly more than Protestantism had. In Germany, for instance, the heroic struggle of labor that Niebuhr described was supported more by Catholicism than by Lutheranism, suggesting an inherent Catholic social conscience despite that church's flaws.[50]

The crux of Niebuhr's broadly sweeping criticism of the Protestant church and of modern industrial civilization in general always came back of course to the worker, to the individual humans who collectively made up the "masses." This was not because Niebuhr saw the world so much as an arena of class conflict, although increasingly during the late 1920s and early 1930s he did. Rather it was because in Niebuhr's interpretation of society and history the worker as an individual had been most robbed by the industrialized world of a sense of connection, of value, of personality. Thus Niebuhr's hopes for social change focused, by the last years of the 1920s, on the advent of a revitalized Protestantism, one that could fulfill what he saw as religion's proper role as the "champion of personality in a seemingly impersonal world." A renewed Christianity, eschewing Protestantism's spiritual enervation for a dose of Catholicism's symbolic passion, could inspire the necessary "mystical reverence" for human personality. By doing so it might persuade individuals to uncover "personal values in the universe," having already found evidence of the "transcendent value of personality" in the lives of their fellow humans.[51]

Unlike other Christian social reformers of the time, Niebuhr did not feel that an "immediate reward" would necessarily issue from each ethical action, and religion did not and ought not promise this. What it should do, he declared, again echoing an insight he had first articulated at Yale nearly a decade and a half before, was give a person the "final satisfaction" of being assured of the existence of a universe cognizant of the values for which the highest price was demanded, a universe not indifferent to the individual's struggle.[52] A church that could move the individual, that could make the individual feel connected to the social process, to something important and transcendent, would fulfill what Niebuhr believed to be its primary task.

By the end of the first decade and a half of his career, Niebuhr, like Wallace, had fashioned a sweeping assessment of the modern industrial world. Unlike Wallace's sense of place, however, the wellsprings of Niebuhr's outlook were the early doubts he had felt about his own place in American society. Those doubts made him amenable to the logic of reality and human action that the writings of James had first suggested to the young Yale divinity student, just as James had helped mobilize the young Wallace to attempt a fusion of science with religion. But despite certain parallels and similarities with Wallace, Niebuhr was moved by James's logic to a growing skepticism about any ideology that too idealistically promised society's inevitable salvation, while his awareness of self made him extraordinarily sensitive to issues concerning the individual's sense of place in the scheme of things. At the same time, Niebuhr's personal and professional uncertainties in turn impelled him to articulate his social criticism in forums outside his own denomination.

Niebuhr's writings had not yet attained the range of publication that they would within the next decade. Yet by 1930 he was writing on a regular basis, as a contributing editor for both the *Christian Century* and the *World Tomorrow*, while still contributing columns to the *Detroit Times*. He was writing as well, if not with the same frequency of publication, for more mainstream periodicals such as the *Atlantic Monthly* and *The Nation*. Niebuhr in other words had already gone a long way toward building a personal bridge out of his self-perceived cultural isolation.

By the late 1920s Niebuhr had fashioned a critique of industrial civilization that encompassed the affairs of the city he lived in, of his own nation as a whole, and, ultimately, of the international arena. That critique left him, however, in an appropriately ironic situation. Despite his desire to experience himself within the flow of mainstream American culture, it was that very culture he was becoming increasingly critical of. Even though much of his commentary focused on postwar German society, by the early 1920s Niebuhr began to see America as the epitome of the modern urban-industrial civilization that so degraded personality. He was caught in a self-fashioned paradox of attacking that which he so much wanted to feel a part of. Perhaps not so surprisingly, it would be events in Germany during the subsequent decade—as well as the coming of World War II—that enabled Niebuhr to overcome this new personal dilemma.

4

A "Pitchfork against the Belly" of Europe

Wallace and Niebuhr on the Ironies of Global Interdependence

⟶⋅⟶

In MARCH 1933 Wallace began what was in effect his third career. Once more following in his father's footsteps, the agricultural scientist turned farm editor now entered national affairs for the first time as a policy maker, as Franklin Roosevelt's secretary of agriculture. For Niebuhr the 1930s were the years when he came into his own as both a theologian and nationally respected political-cultural commentator. He already had more than a decade's experience behind the pulpit in Detroit and by 1930 was established as a professor of Christian ethics at the prestigious Union Theological Seminary in New York City. Yet his outsider's perspective remained apparent, particularly in his tendency to draw on developments in Germany as substance for his social and political commentary. Although in several instances the two men focused on the same issues during these years—particularly on questions of international economic relations—they often addressed entirely different topics in their commentaries. Wallace of course was most concerned with issues connected to American agriculture, although he began to move from his direct concern with place and "the land" toward a more diffuse focus on questions of "community" and culture on a national and global scale. Moreover, as a leading member of the Roosevelt administration Wallace was constrained as a critical commentator in ways Niebuhr was not. Indeed, at times Wallace acted as a virtual cheerleader for New Deal policies, a role that amplified his editorial writer's inclination toward analytical oversimplification. Niebuhr, however, further developed his critical examination of nationalism and power, cheerleader for no one. For him the concept of power became an unchanging absolute in human affairs. In contrast to Wallace's expectations of vast, hopeful changes in human nature and behavior, Niebuhr determined that human nature was not changeable, at least not in the foreseeable future.

By the early 1930s Niebuhr's journalistic output had expanded greatly. He contributed regularly to various mainstream journals of the day, including *Atlantic Monthly, Harper's,* and *The Nation.* He also wrote for major contemporary Christian journals, continuing as a contributing editor at the *Christian Century* while at the same time editing the *World Tomorrow* and *Radical Religion.* In addition, his books were being published by major presses such as Scribner's and Harper and Brothers. By the middle of the decade, through several books as well as from thirty-five to seventy articles and columns per year, Niebuhr had fashioned for himself a multifaceted outlet for the whole range of his commentary.

The best known of Niebuhr's writings from these years was the book *Moral Man and Immoral Society,* published in 1932. Although often seen as a "breakthrough" effort, it was in many aspects a thematic aggregation of much of Niebuhr's thinking, both theological and cultural, since the 1920s. The essential thesis of the book was itself a culmination of Niebuhr's evolving view, first articulated a decade and a half before, that nations were incapable of the altruism sometimes exhibited by individuals. In substantiating this argument Niebuhr rehearsed and extended his commentary on the effects of technology and nationalism on human behavior, on the economic sources of national behavior, on questions of power in society and the relativity of moral values, as well as on the likelihood of international cooperation. In addition, he elaborated his ambivalence toward what he termed idealism in lengthy critiques of liberalism and pacifism.[1]

During the early 1930s both Wallace and Niebuhr spent much time assessing the dire effects of global depression and in certain areas their commentaries were complementary. But despite occasional flashes of optimism, Niebuhr did not share Wallace's often hopeful conclusions.

Niebuhr saw no clear resolution to the predicaments of the 1930s. Although Wallace's vision per se did not become a focus of Niebuhr's critique during these years, the faint beginnings of opposition were there nonetheless. For Wallace the Depression presented an opportunity, a potential portal to the "New Age." For Niebuhr the Depression was not only proof of the failure of industrial capitalism; it also illustrated the inherent and possibly fatal weaknesses of the various other ameliorative ideologies that stood in opposition to capitalism. The perspective that Niebuhr developed in the early 1930s was critical of virtually every political opinion of the day that offered to mitigate contemporary difficulties. In all of them Niebuhr saw crucial flaws, some combination of idealistic absolutism with simplistic or mechanistic thinking. None of these perspectives, in Niebuhr's view, recognized the truly complex nature of both human existence and the dilemmas facing humanity in the modern industrial civilization of the 1930s. Based on such criticisms, Niebuhr's outlook further evolved toward the form and content that eventually came into direct conflict with liberal perspectives such as Wallace's.

Wallace and the Legacies of World War I

Most daunting for Wallace, upon his arrival in Washington, D.C., were the very problems he had commented on for over a decade as a nationally respected farm editor and leader. By early 1933 the Great Depression had reached its greatest depth; unemployment rates in some cities reached 50 percent or more, while farm foreclosures shut down agricultural production across entire regions of the nation. Wallace of course was most concerned with the Depression's effects on American farmers, whose problems were now his direct responsibility. He saw the origins of modern-day agricultural problems in the mid-nineteenth-century revolution in agricultural technology, which, amplified during the early twentieth century, resulted in huge agricultural surpluses, decreased income, and increased, often ruinous debt. Further, Wallace was convinced that the problems of U.S. agriculture were intertwined with those of American industry and, ultimately, the world. Eventually

Wallace came to believe that the entire global economic structure was so badly damaged that the salvation of American agriculture paled in importance next to the need to establish full understanding between classes and between nations.[2]

For Wallace, addressing the global dilemma above all meant facing the two predominant international economic quandaries of the interwar era. The first was itself a twofold problem: the combination of reparations payments owed by Germany to the Allies and the war debts the Allies owed the United States. The second controversy was the ongoing global discord over the network of tariffs governing the flow of exports and imports throughout the world.

Like many other American commentators, including Niebuhr, Wallace believed that much evil had come from the Treaty of Versailles that ended World War I. The primary source of difficulty was the treaty's "war-guilt" clause, establishing Germany's sole culpability for the war. Influenced by English economist John Maynard Keynes's well-known condemnation of the tremendous reparations burden placed upon Germany at Versailles, Wallace declared the treaty to be the embodiment of the "spirit of nationalistic hatred," leading not only to outrageous reparations payments and international debts but to tariff wars as well. And, like Keynes, Wallace believed that France was most culpable for creating this situation. French insistence on restrictive monetary policy and low prices, even in the face of global economic collapse, so that German reparations payments would remain as crushing as possible, seemed to bear this interpretation out. The French, Wallace concluded in 1932, were "the outstanding menace to world peace and prosperity." Compounding the problem, in his view, was the fact that most Americans seemed to agree with the French. Driven by the residual influences of super-patriotic, anti-German wartime propaganda as well as by postwar xenophobia, Americans, Wallace sensed, were more interested in hurting Germany than in helping the United States. In any case, they were not amenable to proposals for easing Germany's reparations burden.[3]

Yet it was not just resistance, American or French, to lessening the reparations burden on Germany that perpetuated global economic problems. The other half of the debt-loan issue was the United States' insistence on the repayment of loans it made to the Allies during the war. The unwillingness of American governments during the 1920s either to forgive or meaningfully decrease the debts of Britain and France was a crucial component in a rather vicious circle. As long as the United States demanded payment from the Allies, they—especially the French—were unlikely to back off on their demands for reparations from Germany. Americans thus found themselves making loans to Germany that effectively were passed on to the British and French in the form of reparations and thence back to the United States as payments on the war loans. While they were willing to make adjustments in payment schedules, Americans and their leaders remained resistant to suggestions that the debts be forgiven. As Calvin Coolidge had pointed out with characteristic terseness, the Europeans had "hired the money" in the first place.

Wallace saw no validity in this sort of reasoning. He understood that the nature of international debt was quite different from that of personal debt, belying logic like that of Coolidge. International debts of such huge scale could not be settled like those between a shopkeeper and a small-town banker. This assessment, combined with his concern for the financial straits of American farmers, led Wallace to favor a real decrease, even a cancellation, of the debts. In his opinion such a policy was vital to any chance that the nations of the world might have of working their way out of the Depression which, not incidentally, was sapping foreign demand for America's surplus agricultural and industrial production.[4]

The decrease in foreign demand for American products was exacerbated, in Wallace's view, by the other crucial source of international economic discord, the U.S. tariff. In the first decades of the twentieth century American tariffs had risen to heights previously unimagined, culminating in the Smoot-Hawley Tariff Act of 1930, part of the American response to the Depression. Despite its wartime transformation into an international creditor, the nation's tariff policy had continued its prewar trend upward. To Wallace the Smoot-Hawley tariff embodied an American refusal to purchase enough European products to allow debtor nations to earn the dollars necessary to pay off their American loans. To the Europeans, he argued, the tariff's passage proved the

United States' intention to profit at their expense. By 1931 the nations of the world were striking back, creating their own impenetrable tariff walls. American economic nationalism, Wallace declared, undermined the global economy, instigating a virtual trade war.[5]

In a related sense this construction of international economic affairs also shaped Wallace's attitude toward the Soviet Union during the early 1930s. If not for the impact of the Depression on international trade, Wallace might have continued viewing Russia from the benign perspective of an agricultural scientist and economist as something of a grand agricultural experiment. But the advent of economic warfare led him to view the Soviets as potential commercial adversaries, ultimately causing him to oppose U.S. diplomatic recognition of the USSR in 1933 as well as to question possible loans to the Soviets that were proposed in conjunction with recognition.[6]

Niebuhr on Postwar International Affairs

Like Wallace, Niebuhr had been concerned since the mid-1920s with the international economic discord arising from World War I. Niebuhr too was particularly critical of American foreign economic policy and viewed tariff barriers and reparations as the greatest threats to global peace. Not surprisingly, such issues remained important topics of his commentary in the 1930s. With their economies in deep depression, the nations of the world were all leaping "instinctively" to tariff protection, Niebuhr insisted, which he believed was no solution at all to the complicated problems of an interdependent world. Niebuhr doubted the Europeans were possessed of the "moral energy and good will" to transcend their animosities, while the United States behaved no better, continuing to demand repayment of the European debt, while refusing through its tariff wall to purchase European products.[7]

Actually, Niebuhr viewed the conduct of the United States in a harsher light than did Wallace. He believed that the international need for American dollars might make it possible for the United States to maintain its high tariff for quite a while even as it amplified anti-American sentiment. But the situation was inherently unstable. To the nations making the various payments required to support global economic arrangements, those payments seemed like "pure tribute." There simply was no valid justification for them in light of the interdependence of the modern world. For Niebuhr American insistence on prolonging this setup was irresponsible and quite dangerous. In the long run, he was convinced, if the United States remained so politically insensitive while in fact increasing its own global economic dominance, the likelihood of another world war would only increase.[8]

If the economic policy of the United States was the most internationally irresponsible, in Niebuhr's view it was Germany, not surprisingly, that suffered most from it. Still a central focus in his cultural criticism of the 1930s, the German situation allowed Niebuhr to describe specifically the damage wrought by American financial behavior. The Germans, he argued, in effect were paying the war debts of all the nations. Germany was being transformed into a "slave nation" just so the Allies would have the funds to pay back the monies they owed the United States.[9]

In Niebuhr's assessment the reparation payments continually undermined the German economy, precluding its recovery from the war's devastation. By 1930 the frailty of the German economy was exhibited in huge deficits, tremendous rates of unemployment, and continually declining wages. Yet as before Niebuhr perceived the bleakness of the German situation not just in economic terms but from a "political and a psychological standpoint" as well. Most frightening to his mind was that German resentment contributed to the rise of both fascist and communist political extremism. At times he was amazed the Weimar Republic survived at all. This relative success he still attributed to German workers, whose Social Democratic Party remained loyal to the republic even in the face of extreme political philosophies. Nevertheless, he feared for parliamentary government in Germany if that country remained under the same economic stresses that pressed it since the end of the war. If no respite came to the German people, Niebuhr speculated in 1931, they might actually undertake a "fascist experiment"—offering militarism as a means of evading social and economic pressures—or become communists and seek relief by aligning their nation with the Soviet Union. Either eventuality, Niebuhr contended, would threaten world peace. And American indifference would stand as the root cause of such a turn of events.[10]

America's International Irresponsibility

In Wallace's criticism of American international economic policy during these years, the overarching implication was that since America was the predominant creditor nation after World War I, its behavior affected the world's economy more than that of any other country. Thus it followed that the United States had a greater responsibility to the world than any other nation, commensurate with its newly attained power. This meant that American intransigence on the war debts issue, in combination with the maintenance of a high tariff, was greatly culpable for the present global economic mess. Wallace continually insisted it was "economic absurdity" for the United States to maintain a high tariff while demanding repayment of the European debt. With somewhat bizarre agrarian imagery, he asserted in a letter that America was trying to have it both ways, "like a person who puts a rope around the neck of another person and tries to draw that person to him while at the same time this person puts a pitchfork against the belly of the other person and tries to push that person away." Such a situation, Wallace noted with understatement, was clearly untenable and likely to lead to disaster.[11]

In Wallace's interpretation the reparations, debt, and tariff controversies offered salient examples of American irresponsibility in international relations as well as a means of measuring the vitality of those relations. They were "barometric in nature," indicative of the chances for reestablishment of international trust. If the United States persisted in its demand for the full payment of the Allied loans, without at least partially rescinding its high tariff, then Wallace feared a total global economic collapse.[12] But if Americans altered their policy, such disaster might just be averted.

In fact, Wallace did not expect disaster. He felt that there was a way out of the growing international economic quagmire through the restoration of trust between the United States and the Europeans.

Moreover, in the global depression he saw not tragedy but rather opportunity. The worldwide economic devastation of the early 1930s was, in Wallace's expansive vision, a watershed in history. The crisis was potentially another portal to the New Age. Wallace fervently believed that America and the rest of the world had a chance to move away from an existence characterized by the paradox of want in the face of abundance—ironically created by the components of modern technological civilization—to a world of abundance for all in a context of international harmony. He could not imagine that the chance would not be taken.

Niebuhr, too, perceived irresponsibility in American foreign policy. World War I had transformed the United States into a great power in the brief span of two years. Recognizing the war's reversal of America's global debtor-creditor status, Niebuhr argued that the tremendous postwar economic strength of the United States established a new type of imperial entity. The American empire was not like historical empires, with dominion based on military strength; its strength derived instead from its wealth. The result of this was ironic: American wealth went out into the world in successive generations of loans, each generation funding those made before, thus reinforcing the foundation of American power. As Niebuhr put it, Americans "are not prosperous because we are imperialists, . . . [rather] we are imperialists because we are prosperous."[13]

Niebuhr reckoned that such dominance had to rankle. It was inevitable, he insisted, that people would eventually despise those whose power controlled their lives, so America gained the world's scorn partly by virtue of its postwar stature. Yet the United States compounded the problem by not wielding its power well. Unlike the British, Niebuhr insisted, Americans possessed no "political grace." The Germans did not either, but in a different sense. In Niebuhr's view the Germans were too much philosophical absolutists in utilizing power while Americans were "too much the engineers." American power and the economic empire that derived from it were the results of American technical know-how. Moreover, Niebuhr argued, America's graceless, engineer-like handling of imperial power was augmented by what he termed the "puritan background" of the United States. The puritan sensibility, by which he meant the "individual virtues of self-discipline," devolved into a cultural tendency to construe all moral and social issues in the simplest of terms. Americans, Niebuhr claimed, had difficulty grappling with the complexity of the world. They were overly moralistic and extraordinarily naive in their approach to international affairs. They made simplistic moral judgments regarding complex international issues, without the slightest consciousness of the ways in which American interests informed those judgments. And they were shielded from an accurate perception of global realities by a still potent "evangelical piety." Niebuhr believed that this combination of traits conspired continually to disappoint Americans, who always seemed shocked that other peoples refused to regard the citizens of the United States as "saviors of the world."[14]

Niebuhr saw no better proof of the way this compounding of mechanistic thinking with moral reductionism informed American perceptions of international affairs than the great enthusiasm in the United States for the Kellogg-Briand pact of 1928. The Kellogg-Briand pact for the outlawry of war, formally known as the Pact of Paris, grew out of a conjunction of the efforts of American peace activists with the desire of the French government to tie the United States diplomatically to the security of postwar Europe. Ultimately signed by sixty-four nations, the pact renounced war "as an instrument of national policy" and promised to resolve international disputes by "pacific means." In Niebuhr's view Americans embraced the Kellogg-Briand treaty as an example of their nation's moral leadership. Once again tacitly acknowledging the importance of ideals, he allowed that the pact was indeed an honest expression of an American longing for peace. But it was also evidence, he insisted, of the American inability to confront the complexities of global affairs, perhaps even of a reluctance to do so. Niebuhr believed that such reluctance was implied by the United States' disingenuous handling of the treaty. American advocates of Kellogg-Briand had inveighed against British reservations to the pact—reservations relating to the integrity of their empire—while at the same time articulating analogous reservations in regard to the Monroe Doctrine. To Niebuhr this proved that Americans were as anxious as the British to protect "imperial interests," even if they did not believe that their nation had any. Instead, Americans perceived their nation's policy as righteous. To the outside world, Niebuhr contended, it appeared hypo-critical.[15]

As an example of America's understanding of foreign relations, the Kellogg-Briand pact was further proof to Niebuhr of the way in which industrial civilization had vitiated humanity's spiritual life, in this case by trivializing it. In the global arena of the 1930s, modern industrial capitalism perpetuated the process of depersonalization that Niebuhr first recognized before World War I. The era of the all-powerful indus-trialist had overwhelmed personality. Figures such as Henry Ford con-vinced people of the glories of laissez-faire economics, which Niebuhr believed enabled industrial leaders temporarily to obscure capitalism's inability to address the great social needs created by industrialization. But by the early 1930s the "absurdity" of capitalism's underlying prin-ciples was becoming apparent in international affairs, just as Niebuhr believed the Depression had made it apparent domestically.[16]

The industrialists' gospel of laissez-faire contributed to America's international insensitivity. It was that insensitivity that Niebuhr offered as proof, in the realm of global relations, of the inability of modern political, economic, and religious thought to grapple successfully with contemporary social dilemmas. Americans did not understand Euro-pean resentment of American economic policy. They could not fathom such emotions issuing from international affairs that, for Americans, were simply "business." Intent on selling their products to the world, Americans considered their behavior not only acceptable but of the highest morality. In Niebuhr's interpretation of the American per-spective, immorality in global relations meant anything that inhibited commercial pursuits. Thus, while Europeans seethed over American un-willingness to purchase European products, Americans went on imag-ining that their country's policies constituted moral leadership. Those imaginings were reified in the American championing of the Kellogg-Briand treaty, with its vague promise to maintain global peace to the benefit of commerce. For Niebuhr such obtuseness was indicative of the "political ineptness of the business mind" that guided American actions. As far as he could tell, the same unreflective style of thinking that so damaged America's domestic life by the early 1930s was wreaking havoc in the world through American foreign policy. The evil of Henry Ford's perspective had an impact far beyond the environs of Detroit.[17]

Wallace on America's "Choices"

During the early 1930s, while Niebuhr adumbrated his view of the commercial and ideological roots of America's foreign policy since World War I, Wallace continued to focus on the transcendent goal of attaining a New Age of American and global well-being. The means of its attainment were implicit and explicit topics in much of what Wallace wrote and said from the moment he joined the Roosevelt administration. Wallace laid out the components of his vision in various places, including three books published in 1934: *America Must Choose, New Frontiers,* and *Statesmanship and Religion.* In these books and elsewhere Wallace asserted his conviction that in order to reach the New Age, Americans had to choose the type of nation they wanted to live in as well as that nation's relationship to the world. Within his writings and public statements one also can discern Wallace's ongoing concern with what he viewed as the necessary "keynote" of the era: a new American spirituality to underpin his social vision, a spirituality that was itself an amalgam of Wallace's scientific outlook and the ideal of cooperation.

One topic in which the central components of Wallace's vision were apparent was the tariff controversy. Indeed, the resolution of the tariff question was to Wallace a crucial step in the climb toward the New Age. The tariff, he wrote, was the product of a "pioneer . . . psychology" that was dangerously anachronistic but that still held great sway in the United States. This notion of Americans perceiving themselves as a pioneer nation long after the image had become outdated was a recurrent construction in Wallace's writing in the early 1930s, along with various anthropomorphic metaphors of national maturation, and was bound up in his vision of the New Age. It suggests a sense of inevitability in Wallace's thinking regarding the evolution of national behavior. By the early 1930s, he argued, Americans had evolved far beyond pioneer culture, their nation was "mature," its "infant industries" grown into "giants." Yet although it was reflected in America's relatively recent change in status to an international creditor, the maturation of the nation was not reflected in its tariff policy. The nation still behaved in an impetuous, youthful manner.[18] Wallace insisted that the manner in which the United States addressed international economic issues would indicate a crucial American choice, implicit in the title of the pamphlet, *America Must Choose*. By 1934 the United States was a decade and a half into its "maturity," while the world was a half decade into the global depression that, according to Wallace and Niebuhr, American irresponsibility helped cause. Wallace claimed it was now time for America, its citizens and its leaders, to decide whether or not the nation would commit fully to participation in international affairs.

Initially Wallace saw "two pathways" for America to follow. The "path of isolation" would mean the continuance of high tariffs, an end to American loans abroad, and weak foreign markets for America's surplus production. Foreshadowing a primary feature of the Agricultural Adjustment Act that he initiated as secretary of agriculture, Wallace predicted that the undermining of foreign markets for American commodities would further require of the United States a reduction in the acreage of the crops whose markets were most degraded. The other "pathway" open to America was the one that Wallace believed led to "world consciousness and world leadership." This was internationalism, the "path of world cooperation": the ultimate stage of the agricultural ethic of cooperation that Wallace had espoused throughout the 1920s. Choosing it meant lowering the tariff, reconsidering the war debt-loan issue, continuing to loan money overseas ("under proper restrictions"), and participating, to some extent at least, with other nations in the League of Nations and the World Court.[19]

The choice Wallace presented to his fellow Americans in 1934, in *America Must Choose*, was more complex. Now three paths faced the United States: the "internationalist" and "nationalist" roads that he had already outlined, along with what he termed "a planned middle course," essentially a compromise between the first two alternatives. Although he admitted that he favored the wholly internationalist route, Wallace posited that America was most likely to pursue the middle road.[20] The important thing for Americans to realize, whatever route their nation took, was that each would demand change and sacrifice from them. Wallace was certain that all three courses would require extensive planning and administration on the part of government.

Of the three alternatives, Wallace reckoned that an economic policy that was "nationalist" or "isolationist" (he used the terms interchangeably to characterize policies aimed at either partial or total national isolation from the rest of the world) would require the most extensive planning and rigid enforcement. If a path of "utter nationalism" were followed, he predicted, the requisite planning would be more complex than that undertaken during World War I. Comprehensive programs would necessitate extensive government controls on individual commercial behavior. Such controls would go well beyond what Americans were accustomed to. Indeed, Wallace insisted that the New Deal's efforts at "social discipline" so far had been mild and democratic in comparison. He hoped that such qualities would persist, but he doubted they could on the isolationist path. Thinking again of the hyper-nationalism of the world war as well as of the powerfully nationalistic aspects of European fascism, Wallace contended that extreme nationalism, once triggered, tended to crush all opposition. While he acknowledged that "certain satisfactions" could be derived from harsh central discipline, there was just as much likelihood of "exalted frenzy." If nationalist controls comparable in nature and extent to those exercised during a war were set in place in peacetime America, Wallace feared that the American spirit would quickly become "as a spring, tightly coiled, and ready to burst out dangerously in any direction." He chose not to speculate on the result of such an explosive uncoiling, although he did wonder whether the nation could survive it.[21]

Of course the internationalist pathway had potential pitfalls as well. By the early 1930s, Wallace admitted, most nations actually were taking the isolationist tack, at least regarding tariff policy. Thus it made sense to assume that going against that flow might prove futile. Even if the United States initially chose the path of internationalism, nationalism might ultimately be forced upon it by global circumstances. However events turned out, Wallace suggested, the "internationalists" had to come to what he termed a more realistic understanding of the global situation. They were too idealistic, he implied, given to speaking in "flowing terms" of international economic affairs. They believed, erroneously in Wallace's view, that American social and economic life could continue as it had, if only foreign markets were regained. What the internationalists did not realize, Wallace argued, was that the world's economy itself had changed. That change was apparent in a development especially pertinent to Wallace as secretary of agriculture: the "tremendous expansion" of European agricultural production since the war. If it did not contract again, the hoped-for foreign markets might never materialize.[22]

For Wallace the answer to tariff walls and trade wars was not some idealized vision of absolute commercial freedom. Rather it was a responsible, well-planned program of international commerce, one much less likely to lead to global strife.[23] The nations of the world, Wallace believed, ought to step off the uneven, haphazard path of acrimonious global economic competition and prepare a new, well-surveyed road to international economic cooperation. The question was not whether centralized planning was called for but what type of centralization would develop. It did not matter if the internationalist course or the middle course was finally taken; either path, to be successful, required extensive planning at the national level to a degree never before seen in American history. Thus both courses demanded a willingness on the part of Americans to accept greater government involvement in many aspects of their lives. In comparison with his vision, Wallace suggested, the New Deal would appear as nothing more than a makeshift complex of trial-and-error policies.

Yet in arguing for centralized planning Wallace was by no means endorsing communism. Indeed, he articulated "profound abhorrence" for much of what communism advocated. Above all, he hated communists' arousal of what he perceived of as a bitter "religious fanaticism" over the differences between economic classes. More important for Wallace, neither socialism nor communism was capable of serving the purpose of carrying America and the world into the New Age. In his view both systems were overly dogmatic, having "an emotional dryness" that he found repellent. They focused too much on a theoretical "economic man," ignoring the physical, spiritual, and artistic aspects of humanity. And Wallace suspected that most Americans felt the same way. He believed that the adherents of socialism and communism, along with fascists, actually displayed great ignorance of American values, scorning America's tradition of "tolerance and liberty." Contending that the radicals' understanding of human nature was too simplistic a foundation for a new civilization, he also was skeptical of any view of human affairs that characterized itself as logically inevitable. As far as he could tell, human history was hardly logical in its course. He doubted that Americans would buy into any philosophy that argued otherwise.[24]

In an ironic foreshadowing of his own political struggles of the late 1940s, Wallace was more alarmed by the Red-baiting tactics of those who in his view hypocritically tagged as communist what were in fact liberal democratic policies. He claimed that these Red-baiters, part of an economic oligarchy, used Red-baiting to frighten or arouse the masses in order to obtain votes and inordinate profits. Their strategy was insidious: they attacked as communistic anything they felt smacked of social or economic regimentation, implicitly denying the actual social and economic regimentation Wallace believed already existed.[25]

Echoing criticisms he made during the 1920s of the urban-industrial culture of the United States, Wallace in fact saw regimentation in many areas connected to big business. He discerned it, for example, in the hated tariffs, "worked out by businessmen" in smoke-filled rooms. And he was not alone in this perception. Richard Pells has pointed out that such Wallace contemporaries as George Soule and Stuart Chase insisted in the 1930s that capitalism was already "half collectivized, with partial government supervision of banking and tariffs, private trade associations and cartels, corporate monopolies, consumer cooperatives, and labor unions." To such observers it did not appear a great leap to advance to a wholly centralized economy.[26] Yet Wallace also perceived in these existing forms of de facto centralization an obstacle preventing the leap to a planned economy. The existent centralization of the American economy was subtle, he contended, and it had persisted for decades, so most Americans did not notice it. It was as invisible "as the air they breathe" and thus did not prepare them to embrace new forms of explicit, planned centralization.

Niebuhr's Critique of Fascism and Marxism

In the Depression Wallace saw the potential for the rebirth of capitalism in a new form, one grounded in cooperative economic democracy. Niebuhr, however, viewed things quite differently. In the context of the Depression the failure of American foreign policy marked for Niebuhr the bankruptcy of capitalism as a social system. By the early 1930s he had concluded that capitalism was moribund due to its inability to contend with the realities of modern industrial civilization. Although capitalism was bound up with the industrialized world, Niebuhr argued, it ultimately undermined the complex relationships of that world, both within nations and between them. Capitalism's focus on the unhindered use of private property not only limited the attainment of "intranational justice," it made "international reciprocity impossible" as well. Since the ravages of capitalism derived from its own fundamental precepts, Niebuhr believed it unlikely that serious reform would come from within.[27]

While some, like Wallace, might believe salvation could be attained by educating people of all sectors and classes to the virtues of cooperation, Niebuhr was deeply skeptical. While the most enlightened capitalists might condemn injustice and perhaps try to ameliorate its effects, even they would not admit that their own system was the source of the problem. The logic of such an admission would require that they remove themselves from power, and this Niebuhr deemed improbable. In his estimation the industrial capitalists holding power in the modern world were not the individuals to look for salvation from the effects of their own efforts.[28]

In a related sense Niebuhr criticized those Marxists and liberals who believed that social injustice would end soon simply because it "ought" to. Such expectations misperceived history, he argued, seeing its movement as inevitable without understanding that it was also "lenient." The evils of industrial capitalism might pass, done in by the judgment of history, but Niebuhr insisted they would do so incrementally. Because those who suffered the most from social injustice were slow both to express and act upon their resentments, history was in no hurry to dispose of that which was ineffectual or harmful.[29]

Nevertheless, in trying to understand the social bankruptcy of capitalism Niebuhr discovered a new inexorability. If he doubted that industrial capitalism would transform itself into an economic democracy, by the 1930s he was sure that capitalism nevertheless was dying, and he was convinced that its demise would be slow and difficult. In a medical metaphor that reflected his "outside expert" stance, Niebuhr compared the laissez-faire capitalism of the twentieth century metaphorically to a "man of robust frame" who ignores an illness until it is too late and then who, even after accepting the fact of his illness, tries quack cures instead of following the advice of a trained physician. Hesitation and self-delusion, so Niebuhr's metaphor went, brought disaster. A doctor might be consulted, but probably not in time, or the patient would be so far gone that he might deny the doctor's prescriptions, deluded by a "delirium of fever" that gave the illusion of recovery.[30]

For the capitalist system that fever dream was fascism. And by the mid-1930s the "patient" most obviously ill was Germany. Once again Niebuhr extrapolated from Germany's experience to the West. In the ascension of the Nazis he foresaw the disastrous future that awaited other industrial democracies. Fascism, Niebuhr contended, could temporarily resolve the problems of a collapsing society and provide the false sense of recovery suggested in the illness metaphor. By combining the techniques of demagoguery with military force, fascism could restore the internal unity of a nation slipping into revolution. As in Germany, capitalist oligarchs, unwilling to yield their power to social and economic reforms, turned for salvation to the demagogue, who then used their support to raise himself to power on the shoulders of the alienated middle class.[31]

Despite the "cheap theatricality" of fascist demagoguery, with its false replication of the organic nature of feudal society, the "patient," Niebuhr predicted, ultimately would succumb. Modern industrial capitalism would fail because the social stresses papered over by fascism would persist. When they reemerged, Niebuhr believed, they would be worse than before. Workers might temporarily be mesmerized by fascist dictators, but the sources of labor's discontent remained. The fascists' temporary reign would ensure that capitalism's demise would be "bloody rather than peaceful." As certain as the leftists were of the inexorable reformation of industrial capitalism into economic democracy, Niebuhr was convinced that fascism virtually guaranteed revolution.[32]

As Niebuhr perceived it the success of fascism arose from the fascists' ability to exploit the fears of an alienated lower middle class while mobilizing the working class with a false promise of revolution. Yet the power of that false promise, so crucial to fascist success, derived from what Niebuhr viewed as another false promise, that of Marxism. By the 1930s, Niebuhr believed, Marxism had failed to bring about its promised regeneration of society. Radical doctrines proved ineffective at attaining the sort of society that could fulfill Niebuhr's transcendent aim, the resurrection of personality. Nevertheless, compared to his condemnation of fascism, Niebuhr's critique of Marxism was that of a skeptical believer. Influenced by the effects of the Depression and his experience in Detroit, Niebuhr accepted much of the Marxist analysis of capitalist society. He even joined the Socialist Party in New York City in 1929 and twice ran unsuccessfully for state office on the Socialist ticket in the early 1930s. In addition, in 1935 Niebuhr became editor of a new journal, *Radical Religion,* whose mission, he declared, was to understand both the "affinities" and "divergences" between Christian thought and Marxism. While it is arguable whether Niebuhr should be characterized as a true Marxist during this period, there is no doubt that he drew heavily on Marxist thought in formulating his critiques of liberalism, liberal Protestantism, and capitalism.[33]

It made sense for Niebuhr to evaluate Marxism's effectiveness in terms of personality, which is to say, in the same terms in which he criticized religion. For Niebuhr religion fundamentally was "the yearning after the ideal which transcends any given situation." In his view Marxism fit this definition, beginning with its teleological "mythology." As Niebuhr construed it, the agent of Marxist faith was not God but a relentless "force in history," one that sought the "triumph of man's highest social ideals." Marxist philosophy perceived history, driven by the force of social justice, as carrying humanity inexorably through various stages of civilization, each punctuated by interclass conflict, to a final classless society. In Niebuhr's construction of Marxism the processes of history became as God.[34]

Ironically, Niebuhr's critique of Marxism also afforded him the opportunity to defend his profession as he had never been able to in the 1920s. In exposing the "religion" of the radicals he also rejected the idea that Marxism was scientific, despite its pseudoscientific jargon. In doing so he argued in addition that science itself was capable only of discovering the minutiae of existence but not of harmonizing those details in a larger philosophy. That task required interpretation and, at some point, faith.[35] Thus, in attacking the scientific pretensions of Marxism Niebuhr also indirectly criticized the scientists, young businessmen, and social scientists against whom he often had unfavorably measured himself during his years at Bethel.

In this context Niebuhr's critique of Marxism became analogous to his critique of American culture. The Marxist world view, he contended, was just as mechanistic in its understanding of human behavior as was the moralistic, engineer's mentality behind American politics and foreign policy. Indeed, Niebuhr believed that it was from its parallels with American liberalism that Marxism's failures derived. Like capitalism, Marxism was the product of a "mechanical civilization," while at the same time, like liberalism, it issued from the rationalism of the Enlightenment. Because of this, Niebuhr felt certain, the restoration of the poetic and the organic to humanity's alienated existence would not come from Marxism.[36]

At least such a restoration would not come from any variety of Marxism that existed in the 1930s. Niebuhr did believe that a "pure Marxism," one without such a "dogmatic historical perspective," could contribute to the improvement of the human condition. Such a Marxism would have an "evolutionary" outlook, a more realistic philosophy, recognizing the complexity of historical change. Such a Marxism would acknowledge that progress usually came in bits and pieces rather than as a result of a crisis. Glimpsing a kindred outlook in Lewis Mumford's *Technics and Civilization*, published in 1934, Niebuhr wrote that Mumford described a "communism [that] is necessarily post-Marxian," by which Niebuhr meant a communism not characterized by "messianic absolutism" or by "slavish imitation of the political methods or social institutions of Soviet Russia." Rather Mumford suggested a communism that was to Niebuhr a logical outgrowth of the "necessity of socializing the ownership of the machine" in the modern world.[37]

In Germany, Niebuhr's perennial case study, he saw no such sophisticated radicalism. Instead, he saw all of Marxism's failures potentially opening the door to fascism. By 1932 Niebuhr held German socialists most culpable for those failures, although he blamed them less for a mechanistic Marxism than for political timidity. In supporting an essentially bourgeois parliamentary government, Niebuhr contended, they effectively undermined the potential political power of the proletariat by driving the less fortunate workers into the more revolutionary ranks of the Communist Party. Political division equaled political weakness, which meant that any subsequent revolution might result in fascism. Nevertheless, Niebuhr did not anticipate revolution in Germany in 1932. At least he believed it was avoidable, if only the former Western Allies would lessen Germany's reparations burden, for if conditions improved in Germany, Niebuhr suggested, then the poorer workers would rejoin the socialists and so strengthen the parliamentary government.[38]

Niebuhr criticized American radicalism for reasons that echoed his critique of the Germans. For Niebuhr American socialists were not prepared to become an "emancipating factor" in American politics. At the same time American communists seemed unable to hold the support of even the most desperate American workers. Moreover, Niebuhr believed, as Wallace suggested, that American radicals also failed when it came to recruiting farmers, alienating them by not acknowledging the principle of "property in land" as opposed to industrial ownership. Niebuhr also argued that American radicalism relied too heavily on its European antecedents—in the communist case, through a dogmatic acceptance of Russian doctrine. He implied that a collapse into fascism, foreshadowed by the likes of Father Charles Coughlin and Huey Long, was in the offing if American radicals did not make an effort to discover their own cultural roots. Again exhibiting his implicit agreement with Wallace's principles, while remaining skeptical of their attainability, Niebuhr suggested that grounding for American radicalism could possibly be found in the "pioneer equalitarianism" of American history. He further posited that "western agrarianism" might be the only hope for America, since it was perhaps the only native form of radicalism in the nation.[39]

If in Germany Niebuhr saw the ideological division among radicals contributing to the rise of fascism, while in America radicals failed by not establishing their ideological independence, in Russian Marxism he saw a different situation altogether. In Russia Niebuhr saw the mechanistic nature of Marxism carried to its greatest extremes, if to different effect than in Germany. By the early 1930s the Soviet Union was the best example for Niebuhr of Marxist radicalism's failure to ameliorate the social effects of industrial civilization.

Niebuhr contended that in other nations where Marxism had attained a level of real influence, such as Germany and Great Britain, it had evolved in its mainstream forms into a part of existing political institutions. Socialism, for instance, had become parliamentary. It was only in Russia, Niebuhr insisted, that the Marxist doctrine of interclass struggle was carried to its conclusion with "rigorous consistency." This was due to several historical factors, he believed, including an inept bureaucracy of aristocrats, the effective absence of a middle class, a politically powerless peasantry, "revolutionary solidarity" among the workers, and widespread political cynicism in the face of a brutal, decaying state. The irony for Niebuhr was that it was "backward," non-industrialized Russia that became the locus of a successful revolution on the basis of a Marxist model intended for a modern industrial nation. The explanation for this irony lay not in the economic and political arenas, however, but in what he termed the "psychological" realm. "Communist zeal," Niebuhr declared, arose from the "Russian soul." With a subtle racism common to the era, he explained that Russia's soul was Asian in its essence, meaning that the Russians lacked "intellectual sophistication," tending to raise the principles of a particular philosophy to the level of a religion.[40]

This suggestion, of a Russian transmutation of Marxist philosophy into a religion, accorded with Niebuhr's assertion of the religious nature of Marxism in general. The difference in the Soviet Union was that Marxism was not the religion of a small part of the population, as it was in the West, but rather of the entire nation. The harshness of Niebuhr's characterization of Russian culture underscores the deeply skeptical and rather simplistic view he already held of the Soviet Union by the early 1930s: Russia was a nation whose culture was "so primitive," so lacking in the meliorating "influences of intellectualism," that it was unable to temper its intense religiosity. Their lack of sophistication allowed the Russians unhesitatingly to accept as true a simple, "apocalyptic" view of the future.[41]

The Russians' unreflective acceptance of Marxist dogma, Niebuhr believed, put at risk all that was truly valuable within Russian culture, enervating the cultural life of the nation and supplanting the ritual and mysticism of the Russian Church. Throwing all of Russia's spiritual resources into the process of industrialization, Soviet leaders had established in effect an "anti-religion," a culmination of what Niebuhr termed the "irreligion" of the industrial era generally. In the 1920s he had described how that irreligion had undermined Western culture. It had turned Protestantism into a sycophantic apologia for industrial capitalism and rendered radicalism impotent. In Russia the Marxist anti-religion had eliminated Christianity, replacing religion with radicalism. As Niebuhr saw it, Marxism in Russia created a new theocracy, one bound up with the rise of industrial civilization and dedicated to the worship of the "God of efficiency."[42]

Niebuhr and John Dewey

Niebuhr's thoroughgoing contempt for what he perceived as mechanistically simplistic ideologies helps explain another element of his commentary during the early 1930s: his vehement attack on one of the dominant figures in the American liberal community, philosopher and educator John Dewey. As with his criticism of the Social Gospel, Niebuhr's attack on Dewey can be viewed as another step in the evolution of the critique that he would make of Wallace in the 1940s.

By the early 1930s Dewey was a well known figure in American Pragmatism, a philosophical movement to which William James also significantly contributed. Since Niebuhr drew so heavily upon James's work in establishing his early intellectual positions, his attack on Dewey appears at first glance somewhat surprising. Like James, Dewey stressed the preeminent value of experiential knowledge in attempting to fathom human existence. Although that valuation of experiential knowledge was the hallmark of all varieties of Pragmatic philosophy, there were in fact real differences between Dewey's and James's thinking. It was upon one of these differences that Niebuhr grounded his critique.[43]

Richard Fox argues that when Niebuhr criticized Dewey in the opening pages of *Moral Man and Immoral Society* in 1932, he was contending not with Dewey but rather with a straw man, "an ideal-type opponent who was easy to take down."[44] Indeed, when one notes the similarities between Dewey's critique of modern technological society and the perspective that Niebuhr had developed, Fox's criticism of Niebuhr seems valid. The work that Niebuhr cited in his opening salvo against Dewey was an essay entitled "Science and Society," published for the first time in 1931 in Dewey's *Philosophy and Civilization*. In it Dewey described the changes wrought by modern technological culture, sounding very much like Niebuhr as he did so. Evoking Niebuhr's earlier assaults on the industrial culture personified by Henry Ford, for example, Dewey implied that while science might have improved the conditions of some individuals, it was just as likely to "depress others," turning them into "slaves of machines operated for the . . . gain of owners." In the context of such an assessment Niebuhr's contention that Dewey had no understanding of the role that the "economic interests of the owning classes" played in creating social injustice, and that Dewey's suggestions betrayed the "confusion of an analyst who has no clear counsels about the way to overcome social inertia," seems overdrawn and harsh.[45]

Yet Niebuhr's assault on Dewey, however exaggerated, makes sense in the context of both Niebuhr's philosophical and his personal development. More than anything else Dewey advocated tempering experiential knowledge in the fire of the "scientific method," particularly in the realm of pedagogy. But Dewey's suggestion that the application of the rigor of the scientific method in teaching America's children would yield Americans with the "right mental attitudes" was vague at best (in a sense paralleling Wallace's argument that education in the principles of cooperation would produce a cooperative society).[46] That vagueness gave force to Niebuhr's contention that Dewey and other liberals like him put too much hope in the belief that education based on the methods of the social sciences would eliminate ignorance and yield a just society. It was a criticism that foreshadowed Niebuhr's attack in the late 1940s upon liberals whom he believed expected the virtually inevitable rise of a just global society. For Niebuhr in the 1930s Dewey's logic relied too much on an implied equation of the social and physical sciences, an idea that he had long viewed as specious.

Niebuhr's disparagement of Dewey's expectations for the attainment of social justice was underpinned by one other factor. Dewey advocated the application of the scientific method to social problems arising from what he perceived to be the persistence of obsolete social attitudes. In explaining this discrepancy between social attitudes and modern industrial civilization, Dewey juxtaposed several implicit and explicit criticisms of the church. He declared, for instance, that there were individuals in "high position in church and state" who resisted using science to solve social ills, trusting instead the "transforming influence" of morals and religion. It made no sense, Dewey argued, to continue the "subordination" of the scientific method to "purposes and institutions" that predated its advent.[47]

Niebuhr of course had developed his own analogous criticism of liberal Protestantism during the previous decade and a half. Nevertheless, Dewey's essay must have reawakened in Niebuhr the old self-consciousness that dated back to the days at Yale when William James's writings had helped him begin to fashion a means of imparting social value to the ministry, in part by deflating positivism. Now, in the 1930s, Dewey was not only advocating science for the interpretation of experiential knowledge but also claiming that what had prevented the scientific method from being turned to such a valuable purpose sooner was the intransigence of backward cultural institutions, notably the church. This must have stung Niebuhr, who had worked so long and hard to establish himself within academic and journalistic mainstreams. Dewey's juxtaposition of the importance of science and the obstructionist role played by religion struck directly at the specific personal and professional doubts that Niebuhr wrestled with during his years in New Haven and Detroit. Whatever the intellectual validity of the criticism Niebuhr made in 1932 of Dewey's brand of Pragmatism, one senses that its intensity arose out of old sensitivities of Niebuhr's dating back to the first years of his career. Those sensitivities enabled Niebuhr to ignore the similarities between his and Dewey's commentaries while at the same time they amplified his perception of the differences. Thus Niebuhr could single Dewey out as an exemplar of all that he disdained in the social sciences and of all that he saw as dangerously simplistic and impersonal in modern technological society.

The argument between Niebuhr and Dewey, which Robert Westbrook has validly characterized as one "absent much direct engagement," continued sporadically through the 1930s, with both individuals to a great extent talking past one another.[48] In what was essentially a response to Niebuhr's attack on him in *Moral Man*, Dewey probably only made matters worse by effectively construing Niebuhr's critique as an either/or proposition between rationalism and religion. If both forms of knowledge were "collective illusions," Dewey contended, then, "illusion for illusion," the scientific method was likely the better alternative.[49] Dewey's implied criticism—that Niebuhr was arguing for reliance on the supernatural as the solution to social ills—misunderstood the essential nature of Niebuhr's commentary. Dewey, like Wallace, was presenting a positive vision of a society to be created. After Niebuhr assailed him in *Moral Man*, Dewey too created a straw man, attempting to fashion Niebuhr's criticism into a competing vision, analogous to his own. But Niebuhr was not countering Dewey's vision with a clearly articulated alternative. Rather he was extending his critique of all ameliorative visions. Dewey, like Niebuhr, assumed an opposition that did not actually exist.[50] When in 1934 Dewey argued explicitly for the value of experiences that were religious in nature, even if they had nothing to do with formal religion, Niebuhr did not see—or at least did not acknowledge—how close their two positions were, that they were both ultimately concerned with the resurrection of personality in modern industrial civilization.[51]

Engendering Cooperation at Home and Abroad

During the mid-1930s, as Niebuhr was engaged in his strange, attenuated battle with Dewey, Wallace continued to tout the promise of long-term central planning in the United States. Yet the closest approach to such planning, apart from some New Deal efforts, remained the back-room, businessmen's regimentation of the economy that Wallace found unacceptable. For both Wallace and Niebuhr the alternatives offered by the left and the right were no better. So for Wallace the question became one of melding the centralized social and economic planning he believed both vital and inevitable with the democratic social discipline he believed America, and ultimately the world, had to attain. He was convinced such discipline could develop only out of a changed social experience, new patterns of behavior among the individual members of society. Democratic social discipline, he wrote, would arise from "the ceaseless action, reaction, and interaction of one individual on another, from the very tangible feeling of give-and-take which develops among the individuals of a group which is on the march to a common objective."[52] The answer was to make the ethic of cooperation into the social norm by practicing it.

Rejecting the Hobbesian precept that people were "born greedy," Wallace, again exhibiting a tendency toward oversimplification, posited instead that the behavior many perceived as evidence of humanity's inherently evil nature was in fact a product of "fear" derived from lives lived at the economic edge. Increasingly common in the depths of the Depression, such fear engendered selfishness, eventually spreading throughout a society tragically characterized by an economy of "denied plenty," its "heaping surpluses" juxtaposed with "bitter hunger." More tragic still, the means for the dispersal of those surpluses existed in the very technology that contributed to the social imbalances. Yet for that technology to be turned to communal ends required a cooperative sense of mutual obligation to overcome the selfishness.[53]

If the Depression amplified selfish human behavior, by the mid-1930s Wallace nevertheless believed there was evidence promising the possible liberation of the cooperative spirit. Several developments fueled his optimism. The New Deal itself, he suggested, ultimately sought "enduring social change," even if its methods and uneven results appeared more haphazard than rational.[54] In addition, there was one area of New Deal policy—the "wheat plan" of the Agricultural Adjustment Administration (AAA)—that Wallace frequently cited as proof that a cooperative human nature was reviving.

The Agricultural Adjustment Act, passed in May 1933, was perhaps the most successful component of the so-called first New Deal. Although it included many features, its centerpiece was the "domestic allotment plan," which essentially paid farmers to reduce their production of crops that were already in surplus. The allotment program was the focus of a great deal of controversy during its first year, when compliance required that large portions of the American cotton crop be plowed under and thousands of baby pigs slaughtered in order to drive up the cotton and pork prices. Indeed, an exaggerated image of food being wasted while Americans went hungry was used periodically to attack Wallace for the rest of his career. In fact, such actions were only taken in the first year, and in the case of wheat they were not necessary at all. The wheat plan worked from the first year, greatly helped by a drought that radically decreased the size of the American wheat crop, augmenting the effects of the AAA's policy. The results in wheat foreshadowed the overall relative success that the entire act attained.[55]

Although Wallace admitted that a likely initial attraction of the wheat plan was the promise of benefit payments, he contended that the cooperative aspects of the plan soon gained ascendancy, as government agents held open discussions with farmers in local meetings. Seeing evidence of a sea change in human nature, Wallace insisted that a new consciousness developed in farm communities as growers increasingly became aware that the plan's viability—and thereby their hope for survival—was their own responsibility. In the end Wallace's hoped-for "economic democracy," the heart of his cooperative vision, seemed to come into existence as "economic rearrangement" took place in hundreds of rural counties across the nation. Declaring the plan an unprecedented success, Wallace became convinced that participating farmers had become cooperators.[56]

In asserting this Wallace exhibited a rather simplistic understanding of human nature. At the very least he confused the idea of altering human nature with the possibility of manipulating human nature to alter human behavior, implicitly undermining his contention that human nature was intrinsically cooperative. This criticism should not be overstressed, however. Even if his terms were vague, Wallace made clear that the Depression constituted a special condition; that is, it pushed the ravages of the modern industrial world to their greatest extremes.

In this context suggesting the need to manipulate farmers' selfishness in order to start them cooperating made sense. Wallace was certain that once people began to behave cooperatively—to practice cooperation—their cooperative natures would reemerge and regain ascendance.

Wallace believed that through their cooperative associations farmers learned how to act collectively on their coinciding interests. Even more significant to his vision was his sense that taking part in the wheat program forced American farmers to begin thinking internationally, to "look beyond their line fences at the world wheat situation." Yet if the active collaboration of American growers in the wheat plan hinted at the possibility of international cooperation, Wallace believed there was even stronger evidence available. He saw evidence, for example, in U.S. "reciprocal trade" policy—bilateral tariff and trade agreements, worked out between the United States and specific nations, regarding specific items—which became a hot topic in public forums in 1934.[57] By that time Wallace had joined Secretary of State Cordell Hull in advocating the policy as a last chance to attain some degree of internationalism in American economic policy. The Trade Agreement Act, passed by the Congress in June 1934, eventually led to eighteen treaties that further fueled Wallace's faith in the possibility of international cooperation, thus augmenting his evolving global vision.[58]

Wallace's faith was given its greatest reinforcement, however, by another international political development of these years. The signing of the Pan-American Treaty on the Protection of Artistic and Scientific Institutions, known as the Roerich Pact, seemed to Wallace to establish cooperation as an international ethic. And it did so while validating both his science and his spiritualism. Named for its creator, Wallace's spiritual associate Nicholas Roerich, the treaty provided for the protection of the cultural treasures of all nations during wartime. When the Roerich Pact became a reality in April 1935, it was as a Pan-American treaty and Wallace, as a member of FDR's cabinet, signed for the United States.[59]

Wallace began publicly championing Roerich's plan in the summer of 1933, shortly before an international conference on the pact was held in Washington, D.C., that November. To a skeptical Cordell Hull, Wallace cited what he believed was evidence of the pact's "extraordinary

progress" internationally. Such evidence included the establishment of
a permanent foundation in Bruges, Belgium, to further the pact's acceptance, as well as two previous international conferences on the pact,
held in 1931 and 1932, in which, as Wallace pointed out, twenty-two
nations participated. In his view the Roerich pact suggested a starting
place from which to attain international cooperation. Its acceptance implied that there were aspects of the human condition over which the
citizens of all countries could and would agree, in this case the "values
of culture." Just as the Red Cross attained international cooperation
regarding people's physical welfare, the Banner of Peace would initiate
cooperation over their "spiritual and cultural" welfare.[60]

Invoking the religious underpinnings of his international cooperative ethic, Wallace insisted not only that the pact was "in conformity
with the deepest, most sacred laws of the universe" but that it would
also serve as the basis for an international New Deal. At the very least it
symbolized the emergence of international relations that emphasized
the highest aspirations of humanity.[61] The signing of the Pan-American
Treaty allowed Wallace to infer that the moment had arrived in which
his cooperative vision had become internationalized while focused on
the aspects of the human condition that he most valued. His long-
sought keynote for the New Age had been sounded. The Roerich Pact
convinced Wallace that international cooperation could work.

The Spiritual Regeneration of the Nation

Wallace's ardent support of the Roerich Pact suggests that he had not
lost his spirituality. Indeed, the widespread social and economic traumas of the early 1930s only convinced him further of the depth of
people's spiritual needs. As the global economy worsened, it seemed
increasingly important to Wallace that "a new religious longing . . .
manifest itself" if the new order was to come about. Behind the economic dislocations, he remained convinced, stood humankind's need
for a renewed sense of spiritual connection.[62]

By the mid-1930s Wallace was more certain than ever of the need
for a new source of spiritual inspiration to provide motivation for the

changes in human nature integral to his vision. Such inspiration was necessary if Americans were to create a new "unity of purpose" for themselves and their nation. No longer a pioneer nation with the "frontier" providing a unifying force, something new was needed. There were several possible alternatives, in Wallace's mind, ranging from "imperialism" to "communism and fascism." Seeming to have forgotten his harsh criticism during the 1920s of U.S. policy in Latin America, Wallace asserted that only fascism was a serious danger in America. At a time when demagogic figures such as Huey Long and Father Charles Coughlin were attaining a frightening degree of public influence by appealing to the fears and hopes of the downtrodden (and by attacking the administration in which he was a leading figure), Wallace suggested another potential source of power that might benefit an American fascist movement. With reasoning very close to Niebuhr's, Wallace pointed out that fascism might "follow a period of national chaos." He argued that the danger existed that the "feudalistic aspect" of fascism would draw the support of "certain industrialists" who wished to attain control of the nation's economic strength. Wallace warned that they, like the German industrialists, would be ready to support an American fascist movement in order to preclude the advent of true economic democracy.[63]

Yet Wallace remained optimistic. He believed that Americans ultimately would reject fascism as an alternative and discover a "new frontier" that would create the impetus for national cooperation. The new frontier would arise, he believed, from the ongoing quest for an economy of abundance. Implying that the transformation of human nature could be accelerated by a reinvigorated spirituality, Wallace insisted that the real struggle would be for the "mind and the spirit." This did not seem unusually daunting to Wallace, for in his assessment such struggles had been waged and won before. Once again exhibiting a rather vague and simplistic psychology, he asserted that it was valid to expect to alter human nature, since it had been done before and the change was often driven by spiritual motivations. For instance, a "vigorous Protestantism," Wallace declared, had underpinned America's pioneer expansion by inculcating a "sense of duty." Evoking Weber's "Protestant ethic," as did Niebuhr, Wallace explained that in early American history people had borne onerous duties willingly as an expression of their religiosity. It was this religion-generated discipline, inspiring many an American to personal sacrifice for economic efficiency, that made the United States what it was by the twentieth century: the world's greatest capitalist industrial nation.[64]

Yet, again like Niebuhr, Wallace sensed that by the end of the first quarter of the twentieth century Protestantism had failed. Instead of providing spiritual guidance for American society, it had become a distilled shadow of itself, contributing to rather than alleviating the "dry hardness" of modern industrial civilization. The Protestant spirit had become distilled into a profit motive. Perhaps a different sort of Christianity was needed. Echoing Niebuhr's ruminations in the 1920s, Wallace wondered if a Christianity more like that of the early church fathers or of the medieval era was necessary. Such a spiritual shift might overcome the powerful individualism of Protestantism and so foster a more communitarian social outlook. The new spiritualism had to engage more than just the individual's drive to be materially successful. While preserving Protestantism's belief in the "sacredness of the individual" was important, Wallace insisted that the new religion would have to stress the social context.[65]

Niebuhr's Critique of Pacifism and the League of Nations

While Wallace speculated hopefully on the advent of a spiritually renewed America leading the world to cooperative community, Niebuhr's evolving critique of mechanistic ameliorative ideologies impelled him to great skepticism regarding international relations. That skepticism was manifested in his break during this period with American pacifism as well as in his criticism of the League of Nations. During the 1920s and early 1930s Niebuhr was a member of the Fellowship of Reconciliation, a Christian pacifist group created during World War I. By 1933 he was the chairman of its executive council. At the end of that year, however, Niebuhr resigned the position, having come to the conclusion that the pacifism of the majority of his fellowship colleagues was too rigid. By 1934, characterizing himself only marginally as a pacifist, he did reject participation in an international war, but only out of his be-lief that such an encounter would be "suicidal" to civilization. With that narrow exception, Niebuhr insisted that he and other like-minded fellowship members were really "not pacifists at all." [66]

In *Moral Man* and elsewhere Niebuhr made clear that his greatest impatience was with pacifists who disavowed any degree of coercion whatsoever. Yet he could not even bring himself to agree with those who rejected only "violent coercion." He perceived in both positions the sort of simplistic acceptance of dogma he rejected in so many other contexts. Neither position took cognizance of the role that force played in social relations at both the national and international levels. The "ethical perfectionism" of the pacifists prevented them from seeing the actual coercion in all political and economic life.[67]

For Niebuhr the ingenuousness of the pacifists was one more manifestation of the mechanistic nature of modern Western political thought. Pacifism arose from the same Enlightenment roots as did lib-eralism, capitalism, and Marxism. Those who partook in such value sys-tems, Niebuhr argued, were unable to accept partial successes while struggling for transcendent ideals. They were driven by the alienating nature of modern life to take limited ends and turn them into absolutes. At some point, Niebuhr insisted, those who adhered to these ameli-orative ideologies finally gave in to an "uncritical faith," a belief that human reason was inexorably attaining the ideal. Evoking his critique of Dewey, Niebuhr suggested that all modern moral theories were built on the assumption that human reason only needed to be liberated by the proper form of education. If this were achieved, then human nature would develop a continually greater capacity for disinterested judg-ment. These modern moralists believed, Niebuhr concluded, that once having inevitably attained this impartiality of judgment, people and nations would be able to assess the issues over which they differed with an objective equanimity and so enter into harmonious coexistence.[68]

In Niebuhr's view the League of Nations was an especially perti-nent product of modern moral beliefs that in effect belied their deter-ministic optimism. As late as spring 1932 Niebuhr himself retained some optimism regarding the League. When the League Assembly rati-fied Secretary of State Henry Stimson's refusal to recognize the recent

Japanese conquest of Manchuria, Niebuhr regarded it as evidence of the League's vitality. The League's action, Niebuhr suggested, might even form the basis for the sort of economic isolation of Japanese-held Manchuria that could ultimately force the Japanese venture to fail.[69]

Nevertheless, in Niebuhr's assessment the League had yet to prove itself a true international "community." It only hinted at such a development. Niebuhr allowed that it was possible that the refusal of the League to validate Japan's actions might lead to the degree of coercion necessary to negate the venture altogether. Like Wallace, he felt that the modern industrial world had become "very closely knit" in terms of economic interdependence. Thus the closing off of a nation from access to the financial reserves of the rest of the world could conceivably be enough to force that nation to comply with the "general will" of the global community. Nevertheless, Niebuhr was certain that if a comprehensive international economic policy aimed at undermining the rivalries of nations was not devised, then the Japanese conquest of Manchuria would not be the last act of its kind. Somehow the world's nations had to devise a system that recognized the complexity of international relations, including the inherence of force within those relations.[70]

As the decade wore on, Niebuhr's doubts about the League grew, intensified by Hitler's accession to power in Germany. The Nazi political victory disturbed Niebuhr greatly, and not only because it did not bode well for the social and political futures of either Germany or the capitalist West. Fascism's success in Germany also destroyed whatever optimism Niebuhr felt concerning the likelihood of League-fostered international cooperation. In Niebuhr's assessment Hitler had been successful because America and the League had not redressed the egregious evils of the Treaty of Versailles. The League's failure to make any meaningful revision of the treaty was a clear indication to Niebuhr that no international community had come into existence, at least so far as preserving peace was concerned. To his mind the League of Nations remained a largely ineffective "league of victors."[71]

If Niebuhr needed further proof of this, then League actions pertaining to the Italian invasion of Ethiopia in 1935 were sufficient. When the British and the French showed themselves unwilling to risk war with

Mussolini over League sanctions against Italy, Niebuhr perceived the undermining effects of pacifist sentiment on collective security. He argued that without British and French willingness to back up sanctions with military force, no League program of international sanctions could succeed. Moreover, he added ironically, without a credible promise of force behind any policy of nonmilitary coercion, the likelihood of actual violence actually increased. If the dominant members of the League refused to act on this premise, Niebuhr concluded, there was little reason for optimism regarding collective security.[72]

By the mid-1930s Niebuhr's commentary implied that the hopes so many liberals placed in the League of Nations were grounded in the same logic as that which underpinned domestic liberalism and pacifism as well as, in some ways, Marxism. It was the same reasoning that lay behind American enthusiasm for the Kellogg-Briand pact. By 1935 Niebuhr believed the values informing such policies ultimately were incapable of grappling with the complexities of international relations, above all with the inherent roles that national self-interest and force played in those relations. The failure of the League to fully back the sanctions against Italy to the point of violence simply drove this conclusion home for him.

For Wallace, however, developments of the early 1930s seemed a basis for optimism. Whatever form it took, Wallace believed that a new, socially oriented spirituality could serve as the foundation for cooperative community within the United States. Spiritual renewal would combine with social and economic policies to liberate the cooperative aspects of human nature and foster cooperative practice. What Wallace termed the "religious keynote" would operate in combination with the "economic keynote . . . [and] the scientific keynote of the new age" to overcome the now outdated individualistic struggle in scarcity. That struggle and its underlying logic could be replaced at last by the "higher law" of cooperation. As Wallace saw it, this was the task of the moment. For he believed the attainment of such changes in America ultimately would prove valuable to other nations. The United States again could be exemplar to the world. Yet just as Wallace was finding cause for optimism in events such as the signing of the Roerich Pact, Niebuhr was growing pessimistic about the immediate future of global relations.

He doubted the imminence of world community. For Niebuhr international affairs in the 1930s epitomized human limitations, tragically revealing the results of the "sinful dishonesty" that informed all efforts to transcend those limitations.[73] One could hope for cooperation, but to expect it might prove folly.

5

Preserving the "Open Society"

Wallace, Niebuhr, and the Coming of World War II

———❖———

In THEIR commentaries of the late 1930s Wallace and Niebuhr further developed many of the themes they had addressed during the first part of the decade. Still sharing the belief that the United States had to take up its global responsibilities definitively, as war approached Niebuhr proved more willing to risk American involvement. For his part Wallace continued to expand his vision of a spiritually grounded, cooperative civilization. A regard for sense of place still underlay his commentary, but his writing about cooperation and community was increasingly removed from discussion of agricultural issues and the land. The return of depression in 1937 only augmented his concern with cooperation at home and abroad, while the arena of international trade remained a primary focus of that concern. Wallace's assessment of global commerce, and America's crucial role in its revival and in the maintenance of a world community based upon that commerce, did not alter greatly as World War II approached. If anything his views only gained urgency.

In his analysis Niebuhr continued to discuss the fate of the West, watching it unfold out of what he perceived as the tragic failures of the various ameliorative ideologies facing fascist aggression, especially their inability to fathom the role of power in politics. The repeated successes of the various fascist movements, as the decade wore on, gave further impetus not only to his increasing disillusionment with radicalism but

112

also to his condemnation of what he considered the simpleminded idealism of both pacifists and liberals, whose expectations for collective security rested upon the increasingly impotent League of Nations. Nevertheless, and with great irony, by the end of the decade Niebuhr found himself staunchly defending the very liberal culture he had so long and so profoundly criticized.

Nationalism and Global Responsibility

In the late 1930s Wallace still characterized international behavior since 1918 as irrational and mutually destructive. Most worrisome was the number of nations pursuing the "nationalist path" he had warned against earlier in the decade, the path most likely to trigger dangerous international responses. In his concern that the United States might take such a course, Wallace again called for the nation to take up its responsibilities and behave as the economic power it had become. It was time for the great creditor of the world to let go of its "debtor psychology" and nurture global commerce. For Wallace the "foreign trade problem" was clearly "domestic as well as international," demanding an increase in consumption at home no less than access to markets abroad. He thus linked the nascent welfare state of the New Deal with the foreign economic policy of the United States, foreshadowing postwar progressive calls for full employment. The solution to international trade problems, he felt, was inextricably bound up with America's domestic recovery, requiring less thought about "favorable balances of trade and more about making goods available to people," whether or not those goods were domestic or foreign. First the United States must eliminate the want at home that persisted in the face of abundance. Having done so, America could then help eliminate it globally as well.[1]

Calling upon government to establish a "unifying principle of balance" in the best interests of what he termed the "general welfare," Wallace in fact reasserted the ethic of cooperation. Although he argued for an increased role for government, his aim was a cooperative community of individuals. Still the insider seeking to establish a sense of place for all Americans, Wallace was not trying to impose an artificial, uniform social equality but rather to create a society of individuals each of whom strove for "unity in diversity." He believed this to be an inherently American aim, what the founders sought during the Confederation period, leading them to create the Constitution. Only the overwhelming changes of the modern era had pushed the nation off the path of cooperation, Wallace contended.[2]

Wallace believed that the establishment of a national culture nurturing of the individual-in-the-community required not only that more emphasis be placed on cooperation but also that emphasis be taken away from the ideal of free enterprise. If the United States was not to go the route of fascism or communism, cooperation had to develop as fully as possible. As he had argued for the previous decade and a half, Wallace insisted in the late 1930s that nationally, and by implication internationally, the ethic of cooperation must "pervade the community." To him this meant developing an "attitude of mind" quite different from one that underpinned a society based on unchecked competition.[3]

Fascist Victories and the Failure of Western Neutrality

While Wallace developed his commentaries on national responsibility and the general welfare, Niebuhr extended his critique of Western society, for which, by 1937, he had a new focus. The Spanish Civil War began the summer before, when fascist leader Francisco Franco commenced his assault on the Spanish constitutional government. For Niebuhr events in Spain during the 1930s captured in microcosm the "whole social history of Europe." But Spain convinced Niebuhr of something else, something that he had first realized after Hitler's unexpected ascension to power in 1933. Niebuhr no longer perceived of fascism as capitalism's dying delirium. Nor had fascism simply co-opted the petty bourgeoisie. Niebuhr now contended that fascism in fact derived from the "social resentments and the political confusion" of the lower middle classes, resulting in a division between the petty bourgeoisie and the workers, the two sectors of modern society that Wallace, in 1942, would label collectively as the "common man."[4]

In addition, the civil war in Spain reinforced Niebuhr's perception of radicalism's failings. In the Spanish case it was anarchists who undermined the cause of democracy, their idealism leading them to attack the constitutional government even as they defended it on the battlefield. At the same time, however, Niebuhr pointed out that the Spanish radicals were not the only ones to blame for their nation's circumstances. Christianity, in the form of the Catholic Church, played into the hands of the fascists by being too bound up in Spain's vestigial feudalism. In Niebuhr's interpretation the Catholic Church in Spain, in its implacable resistance to democracy, helped create the social, political, and spiritual conditions that drove the anarchists. The extremity of the latter's aims in turn fostered the rise of fascism in the nation's lower middle classes.[5]

Just as Niebuhr saw the Spanish fascists as part of a greater fascist threat to Western civilization, he viewed the failings of the Spanish radicals in a larger context as well: the failure of the Western democracies and the League of Nations. In Niebuhr's assessment the League had never proven an effective collective security organization, a view only strengthened by the Western democracies' nonaction in Spain. The leaders of Britain and France, Niebuhr contended, remained committed only to the establishment of international accords not backed up by any threat of force. The extent of German and Italian intervention, however, despite such accords, belied the Anglo-French faith. While Niebuhr allowed that a "thoroughgoing neutrality" might have helped Spain's constitutional government, he felt that the actual, poorly enforced neutrality only aided the fascists.[6]

The ongoing conflict in Asia between Japan and China further reinforced Niebuhr's skeptical view of the League and also illustrated what he viewed as the profound risks of a policy of absolute neutrality. Although the League declared Japan's invasion in 1931 an unprovoked aggression, the lack of any action in proportion to that declaration, Niebuhr argued, proved the League's impotence. By September 1937 little had changed internationally, while in the United States fierce debate continued over American neutrality policy. While Niebuhr explicitly acknowledged the need for absolute Christian pacifism as something of a transcendent standard, he nevertheless insisted that the pacifists were mistaken if they believed that absolute moral standards of human action could stand as a social-political norm. As before, Niebuhr argued that the pacifists in their moral simplicity denied the central reality of politics, domestic and international: politics remained a "contest of power, in which motives are never altogether pure." Moreover, to Niebuhr absolute neutrality embodied an a priori decision to avoid evaluating the relative moralities in a particular conflict. While he allowed that sometimes it was difficult to determine the aggressor in an international dispute, at other times he believed it "terribly easy." For him the Sino-Japanese situation fell into the latter category. Niebuhr was convinced that a decision by the United States and other nations not to apply economic sanctions against Japan because of some mechanistic moral formula was a denial of reality. More than that, Niebuhr declared that such self-imposed national impotency indicated "complete irresponsibility" in foreign policy. The simplistic, pacifist-generated desire to remain not only physically but also morally distanced from all global conflicts contributed in the Sino-Japanese conflict to the defeat of the side that Niebuhr believed actually held a great moral claim to American support.[7]

A Hemispheric "City on a Hill" in a Time of Global Strife

By 1938, as the descent of Europe and Asia into war accelerated, Wallace began to share Niebuhr's sense of doubt regarding international affairs, for a time even becoming skeptical of global cooperation. On the one hand, he could still write that individualism was on the wane throughout the world, which suggested a growing international inclination toward cooperation. On the other hand, as Germany, Italy, and Japan pursued their dreams of empire, Wallace acknowledged that these "preliminary" forms of unity were predominantly nationalistic and not likely to result in the international community he hoped for. So Wallace retreated for the moment from his global vision into a short-lived variation on isolationism. As the international situation deteriorated in the late 1930s, he began to advocate the strengthening of American institutions and the promotion of cooperation within the United States. Americans had to reinvigorate their own political, economic, and social institutions to carry their nation through the uncertain years ahead.

Once more evoking the image of John Winthrop's "city on a hill," Wallace implied that if Americans attained "harmony in the national picture," their nation eventually might still lead the way to global harmony as well.[8]

Wallace did not altogether abandon his vision of international cooperation, however. In summer 1938 the European crisis arising from Nazi Germany's claims on Czechoslovakia moved toward its culmination at Munich. Observing the course of events, Wallace wrote that it was clear that Hitler's aim was "to take a bite at a time." Once the Germans consolidated their position in Europe, Wallace reckoned they would look across the Atlantic, "putting both external and internal pressure" on the United States and its neighbors in the Western Hemisphere. He concluded that it was time to "take the long look ahead" and begin preparations that would allow America and the other nations of the hemisphere to avoid war.[9]

Having briefly narrowed the scope of his vision to domestic affairs, Wallace refocused on the Western Hemisphere. In the face of fascist victories throughout Europe, Wallace was returning to the scene of what he considered one of the true instances of international cooperation, for it had been the nations of Latin America that had officially subscribed to the Roerich Pact and the Banner of Peace in 1935. If the nations of Europe showed little evidence in 1939 of evolving toward a cooperative international community, Wallace thought such an evolution possible among the nations of the Western Hemisphere. For this reason he narrowed his international vision to the limits of Roosevelt's so-called Good Neighbor policy toward Latin America.

Elaborating a policy actually begun by Herbert Hoover, aimed at overcoming the distrust and hatred felt by many Latin Americans toward the United States, Roosevelt and Hull endorsed declarations of the Pan-American Union on the illegality of U.S. interventions south of the Rio Grande and lowered the U.S. tariff wall through reciprocal trade agreements with the various Latin American nations. After the European war began the Good Neighbor policy was turned to developing diplomatic mechanisms for hemispheric cooperation in neutrality and defense. For Wallace the creation of a united, cooperative Western Hemisphere meant that the United States would not stand alone as a beacon to the world, as exemplar of the cooperative future, a hemispheric City on the Hill.

From late 1939 on, Wallace developed the theme of hemispheric interdependence in earnest. He argued that international events were forcing North and South Americans to reconsider their relationship, to develop a new culture, "genuinely inter-American" in character. His proposals manifested the deepening of his vision, already apparent at the signing of the Roerich Pact, of a truly cooperative international community. Wallace's suggestions ranged across the cultural landscape, from literature to theater, from education to film. The ultimate exchange Wallace hoped for was the eventual establishment of a "genuine inter-American university." Such an institution could actually create an international cooperative community in ways that the Roerich Pact only hinted at. An inter-American university, Wallace believed, might become the true birthplace of the "soul of the Pan America that is to be." [10]

However, what remained essential to economic cooperation in the Americas, in Wallace's view, was trade. In an October 1939 magazine article he pointed out that there was already substantial trade between the United States and Latin American nations. He believed the key was to cultivate a truly complementary trade relationship, especially regarding products that would become scarce as the war continued, to create among the nations of the Americas the sort of "middle path" planned economy that he had advocated for the United States in *America Must Choose*. Balance was still crucial, Wallace implied, insisting that science, capital, and management, directed by sympathetic governments, could all help create a cooperative hemispheric community. If this could be done, then the New World could slowly break its dependence on the Old. [11]

Foundations of a Cooperative Hemispheric Defense

In 1940 the war in Europe was going against the western Allies. France capitulated to the Nazis, while Great Britain hunkered down for a siege that many doubted it could survive. Like many Americans, Wallace still hoped that the United States would not enter the war. But if America was to stay out, Wallace believed it would be necessary to prepare American and hemispheric military defenses while giving thought to a future in which Germany, at least for a time, would dominate Europe. It was with such aims in mind that Wallace further elaborated his vision of hemispheric solidarity in the summer of 1940, as a main theme in a book entitled *The American Choice*. Invoking the title of his 1934 book *America Must Choose*, Wallace implied that inter-American cooperation now was the "path" for the United States to take.[12]

Although in *The American Choice* Wallace conceded that Germany might very well win the war in Europe, he believed that the era of German domination would be only temporary. Once again exhibiting the influence of Thorstein Veblen on his thinking, Wallace insisted that alleged German superiority in "science, factory production and war" could be easily explained in terms of propitious historical timing. Making use of scientific procedures and methods of factory production pioneered elsewhere, Germany had leaped from the "feudal age to modern times," saving a generation of wasted time. The Germans were no race of "supermen" and Americans had to understand that if the Western Hemisphere were to remain a locus of human freedom and progress in an uncertain future. Rejecting the Nazis' false racial logic, he insisted it was necessary for Americans to grasp what he termed "genetic equality": in terms of inherited traits, the children of one nation were no more naturally intelligent than the children of any other. This "genetic basis of democracy" was entirely in opposition to the temporarily ascendant racial ideology of the Nazis.[13] What Wallace did not seem to realize was that, in attempting to deflate the power of the Nazis' "super race" ideology, he inadvertently was making an argument for doing nothing, for simply waiting until Nazism collapsed under the weight of its own lies.

This principle of genetic equality and its corollary, that Nazi race theory was groundless and thus German dominance transitory, underpinned Wallace's propositions regarding hemispheric cooperation. Whatever the outcome of the European war, Wallace was convinced, the Western Hemisphere would be in the best shape, economically and spiritually, of all the regions of the globe. This being the case, he contended, the nations of the Western Hemisphere ought to be extremely cautious in their economic intercourse with a German-dominated Europe, now or later, since even a victorious Germany was sure to fall from power.[14]

The main thing was that American business not face the centralized forces of a Nazi-controlled Europe "headlong [and] haphazardly" as it had tended to do in the past. To enter into trade with such a "terrifically concentrated" bargaining power on the other side, while leaving themselves vulnerable in their disunity, Wallace suggested, would be little more than commercial suicide for the nations of the Western Hemisphere. The only way to trade with German Europe safely, Wallace insisted, was in a "planned, organized way," and that would require an increased level of government involvement. While this might strain the North American penchant for individual initiative, Wallace viewed it as absolutely necessary until totalitarianism failed and a "New World Order" gained sway.[15]

As Wallace saw it, the first task in creating a pan-hemispheric approach to Europe was to preempt the diplomatic and commercial incursions Germany was already making in Latin America. And the best way to preempt the Germans, Wallace argued, was to strengthen inter-American ties. That meant establishing the bonds of hemispheric cooperation; that is, creating the means by which the peoples of the various American nations would develop the habit of cooperation through its practice. That in turn meant learning more of one another's culture, as he suggested in 1939, in order to foster the sort of mutual understanding that would strengthen trust and interdependence. Desiring to undercut any North American sense that the traditions of Latin America were too vastly different from those of the North for such harmony to develop, Wallace once more indulged in historical reductionism, arguing that the cultures of the Latin American nations were no more Spanish than that of the United States was English. Having asserted this, he could ignore the complexities of various cultures and portray Latin Americans as sharing the beliefs of the citizens of the United States regarding social, political, and economic institutions. Engaging in the common Western practice of assuming that all peoples were simply North Americans in the making, Wallace suggested that the cultures of the Western Hemisphere all shared an "American belief in a democratic progressive future." Implying a common revolutionary heritage, Wallace evoked the clichéd image of Simón Bolívar as the George Washington of South America and declared that Bolívar and other Latin American liberators had gained many of their revolutionary ideas from the United States. In Wallace's mind such presumably shared ideals were the ready bases for inter-American unity. It was an easy matter of tapping sources of cooperation that already existed.[16]

As Europe slipped back into its traditional quagmire and threatened to drag the Americas down as well, Wallace declared it time to assert the "New World way of doing things." Whatever the outcome of the new European war, the nations of the Western Hemisphere had to prepare themselves to meet the future in ways never before attempted. As Europe burned, it was time to go "on into a new world" with the "determined will to make it a better one."[17] While Niebuhr moved toward an increasingly interventionist stance by 1940–41, Wallace retreated into a hemispheric perspective, transforming Nazism into simply one more manifestation of a larger European menace to New World virtue.

Wallace in Mexico

Wallace's inherently American vision of Pan-American interdependence fit well with the Roosevelt administration's strategic aims in the region. By summer 1940 Roosevelt and Hull were deeply concerned with the threat of Nazi incursions in the Western Hemisphere. In July, at around the same time that Wallace was completing *The American Choice,* the Department of State called for a Pan-American conference to be held in Havana in order to line up Latin American support for U.S. policy opposing the transfer of control of any New World territory from defeated European nations to the Germans. Wallace saw great promise for hemispheric cooperation in the conference's subsequent pronouncement against any such changes of authority in the European colonial holdings in Latin America. He believed Pan-Americanism might just be the foundation of a new hemispheric order analogous to that established by the former Anglo-American colonies in 1789.[18]

After his election to the vice presidency in November, Wallace was given the opportunity to contribute to the realization of his hopes for hemispheric cooperation when Roosevelt appointed him "Ambassador Extraordinary and Plenipotentiary" to head an American delegation to the December 1 inauguration of Manuel Ávila Camacho as president of Mexico. Wallace was an excellent choice for the mission. As his interest in Latin America blossomed over the prior several years, he had become in typical fashion an ardent student of Latin American culture as well as the Spanish language. By the time he left for Mexico he was fully conversational in Spanish, which greatly impressed the Mexicans. His penchant for visiting with the common people as well as his ability to communicate in the native tongue drew enthusiastic responses wherever he traveled.[19]

While in Mexico Wallace conducted an extensive correspondence with Washington. His letters from Mexico showcased his hopes for Pan-American interdependence. The centerpiece of this correspondence was a twenty-one page dispatch sent from Michoacán on December 16 to Secretary of State Hull. In it Wallace gave a thorough assessment of Mexican culture, politics and economy, along with an analysis of the central issues of Mexican-American relations at the time.[20]

Among other questions, Wallace addressed the long-term influence of the reformist policies of the outgoing president, Lázaro Cárdenas. It was Cárdenas's administration that had expropriated foreign—including U.S.—oil companies' holdings in Mexico in 1938, causing an international dispute that seriously threatened the viability of the Good Neighbor policy throughout Latin America. In his long dispatch Wallace contended that the new Mexican regime was likely to be amenable to reaching some sort of final settlement of the oil issue (as eventually was the case). Doing so would in turn open the door to further Mexican-American cooperation. That cooperation could take many forms, from joint meetings of national chambers of commerce, to the establishment of a U.S.-style agricultural experiment station in Mexico, to the creation of a joint U.S.-Mexican commission to address the various other problems existing between the United States and Mexico. Wallace even hoped the joint commission might prove a model for similar global arrangements.[21]

Wallace advocated such joint Mexican-American policies because he believed they would enable the two countries to resolve the various sources of discord between them, allowing the two nations to conduct a mutual defense against a dangerous world. More than this, relieving tensions and strengthening ties with Mexico could establish a precedent in which Mexican-American cooperation would form the basis of a wider U.S. hemispheric policy. If real stability could be attained in U.S.-Mexican relations, it would enhance the Good Neighbor policy throughout the region, Wallace argued. And that would indeed make the New World the bastion of "light and hope" that he envisioned.[22]

From Versailles to Munich: The Failures of Western Liberalism

Despite the ominous and tragic events of the late 1930s, Wallace continued to envision a cooperative regional and, eventually, global society. Niebuhr, however, saw events bearing out his critical prophesy of the West's doom. He perceived the situations in Spain and Asia as results of, among other things, the too-simple rationalism of pacifists and isolationists. That perception fell within the larger context of his transcendent critique of Western liberalism since Versailles. For Niebuhr it was all part of a tragic tale that led more or less directly to Munich in 1938. He believed the "capitulation" of the Western democracies at Munich in September to Hitler's demands regarding Czechoslovakia issued partly from the relationship of fascism and capitalism. The Munich agreement displayed an "essentially treasonable" action taken by industrialists hoping to preserve industrial capitalism from the revolution they believed would follow another global war. In other words, it was more an act of class interest, an example of the industrialists' belief that their best hope of preserving themselves lay in cooperation with fascists. By September 1938 the sinful coupling that had occurred in Germany five years earlier was being replicated internationally.[23]

Yet Niebuhr believed Munich to be more than just another example of the treachery of capitalists; it was also the product of "liberal confusions" that helped enervate any serious opposition to the policies of the industrialists. And those confusions arose out of the most basic assumptions of modern liberalism. Implicitly discounting Wallace's logic regarding the resurrection of a cooperative human nature, Niebuhr argued that such liberalism, grounded in the "rationalistic optimism" of the liberalism of the eighteenth and nineteenth centuries, always expected humanity to eventually overcome its primitive violence and learn to "substitute reason for force." At the same time, Niebuhr insisted, democracy also reflected the realities of power that liberalism's illusions failed to grapple with. Democratic government was the only way to rein in the will to power of those who rose to power within democratic society. So democracy was more than just the product of liberal delusions of human perfectibility; it was also a "perennial necessity" because the attainment of justice would always demand that the "power of government be checked as democracy checks it." In describing this dynamic of democracy, Niebuhr moved toward the typically ironic and terse dictum he would articulate five years later: "Man's capacity for justice makes democracy possible; but man's inclination to injustice makes democracy necessary."[24]

At that moment in 1939, however, democracy's capacity to balance the dynamic of power was not in ascendancy, Niebuhr contended; rather the simplistic and overly optimistic liberal delusions that had dominated since Versailles were. The nature of liberal capitalist culture was to deny its inherent inequalities and the profound tensions they created, and from Niebuhr's perspective this denial was no more clearly manifested than in the unjust peace of Versailles. All the old problems of industrial society remained, even though liberals believed that the war and the peace treaty had eliminated them.[25]

Never in fact gone, the evils of industrial capitalism had festered for two decades. Drawing on Niebuhr's own occasional penchant for medical metaphor, one might say that his commentary of the 1920s and 1930s had in fact been something of a running diagnosis and prognosis of the deepening infection in the collective body of Western society. Munich was one more symptom, but one that re-created in microcosm the entire course of the illness. The "peace of Munich"—in reality a new injustice, a new "capitulation to tyranny"—proved that it was not possible to correct the "injustices of conquest" that Versailles embodied. For Niebuhr, as physician to the Western world—that is, as objective, expert outside observer—Munich strongly suggested the likelihood that the sickness of modern capitalist civilization was reaching its ultimate crisis.[26]

The outcome of the Munich conference revealed to Niebuhr that the Western democracies still did not understand the implication of force that he believed underpinned all politics. Behind any effective political agreement there had to be a threat of violence. But behind Munich there was none, at least not on the British and French side. There was only surrender. Even if the motives of Neville Chamberlain and Edouard Daladier were those of the capitalist oligarchy rather than loyalty to democratic principles, it was those principles most liberals believed to have gained ascendancy in the Munich agreement. In fact, it was not such principles but rather blind devotion to them that Niebuhr denigrated. For if the foe that was negotiated with viewed war as the "ultimate good," then the naive liberals sacrificed their peace for a settlement with an enemy who in the end planned to annihilate them anyway. As Niebuhr put it, "peace [was] lost for peace's sake."[27]

The Meaning of Munich

In asserting this Niebuhr articulated a prototype "Munich analog" in the very wake of Munich. Turning the specific circumstances of the confrontation over Czechoslovakia into a principle of political science, he implied that in such situations liberals would always lose the peace. They would lose it, he believed, because they failed to realize that at certain critical junctures the threat of force underlying all political struggle had to be made explicit, and it had to be made so by those who valued peace the most.

At Munich the threat of force was raised not by the peace-craving Western democracies but by Hitler, who, Niebuhr insisted, "glories in the threat." The liberals and pacifists missed what Niebuhr believed was apparent by 1939: that in fascism, particularly Nazism, they faced something new under the modern sun. Nazi Germany was not a society that pursued war rationally, as a means to self-interested ends. Rather it was a throwback to barbarism, a culture with a blood lust. Nazism was, simply, "the worship of power for its own sake." Niebuhr viewed Nazism—like Marxism and, to a lesser extent, liberalism—as a religion. But the Nazi religion was an essentially "pagan faith." In agreement with Wallace, who by 1942 would identify Hitler and the Nazis as "stooges" of "Satan," Niebuhr characterized Nazism as a form of "modern devil worship." After all, the devil, as Niebuhr pointed out, was an angel whose fall from heaven issued from his attempt at usurping God. Likewise, the Germans construed their nation as God, which for Niebuhr was as false a usurpation as that which Satan had attempted.[28]

What is interesting in this context is that Niebuhr did not make a similar judgment of the Soviet Union. He had long argued that the essence of Marxist "religion" was its replacement—that is, usurpation—of God with the historical dialectic. Yet he did not characterize Marxism, Soviet or otherwise, as devil worship, implying at least for the time being that the Nazi usurpation was somehow more purely evil than that of the communists in Russia. This could not have been due, in 1939, to any noticeably darker image held by liberals of Nazi German than of Soviet society. What was known and generally only rumored of Nazi atrocities by that time was no worse than the substantiated knowledge of Stalin's depredations of the 1930s. In part Niebuhr's less harsh evaluation of Soviet communist culture derived from his affinity for Marxism, integral as it was to his critique of liberalism. He was sympathetic to Marxism's prophetic insights of catastrophe; in those insights he saw real, if flawed, wisdom.[29]

It seems likely that Niebuhr's characterization of Nazi culture derived much of its extraordinary virulence from the old tension that still existed within his commentary and self-perception regarding Germany. By the time World War II began in late summer 1939, one senses that events in Germany since 1933 in some ways had overwhelmed Niebuhr. It is true that by the mid-1930s he developed a calm, cogent explanation of Nazism's ascendancy, attributing it in great part to the failure of German radicalism. He even prophesied the war that finally was occurring. Nevertheless, by 1939 Niebuhr's writings betray something like a subtle shock in his realization that modern civilization had finally come to such a crisis and, especially, that Germany was its catalyst. Reminiscent of his similar ambivalence regarding German-Americanism in World War I, it was as if Niebuhr was struggling within himself for a more complete explanation, one that was beyond the detached perspective of the outside observer.[30]

This tacit shock and uncertainty was reflected in Niebuhr's condemnation of Nazi ideology as devil worship and in the telling absence of a similar condemnation of Soviet communism. The tension was apparent in the extremity of the language and imagery Niebuhr used in describing Nazi German society: Nazi culture was "tribal," a recrudescence of "barbarism" in the modern world, possessed of a "racial mania and fury" that flew uncontrolled in the face of Western civilization. But more than anywhere else Niebuhr's dilemma was manifested in a curious, almost contradictory dualism he created concerning the meaning of Germany after Munich. One side of the dualism was his suggestion that Nazi Germany's "religious racialism" was only different by degree from the nationalism of any modern nation, that it was related to the "cultural decadence" of European society in the same way that the politics and economics of fascism were related to the "structural decadence" of Western technological civilization. Nazism was evil that arose from the heart of modern industrial society.[31]

At the same time Niebuhr argued that Nazism was something horrible in and of itself. While perhaps arising out of the flaws of Western liberal civilization, Nazi culture exaggerated those flaws insanely. Britain, France, and America still preserved "certain values of civilization"; Nazi Germany did not. It was a "terror . . . sweeping over Europe," not a civilization. Throwing off his own coolly rational historical understanding of events since 1918, Niebuhr declared in late 1939—implicitly criticizing Wallace and others who still invoked the errors of Versailles—that any moralistic logic that attempted to obscure the totality of Nazi evil was "perverse."[32] Prior to 1933 Germany had been for Niebuhr the measure of whatever promise liberal capitalist civilization held. While he did not abandon this view altogether, after Munich Niebuhr stressed the perception that Hitler and the Nazis had transformed Germany. What they created might have issued from the West's failures, but in Niebuhr's view the extremity of Nazi evil carried it beyond any reasonable comparison.

Niebuhr's placement of Nazi German culture beyond the pale of relative morality was extraordinary for him, and it marked a crucial juncture in the evolution of his thought. By making such an evaluation of the evil of Nazism, Niebuhr raised the possibility that, despite their failings, the morality of other nations might be so much greater than that of Germany as to make the distinction effectively absolute. He was, in other words, implicitly rejecting the differentiation he had made between the morality of individuals and that of communities, the construction that characterized his writing from its first appearance, in his bachelor's thesis of 1914, through the 1930s, most notably in *Moral Man and Immoral Society.*

This suggestion—perhaps in 1939 it was no more than an implication—of the possibility of relative communal morality was the first step in a logical process that culminated in Niebuhr's classic cold war writings of the late 1940s and early 1950s, including *The Irony of American History,* published in 1952. As it developed, this logic crucially supported his attacks on the Soviet Union from 1946 on, making Niebuhr for many Americans the complete cold warrior and in fact an archetypal cold war liberal.[33]

The Open Society

After 1939, having diluted his logic of national immorality, Niebuhr could argue that Western capitalist democracy, despite his own decades-long criticism, was unquestionably worth saving from the fascist threat. It did not matter that one could point out "how undemocratic America is" or that "England is not a democracy and never will be." As far as they went such criticisms were true. But the Nazi threat made that truth *relatively* unimportant. The quite real flaws in the political, economic, and social systems of the Western nations did not lessen the far greater danger of the "fascist negation of justice."[34]

By 1941, Niebuhr insisted, Atlantic culture had been evolving for a millennium. What differentiated this civilization from any other—what made it in Niebuhr's view worth preserving despite its failings—was that within its bounds men and women created their nations "on the basis of consent rather than . . . force." Echoing his World War I contention that America was an ideal in the process of realization, Niebuhr declared that the Western democracies embodied the "open society," characterized not by social or political perfection but rather by the encouragement of "criticism of itself in the light of universal standards."[35]

One suspects at this point that Niebuhr was reflecting on his own rise. He had climbed, after all, from a moderate-sized parish of a fairly obscure, non-Anglo-Saxon Christian denomination to the heights of American academic theology as well as mainstream political journalism. And he had done so in great part by making a relentless critique of American and Western European religion, politics, and society. Niebuhr must have realized that he could never have produced such a commentary had he been living in Nazi Germany. He must have known if he had tried to do so he would have ended up in exile, in a concentration camp, or dead. For Niebuhr America and the West had indeed proven to be the open society: the one that allowed "its most independent minds and its bravest spirits"—among whom he implicitly included himself—to speak out at will without fear of state-controlled terror associated with both fascism and Russian communism.[36]

It was this freedom of expression, with its potential for social improvement, that was the "rich inheritance" of the West. This is what a Nazi victory threatened to destroy so unhesitatingly and so completely. The rise of Nazism, culminating in the Western democracies' capitulation at Munich, ironically forced Niebuhr to defend explicitly the most central ideals of the liberal capitalist culture he had consistently derided during the prior two and a half decades. Yet it was only in the survival of that culture, of those ideals, that Niebuhr now saw any hope whatsoever for modern civilization.[37]

Niebuhr's epiphany in 1941 regarding the supreme value of the West's "open society" was another milestone on his path to becoming a cold warrior. It was one of the first signs of what became his habit of characterizing cultures (such as American and Soviet) in ideal absolutes, an ironic development in light of his own critique of philosophical idealism. His unreflective use of such totalizing myths in discussing international relations in the 1950s would be condemned as "completely unreal" and thus unjustifiably dangerous by commentators in the 1960s.[38]

The manner in which Nazi Germany and the Munich episode reshaped Niebuhr's assessment of relative national morality helps explain why his critique of Soviet Marxism did not attain the same degree of harshness as did his attack on Nazism. It was not, however, as if Niebuhr eased up on his critique of Marxism's mistakes or, more specifically, of Soviet tyranny. Niebuhr believed that Marxists, like liberals and pacifists, ultimately failed to understand the role power played in society. They saw it not as Niebuhr did, as a "necessity of social cohesion," but rather and simply as a tool for class oppression. Thus Marxists could look forward to the workers' utopia: once the proletarian revolution had occurred, social relations would no longer need the mediation of the force inherent in politics. In this sense Marxism became for Niebuhr a subset of liberalism, partaking in nearly all "liberal illusions."[39]

That Marxism shared liberalism's ultimate ideals is what distinguished it from Nazism in Niebuhr's mind. That it did so based upon its presumption of capitalism's inevitable demise, however, was what he viewed as Marxism's dangerous flaw. Niebuhr could not construe communism as being as profoundly evil as Nazism, but Marxist idealism could engender tyranny nevertheless. In Russia the brutalities of Stalin's dictatorship ultimately degraded the ideals implicit in Marxism, because the power of those ideals underpinned Stalin's regime. Niebuhr perceived real tragedy in the thinking of those Westerners who could not disabuse themselves of their faith in the Soviet Union. Yet he still felt that their belief in Russia, though grounded in an "unbelievable credulity," was essentially more sophisticated than the perspective of the liberals. It was a faith issuing from an understanding of the "tragic realities" of modern civilization. The irony of the credulity of such fellow travelers lay, however, in their own ultimate liberalism, which also underlay the Marxist belief in the workers' utopia.[40]

Niebuhr's comparison of the evils of Nazism and Soviet communism left him cynical of Russian foreign policy. He thus was not especially shocked by the Nazi-Soviet nonaggression pact of August 1939. In fact, the Hitler-Stalin agreement made a lot of sense to Niebuhr.

Those who failed to see its logic denied the true nature of Soviet society. By confusing a nation with an ideal, Niebuhr insisted, Western communists and fellow travelers were unable to imagine the Soviet Union following a policy based on the requirements of national survival rather than loyalty to a universal cause.[41]

Anticipating the explanation of Cold War origins articulated by historians such as Arthur M. Schlesinger Jr. in the 1960s, Niebuhr contended that it was exactly concern for national survival that led Stalin to accept the treaty Hitler proffered. The Munich accord, he argued, implied to the Soviets that the Western nations wholly subscribed to the law of the jungle, compelling Stalin to seek a *modus vivendi* with Hitler. It was the democracies' collective cowardice, Niebuhr concluded, that led to the Nazi-Soviet pact.[42]

This is not to say that Niebuhr approved of the Soviet policy in an absolute sense. In fact, he, along with many other left liberals, was quite disgusted with the contortions that many Western communists put themselves through in justifying the pact. For instance, he severed his editorial connection with the *Protestant Digest* because of its support of the pact, characterizing its editorial policy as "covert pro-Nazism." He then went on to condemn any group that "went out of its way to defend Russia," while denying the "obvious fact that the Nazi aggression was unleashed upon the world through the Nazi-Soviet Pact."[43]

Global Internationalism and American Complacency

During the period of Niebuhr's intellectual transformation on the issue of national morality, Wallace continued to think a great deal about inter-American relations and to preach Pan-Americanism. He persisted at this even after the United States entered World War II.[44] Nevertheless, before the Japanese attack, a shift occurred in his thinking. As we will see, American entry into the war had the overall effect of turning Wallace's cooperative vision outward again, until it encompassed not just the Western Hemisphere but once more the entire globe. This shift in Wallace's commentary was already apparent by spring 1941, after Roosevelt committed the United States, by way of the Lend-Lease program, to becoming the "arsenal of democracy." In this context Wallace no longer focused solely or even centrally on the need to make the Western Hemisphere a stronghold of economic and political democracy for the other nations of the world to look to when they finally came to their collective senses. Instead, he began to speak and write regarding the United States' postwar responsibilities as a fully engaged participant in global affairs. Much of what he argued, not surprisingly, was articulated in the terms of his cooperative vision. It was amplified, however, by his understanding of the Nazi threat. In Wallace's assessment— which was strikingly similar to Niebuhr's condemnation of the cultural insensitivity of Marxist radicalism—the Nazis helped create a new opportunity for attaining global cooperation not just by starting a war but by virtue of ironic example. The Germans' seemingly slavish willingness to put themselves at their nation's service suggested to Wallace the task that lay before the United States and other democracies. Democracy needed to instill in its adherents a sense of duty analogous to that of the Germans but grounded in cooperation, not coercion. Wallace believed that the manner in which the democratic nations—America most of all—fostered cooperation during the war would go a long way in determining what sort of world would come into being at the war's end.[45]

Niebuhr of course also insisted that the United States held no small share of the guilt for the "mistakes" of the Western democracies. By asserting this in 1941 he actually was summarizing much of his own commentary of the previous decade. Beginning with America's rejection of the League of Nations in 1919, continuing through the 1920s and 1930s with the international economic policy that he, like Wallace, so powerfully condemned, and culminating in the United States' unwillingness to take an effective stand on the Sino-Japanese, Italian-Ethiopian, or Spanish conflicts, Niebuhr viewed U.S. foreign policy since World War I as one long tale of irresponsible behavior in the international arena. In the eyes of the world, Niebuhr argued, America had miserably failed to fulfill Woodrow Wilson's promises. The faith of the smaller nations of Europe in America was misplaced. Yet despite profound disappointment created by the nation's failure to fulfill its promise, the world's nations continued to believe in the United States as the champion of democracy. Niebuhr feared that such international faith in American righteousness might once again prove ill-founded.[46]

In Niebuhr's assessment the likelihood that America might once again fail in its international responsibilities was suggested by the continued efforts of American pacifists and isolationists, who were allied by summer 1941. More than that, Niebuhr perceived a distressing complacency in the American people generally. That fall public opinion polls demonstrated that most Americans agreed with Niebuhr and Wallace, doubting that American democracy could long survive a complete Nazi victory in Europe. But the same polls also made clear that Americans still strongly wanted to stay out of the war. On this issue Niebuhr broke with Wallace's optimistic hopes. To Niebuhr the tension between Americans' loathing Nazism and their unwillingness to commit to the struggle against it only proved once again the simplistic inability of liberal society to understand the dynamics of power. The problem was that Americans did not feel moved to action by a threat that was "ultimate" rather than "immediate" in nature.[47]

By late 1941 Americans recognized that Hitler posed a real threat to their country if he were to defeat the British and Soviets. But to Niebuhr's great frustration they still would not approve any actions that might actually turn the tide against the Nazis; they would only accept halfway measures. He speculated that a British and Russian victory might still come about in the end, despite American recalcitrance, but if it did it would have been bought with "British tenacity and Russian blood." Americans would benefit from a peace that came dearly to others but cheaply to themselves.[48]

Distressed by American complacency, Niebuhr did all he could throughout 1941 to upset it. He became, for instance, an extremely vocal supporter of Roosevelt's Lend-Lease policy, testifying before Congress in January 1941 in favor of the Lend-Lease bill. Niebuhr praised Lend-Lease because it directly addressed what he considered the specific nature of U.S. complacency toward the war, combining the American desire to give "all possible aid" to Britain with the possibility of staying out of the war. By providing the maximum level of American material aid to the Allies, Lend-Lease at least lessened the effect of the continuing American reluctance to confront a threat that for them remained theoretical rather than immediate.[49]

Union for Democratic Action: Formation and Context

Although Niebuhr saw some reason for hope in the Lend-Lease bill, he remained deeply concerned about persistent American reluctance to commit to the fight against fascism. Lend-Lease, he feared, might prove too little, too late. At the same time, the debates over the legislation demonstrated the continuing ominous presence of a "stubborn . . . isolationism" in the nation. Such doubts gave impetus to Niebuhr's decision to take a leading role in the formation of the Union for Democratic Action (UDA) in spring 1941. At the time of its founding Niebuhr, the new organization's chairman, described the UDA as a locus for the unification of Americans "on the center and left" who believed as he did in the vital need to preserve democratic society. But the UDA as Niebuhr conceived it looked to the future as well. In words that Wallace must have appreciated, Niebuhr insisted that democratic forces had to organize themselves now, during the war, if there was to be any hope for establishing a "new world order" later.[50]

Not actually a political party, the UDA received much of its support from American leftists disgusted with the isolationism of Norman Thomas and the Socialist Party. Its leadership included progressive intellectuals and reformers, including Niebuhr, the historian Arthur Schlesinger Jr., *The Nation* editor Freda Kirchwey, the romance-language scholar James Loeb Jr., and John Childs of Columbia University's Teachers College as well as leaders from organized labor, such as Murray Gross and Lewis Corey of the International Ladies' Garment Workers' Union and George Counts of the American Federation of Teachers. The organization became what one writer has called a "halfway house for anti-Fascists eager to defend Britain and groping for a non-Socialist yet still progressive vantage point on domestic issues." In other words, the UDA brought together New Deal and leftist reformers who favored the strongest possible support of the British war effort but who wanted to distance themselves from doctrinaire leftist radicalism. The UDA's "educational" aim was to get its positions into print as frequently as possible, which for Niebuhr by this time was practically second nature.[51] In this sense the activities of Niebuhr and the UDA dovetailed nicely with Wallace's efforts in speeches and articles to gain public support for both FDR's foreign policy and plans for postwar global organization.

The UDA has been described as a prototypical "liberal, anti-Communist organization." This is because communists could not become members, although at the time of its creation it did not yet explicitly condemn communist ideology or nations. In fact, the UDA represented the institutionalization of "cold war liberalism" well before the cold war began. At its inception the UDA embodied three themes: advocacy of "all aid short of war in support of the Allies" (which became, after American entry, "whole-hearted support of the nation's military effort"); nurturing "democratic left-wing unity" in preserving and extending the programs of the New Deal; and pursuing the first two aims while firmly rejecting communism. Transforming this constellation of aims into "cold war liberalism" only required the short leap from strong support of American wartime military policy to strong support of postwar, militaristic American hard-line policy toward the Soviet Union, a leap that was quite likely in light of the group's distrust of communism from the outset. Indeed, this transition is exactly what took place after the war, culminating, as we will see, in the formation of Americans for Democratic Action in 1948.[52] Just as the Munich crisis began the process of altering Niebuhr's assessment of the relative morality of nations—a transformation crucial to his cold war commentary—the creation of the UDA established the institutional framework within which that commentary attained its greatest sway.

Much of the context of Niebuhr's secular commentary of 1941—his concern with politics, culture, and international affairs—as well as of the founding of the UDA was discernible in his prestigious Gifford lectures, given at Edinburgh University in 1939 and published as two volumes, in 1941 and 1943, entitled *The Nature and Destiny of Man*, the best-known of his books and certainly his theological magnum opus. The first volume, *Human Nature*, was widely hailed upon its release, raising Niebuhr's stature as a theologian while definitively establishing his theology as a basis for cultural criticism.[53]

As with many of Niebuhr's books *Nature and Destiny* restated various components of his discourse that he already articulated in articles, speeches, and sermons over the years. Indeed, as Richard Fox points out, the fundamental structure of the argument of *Nature and Destiny* was "already laid out in Niebuhr's BD thesis" nearly thirty years before. Within an extended discussion of classical and modern philosophical and theological thought, for example, one discerns Niebuhr's longstanding critique of modern culture, including his views on idealism and liberalism. Idealism, Niebuhr thundered, whether Christian or secular, was "completely irrelevant to the tragic facts and problems of history" and in the end often served to aggravate those problems rather than solve them. Thus modern tyrannies issued not from a long sequence of tyrannies, each worse than the preceding, but rather from the "corruptions of a mature civilization" in which the instruments of supposedly beneficent technology became the tools of tyranny. In a similar sense, from its inception modern bourgeois liberal culture, grounded on assumptions of individuality, undermined that individuality by virtue of the "enslaving mechanical interdependencies and collectivities" it created.[54]

Nature and Destiny also contained by now familiar Niebuhrian interpretations of fascism and Marxism in the context of modern capitalist culture. The romanticism of the lower middle class culminated in fascism while industrial workers gravitated "naturally" toward communism. Niebuhr again characterized fascism as "demonic" for its replacement of "God with race and nation," while Marxism, he once more insisted, erroneously determined that a historical dialectic, accessible to human reason, was the driving force of human existence. Yet Niebuhr still expressed an appreciation of Marxism. He still insisted that, unlike fascism, Marxism was constructive and inherently rational, even if its logic was overdrawn. What Marx failed to see, according to Niebuhr, was that bourgeois culture shared its ideological element with all classes of society and that each asserted the universal significance of its particular values.[55]

Nature and Destiny also exhibited the normative role that Niebuhr's concern for personality still played in his thinking. In the end, Niebuhr argued, God as "will and personality" was the "only possible ground of real individuality," not the false assumptions regarding freedom held by idealistic moderns. True self-understanding only issued from faith that one was "understood from beyond" oneself, that one was "known and loved of God" and found oneself "in terms of obedience to the divine will." Niebuhr believed that real individuality, by which he meant personality, had achieved its highest development within Christianity, before Renaissance and modern thought sought to extend the idea of individuality beyond its valid scope. Only Christianity, Niebuhr insisted, in which "the individual is absorbed into the divine," actually saw and established the human spirit in its "total depth and uniqueness." In tracing the rise of modern Western society Niebuhr analyzed the ways modern cultures and ideologies undermined personality-grounded individuality. It was destroyed, in the name of individual freedom and equality, by the "mechanical and impersonal elaborations of a commercial culture" that reached their culmination in industrial civilization. Instead of nurturing personality, bourgeois modernity led to a "general pattern of social anarchy."[56]

In *Nature and Destiny* Niebuhr tied the threads of his theology and his evolving political philosophy together, if often only implicitly. For instance, in arguing that human personality—true individuality—could only attain its fullest realization within an interconnected, spiritually potent community, he was implying that some communities might at least be partially moral. In this sense, Niebuhr acknowledged somewhat hopefully, social recognition of "brotherhood" in terms of custom and law did evolve through history, if slowly. Because of this, societies arose in which negotiations of interests between groups and between individuals occurred without the mediation of a superior power. It was not quite an invocation of the open society, but it was moving that way.[57]

The UDA's Attack on American "Fascism" and the Coming of War

As his star rose in 1941 with the publication of the first volume of *Nature and Destiny*, Niebuhr continued his vigorous commentary on issues connected to American support of the British and Soviets. He strongly advocated the repeal of the Neutrality Act of 1939, arguing that it was another dangerous product of America's international irresponsibility. He even went so far as to argue that the U.S. Navy should join the British in battling the Germans in the North Atlantic. He justified this advocacy of actual if undeclared belligerency on the part of the United States by arguing that it was the only acceptable response to the situation. America, Niebuhr declared, faced a rare opportunity. Such a chance to "rid the world of tyranny" might not come again for "a thousand years."[58]

In addition, Niebuhr and the UDA began a preemptive attack on what they perceived as nascent fascism in the United States in the context of their interventionist crusade. In so doing they contributed to what one historian has described as a domestic "fascist scare" that began in the United States during the early 1930s. It grew out of falsely perceived connections between actual European fascism and various American extremists, including the German-American Bund, William Dudley Pelley's American Silver Shirts, and Father Charles E. Coughlin, the Detroit "radio priest." By 1941 the fascist scare was manipulated by liberal interventionists and aimed at new targets, including aviator and isolationist Charles Lindbergh and the America First organization.[59] The UDA, for example, attacked Lindbergh and America First's opposition to U.S. involvement in the war by indirectly and directly imputing to them both fascist tendencies and a willingness to actually collaborate with fascist regimes. With some exaggeration they suggested that the organization was made up of individuals whose political behavior was similar to that of French collaborationists and who publicly supported fascist regimes in Germany and Spain. Lindbergh was castigated for his "cordial relations with nazi leaders" and for being an "apologist for nazi racial theories."[60]

In denouncing America First the UDA formulated a scenario of how fascism might develop in the United States. It was a scenario clearly influenced by Niebuhr's interpretation of the rise of fascism in Europe. It also owed much to the devil theory of the 1920s, which was strengthened in the 1930s by the Nye Committee investigations of war profiteering, which established a public image of calculation, conspiracy, and callousness on the part of certain American and international corporations. At the core of American conservatism the UDA discerned the assumption that the needs of "monopoly business" superseded those of "democracy and national defense." Reflecting the power that the Munich analog already had attained in liberal thinking, the UDA argued that such assumptions contributed to a desire to appease fascism. Such a desire was apparent in suggestions made by isolationists and conservatives that the United States had to learn to coexist with Nazi Germany. At home, the UDA warned, these protofascists feared progressive economic change and the strengthening of democracy, particularly in relation to labor. Nascent American fascism was construed as big, monopolistic business interests that were willing to cooperate with demagogues, right-wing extremists, and foreign fascists in order to maintain control of American society, especially the economy.[61]

Nevertheless, despite efforts by Niebuhr and the UDA to exhort Americans to greater and more direct support of the Allies, it was ultimately the Japanese attack on Pearl Harbor that galvanized the spirit of their fellow citizens. If earlier the fascist threat had seemed distant, Pearl Harbor finally created the sense of immediacy that Niebuhr had found lacking. "History," Niebuhr wrote a few weeks after the attack, had "overtaken" America while Americans had done no better than irresponsibly and endlessly debate whether or not to take up the international obligations that to him were so obvious and compelling.[62]

For Wallace American entry into the war meant a full-fledged return to global internationalism, in the terms of his cooperative ethic. But his perspective had evolved greatly in its scope. Shifting his commentary farther and farther from his midwestern roots during the 1930s, Wallace by 1942 had evolved into a full-fledged internationalist. During the war he would become as much a citizen of the world as an American leader, in that sense beginning another transformation, from a quintessential American type into an outsider himself. Moreover, the more removed from the physicality of the Midwest Wallace's discussion of cooperation and community became, the more it resembled Niebuhr's conception of personality, in the sense of stressing an individual's need for vital connection to the group. The essential difference lay in the fact that the essence of Wallace's ethic of cooperation lay in practice, while the essence of Niebuhr's conception of personality was spiritual.

Because Niebuhr saw too many practical obstacles—in terms of power, politics, and nationalism—to the advent of the sort of co-operation that Wallace envisioned, he did not view the war as the wide-open portal to the "New Age" that Wallace perceived. For Niebuhr, the modern world remained as tragic a place as ever; the war that now engulfed it had been born of the many failings of modern industrial civilization that he had denounced for the last quarter century. Nevertheless, he could still assert with conviction that it was "not a world from which God has fled or from which He averts His eyes."[63] The portal perhaps remained open a crack.

PART 2

6

"A New World . . .
or a New World War"

Fighting the War with an Eye on the Future

———◆———

For WALLACE, Niebuhr, and other liberal internationalists, the United States' entry into World War II was an exhilarating, vindicating event. The UDA *Bulletin* of December 1941 went to the printer's just before the weekend of December 7, so the editors inserted a sidebar on the first page declaring that despite the contents of some of the articles, the international situation had vastly transformed. "Over the weekend, . . . Japan attacked. Now . . . OUR JOB BEGINS!"[1] No longer did the UDA need to convince Americans that their nation should do more in the global battle against fascism. With the question of war settled by the Japanese attack on Pearl Harbor and the German and Italian declarations of war, liberals could turn their full energies to America's role in the struggle.

This they did, but with an illuminatingly divided emphasis. As the United States became a formal belligerent in 1942, Wallace, Niebuhr and the UDA, and other liberal internationalists began to focus as much of their attention on the question of international relations after the war as they did on the war itself. In this sense as well as others, American liberal responses to events after Pearl Harbor underpinned postwar developments within the liberal community.

For example, during the war years both Niebuhr and Wallace reiterated their arguments regarding the need for the United States to fulfill its international responsibilities, but now with the focus of their critiques shifted from the need to enter the war against fascism to the need for the nation to stay involved internationally after the war's end. Like most American internationalists, neither man foresaw any hope for a peaceful postwar world should the United States revert to its prewar unilateralism. In addition both men, as well as the UDA, continued to warn their compatriots of the potential threat of domestic fascism that might arise in the context of a wartime economy, threatening the postwar peace.

Wallace continued to articulate his cooperative vision, now almost entirely focused on the international realm, with virtually no connection left to the landed sense of place from which his vision had originated. Nor did he recognize the extent to which he was attempting to apply an essentially American set of cultural assumptions to the behavior of other nations. For his part Niebuhr remained skeptical of global cooperation, although not yet wholly pessimistic. Wallace spoke broadly, if in a culturally blind fashion, on various aspects of cooperation, such as economic development and intercultural convergence and exchange. Niebuhr, however, persisted in focusing narrowly on the constraints of power in international relations. Viewing power as a virtual absolute, he often did not seem aware of its variability, grounded in just the sort of economic and cultural factors that so interested Wallace. Moreover, although Niebuhr's ideas profoundly influenced the UDA, Wallace's did as well. Indeed, throughout the war years Niebuhr remained somewhat on the outside of the liberal internationalist discussion, with most liberals seemingly more attuned to the hopeful vision of international cooperation laid out by the vice president.

Liberal Internationalism and Wartime Strategy

If American liberals' attention to the policy of war making was divided, it still displayed the qualities of their internationalism, often indicating the nature of their postwar expectations. Wallace, for example, developed a fairly wide range of strategic interests, both in his official capacities and from personal inclination. Not surprisingly, his passion for Latin American culture remained apparent even in the midst of a war effort focused upon Europe and the Pacific. Returning from an official and highly successful goodwill tour of several Latin American nations in early May 1943, Wallace wrote fervently about his experience, noting that Mexico was still his "first love" in the hemisphere, and he re-articulated the theme of hemispheric cooperation in a new strategic context, noting that Ecuadoran balsa was used in the construction of British bombers, while rubber harvested in Peru, Colombia, Costa Rica, and Panama was being used to manufacture tires for American combat vehicles.[2]

If personal inclination continued to draw Wallace's interest to strategic questions regarding areas like Latin America, there were also areas of strategy to which his attention was compelled by his official duties. Indeed, the most important and wide-ranging strategic activities Wallace undertook during the war were those connected to his role as director of the Board of Economic Warfare (BEW). Established by Roosevelt in July 1941, originally as the Economic Defense Board, the agency was responsible for locating and obtaining items of strategic importance to the United States from all over the globe. As director of the BEW, Wallace came into direct and highly visible bureaucratic conflict with Secretary of Commerce Jesse Jones, who was also director of the Reconstruction Finance Corporation (RFC) as well as, ultimately, federal loan disbursement in general. The story of that conflict, finally resolved in 1943 with the termination of the BEW and any official role for Wallace in strategic policy making, has been related in detail elsewhere. It has validly been portrayed as a personification of the struggle between the conservative and liberal wings of the Democratic party, foreshadowing the politics that in 1944 drove Wallace from the vice presidency. Indeed, Torbjörn Sirevag has argued that Jones's appointment as secretary of commerce in August 1940—replacing ardent New Dealer Harry Hopkins—was a symbolic "antidote" for conservative Democrats poisoned by Roosevelt's successful insistence on Wallace as his vice president at the 1940 national convention.[3]

The points of contention between Wallace and Jones highlight Wallace's wartime strategic thinking and the manner in which it was informed by his internationalism. The main circumstance behind the controversy was that the RFC controlled the BEW's funding, which meant that disagreements over procurement were likely to lead to classic bureaucratic battles. For Wallace there were two interconnected concerns forming the crux of the conflict: efficient matériel procurement and the assumption that procurement policies had to be socially just, not only for humanitarian reasons but to attain optimum efficiency. One problem was that Wallace and his subordinates at the BEW assumed that the simple circumstance of being at war meant that peacetime assumptions regarding the flow of goods had to be left behind; the exigencies of war fighting demanded innovation and particularly might mean forgoing what would normally be considered sober business practices. For Wallace's BEW the profit motive was not a driving strategic principle, but for millionaire Texas businessman Jones and his like-minded team, following sound business practices was of paramount importance.[4]

If efficient procurement of matériel measured in strategic rather than business terms was Wallace's main concern at the BEW, there was one qualification to this concern that reflected his larger social and political philosophy, particularly his views regarding technology and industrial society. Having argued by the late 1930s that modern industrial civilization was in its nature inherently cooperative, by 1942 Wallace included industrial technology as a full-fledged component of his cooperative vision. Modern urban-industrial society, specifically the tremendous productive capacity of new technology, seemed to proffer the "shared abundance" that Wallace had so long hoped for. In a phrase that has often been taken out of context, Wallace asserted in his famous speech of May 1942, "The Price of Free World Victory" (often known by one of its key phrases, "the Century of the Common Man"), that modern technology was now capable of ensuring "that everybody in the world has the privilege of drinking a quart of milk a day." The universal availability of good nutrition meant a great deal to Wallace, who was still very much the scientist. Children who ate well would learn well, well enough to master the technology that would industrialize their nations, enabling those nations to participate in the postwar global prosperity Wallace envisioned. Worldwide industrialization would create, one might say, dietary democracy, which would in turn be the foundation for cultural and economic democracy.[5] In suggesting such possibilities Wallace was in effect romanticizing and globalizing current

American history. In Wallace's vision this democratic dialectic was the American experience, or, in the context of the New Deal, was becoming the American experience. He believed it could be the world's experience as well.

In terms of the BEW's responsibilities Wallace's advocacy of dietary democracy was manifested in his regard for the well-being of the workers producing the supplies the BEW sought to procure, especially in Wallace's beloved Latin America. This regard did not contradict Wallace's concern with strategic efficiency. To Wallace the cause—in this case, the health—of the "common man" was bound to the question of efficiency. What was humane ultimately made the best business sense. This set of assumptions was translated into BEW policy in the form of labor protection clauses within procurement contracts that promised adequate living and working conditions for workers, ensuring that production goals were not compromised by the weak or ill. Jones and the RFC insisted that the clauses should not be invoked unless there was clear evidence that poor conditions were impeding production and supply. The clauses were regularly included in BEW-negotiated contracts by 1943, with the RFC essentially disavowing responsibility for them.[6]

For Niebuhr and the UDA concern with strategic issues was assumed once the United States entered the war. Such concern was simply an extension of one of the organization's central reasons for existence. When in May 1941 Niebuhr, as chairman of the UDA, urged that the United States government employ convoys to protect American shipments of war supplies to Great Britain, he was advocating a military strategy for the United States well before the nation was a formal belligerent. Similarly the UDA addressed strategy when it accused the Department of State of "appeasing fascism" for cooperating with the collaborationist Vichy government in France (also making apparent the power that the Munich analog already held). It thus made sense when James Loeb, UDA executive secretary, wrote to members on December 8, only minutes after the American declaration of war on Japan, asserting that the entry of the United States into the war meant "a new importance and a new significance" for the organization but not a new role altogether. In Loeb's view the UDA already was the nation's "only democratic organization with a full program of real anti-Fascist content." Since its inception the UDA had been at war with the Axis powers. The rest of the nation had finally joined up.[7]

The UDA and the Dies Committee

In May the UDA revived its assault on domestic fascist fellow traveling at home in a "special supplement" published in the *New Republic,* a joint effort of the magazine and the Union. The supplement, entitled "A Congress to Win the War," was an analysis of the voting records of both houses of Congress on various international-affairs issues over the prior four years. Specifically naming several members of Congress and portraying them as reactionary obstructionists and even protofascists, the study attacked these individuals in harsh, sometimes exaggerated terms. Their opposition, for example, to Roosevelt administration policies such as Lend-Lease was characterized not as political opposition but as "slander" on the "government" (as if they were not part of it but rather were criminals of some sort) and even implicitly as treason, when they were accused of "playing the Nazi game."[8]

Crucially, one of the UDA and the *New Republic's* central targets in the piece was the conservative Democratic congressman from Texas Martin Dies. Dies chaired the notorious Special Committee on Un-American Activities, the so-called Dies Committee, precursor of the infamous House Committee on Un-American Activities (HUAC) of the late 1940s and early 1950s. The supplement attacked Dies and his committee as well as other noninterventionists in Congress for using the committee's investigatory powers to badger liberals in the administration and confuse the public. Once again imputing something like treason, the piece insisted that Dies's harassment of government officials had in some cases compelled those officials to suspend "essential war business in order to defend themselves." The article further noted that Dies's efforts had been of such obvious benefit to the Axis powers that he had become the "most frequently quoted American" in Axis radio broadcasts beamed to the Western Hemisphere.[9]

The publication of the supplement, meant to help drive reactionaries and isolationists from office in the November election, triggered a predictable if ironic response from some of its targets, particularly Dies and his associates, a response that seemed to catch the leaders of the UDA and the publishers of the *New Republic* off guard. The liberals had used overdrawn, ad hominem methods to make their attacks on the anti-interventionists, in effect taking a page from Dies's "book" that was then turned back upon them. If their assault was somewhat exaggerated, the response was extremely so.

True to form, Dies attacked the UDA as a communist front organization aiming to "discredit and obliterate Congress" and so undermine the Constitution. He and his fellow committee members absurdly portrayed the UDA as a nest of communist subversives. Then, having made the usual charges of communist subversion against their political enemies, Dies and his associates asserted with an injured air—and not without some truth—that the UDA and others were engaged in a purge of Congress, hoping to eliminate members because they opposed Roosevelt's policies. In the best populist-demagogic fashion, the Dies Committee concluded that this was a battle over nothing less than the "preservation of the political institutions of free men."[10]

The UDA's leaders reacted with indignation, as if they were surprised by the nature of Dies's counterattack. The *UDA Bulletin* declared Dies's attack a Red-baiting "smear," while UDA president Frank Kingdon suggested the absurdity of characterizing his organization as a communist front. In agreement with the *New Republic,* the *Bulletin* suggested that the Dies Committee attack itself arose from a larger complicity against the UDA, emanating from the isolationist press and the State Department, which was still embittered by UDA allegations that it had appeased French fascists.[11]

The UDA responded to the conservative counterattack by rallying a great deal of liberal and moderate support in the press while calling for a congressional hearing to clear its reputation. Many moderate and liberal journals published editorials disparaging the Dies Committee's charges. Meanwhile, UDA members were urged by the leadership to register a "barrage of protests" to the Dies Committee itself. Chapter officers across the nation received information sheets enabling them to respond locally to further attacks, while "factual statements" explaining the episode were prepared for circulation to sympathetic electoral candidates.[12]

In March 1943 Niebuhr entered the fray directly, with a strong critique of the Dies Committee. It was nevertheless made in more measured terms and was less volatile and exaggerated than the exchange
between the UDA and Dies had been the previous year. The analytical quality of Niebuhr's attack on Dies illustrates Niebuhr's ability to
maintain a position outside of a debate in which he was in fact directly involved. In a radio address Niebuhr condemned Dies for breaking "moral law," specifically the biblical injunction "thou shalt not
bear false witness against thy neighbor." Niebuhr insisted that the
Dies Committee had "never seriously investigated anything," engaging
rather in innuendo and slander. Niebuhr allowed that this was a human
tendency, particularly in political forums, but Dies and his associates
carried this tendency beyond the pale, their actions perverting the authority of Congress. This, Niebuhr argued, was far more dangerous
than the normal sort of political exaggeration, for lies told with such
authority were more powerful than those told by individuals.[13]

In discussing the specifics of the Dies Committee's attack on the
UDA, Niebuhr's analytical detachment did waver slightly, subtly reflecting the UDA's extreme indignation the year before. Yet Niebuhr's account of the original UDA–*New Republic* supplement constituted an
illuminating sin of omission: it lacked any mention of the extraordinarily harsh, exaggerated nature of the piece. He failed to mention that
the article had attacked several opponents of the administration's foreign policy—on the basis of their opposition alone—as virtual Nazi
sympathizers and traitors. Instead, Niebuhr rearticulated the UDA's
antitotalitarian and, especially, anticommunist credentials and then recounted what he characterized as the Dies Committee's "falseness" and
"baseness" in promulgating its "preposterous" accusations against the
UDA. Niebuhr noted, in a particularly aggrieved tone, the details of
the committee's attack on himself. He pointed out that he was charged
with membership in four communist organizations, three of which he
had never belonged to and the fourth of which he had resigned from
when communists gained control of it. Somehow in Niebuhr's critique
the battle shifted from a noble defense of the sanctity of government
institutions to a faintly sordid nit-picking over how many communists
Niebuhr had or had not associated with in the past. He weakly if obvi-

ously concluded that the reason for Dies's assault on the UDA was "simple": it was because the UDA had published the voting records of all members of Congress and advocated voting some members, "including several members of the Dies Committee itself," out of office.[14]

The Dies Committee episode was important for two reasons. First, it foreshadowed the techniques that the UDA used—including in its cold war incarnation as the Americans for Democratic Action (ADA)— against political opponents. The UDA attack on Dies and his associates in 1942 rehearsed methods of political calumny used by the ADA against Henry Wallace by 1948. The episode also exposed the increasingly sensitive—perhaps after this incident, hypersensitive—anticommunist reflexes of Niebuhr and the UDA (and so, later, the ADA). The leaders of the UDA believed that in confronting Dies they had taken an action well within the bounds of mainstream contemporary American politics: condemning fascist fellow traveling. For their righteous action they were rewarded with the accusation of being communists, that is, of being that which they detested most of all, their antifascism notwithstanding. Such an outcome may have amplified their already extant anticommunist reflex, beginning its transformation into a postwar obsession.

Germany and "Total War"

If during the first year after American entry into the war the UDA seemed to focus on obstructionism and fascist fellow traveling, for Niebuhr the war against fascism had another dimension. For him it once again raised implicitly personal questions about Germany. His longstanding concern with that nation was only augmented by the state of hostilities now existing between the land of his birth and the land of his heritage. Germany thus became a frequent topic in Niebuhr's writings directed at questions of strategy. The old tension was in him still.

For Niebuhr strategic issues became bound up with larger moral questions, particularly those surrounding a relatively new concept of "total war." Indeed, by its very nature the logic of total war removed any absolute distinction between questions of strategy and of morality.

To Niebuhr's mind this war was obviously "total," with few regions of neutrality and weaponry far more advanced than that of World War I, which he had so powerfully condemned. In addition, Niebuhr noted, the present war involved civilians as both participants and casualties to a degree never before seen in history. Moreover, the outcome of this war would also be "total," in terms of both "victory and defeat": because Nazi domination was total, its destruction would likely leave the German nation completely paralyzed at war's end.[15]

Niebuhr saw the age of total war epitomized in the strategic bombing of the enemy's cities, raising a great moral dilemma for the modern industrial world—a dilemma in many ways familiar to him. Such destruction, Niebuhr argued, however successful in strategic terms, ought not be gloated over. Nevertheless, even a full acknowledgment of the level of devastation wrought by Allied bombers, along with a concomitant level of sorrow for its effect on human lives, did not justify the pacifist argument that such violence was uncalled for. Rather, strategic bombing of cities was a "vivid revelation" of the "moral ambiguity" of warfare: it was impossible to defeat an enemy without causing the innocent "to suffer with the guilty." In the end, Niebuhr concluded, humans could not expect to "move in history without becoming tainted with guilt."[16]

The level of destruction being visited upon Germany in the course of fighting a total war raised in Niebuhr's mind the questions of guilt and forgiveness at war's end in a manner hinting at his personal ambivalence toward Germany. He allowed that Germany had committed perhaps the ultimate "crime against civilization" but argued that there existed no punishment that could reverse the evil of that crime. In addition, the circumstances of defeat in a total war would in themselves be punishment almost beyond comprehension. Whatever the Allies might plan for Germany after the war, Niebuhr predicted, the exigencies of "averting total chaos" in that nation after its defeat were likely to overwhelm all plans. Finally he raised the great question of the twentieth century, which was being brought into bold relief by growing knowledge of the Holocaust: where does responsibility lie in mass society? "What standards," Niebuhr asked, should be used in judging Germany to "distinguish individual from collective guilt? Shall we punish the lieutenant who obeyed an order or the general who gave the order?" What laws were to be used to judge a whole nation? In resolving such questions Niebuhr believed humanity faced tragedies "too deep for any system of morals or law." When viewed from a post–cold war, post–containment doctrine perspective, it is ironic that he concluded Germany would eventually have to be restored to the international community, because Europe could not "be made into a jail." [17]

Wallace approached the issue of total war more obliquely than did Niebuhr and without Niebuhr's sense of moral ambiguity. His perspective on it is seen best in his articulation of the meaning of the war in "The Price of Free World Victory." In that speech Wallace made clear that the Nazis embodied the antithesis of the world he envisioned, rendering this war a fight of good versus evil, clear-cut. Total war was justified by the degree of evil the Allies faced as well as by the postwar order he envisioned. The Germans might believe that America did not have the heart for the fight, but they would discover the opposite. "The American people," Wallace prophesied, "will fight with a relentless fury which will drive the ancient Teutonic gods back cowering into their caves." But the United States had entered the fray of total war not simply to attain military victory. During and especially after the war Wallace presumed that it would be America's opportunity to illuminate the path to the New Order. The battle would be total, but the United States would fight for a "complete peace as well as a complete victory." [18] For Wallace as well as Niebuhr total war had to be considered not only in terms of the present threat but also in terms of the world that the victors would create once that threat was destroyed.

Wallace, American Know-How, and the Postwar World

Understanding this—that for liberals justification of this war was bound up with expectations regarding the postwar world—makes clear the arbitrariness of attempting to draw a complete distinction between their strategic concerns and their hopes for the postwar world. Even when they addressed questions of immediate strategy during the war, liberals continually looked toward the future. Indeed, this eye-on-the-horizon perspective was quite common in the United States during the war years. As Robert Divine has shown, the experience of the interwar era convinced many Americans that in this war the nature of the peace to come was as important as victory.[19]

If support for postwar internationalism was generally prevalent in America during the war, it was the predominant theme among liberals. Even before Pearl Harbor Wallace began to speak and write about the United States' postwar responsibilities as a fully engaged participant in global affairs. As he had done in the 1920s and 1930s, Wallace once again indicted the nation for rejecting its responsibility for the fractured world it helped create. This war, however, brought opportunity along with tragedy. It presented a "second chance" for America to step into international relations, to try again "to make the world safe for democracy." For Wallace World War II, like the Great Depression, offered another portal to the New Age.[20]

As the United States transformed itself into an official belligerent in 1942, Wallace elaborated his vision of the postwar world, including the special role that America would play in creating it. He believed that the manner in which the democratic nations fostered cooperation during the war would go far in determining what sort of world would come into being at the war's end. Invoking the image that became his greatest political legacy, Wallace proclaimed that the January 1, 1942, "Declaration of the United Nations" had created a "worldwide alliance of the common people" to a degree never before seen in history. The soldiers of the Allied armies—"young men of different nationalities"—attained the intimacy of battlefield comrades, perhaps the most direct form of international cooperation. And the citizens of the soldiers' homelands, although prevented by the war from personal contact, were coming to know one another as well, modern technology making comrades of them all.[21]

The Henry A. Wallace of the 1920s, all-out champion of American rural culture, was greatly transformed by 1942. He was convinced that industrialization was the road to the future, first in winning the war and then in achieving higher standards of living for common people the world over. He had become a champion of urban-industrial civilization based on an American model. Instead of being the nemesis of rural culture, he believed, modern technological society became a means of preserving the best of that culture and its inherent values, which for Wallace embodied America's essence. His social, political, and international perspectives were now themselves "industrialized" in the sense that Wallace increasingly viewed the West's industrial and technological know-how as both an impulse toward and a means for creating global economic and social democracy.

In Wallace's assessment the historical moment for attaining a world of multifaceted democracy had arrived in the form of this second global war, and as the epitome of modern industrial civilization, with its great promise of democracy, America again would become the City on the Hill. But in Wallace's vision it would be an industrial city of the twentieth century standing as exemplar to the world. "Older nations," such as the United States, would be obligated to assist the "younger nations"—by which Wallace meant the less industrial ones—in the process of industrialization. It was an ironic conclusion for Wallace to draw, considering that less than a decade before he had viewed America as having only reached its adolescence. Having fully embraced technological society, Wallace now viewed the United States as a mature model of political and economic democracy, despite its flaws. Wallace did insist that the assistance given by the older nations to the younger must come without either "military or economic imperialism." Yet he believed that the United States had an unusual responsibility. What Americans had learned in the industrialization process they were obligated to pass on.[22]

Wallace did not realize that despite his disclaimers he was in essence extrapolating his vision of domestic American society to the rest of the world, advocating at the very least cultural imperialism. Like many American internationalists, he could not imagine that the peoples of these admittedly less industrialized countries might hesitate to acquiesce to the changes incumbent in the process of industrializing on an American model. Wallace's inability to perceive the possibility of such reluctance was ironic, for hesitation on the part of less industrialized nations to embrace wholeheartedly the American paradigm of industrialization was analogous to Wallace's own reservations during the 1920s regarding the impending absorption of American rural culture into modern urban-industrial civilization. By the 1940s Wallace was unable to comprehend that the community of nations he envisioned was cast in an American mold that might prove an unacceptably rigid fit for some.[23]

Liberal Internationalism and "Full Employment"

One of the reasons that American liberals were so concerned during the war with the postwar world was their collective fear that the United States might slip back into profound economic depression at the war's end. When Wallace, Niebuhr, and others spoke of America's international irresponsibility during the interwar years they often meant economic irresponsibility: the nation had not fulfilled its obligations to global economic interdependence. Similarly, when Wallace wrote of likely American obligations to Asia or Latin America in the postwar era, it was in terms of helping those regions to become full players in the global economy, precluding future economic dislocations abroad and at home.

Liberals' concerns regarding the postwar global economy created in their wartime thought an important confluence between international relations and domestic reform. A significant focus of this confluence was the issue of "full employment" that culminated in 1945 but developed throughout the war years. Wallace was concerned about full postwar employment in the United States as early as May 1941, after receiving a letter from Federal Reserve Board member Alvin Hansen insisting that full employment was integral to the postwar peace. By February 1943 Wallace believed the American people viewed full employment as a crucial postwar goal. A year later he was a full-fledged champion of the employment cause, outlining his views before a meeting of the Congress of Industrial Organizations' Political Action Committee (CIO-PAC). Established by the CIO's executive board in July 1943, CIO-PAC was created to mobilize labor's electoral strength against what its founders viewed as a rising tide of conservatism in the United States. It became what one historian has characterized as a "spearhead" of the liberal-labor alliance. In his speech to CIO-PAC Wallace unequivocally asserted the connection between postwar global cooperation and full employment at home. He declared that without global peace it would be impossible to count on vigorous international commerce, and without that, domestic unemployment was certain. This meant that the most important actions taken by American leaders toward guaranteeing jobs for all workers at war's end were not those taken domestically, but rather those aimed at establishing postwar international economic and political cooperation. Wallace also began a crusade against those American industrialists that he, like the UDA, termed variously isolationists, monopolists, cartelists, and fascists. He warned American liberals that such individuals intended to reestablish a high tariff behind which they could hold down production in order to elevate prices. And they fully expected to conduct their "monopolistic operations" all over the world. If successful, Wallace cautioned, these "American fascists" could decrease domestic employment and increase international tensions, perhaps starting a third world war.[24]

Like other liberals, the members of the CIO-PAC viewed wartime strategy in terms of postwar possibilities, seeing no separation between "planning for war and planning for peace." The leaders of the committee took up the cause, completely intertwining the dual goals of full employment and postwar international cooperation. Attaining them required both defeating the fascists and establishing "international arrangements for a just and enduring peace." As did Wallace and Niebuhr, the members of the CIO-PAC recognized the transformation of international society by modern technology and the rise of global economic interdependence. In early 1944, before the Dumbarton Oaks conference issued its draft charter for the United Nations Organization, the CIO-PAC advocated the establishment of an international organization open to all nations for the maintenance of "international peace and security." At the same time, before the Bretton Woods conference establishing the World Bank and International Monetary Fund—and in a manner that shared both Wallace's vision of cooperation and its inherent cultural imperialism—the CIO-PAC came out in favor of the creation of international agencies to make long-term loans "to industrially-backward nations." This would allow such nations to develop industrial prosperity along the lines the CIO-PAC envisioned for America. While the CIO-PAC, again like Wallace, insisted that the

United States had to avoid any "American imperialism," their call for the nation to help "backward peoples of the earth to modernize" nevertheless suggested that their outlook also shared Wallace's unspoken assumption of the inherent superiority and eventual benevolent triumph of American cultural institutions. It certainly shared the belief that creating a stable international economy on American principles would bring about the desired goal of full postwar domestic employment.[25]

The UDA also took up the full employment torch. Its members still saw the same threat of domestic fascism they had in 1941, with its potential to undermine hopes for full postwar employment. Like most internationalists, the membership of the UDA believed that by 1944 the connections between global depression, fascism, and world war were obvious. That connection led them, like Wallace and the labor leaders, to the conclusion that full employment was crucial to world peace. War production and the nearly full employment it engendered had demonstrated what an "economy of abundance" could be like. The danger from American fascists lay in the fear held by American workers that when the war ended so might their jobs. In the UDA's view such fears could be manipulated by the "political Fascists" to obstruct constructive policy-making by liberals, undermining any chance of establishing either a sound domestic or international economy.[26]

Niebuhr's Perspective on the Postwar World

Niebuhr's wartime vision of the postwar world was more ambivalent than that of other liberal internationalists, including many in the UDA. Certainly it lacked Wallace's quality of inexorable optimism. Nevertheless, Niebuhr's outlook continued to exhibit the mellowing of his critique that began after Munich, impelled by the meaning he took from the rise of Nazism. Where he had before condemned the Western nations, he now critiqued skeptically and did so with an inconsistent but apparent undertone of hopefulness. Niebuhr at least saw the possibility of what Wallace had termed the world's second chance. He posited the war's capacity as a catalyst for change in international affairs during the first weeks after the German invasion of Poland, arguing that if the war were sufficiently horrific it might compel nations to yield enough of their sovereignty to render a postwar international community viable. By early 1942 Niebuhr was certain that the war would be long and horrible, and just might trigger a "thoroughgoing repentance and conversion, from those sins of the democratic world" that had engendered the conflict in the first place. Perhaps the war could provide a transforming fire of the sort that Wallace and others envisioned.[27]

At the very least, Niebuhr believed, the war forced Americans to accept mechanisms of "international cooperation" integral to the wartime alliance, mechanisms they would not accept otherwise and in fact continually rejected during the interwar era. What might finally issue from the crucible of war in terms of postwar international community was hard to predict. Niebuhr invoked the American revolutionary and early national eras in his speculations, pointing out that the U.S. Constitution had issued from the experience of the American Revolution and the "inadequacies of colonial particularism." He implied that World War II exposed an analogous international particularism that might issue in cooperation, now that the United States had taken up its international obligations.[28]

Like other globally minded liberals, Niebuhr also believed that America and the other democracies had to address their domestic social and economic ills in order to attain a peaceful world society. It was after all the internal flaws of Western society that had engendered war. Niebuhr expected that the depredations of this war would amplify the problems that stemmed from the skewed distribution of wealth existent in virtually all Western nations. He was as usual skeptical, yet still faintly optimistic in late 1941 that the war's circumstances might at last "persuade the privileged to accept new social demands" that would arise out of the war.[29] For the United States it was time to address national responsibilities at home as well as abroad.

Niebuhr, like Wallace, had long argued that American foreign policy after World War I had been profoundly irresponsible and, by virtue of what that irresponsibility had contributed to, immoral as well. Again eschewing his once central distinction between the morality of individuals and that of nations, Niebuhr assessed the immoral behavior of the United States and the other Western democratic nations in terms of the individual's moral responsibility to the community. In doing so he implicitly resurrected the concept of "personality" as a standard for social behavior. Moral behavior in the individual demanded acknowledgment of one's obligations as a member of a community. To deny or ignore those obligations was to be "immoral." Understanding this was to understand the individual's profound need to experience him- or herself as meaningfully bound up within the larger life of the community, the essence of personality. Having asserted this standard of social morality for the individual, Niebuhr now felt justified in extending it as a standard for the behavior of nations as well: "as with men, so with nations. An irresponsible nation is an immoral nation, while a nation [hopefully the United States] that is becoming dimly aware of its responsibilities and acts accordingly is moving toward morality." [30] If recent history had shown that privileged individuals in the West had to accept new social responsibilities and so acknowledge the interdependence of personal life, it had also made clear that privileged and powerful nations faced a similar obligation. These nations had to accept the demands of their society—which was the international community—and recognize the interdependence of nations. The implication was that a nation whose privileged citizens accepted their social responsibilities at home would probably accept its obligations as a nation in the world order.

Without Wallace's unalloyed optimism, by the early 1940s Niebuhr clearly saw the war's potential as a catalyst for social change, both nationally and internationally. Whether a world community based on "mutual responsibility" could be created remained to his mind unanswerable at present, but Niebuhr did suggest that the potential framework for such a community was being formed in the various councils of the alliance. If not all the problems of the postwar era were being resolved within them, he insisted that there was not a "single problem of world-reconstruction" on which some aspect of wartime international relations did not touch. [31]

Questions of Cooperation, Justice, and Power

On December 28, 1942, Wallace gave an address over national radio in honor of the eighty-sixth anniversary of Woodrow Wilson's birth. In the talk Wallace brought together several themes that for the past decade and a half had informed his commentary on international affairs. He suggested that the defeat of the Axis powers was only a matter of time and effort, and that when that defeat was attained an "entirely new phase of world history" would commence. In other words, the end of World War II would mark the beginning of the New Age that Wallace had looked for since the late 1920s. Moreover, victory in this war would be victory for the common man, for this was a "worldwide people's war." [32]

Wallace also invoked the American revolutionary era for historical guidance, but he took the lesson farther than had Niebuhr. Implicitly accepting the venerable American myth of postrevolutionary crisis, Wallace explained that the citizens of the newly independent United States had quickly perceived the fatal flaws of the Articles of Confederation and thus decided they needed to create a stronger union if their young nation was to remain intact. In an analogous sense, Wallace claimed, the nations of the world had realized during the interwar era that the League of Nations, like the American confederation, was crucially flawed. The successive traumas of global depression and world war had overwhelmed it. Once these two disasters were overcome the global community would have to fashion a means for preventing their recurrence. As the fledgling United States had discarded the Articles of Confederation and created a stronger union in the Constitution, so the nations of the world would have to leave behind the failed League and forge a more viable international community. Woodrow Wilson's legacy, Wallace implied, would be resurrected by the United Nations. [33]

Niebuhr sympathized with this contention. He too declared the creation of some kind of international association, acknowledging the realities of the modern global society to be the most "compelling command" of the day. Yet his guarded optimism regarding the possible influence of the war on postwar world cooperation was informed by his characteristic skepticism of what he considered overly idealistic expectations for the solution of humanity's dilemmas. It led him to attack the very analogy that Wallace and others were suggesting as a basis for optimism regarding global affairs. In fact, by the time Wallace articulated the Articles-to-Constitution : League-to-United Nations analogy,

Niebuhr already had insisted upon the analogy's limits. He criticized it in terms similar to those in which he had assailed the logic of liberals and pacifists throughout the 1930s. As with "idealists" in earlier periods, Niebuhr declared, those who were now fashioning plans for postwar international organizations often did not perceive the real roots of authority or understand the "problem of power." When they did think about such questions, they usually did so by positing a "central pool of power" but never by asking what "tributaries" were to fill it. Generally, Niebuhr claimed, the idealists invoked the "creation of American nationhood as analogy and proof of the possibility of creating such a new authority." While he still allowed that early U.S. history did conform more closely to the current situation than did any other nation's history, he insisted that the conformity was less substantive than those who invoked it realized.[34]

The implication of Niebuhr's pronouncements by 1942 was that he was profoundly skeptical, if not pessimistic, that international cooperation could come about in the manner expected by liberals such as Wallace as well as many members of the UDA and CIO-PAC. He could not keep himself from blaming such liberals for much of the evil that had come about in the world. No matter how much rational insight they may have brought to the understanding of global events, in Niebuhr's view idealistic liberals had always been too caught up in simplistic moralisms to adequately address the threats facing society. The most they could do, he claimed, was "wring their hands in holy horror when the tortuous processes of history do not conform to their ideal demands." Liberals had been so preoccupied with condemning nations for defying the requirements of global community, Niebuhr asserted, that they had been oblivious to immediate perils facing their civilization.[35]

Buried in the language of this criticism of idealists, liberals, and pacifists was the warning of the Munich analog, by 1942 thoroughly assimilated into Niebuhr's commentary. In assailing liberal idealism in this fashion, Niebuhr was further establishing the principle he had first articulated in the wake of the Czechoslovakian crisis of 1938. For Niebuhr the logic was clear: in the 1930s liberals and pacifists, driven by their idealism, had apologized for and legitimated the Germans and then allowed them to act as they pleased until the debacle of Munich had occurred. These idealists were so busy forgiving Hitler's aggression, on the basis of the moral dubiousness of Versailles, that they were unable to confront and arrest what Niebuhr considered the absolute evil of Nazism. Behind Niebuhr's great ambivalence by the end of the United States' first year at war lay his apprehension that the idealists were incapable of not doing the same thing again and again. He feared that in the postwar era the simplistic moralism of the liberals might once more prevent the establishment of policies that would preclude the rise of another entity like Nazi Germany.

Niebuhr's writings during the early 1940s were substantively supportive of calls like Wallace's for the establishment of an international cooperative community. Nevertheless, Niebuhr's logic of skepticism undermined such positions within liberal discourse, even as Wallace and others voiced them. Niebuhr based his outlook on international affairs by late 1942 on his understanding of Munich, which itself was bound up in his own life experience as well as in the nature of the commentary he developed during the previous twenty-five years. That outlook was inclined toward caution to such an extent that it effectively militated against the practice of international cooperation that liberal internationalists—including Niebuhr himself, in the context of the wartime alliance—viewed as so crucial to the creation of habits of cooperation.

This pattern of ambivalence in Niebuhr's perspective on the postwar world—occasional admissions of hope strongly tempered by skepticism and at times pessimism—continued to appear in his commentary throughout the war years. Indeed, if anything Niebuhr's skepticism increased. In part this was due to the fact that he did not perceive any fundamental changes in human nature arising out of the experience of war. He remained critical of rational idealists, those who in his view continued to believe that simply by recognizing the errors of humanity those errors could be righted. Moreover, he saw little positive change in the aspects of modern mass civilization that had so undermined human society by degrading "personality." Where more optimistic liberals like Wallace saw in modern communication technology, for example, the potential for universal education and international cooperation, Niebuhr saw a society that had created mass literacy without a "general basis for a profound culture." Just as he had in the 1920s, Niebuhr still insisted in the 1940s that modern means of production robbed the individual of his or her skill, contributing further to human alienation. This most modern of wars proved to Niebuhr, perhaps even more than had World War I, that modern society was overly rational and mechanical, that science was given too much prestige over what he once termed poetic knowledge. With this dark perspective in mind it is not surprising that Niebuhr did not share the sense of optimism held by other liberals regarding the potentialities of the postwar world. His remained a voice of prophetic foreboding.[36]

Still there remained signs of hopefulness in Niebuhr's outlook. If the coalition of Allied powers could be maintained after the war, a durable peace was possible. Niebuhr continued to argue that the activities of the UN as a wartime alliance might form the basis for international organization after the war. He could agree with Wallace that postwar global relations were "being fashioned by the actual practices" of the Allies during the war. Yet Niebuhr nevertheless found relations among the Allies unreassuring. The UN remained essentially a "paper organization," with various official councils, boards, and conferences but not much substance as far as Niebuhr could tell. A large part of the problem, he believed, was the lack of natural affinities between the Allies, the sorts of affinities that would transcend the defeat of a common foe and bind the Allies together after that defeat. What was required, Niebuhr concluded, was highly imaginative statesmanship capable of using the exigencies of war to create the basis for postwar coalition.[37]

Unlike other liberal internationalists, including many members of the UDA, Niebuhr was willing to accept a peace based on "preponderant power," that is, on agreements reached by the great powers. The ultimate aim in his view was to attain both "justice" and "order." Order, Niebuhr believed, was a reasonable expectation that could issue either from friendly or tense agreements among the great powers. Justice, conversely, was a much more difficult goal only to be attained if the great powers exercised "conscience and imagination," setting up international mechanisms guaranteeing the rights of weaker nations. Niebuhr remained doubtful of such an eventuality, since it would require the great powers to surrender an unprecedented degree of sovereignty. Nevertheless, despite the inherent dangers of international organization based upon preponderant power, Niebuhr was more comfortable with it than with any of the idealistic but to his mind vacuous "world constitution" plans that were promulgated during the war. He was sure that such plans would fail to compel the large powers to take up their international responsibilities, for in the final analysis Niebuhr was convinced that "power and responsibility must be made commensurate in the new world order."[38]

The UDA and Hopes for Postwar Internationalism

The UDA, Niebuhr's organization, was concerned from its inception with the world that would exist at war's end. The group's introductory pamphlet, circulated among liberals in spring 1941, insisted that planning for the peace had to be incorporated into wartime strategy. After American entry into the conflict, the UDA's leaders quickly set about the process of formulating the association's positions on postwar issues. By summer 1942 they had commissioned a series of studies by various experts on diverse aspects of postwar reconstruction. The UDA published the studies as pamphlets over the next three years.[39] By early 1944, after a conference on foreign policy held in conjunction with the Committee for a Democratic Foreign Policy, the UDA articulated a wide-ranging outlook that intertwined wartime foreign policy with a vision of postwar international relations. Despite Niebuhr's tremendous influence in the UDA, that vision was more optimistic than his. The influence of his skepticism, however, was often apparent.

Most members of the UDA shared Niebuhr's assumption that the wartime alliance of the United Nations was the most likely basis for postwar collective security. What was immediately necessary in spring 1944 was strengthening the UN as a location for taking common counsel in solving global problems. The UDA believed the tendency of the great powers toward independent action—something that Niebuhr by this time viewed as virtually inevitable—had to and could be stopped. Like both Niebuhr and Wallace, the UDA recognized a special American responsibility in creating more cooperative international relations.

With Niebuhrian logic they noted that the United States had more immediate security than most nations but no more "ultimate security" than any other nation "in a world of international anarchy." It was the immediate security that tempted America to international irresponsibility. The UDA hoped that two world wars had demonstrated for all time the error of yielding to that temptation.[40]

Also like Niebuhr and Wallace, the UDA made statements that asserted that America's international responsibilities were bound up with its domestic life. Certainly this was implied by the Union's advocacy of full employment. But UDA literature suggested that there were additional conditions within American society that acted as obstacles to a liberal peace. The UDA argued, for example, that such obstacles arose from "national origin blocs," from the prejudices and loyalties still held by first- and second-generation Americans and their potentially chilling effect on national unity and so on the success of foreign policy. In a different sense the UDA evoked Wallace's commentary of the 1920s when it contended that American workers had to disabuse themselves of the long-honored but false assumption that their standard of living was dependent on high tariffs.[41]

While UDA statements suggested that these and other problems impeding cooperative international relations could be overcome, by 1944 the organization's outlook increasingly inclined toward Niebuhr's skepticism. Despite the fact that the United Nations were winning the war, the leaders of the UDA believed that the prospects for the eventual peace were "not as bright," that the peace was already threatened. Above all it was in danger of being an undemocratic peace, a peace imposed by the great powers executing agreements made among themselves and often in secrecy at places like Cairo and Tehran. At the same time the alliance exhibited "considerable disunity," manifested, for instance, in disagreements over recognition of Charles de Gaulle's Free French as well as in relations with similar groups from Poland, Czechoslovakia, and the governments of Yugoslavia and Greece. And despite explicit praise of the Soviet Union in fighting the Germans, the UDA already expressed grave misgivings regarding Soviet policy toward Poland. Perhaps most dangerous of all, the UDA feared the triumph in American domestic politics of the sort of "narrow nationalism" that might lead the United States to fail once again in its international responsibilities, if not from a resurgent isolationism then by establishing an American imperialism.[42]

There were many postwar problems to be faced, but what the members of the UDA—in this sense led by Niebuhr in fact as well as spirit—despaired of most was the "paucity of vision, imagination and courage" among the people of the United Nations and their leaders. In words that strangely mixed Niebuhr's pessimism with Wallace's hopeful vision, the UDA insisted that all of the world's peoples were tied "by a thousand fetters" to the "old, rotten world" that had engendered this war. The present generation had to break those fetters completely. "This war," the UDA declared, "will either bring a new world or it will bring a new world war."[43]

Tentative Hopes for U.S.-Soviet Cooperation

At the heart of liberal concern with the postwar world of course lay the issue of relations between the United States and the Soviet Union, upon which most American internationalists believed the likelihood of global community depended. All hopes for permanent peace and global organization were predicated upon the mutual participation of the two most powerful nations in the world.

By 1943–44 Wallace seemingly had forgotten his doubts of the early 1930s regarding the Soviet Union as a U.S. trading partner. Indeed, he saw a whole range of areas of potential cooperation, from the economic to the agricultural, between the two countries. Toward that end Wallace drew on his Pan-Americanist past in proposing the development of diverse U.S.-Soviet cultural connections. As he had once suggested regarding intrahemispheric relations, he now argued that a better foundation for postwar cooperation between Americans and Russians could be built if more Americans studied the Russian language, attended Soviet universities, and lived in Russian communities. At the same time all steps should be taken in the United States to enable Russians to attain similar experience of life in America. In Wallace's view there was a direct connection between the establishment of such cultural ties and world peace. "The more first-hand contacts" there were between the people of the two nations, he insisted, the "less likely we are to have World War III." [44]

The concern with potential domestic fascism he shared with other liberals during the war also influenced Wallace's perspective on postwar U.S.-Soviet relations. Foreshadowing arguments he would make in 1946, Wallace feared in 1943 that the West might "double-cross" Russia, particularly if "fascist interests" driven by a hatred of the Soviet Union were to gain control of the U.S. government. Shortly before the war ended Wallace declared that fascism remained a global threat whose greatest threat to America would come, ironically, "*after the war.*" He worried that postwar fascism would push the United States farther and farther toward imperialism and war with the Soviets. Wallace believed such a turn of events all the more likely in the face of American ignorance regarding Soviet history and society, a belief that underscored his call for extensive cultural exchanges between the two nations. The Soviet Union's "valiant stand" against the Nazis, he insisted, had been a gift to the United States of the "lives and futures of a million American boys." The Soviets' exertions on behalf of the enemies of fascism stood as clear proof to Wallace that cooperation was possible. But it required overcoming prejudices born of ignorance, prejudices that fascists could easily manipulate once the war ended. [45]

For the CIO-PAC, cooperation with the Soviets remained mostly implicit in discussions of postwar international relations, probably due to domestic tensions over the issue of communists in the labor movement. In its pronouncements regarding Soviet-American relations the political action committee asserted the paramount importance of preserving and strengthening the "coalition of the United Nations" after the war's end to further American and Allied objectives. Policies aimed at attaining these aims, the CIO-PAC declared in Wallace-like language, had to be grounded upon "deepening friendship and ever closer cooperation" among the "governments and peoples" of the United Nations. [46]

In a manner that combined Wallace's call for a democratic peace with Niebuhr's acceptance of great power predominance, the CIO-PAC did call for cooperation between the United States and the Soviet Union in establishing postwar collective security while the bases of the peace were worked out. American arms were to be used only *"in co-operation with other nations"* to prevent armed international aggression after the war was over. The CIO-PAC anticipated America becoming one of several world policemen, not a lone ranger.[47]

Niebuhr's wartime perspective on postwar U.S.-Soviet relations was a subcategory of his overall outlook on postwar international affairs and so was characterized by his usual skeptical ambivalence. By 1942, he contended, if the war against fascism compelled America to accept internationalism, the viability of that internationalism as well as the possibility of international community after the war was contingent upon Soviet-American cooperation. This was despite his prior disgust with the Nazi-Soviet pact of 1939. In 1942, with the Soviet Union now an ally against the Nazis, Niebuhr's anger receded, leaving him relatively optimistic if still skeptical regarding the likelihood of good relations with the USSR after the war ended. It was this "fateful comradeship of arms with Russia" that moderated his doubts. Already the British and the Soviets, with American cooperation, had at least temporarily dispelled disagreements over postwar territorial claims that had threatened the integrity of the alliance. This issue had been resolved, Niebuhr believed, because the Russians were convinced by British and American assurances that the Soviet Union would not be isolated after this war as it had been after World War I, which in turn suggested that Russia was not inherently imperialistic. In this context Niebuhr felt that the Anglo-Russian pact laid the groundwork for substantive cooperation among the Big Three.[48]

Moreover, even if the partnership between the Soviets and the Western democracies was born solely of strategic necessity, Niebuhr allowed that it could evolve into a deeper relationship. Implying a logic similar to Wallace's regarding the effects of practicing cooperation, Niebuhr suggested that long-term associations between different national cultures might lead to fundamental changes beyond the scope of the original association. "If maintained long enough," he wrote, alliances could engender "common political ideals." The Soviet Union might change owing to its relations with the Western democracies. Suggesting the value he still saw in Marxism, Niebuhr also thought it conceivable the democratic nations "might learn something from Russia."[49]

In the long run, however, it did not matter, Niebuhr claimed, if

Russia became more like the Western democracies. An international community was no more contingent on the "internal structure" of its member nations than was the wartime alliance. Evoking the relatively new theory of "geopolitics," Niebuhr posited that it was entirely possible that "geographic and other considerations" could prove more central to successful community than the existence of similar political systems. While he acknowledged that the Soviets might attempt to gain control of Germany and eastern Europe after the war, in 1942 Niebuhr doubted this would come to pass. For one thing, he reckoned that Russia, like the rest of the victors, would be too exhausted to consider further military action. But more than that, Niebuhr believed, as an "imperialistic religion" communism was probably a "spent force." Sounding like the stereotype of idealism later identified with Wallace, Niebuhr wrote that he expected the Soviets to be ready and willing, as they had been in the past, to join in "genuine constitutional arrangements" with the other victors. It was time for Western liberals to "learn that history does not move with perfect logic or . . . consistency." Nations with different cultures, even vastly different, "had to learn to live together." It would probably prove easier to do so without holding high expectations of cultural transformation.[50]

This relative optimism in Niebuhr's skeptical view of relations with Russia persisted through the next two years of the wartime alliance. He continued to believe along with most other liberals that it was imperative the United States and Great Britain reach some basic understanding with the Soviets if a third world war were to be avoided. He worried about liberal idealists who demanded either perfect international mechanisms or no international association whatsoever. He also disdained fellow travelers who placed too much of the blame for U.S.-Soviet tensions upon the United States. Either group, Niebuhr feared, could undermine realistic arrangements between the two great powers. And while he had not stopped blaming the Soviets for loosing the demonic evil of Nazism on the world in 1939, he saw the possibility of cooperation between Russia and the United States. Although the Russian government remained a totalitarian dictatorship, Niebuhr felt compelled as he had in the late 1930s to distinguish between it and Nazi totalitarianism. Above all, he reasoned, the communists believed in "universal standards of judgment," which separated them altogether from the Nazis and highlighted their historical connection to Western liberalism.[51]

Niebuhr also continued to argue that good relations between Russia and the Western democracies were not predicated on the development of a common culture. Such an expectation of perfection was another characteristic of the liberal idealists that he so disdained, individuals who imagined the attainment of universal norms a simple process. There had to be agreement on some minimum "standards of equity," Niebuhr allowed, but he insisted that coincidence between diverse national self-interests and the "requirements of peace" in international organization was more important. For Americans this meant tolerating cultural differences that might seem quite distasteful, especially in terms of political economy. They had to learn to accept systems that did not fit the American mold, that might seek to "combine collective forms of economy with political freedom." Such an adjustment required the repression of the American habit of supporting conservative and fascist regimes that appeared relatively "decent"—Franco in Spain and the Vichy French were the most recent examples—particularly because it might alienate the people who had lived under them, perhaps driving them toward communism.[52]

There were traces of doubt regarding the likelihood of a postwar understanding with the Soviets in Niebuhr's commentary. For one thing, the persistence of the Soviet Union in maintaining the international Communist Party raised doubts about the sincerity of Russian cooperation with the West, despite Niebuhr's assertion that communism was a spent force. It was not that he feared the party would win the Soviet Union important victories internationally. Indeed, he continued to discount communism both in the United States and elsewhere. The danger of the party lay in its being a potential embarrassment to good relations between America and the Soviet Union. The Soviets' insistence on maintaining an international Communist Party as a justification for Soviet foreign policy—that is, that Soviet policy was for the benefit of the international workers' revolution—insured American conservatives' and reactionaries' rejection of international policies that actually might benefit both nations.[53]

For Niebuhr the ultimate concern, transcending ideologies, remained the "vexatious problem" of social and political justice, a problem not far removed from his long-standing concern with the degradation of personality. In 1943 he still claimed that neither America nor the Soviet Union had resolved the problem, that both societies remained deeply flawed. Moreover, the power of nationalism in both nations threatened to undermine each one's potential as a champion of internationalism. The Soviet Union's "generous impulses of communist universalism and internationalism" had been subordinated by late 1943 almost entirely to Russian nationalism, while the United States had similarly betrayed the Christian and liberal universalism of its culture. Isolationism may have been laid to rest at Pearl Harbor, but to Niebuhr's mind it was far more likely to be replaced by American imperialism than internationalism.[54]

"Children of Light and . . . Darkness"

Niebuhr raised these and other concerns in his widely read 1944 book *The Children of Light and the Children of Darkness,* which can be read not only as another recapitulation of much of his commentary as it developed since the early 1930s, but as a distillation of much of *Nature and Destiny* as well. In its pages, for example, he once more revisited his explanation of the corruption of Western democratic capitalism and the obliviousness of Western liberals, the "children of light," to that corruption. And he again explained the contribution of those phenomena to the rise of fascism in Europe, the ascension of the "children of darkness." In that context Niebuhr continued to describe Marxism, as he had in the 1930s and in *Nature and Destiny,* essentially as a variation on liberal utopianism.[55]

The failings of the children of light obviously were not new revelations for Niebuhr. As in prior years he again pointed out that Western bourgeois liberals' shortcomings arose from their lack of self-awareness. They sought to bring individuals' self-interests under the control of "universal law" and into "harmony with a more universal good" but failed to take into full account the power of their own self-interests. For Niebuhr the political implication of this flaw—an inability to discern the power of class interests—was bound up with its religious implications, with the failure of liberal Protestantism. The modern rejection of the doctrine of original sin had preempted the capacity for self-criticism, leading moderns to believe, as Wallace did regarding Soviet-American relations, that social and political problems arose only out of ignorance.[56]

Also apparent in *Children of Light* was the evolution, since 1932 and *Moral Man,* of Niebuhr's thinking about the morality of nations, an evolution clearly influenced by the rise of Nazism. He rearticulated his old axiom, stating that no society, democratic or otherwise, was great enough or good enough to be the "final end of human existence." Nevertheless, despite its flaws, Western liberalism, by making the creation of a democratic society humanity's highest aspiration, came relatively close. As he had noted in the wake of Munich, Niebuhr asserted that democratic society at least allowed "criticism of its life and pretensions," that it still remained an open society. Even though he continued to believe that nations were by nature more "consistently egoistic" than individuals, he was now willing to allow that social behavior might be moral.[57]

At the forefront of Niebuhr's analysis—literally in the book's first pages—once more appeared his concern with the individual's connection to the community, that is, with personality or something very like it. Western bourgeois society, he claimed, gave too much attention to individual freedom, forgetting that humans were inherently social as well as free creatures. Echoing Wallace's "unity in diversity" theme, Niebuhr insisted that the great need in democratic society was to find ways for diverse groups to express themselves without destroying the unity of the community, a point that clearly underpinned his assertion of the need for greater toleration in international affairs.[58]

Indeed, Niebuhr insisted in the book's last chapter that the "most urgent" issue of the era was humanity's need to extend the "principle of community" from the national to the global level. What made this need so great, Niebuhr contended, was the convergence by the 1940s of two historical "universalities" in the modern world. One was old: a sense of "universal moral obligation." The second, newer universality was one that both Niebuhr and Wallace had recognized since before the war began: the advent of a modern, "technical civilization" that had rendered the world effectively smaller, establishing the potential for a world community.[59] The need for such a community seemed obvious; its fulfillment now seemed possible.

Niebuhr's internationalist commentary in *Children of Light* maintained his wartime ambivalence, his characteristic combination of profound skepticism tempered by mild but persistent optimism. He noted, for example, that the step from national to international community represented a difference of kind, not degree as some internationalists implied. The international community lacked the cohesive cultural-historical forces that were the bedrock of nations, negating contemporary expectations of a world federation based on hopes for global constitutions and other such mechanisms. What did exist, however, was a shared fear of anarchy, which suggested the preponderant power of the great powers as the potential if somewhat distasteful replacement for cultural cohesion at the international level. Even if a global community came into existence in some form at the war's end, Niebuhr expected it might be a community in which order was "purchased at the price of justice." Nevertheless, he still held a faint hope that if international arrangements were made carefully, taking care to protect the interests of smaller nations, then constitutional principles might eventually become part of the "organic processes of history" and so underpin a true world community.[60]

In the end Niebuhr remained truly ambivalent. In the book's last paragraphs he again asserted that the task of building such a community was "man's final necessity" but that it was also "his final impossibility." It was an insight into international affairs that was deeply colored by his theology, by his understanding that Christianity's essential meaning was paradoxical. Christ's goodness was a norm for humanity's existence in history, a goal to be striven for but unlikely to be attained.[61]

By 1944 Niebuhr, in his doubtful ambivalence, was out ahead—or at least still somewhat on the outside—of the liberal discussion of postwar international relations. As the presidential campaign of 1944 approached and as the United States' third year at war neared its close, the liberal community was still essentially cohesive. And in that cohesiveness most liberals, including Niebuhr's associates in the UDA, inclined much more toward Wallace's optimism than Niebuhr's skepticism.

7

"Light and Peace" or "Darkness and War"

The Atomic Portal to the New Age

———◆———

DURING SUMMER 1944 Wallace remained America's leading liberal internationalist, but his hold on the vice presidency was tenuous. His failure to gain renomination in July resulted from tensions between liberal and conservative Democrats that had dogged him throughout the New Deal years as well as during his directorship of the BEW. Within the liberal community, however, Wallace's star still shone brightly as the United States entered the last year of the war. For liberals the period bracketed by Wallace's two "removals"—from the vice presidency in July 1944 and from the cabinet and government altogether in September 1946—saw the continuing evolution of various themes that had been developing since the war began in 1939. Liberals remained concerned, for example, with connections between the domestic economy and foreign relations. The urgency of such concerns, however, was greatly amplified by the advent of the atomic bomb, as were liberal worries regarding U.S.-Soviet relations.

Wallace and Niebuhr remained, in their different ways, at the center of liberal discussions during the 1944–46 period. Wallace continued to hope for international cooperation, while Niebuhr's skepticism persisted, grounded in his perception of the essentially unchanging influences of power, nationalism, and human nature upon human affairs. In liberal battles for policies such as "full employment," Wallace remained both a participant and a symbol, particularly as he struggled in 1945 for congressional confirmation of his nomination as secretary of commerce.

175

This was also a period in which several episodes occurred foreshadowing later events in liberal politics. During such episodes Wallace's naïveté regarding public relations augmented a growing tendency in the press to portray him and his positions in simplistic, often exaggerated and even inaccurate terms. This in turn contributed to nascent doubts in the minds of many liberals, including Niebuhr, regarding Wallace's views on international affairs and thus his qualifications as a national leader.

Liberals and the Campaign of 1944

In May, as the nation moved into the electoral season, the UDA and *New Republic* published another joint supplement, "A Congress to Win the War and the Peace," on congressional voting patterns, indicating that the liberals put as much importance on congressional elections as they did upon presidential and vice presidential politics. In addition, the supplement demonstrated again their belief that fighting the war was as much about the nature of the peace to come as it was about defeating fascism.[1]

The 1944 supplement maintained much of the vitriolic quality of the 1942 piece that had triggered the Dies Committee episode. Able and progressive members of Congress were overwhelmed, it declared, by "petty men" who mistook "ambition for capacity, bluster for work, blindness for vision and passionate hatreds for patriotism." Attacking conservative Democrats as well as Republicans, the UDA–*New Republic* article once again implied that the Roosevelt administration's political enemies approached treason in their attempts to "sabotage" administration policies during a war. The 1944 piece did not contain quite the ad hominem quality of its predecessor, although it did urge readers to draw conclusions about the "integrity and patriotism" of individual members and managed another oblique swipe at Dies.[2]

In addition, the supplement contained a fully articulated "platform for progressives" aimed at the upcoming national conventions, laying out both domestic and foreign policy objectives and making clear how thoroughly intertwined the two categories were in progressive liberal thinking. Many of the platform's components reflected positions Wallace had advocated since the war began. It called for a peaceful world in which all nations turned their energies to the production of a "high level of prosperity" for all their citizens—in other words, Wallace's world of "shared abundance." And, like Wallace, the progressive platform saw such a world attainable by means of the modern technology that had created the possibility of a "comparatively high level of living for everyone." With an optimism one cannot imagine Niebuhr fully sharing, the platform declared that poverty was "technically obsolete."[3]

In discussing foreign affairs the supplement insisted on the importance of a "world organization" for establishing postwar peace. In full agreement with both Niebuhr's and Wallace's long insistence on the need for the United States to take up its international responsibilities, the platform insisted that an effective world organization required American participation. At the same time it acceded to Niebuhr's logic of basing a postwar organization upon preponderant power. It also made an attack on the international monopolies that Wallace saw as so damaging to both domestic and international affairs while advocating international economic agencies to promote an expansive international economy, bringing prosperity to all.[4]

If the United States was to participate fully in postwar international affairs it was necessary that it expand the general prosperity attained during the war. Thus the UDA–*New Republic* platform also called for extending the New Deal, insisting on supports for agriculture, additional regional development programs on the model of the Tennessee Valley Authority, and the expansion of the Social Security system. Most important, however, was a peacetime industrial production program comparable in scale and effect to the nation's mobilization for war, which above all meant full employment, a goal that gained significance as the year wore on.[5]

As the Democratic convention opened in July, the UDA supported Wallace's renomination. In a letter to Democratic National Committee chair Robert Hannegan, UDA Executive Secretary James Loeb argued that the main threat to the Democratic party was voter apathy, which, he insisted, Wallace's renomination could help overcome. Wallace's stature, Loeb declared, had only risen in the "minds and hearts of the 'common man'—the voter." As the struggle over the vice presidential slot heated up, the UDA remained loyal to Wallace, although doubts arose regarding the party itself. Whether or not he remained vice president, it was clear that the leaders of the UDA viewed Wallace as the U.S. champion of progressive liberalism. Niebuhr himself, in a telegram addressed to Wallace at the convention, declared the latter's renomination "absolutely essential," not only for a Democratic victory in November but also for the campaign to "have meaning for the future." As the efforts of conservative Democratic party pols to abandon Wallace became apparent, Loeb became pessimistic of progressive victory in the near term but maintained hope for the future, hope dependent on Wallace's political fortunes. In what may have been the genesis of Americans for Democratic Action, if not the Progressive Party of 1948, he wrote of the many liberals who might be brought together to create a "movement." If Wallace were pushed out, it was time to make a stand. Liberals, Loeb felt, could not go on "retreating and retreating and retreating," at least not without pursuing a "little guerrilla action behind the enemy's lines."[6]

His pessimism regarding Wallace's renomination having proven valid, after the convention Loeb expressed his doubts about the November election. Nevertheless, his support for Wallace remained vital, and he argued that all possible influence ought to be brought to bear upon Wallace to persuade him to fight on through the fall and beyond. After the November victory Loeb began to pursue his idea of creating an independent movement of progressive liberals with Wallace at its head. After a small conference of progressive leaders, Loeb wrote Wallace that all the participants were eager for his counsel, believing him the "leader of the American progressive movement."[7]

Linking the Domestic to the International

That Wallace was viewed by liberals as the leader of progressive liberalism became even more obvious by early 1945, in the culmination of two domestic political battles with implications for postwar liberal internationalism. The first was over the issue of "full employment." The second was over Wallace's confirmation as secretary of commerce. Concern with full employment in the postwar era arose before the United States actually entered the war, once the impact of war production had substantially reduced the unemployment levels of the Great Depression. The call for full postwar employment gained impetus during the war as liberal and labor leaders began to worry about the fate of American workers once the war and war production ended. As we have seen, by early 1944 Wallace and others had connected the intertwined causes of full employment and full production not only to fears of a return to domestic depression at war's end but also to various issues in world affairs, including international industrial development, balanced foreign trade, and the elimination of international cartels.

A year later progressive liberals remained concerned about these interconnected questions. In early 1945, for instance, Wallace reasserted his association of open foreign trade, international peace, and full domestic employment. Throughout the year, in speeches on full employment, in congressional testimony connected to his confirmation as secretary of commerce, and in his widely read 1945 book *Sixty Million Jobs,* he continued to champion these causes. He advocated, for example, federal budget legislation to provide public-works jobs as a final guarantee of full employment. In this context Wallace also called for full United States participation in the United Nations as well as cooperation with and toleration of the Soviet Union. In doing so he began developing a logic of U.S.-Soviet relations that eventually carried him out of government in 1946 and ultimately into the electoral debacle of 1948. Seeming to forget his own strong opposition to U.S. recognition of Soviet Russia in 1933, he suggested that anyone knowledgeable of the "bungling policy" of nonrecognition prior to 1933 could understand the sources of Soviet suspicions of America in 1945. He also contended that the Soviets were ready to meet the United States half way. While Americans might not approve of the Soviet system of government, Wallace allowed, it was not likely to disappear soon, which made some degree of mutual acceptance essential.[8]

The overarching point for Wallace was that questions of postwar reconstruction and development had to be addressed in their domestic and global contexts at the same time. Postwar industrial expansion of the United States had to be undertaken with the development of the whole world in mind. In the end his logic came a complete and typically liberal internationalist circle: full employment for American workers after the war promised prosperity not only to the United States but to all nations, yet full employment at home was only possible if the whole world shared in American prosperity.[9]

The UDA concurred with Wallace on virtually every point he made regarding full employment in both its domestic and international contexts. By 1945 the organization declared that the United States confronted two essential long-term responsibilities: cooperatively organizing "a permanent peace on democratic foundations" and securing a "stable and expanding domestic prosperity." Attaining these two aims was predicated on by now familiar factors. Above all the UDA stipulated a need to avoid a return to depression, which meant the primary prerequisites of postwar domestic and global prosperity were full employment and full production in the United States. By summer 1945, while the Grand Alliance was still vital, the UDA declared that it was America's responsibility to turn its financial and industrial resources toward rebuilding Europe and Russia. The resurrection of European industry along with the expansion of the European economy would provide just the sort of vigorous foreign commerce that the UDA, like Wallace, viewed as crucial to American prosperity, while the establishment of new industries in less developed regions would underpin "real independence" in those areas. Also like Wallace, the UDA called for American support of United Nations and other international economic and social programs as well as a reduction of U.S. tariffs and a "progressive rise in American imports." Liberal internationalism had come around to unequivocal support of the policies that Wallace had advocated since his days editing *Wallaces' Farmer*.[10]

By early 1945 the UDA was already pushing hard for a national full employment policy. In doing so it drew Wallace to the center of the full employment struggle just as the latest battle of the liberal-conservative wars within the Democratic Party and Congress was taking place over his confirmation as secretary of commerce. For liberals the two issues— Wallace's confirmation and full employment—were inextricably intertwined. Niebuhr himself insisted that the struggle over Wallace was a "preview of the political battles which will agitate this nation for decades to come." Conservatives might seek to label Wallace a "dreamer" for the policies he advocated, but Niebuhr viewed him—at least on domestic issues—as a rock-hard realist. For Wallace understood that a modern, highly technological society, with its "vast system of interdependence," could not return to the unregulated mechanisms of early capitalism without disastrous consequences.[11]

Thus in January 1945 Niebuhr and the UDA once more joined forces with the *New Republic,* this time to sponsor a testimonial dinner honoring Wallace as the nation's leading progressive. Niebuhr and *New Republic* editor Bruce Bliven were cochairs of the affair, and sponsors included Eleanor Roosevelt and labor leaders David Dubinsky, Philip Murray, and A. Philip Randolph. Niebuhr and the other organizers hoped to mobilize support for Wallace's confirmation as secretary of commerce, for the cause of full employment, and for other progressive ideas for which they believed Wallace to be "America's most effective spokesman." Wallace was also invited by the UDA to participate in a high-level progressive strategy and fund-raising meeting the day after the dinner. Shortly after the banquet and meeting Niebuhr and the UDA held a widely publicized rally at Town Hall in New York City in support of both Wallace's nomination and the full employment bill. The announcement for the rally made clear the role Wallace played in the symbolic politics of the progressive liberals. It declared that all progressives understood that opposition to Wallace's appointment was less aimed at Wallace than at the policies he advocated. His opponents, the announcement asserted, were against the attainment of shared abundance, and their selfishness was likely to bring on a new depression.[12]

By spring Wallace was confirmed as secretary of commerce after a bloody congressional battle, while the UDA's full employment drive accelerated, with Wallace remaining a symbolic focus. The group conducted a tremendous campaign, replete with nationally distributed posters, pamphlets, and buttons. Plans were made to present the first of the full employment buttons to the new secretary of commerce on the day *Sixty Million Jobs* came out. Yet despite the best efforts of the UDA and other progressive groups, the fight for full employment ultimately ended in early 1946 in a compromise bill that was acceptable to conservatives. The bill jettisoned the central progressive assumption of federal responsibility to guarantee employment by means of the national budget and, implicitly, public works projects, replacing it with a vague pledge for the federal government to do its best to "promote maximum employment, production and purchasing power" and with the establishment of a Council of Economic Advisors to provide appropriate guidance. The UDA condemned it as a virtual betrayal of American workers by the Truman administration. Wallace for his part accepted the final bill with equanimity, insisting that the greatly diluted Employment Act of 1946 was but a "preamble" to victory later on.[13]

Liberals and the United Nations Organization

Debate of foreign relations did not cease during the drawn-out struggles in 1945 over the full employment bill and Wallace's confirmation as secretary of commerce. During the same months that progressive liberal internationalists defined their positions on domestic postwar social and economic problems they also took stands on international political developments that would determine the nature of the peace. The battle for full employment indicated the still general cohesiveness of the progressive liberal community in early 1946, at least on issues of domestic reform that were connected to visions of the postwar world. Discussions of international questions, however—particularly those connected to the establishment of the new United Nations Organization (UNO) or the control of atomic energy—exhibited nascent divisions among progressive liberals, even within the UDA, over foreign affairs.

From the start American liberals generally supported the Dumbarton Oaks plan for the UNO. They believed its structure, particularly the proposed General Assembly, would provide a global analog to Anglo-American representative democracy. As such it would furnish an engine for progressive reform at the international level. The Dumbarton Oaks proposals, the UDA declared, if implemented, would create an international environment in which liberals could militate for "progressive social and economic change, for justice to small nations and exploited peoples, and for a steadily expanding area of cooperation among all powers."[14]

This expectation of future improvement was significant, for it reflected a certain skepticism among liberal internationalists regarding the UNO, particularly in the wake of the Yalta summit of February 1945. The leadership of the UDA harbored mixed feelings about the Yalta accords. They acknowledged that the Big Three conference resulted in greater agreement than anticipated, but they nevertheless believed the United States and Great Britain had compromised important principles, and they particularly deplored the proposed postwar boundary between Poland and Germany. In a similar vein some of the UDA leadership were wary of the Dumbarton Oaks plan. They noted that the proposed organization in no way promised the advent of world government, that it was rather a "Great Power alliance for the promotion of peace." This fact did not condemn the proposed UNO a priori, but coming to terms with it did demand a certain degree of Niebuhrian skepticism. While the new organization did not promise the extent of international democracy that some liberal internationalists hoped for, it at least established a basis for hope by creating a postwar forum for international discussion.[15]

Viewing the UNO at its inception as essentially a strengthening of the Big Three alliance represented partial assimilation within the UDA of Niebuhr's acceptance of peace based on "preponderant power." The UDA acknowledged that the Dumbarton Oaks plan was "not perfect" but insisted that compromise was crucial to international agreement. In language echoing what could be termed Niebuhr's "organic imperative," the UDA insisted that mutual international security of a more democratic nature had to issue from "common experience and growing trust," that is, from organic cooperative experience.[16] At some point in the future it was possible that world government could arise from such a source. For the time being, however, simple cooperation among the great powers was the most that could be expected.

Niebuhr himself continued to develop the logic of preponderant power throughout the period of the UNO's establishment, maintaining all the while his characteristic skepticism. Tying his analysis of great-power politics to his overarching critique of modern industrial society, Niebuhr insisted in late 1944 that the dominance of the Big Three was grounded in their mastery of the "mechanization of modern warfare." For all of its flaws, he wrote, the Dumbarton Oaks plan did the best job of recognizing the realities of that dominance. But he still questioned the likelihood of the plan's success, for two reasons. Niebuhr feared that Dumbarton Oaks's provision for regional global arrangements opened the door to "spheres of influence," and he worried, with logic that the UDA assimilated by the following spring, that the plan lacked any real international democracy. In the end his skeptical advocacy of Dumbarton Oaks—and of liberal internationalist hopes in general—tied back to the central thesis of *Moral Man*. Individuals might see that the Dumbarton Oaks plan was flawed, yet collected in their nations they lacked such perspicacity. An individual might view international affairs from an altruistic perspective, but nations could not. Niebuhr had suggested earlier in the war that if the conflict were horrible enough, if it shook nations "to their foundations," they might transcend their inherent immorality. But by the end of 1944 he doubted that the requisite concussion had occurred. Indeed, he wondered if such a transformation were possible at all. If, as we have seen, by the late 1930s the brutality of Nazism had led Niebuhr to a partial if significant modification of his understanding of the morality of nations, the themes of *Moral Man* still inhered in his commentary of the mid-1940s. In the end it remained a question of virtually immutable human nature for Niebuhr. The imagination of "collective man" was so limited and the "moral inertia and complacency" so great that even this war, one of the "greatest tragedies of history," could not overcome them.[17]

For the UDA, acceptance of the associated principles of preponderant power and the organic imperative was partly driven by the organization's fundamental rejection of American isolationism. With the approach of the San Francisco conference in spring 1945, liberal internationalists anticipated that isolationists were preparing for a last-ditch defense. Once more raising connections between isolationism, racism, and fascism, the UDA declared that because isolationists heard their death-knell tolled at Dumbarton Oaks they were "building new soap-boxes and priming their clansmen" for the final battle. Evoking both Wallace and Niebuhr, however, the UDA argued that the advent of modern industrial civilization meant that isolationism's era was irrevocably over. Because of modern technology and global commerce, the world's nations were becoming the "neighborhoods" of the twentieth century.[18] In the background of this revelation lay Wallace's and Niebuhr's corollary insistence that in such a global neighborhood no nation, above all the United States, could shirk its global responsibilities.

Doubts at San Francisco

Once the San Francisco conference began in late April 1945, the liberal internationalists of the UDA returned to these and other recurring themes. They continued to insist, for example, that the UNO could succeed only if it became a mechanism for attaining greater international democracy. As Wallace had argued since the 1930s, the UNO had to offer not only international political democracy but also economic democracy, which meant adopting "economic measures" that underpin political democracy. International acceptance of the UN charter was not enough; acceptance of economic institutions such as those entailed in the Bretton Woods agreements was crucial as well.[19]

Great-power cooperation, however, remained the UDA's paramount concern during the conference, the sine qua non of peace. That concern was heightened by the actual deterioration of great-power relations during the charter conference. By May 1945 problems among the Big Three, particularly between the United States and Russia, in the context of UN charter debates had become obvious. Despite the shared joy of victory in Europe the Allies were at loggerheads over European occupation policy as well as certain specifics of the charter itself. The danger of a serious breach seemed so great that Niebuhr, as chairman of the UDA, felt compelled to declare publicly that "mutual trust and confidence" had to replace the "warlike statements" the Allies were making on a range of issues. Niebuhr's statement contained a balanced,

Wallace-like assessment of blame for U.S.-Soviet tensions, remarkable in light of the staunch anti-Soviet position he took less than a year and a half later. Niebuhr suggested that the problems between the two nations were amplified by oversimplification, a situation worsened by those in the West who felt that the Soviets could "do no wrong." But such individuals were more than balanced by "far more powerful sections" that were convinced that "Russia can do no right." Responsibility for the tensions, Niebuhr insisted, was mutual and the only way to overcome them was to break the "vicious circle of distrust" that had come to characterize U.S.-Soviet relations.[20]

Niebuhr acknowledged that the Soviet Union had given even its friends in the United States cause for alarm through its actions in central Europe, some of which were in seeming contradiction of the Yalta accords. Nevertheless, his critique of American and British policies was harsher, perhaps because he expected more from the leading Western democracies than he did from Russian communists. The Western allies, Niebuhr argued, had given "ample cause for distrust" by consistently being in the wrong on many questions. In liberating western Europe from the Nazis, they appeared always to support the "status quo" or, even worse, reactionary forces rather than the various national resistance movements. And at San Francisco, Niebuhr contended, the United States seemed to have lost altogether its "moral leadership in world affairs." It rejected the use of the word "independence" in addressing the question of colonies in the charter; it took conservative stands on the issues of trusteeships and military bases; and its delegation opposed an international statement on full employment. The delegates from the United States, Niebuhr proclaimed, stood before the peoples of the world at San Francisco as the "champions of reaction."[21]

To Niebuhr and the UDA, however, the most damning action taken by the United States at San Francisco was its advocacy of the admission to the UNO conference of the "clearly fascist" government of Argentina. The question of Argentine inclusion also marked the nadir of Soviet-American relations at the conference. It arose when the Latin American delegations at San Francisco insisted that Argentina—uncooperative in the war against Germany and a latecomer to the wartime alliance—be seated before they would vote in favor of seating White Russia and the Ukraine as the Soviet Union had demanded. The Soviets declared the quid pro quo "incomprehensible" in light of Argentine temporizing during the war. U.S. insistence nevertheless led to Argentina's admission, while the episode made clear the growing rift between America and the Soviet Union, quite foreboding to American internationalists. The journalist Walter Lippmann later likened the American action regarding Argentina to a "steamroller" being driven through the conference.[22]

To liberals like Niebuhr and the UDA, American support of Argentine inclusion constituted an unconscionable "Argentine hoax." They drew a parallel between it and the ongoing international dispute over the Soviet-backed "Lublin Pole" government of Poland, arguing that neither the Argentine nor the Polish regime ought to have been admitted at San Francisco. The Soviets were wrong not to live up to the Western reading of the Yalta accords, but that did not justify the "appeasement of Argentine fascism." Demonstrating once more the pervasiveness of the Munich analog, the UDA declared that American policy regarding Argentina might go down in history as the "New World's Munich."[23]

The leadership of the UDA did not use the term "fascism" offhandedly in regard to Argentina. They insisted that fascism had a long history in that nation, that "fascist forces" had been gaining power for more than fifteen years, and that the seizure of power by the Farrell-Peron regime in 1943 had been the culmination of a long evolution of Argentine fascism. In fact, behind the stridency of this UDA commentary on the Argentine hoax lay aspects of the old American liberal fear of potential domestic fascism embodied by corporate interests. While the UDA acknowledged diplomatic reasons for American policy, they insisted that it was American business interests as well as related fears of Latin American revolution that really impelled U.S. policy. "Appeasement" of the Argentine government would regain for the United States Argentine trade that was being lost to the British; it would establish a basis for cooperation between American and Argentinean "tycoons"; and it would place U.S. power behind the Peron government, helping to stave off a potentially destabilizing revolution in Argentina.[24] To the members of the UDA, the Argentine hoax bore all the earmarks of the protofascism they so feared at home.

Atomic Bombs and Vetoes: Division within the UDA

Through summer 1945 the views held by various leading members of the UDA, including Niebuhr, regarding the UNO differed little from one another. But during autumn and winter, in the wake of U.S. use of atomic weapons against Japan, a serious division developed within the group, foreshadowing division within the larger liberal community over the next two years. It was a split that highlighted the range of liberal viewpoints regarding the UNO itself as well as more transcendent issues such as world government and practical politics.

Niebuhr recognized immediately the transformation that atomic weapons wrought upon both domestic and international society. Above all, he understood that they carried the dilemma of existence in technological civilization to a new, terrifying level of complexity. Moreover, the bomb's "indiscriminate destruction" proved that total war was not an invention of the Nazis. Niebuhr claimed that the Allies' justification of the bomb with the argument that it mercifully hastened the end of the war only echoed Nazi justifications for especially brutal actions taken in places like the Netherlands and Poland. American use of the bomb, Niebuhr concluded, was "merely the culmination" of total war.[25]

Presaging later debates regarding the American decision to use the bomb, Niebuhr initially argued that the United States ought to have demonstrated the weapon to the Japanese instead of dropping it by surprise on major population centers. He believed that by forgoing such a demonstration America had damaged its moral position. In asserting this view, however, Niebuhr did not forget historical context. Recalling that the bomb was developed in a desperate race with Nazi Germany that had its own momentum, he contended that once the bomb was built it would have been almost impossible not to use it. A similar sense of inevitability underlay Niebuhr's speculation regarding the bomb's future implications. He doubted atomic energy would strengthen the unity of the Big Three. Already, by fall 1945, he saw evidence that the Americans and British did not intend to share their atomic knowledge with the Soviets, which he feared would exacerbate Russian mistrust of the West. In full agreement with the position Wallace articulated the following summer, Niebuhr suggested that Americans needed to put themselves in the Soviets' place and "imagine that they had the bomb secret and had announced that they would keep it as a trust." Such an insight might render Soviet fears more understandable, if not completely valid.[26]

Initially the rest of the UDA leadership was in full agreement with Niebuhr regarding the implications of the atomic bomb. After the breakdown of the first meeting of the Council of Foreign Ministers in London in October 1945 they saw little accord between Russia and the Western allies, which in the new atomic context threatened "mutual destruction." Such fears led the UDA to embrace Niebuhr's principle of preponderant power in order to resolve issues that already seemed beyond the reach of the UNO.[27]

By early in the new year, however, there was dissent within the UDA, arising from fears created by the bomb. UDA national board member Anthony Smith, for example, foresaw imminent international conflict: a "third world war" with atomic weapons that might "mark the end of civilization." The perception of a danger of such magnitude led Smith along with other members of the UDA board to advocate a fundamental revision of the UN charter to give the organization authority to enact real international law. Smith and the other dissidents on the national board, including Ethel S. Epstein and Alfred Baker Lewis, believed that it had become too dangerous to human survival to leave everything to the great powers. Rejecting Niebuhr's principle of preponderant power and the gradualism implicit in UDA policy, they called for the immediate transformation of the UNO into a world government that could compel the great powers to behave in an orderly, cooperative, moral fashion.[28]

For Smith and his fellow UDA dissidents, re-creating the UNO as a true world government above all required the abolition of the veto power held by the permanent members of the Security Council. If the transformed UNO and the laws it created were to have any real meaning, Smith reasoned, then the UN secretary-general would have to be able to enforce those laws "without veto" against any offending nation or individual. Lewis argued that anything less was only old fashioned "power politics." In a letter to Niebuhr he insisted that abolishing the veto was the position the UDA should take and expressed his hope that Niebuhr, with his international reputation, would join the fight.[29]

Epstein meanwhile attacked what she viewed as the contradictory outlook of the UDA foreign-policy committee, which held an essentially Niebuhrian opposition to abolition of the veto. She noted that the committee acknowledged that there could be no effective world government while the veto power remained in place. Yet she pointed out that the committee members also believed that the Soviets would actually perceive abolition as a threat. Epstein insisted that Russian as well as other nations' fears could be assuaged, although she was unclear as to how this would be done. In any case, she argued that international reassurance was certainly not accomplished by the sort of great-power agreements that effectively eliminated the rights of smaller nations. The logic of preponderant power, she argued, buttressed by the Security Council veto, only gave impetus to the race for spheres of influence. At some point, Epstein warned, the racing antagonists "must meet."[30] For UDA dissidents such as Smith, Lewis, and Epstein, in the now atomic world it was no longer possible to live by Niebuhr's logic. There was no time to wait and see if real international democracy would arise organically from a peace enforced by great-power cooperation. Rather, it was crucial that international justice be established immediately, with the great powers subject to the same international law as everyone else.

As the dispute crystallized, James Loeb feared that it might split the UDA. He warned Niebuhr that Epstein and Smith completely disagreed with the organization's established position on world government and that they could potentially carry other influential members along. Niebuhr rejected the dissenters' position, explaining that all his "political instincts" warned him off the idea of immediate world government, while he fully believed the Soviet Union desired the veto power for its own protection. He finally asserted that if the Smith-Epstein position carried the day, he would leave the organization. While admitting great respect for his colleagues, he insisted he would "never go along if the world government position wins in the UDA."[31]

The foreign-policy statement finally issued by the UDA's national board in early summer 1946 was partly a compromise between Niebuhr and the dissenters, but in an important sense it was a victory for Niebuhr. The statement spoke to concerns most liberal internationalists shared, particularly regarding economic and political democracy. At the same time it insisted on the need to continue to seek cooperation with the Soviet Union. It was in regard to the issue of atomic energy, however, that the UDA foreign-policy statement went farthest in favor of the Epstein-Smith group. The statement insisted on civilian control of atomic energy in the United States and called for the creation of a UN "Atomic Development Authority." Most importantly, the statement explicitly demanded the elimination of the Security Council veto as it applied to all aspects of atomic energy. In addition, it declared that the nation's progressive movement had to join in the cause of world government.[32]

Nevertheless, despite articulating such aims regarding the transformation of the UNO, the UDA foreign policy statement clearly took a Niebuhrian position. No matter what sort of international political mechanisms the organization worked for over the long term, the statement insisted, the UDA had to prevent those "more ultimate demands" from interfering with the achievement of an "immediately operative system of mutual security" that could function until a more ideal system replaced it.[33] Niebuhr's logic of international relations had won this brief battle within the UDA for the heart and soul of liberal internationalism. The dissidents could dream their dreams of world government, but the UDA would spend its greatest energies on international relations working within the confines of the principle of preponderant power.

The "Tragedy of Liberalism"

The relatively brief episode of division within the UDA in early 1946 foreshadowed the greater division developing within the larger liberal internationalist community over U.S.-Soviet relations. The settlement of the dispute within the UDA on Niebuhr's terms prefigured the course events would take within that community after Wallace's departure from the cabinet in September. In fact, at around the same time as the debate within the UDA was being resolved, Wallace became embroiled in a controversy that made such a course of events much more likely.

The controversy originated in remarks Wallace made in what he naively thought was an off-the-record interview, in March 1946, regarding the relatively minor matter of U.S. military bases in Iceland. Wallace's comments made their way into a *New York Times* article asserting that Wallace, as secretary of commerce, believed U.S. troops should be withdrawn from Iceland. The piece accurately quoted Wallace as saying the Soviets would likely view American forces in Iceland as a threat.[34]

In May, because of his remarks and in the wake of Iceland's ultimate refusal to renew U.S. leases on the bases, Wallace appeared as a central character in a lengthy *Life* magazine article entitled "The Tragedy of Liberalism," written by well-known liberal journalists Joseph and Stewart Alsop. Because of its tone and content it is likely that the high-profile piece began the process of turning many within the liberal community against both Wallace and any U.S. policy of moderation toward the Soviet Union. In this sense the Alsops' article can be viewed as an opening salvo of cold war liberalism. Indeed, the Alsops' article was essentially sympathetic toward liberals like Wallace. The problem, the authors contended, was that Wallace and others, having been "deeply stirred" by the Soviets' experiments in social planning as well as the nation's heroic struggle against Hitler's armies, were too idealistic and did not understand the Russians' true nature or realize that Soviet imperialism extended the methods of the Nazis. Like Niebuhr, the Alsops viewed Soviet-American relations through the lens of Munich, declaring that liberals such as Wallace failed to see that "appeasement is always wrong" for it inevitably led to a situation in which "you must fight or knuckle under forever." For the Alsops there was neither a middle alternative nor any need to take account of the Russian perspective. Ignoring the fact that Wallace consistently had argued that America and Russia shared blame for the tensions between them, the Alsops unfairly castigated Wallace for blaming the United States alone.[35]

In "The Tragedy of Liberalism," following their critique of Wallace, the Alsops further attacked what they considered another example of misguided American liberalism, the "Win-the-Peace" conference, held in early April in Washington, D.C. The fact that the meeting convened in the Department of Commerce auditorium implied that it had Wallace's approval. The meeting of nearly 1,000 delegates, speakers, and sponsors included some well-known communists and fellow travelers as well as many non- and anticommunist liberals from within and without government. It was, in other words, a "popular front" convention. Various progressive resolutions were passed, ranging from opposition to Universal Military Training to calling on the United States to work for the freedom of colonial peoples as well as one attacking the U.S. policy of establishing overseas bases—including the ones in Iceland—as hostile to the Soviet Union.[36]

While many noncommunist progressives participated in the Win-the-Peace meeting, their numbers notably did not include the leadership of the UDA. In fact, the UDA explicitly attacked the conference as an example of communist manipulation of "unquestioned progressives." The attack clearly indicated that despite the ambivalent tolerance it had sometimes shown for the Soviet Union in international affairs during the previous year, the UDA was as staunchly anticommunist as ever. Moreover, the manner in which the attack was articulated laid more of the foundation for later assaults on popular front liberals, including Wallace. The UDA statement insisted that the Win-the-Peace conference represented a new threat to American liberals, one that could ultimately "destroy their influence [in American society and politics] completely" and render American liberalism "subservient to the purposes of the Communist Party." The UDA also contended that some of the leading American liberals had signed the conference's resolutions but only because they were drawn into a (presumably communist) "trap" by, among other ploys, an "unscrupulous appeal" to the memory of FDR.[37] This last was a claim that would be made repeatedly and rather viciously against Wallace and the Progressives in 1948. In April 1946, however, it represented an early, less hostile version of a particularly potent cold war liberal construction: that of the overly idealistic, well-intentioned progressive who was somehow duped by the communists into supporting essentially communist, pro-Soviet policies. It was an effective image, despite the fact that it ignored the intelligence and political perspicacity of many of the individuals whose behavior it was used to explain or criticize.

By placing such significance on the Win-the-Peace conference and by immediately juxtaposing it with their critique of Wallace, the Alsops began the process of associating Wallace in liberals' minds with this still inchoate communist-dupe construction. Moreover, considering the vitriol expended by the leadership of the UDA toward the conference, the Alsops' article probably helped weaken what was still a strongly favorable perception of Wallace within the UDA's ranks. The article, like the UDA debate over the Security Council veto, testified to the increasing division among liberals regarding international affairs, while both episodes suggested a growing urgency among liberals regarding the resolution of the major global problems facing the nation in 1946. Both episodes also implied the transcendent source of that urgency. For the Alsop brothers and Niebuhr, as well as the UDA dissidents, the atomic bombing of Japan had transformed international relations: America had no time to lose. By early in the year the various questions connected to atomic energy—particularly those concerning domestic and international control of weapons matériel and technology—formed the context for virtually all liberal discussions of foreign relations. They also formed the context for the culminating controversy of Wallace's government career.

Domestic Control of Atomic Energy

Like Niebuhr, Wallace understood immediately in fall 1945 that the atomic bomb had greatly altered international affairs. The day after Hiroshima he presciently predicted that the struggle to control the new form of energy would be "one of the most unusual . . . the world has ever seen." Also like Niebuhr, he saw the possibility that an American monopoly on the weapon, however temporary, could transform the nation, or at least alter the nation's image, with dangerous implications. Wallace feared that its atomic monopoly made the United States appear aggressive, whether or not that was the case. That appearance could affect other nations' behavior toward America, undermining the UNO. Such a prospect led Wallace to conclude, along with the UDA dissidents of early 1946, that the UNO would have to be "redesigned" to take into account the existence of the bomb and its influence on international politics.[38]

American possession of the bomb also triggered Wallace's and other liberals' fears of domestic protofascism. In some of his earliest writing about the various ramifications of atomic energy Wallace expressed concern that either the military or what he termed "vested interests"— which could include monopolistic capitalists—might gain control of the nation's atomic technology. Wallace believed that either group would prevent the development of civilian applications that he was sure could beneficently transform the lives of common people. He also warned that such restraint might allow other nations to move ahead of the United States in the field of atomic science, with dangerous strategic and economic consequences. The UDA articulated a similar fear in the first days of the atomic era, also warning of "vested special interests" that might try to "suppress" the use of atomic discoveries for the common good.[39] Both Wallace and the UDA, in other words, saw the possibility that atomic technology might strengthen the positions of American militarists and protofascists. It was this and related concerns that led them to staunchly advocate civilian control of atomic energy domestically and the sharing of American atomic science knowledge internationally.

Wallace, for instance, roundly and repeatedly condemned the May-Johnson bill, the first piece of legislation proposed in 1945 for regulating the domestic development of atomic energy. Drafted by the War Department, May-Johnson would have placed all atomic research and development under military authority. In letters to Truman as well as in testimony before Congress Wallace insisted that the bill transgressed the nation's democratic traditions, particularly that of civilian control of the military. He was especially concerned that under the bill's provisions the director of the Atomic Energy Commission would be appointed by the commission and not by the president, and that the president only with great difficulty could remove either the director or members of the commission itself. This fear took immediate substance from the control that Manhattan Project military director General Leslie Groves still maintained over atomic bombs and atomic bomb materials in the months after the war's end, as well as from Groves's truculent comments regarding FDR's handling of atomic policy. Wallace urged Truman to quickly establish a new authority, one that would put the supervision of atomic energy matériel under an individual who answered directly to the president himself. With Groves's example in mind, Wallace warned that the tenets of May-Johnson could place Americans—and "even the world"—at the mercy of a "small group of men, perhaps a military clique," who might utilize atomic energy to impose "authoritarianism and imperialism."[40]

Along with many members of the American scientific community Wallace also feared that May-Johnson would curtail what otherwise would be the natural course of atomic research, that its proposed security regulations would stifle scientific research. Implicit in such worries were Wallace's wide-ranging hopes for atomic energy, hopes that were shared by many individuals within the scientific community as well as thousands of other Americans who placed great faith in science and technology. Paul Boyer has written at length about the concerns regarding atomic energy that Americans, including American scientists, had in the immediate postwar era. He has shown how initial American perceptions of atomic energy ranged from outright terror to exaggerated expectations of techno-science utopias and has argued that this oscillation between nightmares of nuclear Armageddon and bright visions of a benevolent atomic future defined the entire discourse of the early atomic era.[41] Because of his eclecticism Wallace exemplified virtually the entire spectrum of that discourse. He expressed great fears regarding the destructive potential of atomic weapons while, as a spiritually inclined scientist, he also articulated a powerfully optimistic vision of an atomic future attainable if Americans made the right choices.

Wallace viewed the atomic era as another portal to the New Age he had so long searched for. If the atomic genie were not bottled up by the militarists and monopolists, then a new civilization beckoned. The future could become a "golden age of abundance" for all. For Wallace the discovery of atomic fission made it seem as if "God were saying to us, 'Enter now into the land of abundance and enjoy all its fruits sharing joyously with one another of the riches which are there for everyone.'" The atomic sword, however, was double edged. Atomic energy, Wallace was convinced, could allow humanity to advance rapidly in terms of technology. But if Americans and the rest of the world did not learn to cooperate, to "understand the social rule of abundance," God would turn this power of "light and peace" into one of "darkness and war." Then humanity's existence, Wallace warned, would be more miserable than ever. The atomic era, in Wallace's view, was both the most promising and most hazardous portal to the New Age yet confronted.[42]

Like Wallace, the UDA strongly opposed the May-Johnson bill. Evoking the protofascist specter, the UDA also expressed disgust for the legislation's proposal of a "9-man scientific-military dictatorship" and called instead for legislation mandating civilian control to prevent atomic energy's exploitation by unsupervised "private monopolies."[43] By January 1946, however, another bill was under consideration that initially seemed to resolve liberal fears of protofascism and the suppression of science. The McMahon Act, eventually passed as the Atomic Energy Act of 1946, proposed a wholly civilian Atomic Energy Commission in which all members were directly answerable to the president with the advice and consent of the Senate. In congressional testimony, Wallace declared that this bill maintained American "traditions of democracy" by placing the control of atomic energy in the hands of the people's representatives while also establishing unhindered scientific research.[44]

The UDA was more skeptical than Wallace, at least at first, of the McMahon bill. It was a skepticism not so much of the bill itself, which seemed to offer just what the UDA was demanding, but rather of what the group imagined would be the legislation's eventual form if passed. Observing the efforts of Groves and his associates in lobbying for military control, the UDA feared that militarists in government would manipulate the McMahon bill in such a manner as to render what appeared to be civilian control into an "'inside' military rigging" just as dangerous as the tenets of May-Johnson. Explicitly invoking Wallace and his characterization of the domestic control issue as the "moral issue of the century," the UDA insisted that renewed public outcry was the only hope for preventing such a subterfuge. Their fears were amplified in April, when Truman appointed millionaire industrialist and staunch anti-Soviet, anticommunist Bernard Baruch as the American delegate to the new UN Atomic Energy Commission. For the UDA the ascension of "Baruch and the bankers" was proof that private interests and militarists were attaining control of American atomic policy. Nor did matters improve during the summer. By July the UDA claimed that the McMahon bill had been amended to the point where it was worse than May-Johnson, ensuring military domination of all aspects of U.S. atomic energy supervision and production.[45]

By as early as February, in fact, the McMahon bill had been amended so extensively that in certain respects it was little different from its predecessor, giving extensive influence over atomic energy control to the military. Wallace recognized the import of the changes, fearing not only that they would cause the United States to fall behind in atomic energy development but also that the military would gain dominance over American foreign policy making. To Wallace such a level of military control made war with the Soviets "inevitable." Wallace was joined in this concern by other liberals. In March, for example, the progressive liberal National Citizens Political Action Committee (NCPAC) declared its deep concern over "military domination" of atomic energy. Established in 1944 as a mechanism for independent political action for a wide range of progressives, NCPAC's membership included business people and professionals as well as farmers, consumers, and workers of all religions and ethnicities. By early 1946 they too were alarmed by developments regarding both McMahon and May-Johnson. And they too insisted that the McMahon bill in its amended form was as dangerous as May-Johnson seemed at the outset.[46]

The McMahon bill was finally passed in July and was at best what one scholar has called a "qualified triumph" for those opposed to military control of American atomic science. In contrast to Wallace and NCPAC, the UDA was strangely accepting of the final version of the bill. Indeed, despite repeated, harsh criticisms throughout the spring and summer, by August the UDA leadership termed the Atomic Energy Act of 1946 a "major victory for maturity and enlightenment" as well as "sound and worthy" legislation.[47] By heaping such accolades on the legislation just as other liberal internationalists were condemning it, the UDA's leaders may have been attempting to position their organization politically, to make it appear realistic in its judgments on policy and politics. Whether or not this was the case, the group's conclusions regarding the McMahon bill evinced a division within the liberal internationalist community that also was apparent over the question of international control.

The Question of International Control

Wallace's support for the original McMahon bill in great part arose from his belief that it assured a domestic program on atomic energy consistent with American international policy, which he viewed as vital to the free international exchange of scientific information.[48] He embraced this position within weeks of Hiroshima and by doing so placed himself in the midst of a nascent and acrimonious national debate over the sharing of atomic science information. Wallace's role in that debate and the manner in which it was publicly construed—and misconstrued—added to the increasingly negative image of him held not only by his enemies, but more and more by those who shared his actual views.

The first and perhaps most damaging episode in this debate took place within the administration in September 1945, when Truman's cabinet began discussing international development of atomic energy. The stark divisions within the cabinet were apparent on September 21 in a meeting Truman called specifically for the purpose of debating whether or not the United States ought to share "scientific information regarding atomic energy" with the other members of the United Nations and particularly with the Soviet Union. The discussion was explicitly *not* about sharing technical knowledge regarding bomb construction. The centerpiece of the meeting was a lengthy memorandum on the topic written by soon-to-retire Secretary of War Henry Stimson. Drawing on the opinions of atomic scientists who argued that attempting to suppress either the technical secrets or the theoretical science behind the bomb was impossible, Stimson contended that avoiding open discussion with the Soviets of the development of atomic energy would exacerbate the already dangerous tensions between the two nations. Several members of the cabinet strongly opposed Stimson's position, Secretary of the Navy James Forrestal the most vehemently. To Wallace, however, Stimson's logic made perfect sense, meshing thoroughly with his own. At the meeting Wallace spoke to the issue in broad terms, foreshadowing his positions of the following year. He outlined the history of atomic science and suggested the futility of trying to suppress the dispersal of scientific knowledge. He then strongly advocated the international exchange of scientific information but argued against the "interchange of techniques," that is, the technical knowledge necessary for building bombs. He also insisted that the United States should make its theoretical knowledge available to the Soviets only if they gave American scientists full access to Russian laboratories and knowledge.[49]

News of the cabinet meeting was leaked in rather distorted form to the national press by the next day, and the episode quickly became another component of the growing image of Wallace as too tolerant of the Soviet Union. In several national newspapers, including some sympathetic to him, Wallace was portrayed as having proposed that the United States "reveal the secret of the atomic bomb to Russia." The journals that already opposed him pulled out all the stops. The *New York Daily Mirror,* for example, characterized the nonexistent proposal to give up the bomb as the brainchild of "Russia's No. 1 Special Pleader in our government, Secretary of Commerce Henry A. Wallace, pet of the pinks." The *Mirror's* editorialist went on to express great relief that Wallace had not retained the vice presidency in 1944, since his (alleged) behavior regarding atomic energy suggested that as president he would have delivered the nation "hand and foot, atomic bomb and everything, to Stalin's imperialistic, thieving slave state."[50]

Wallace was perturbed by the leak and the manner in which he was portrayed in the press, so he acted during the subsequent weeks and months to clarify his views on atomic energy. In a letter to Truman written three days after the fateful cabinet meeting and one day after conferring with atomic scientists in Chicago, he fully reiterated his support for Stimson's memorandum, arguing that the sooner the United States shared its scientific knowledge, but not its "industrial and engineering information," the sooner world cooperation would be attained.[51] Later, in November and December, Wallace asserted his agreement in principle with the joint declaration made by Truman and British and Canadian prime ministers Clement Atlee and Mackenzie King proposing international control of atomic energy.

Yet Wallace's agreement with the joint declaration was limited in ways that further clarified his outlook. In a speech given at Madison Square Garden in New York City to the liberal Independent Citizens' Committee of the Arts, Sciences, and Professions (ICCASP) he insisted that the proposals embodied in the declaration "must succeed," but he still expressed great doubts regarding the declaration's viability. He was particularly skeptical of the process propounded by the three leaders, built around a proposed UNO commission that would oversee the development of atomic energy by a series of "separate stages." As each stage was completed to the satisfaction of the commission, international development would move on to the next. The implicit paternalism of the proposed sequence of stages, Wallace feared, would deeply offend the Soviets, leading them to reject the plan.[52]

In a sense Wallace used the occasion of the Truman-Atlee-King declaration as a basis for promoting his own wider-ranging vision of international cooperation on atomic energy. In the speech to ICCASP, for instance, he quickly stated his support for the declaration and then moved on to an extended discussion of various issues connected to atomic energy. He once more pointed out that there were no real secrets in atomic science and no likelihood of a viable defense against atomic attack, which meant that failure to reach an international agreement would be "catastrophic" for all nations. Wallace also invoked the protofascist bogey, warning of the danger that threatened if the control of atomic energy were dominated by special interests hidden behind a "military or industrial cloak" and using their control to bring the world under the domination of "Atomic Imperialism." He again spoke of the potential impoverishment of American science if the nation tried to suppress the international exchange of information and keep its knowledge to itself. Finally, Wallace rearticulated his cooperative, spiritually grounded vision of global abundance in a new atomic age. The discovery of atomic energy, he concluded, was a "unique opportunity" to establish a "single, human community of the highest spiritual level, accompanied by unlimited material facilities," if only humanity accepted the "social rule of abundance."[53]

By March 1946 the Truman-Atlee-King declaration gained substance when the administration proposed an actual program for the international control of atomic energy. The Acheson-Lilienthal plan—named after Undersecretary of State Dean Acheson and Tennessee Valley Authority Director David Lilienthal, who jointly headed the committee that developed the proposal—laid out a series of stages, reminiscent of the joint declaration, through which the UNO would establish international control of the atom. Under Acheson-Lilienthal the United States would continue to possess the only atomic bombs while other nations would allow international inspection of their atomic energy facilities. The plan's creators understood that their program's success might be undermined by Russian veto power in the UN Security Council, so they took Soviet concerns into account by proposing to obtain Russian agreement on general principles of international control while leaving potential veto problems to be worked out later.[54]

Controversy over the "Baruch Plan"

This relatively tolerant approach toward the Soviets changed in April when Truman chose Bernard Baruch to head the American delegation to the UN Atomic Energy Commission. Baruch was displeased with the Acheson-Lilienthal proposal above all because it did not explicitly address the possibility that the Soviets might use their Security Council veto to prevent either facility inspections or sanctions. After obtaining Truman's agreement, Baruch crucially altered the U.S. plan in a dramatic speech given to the first meeting of the Atomic Energy Commission on June 14. The control of atomic energy, he declared, would take place through international administration of raw materials and the inspection of atomic energy facilities by international agencies. He then stipulated that there would be no vetoes allowed of either matériel control mechanisms or inspections and majority vote in the Security Council would carry. Under Baruch's altered plan the development of atomic energy for peaceful uses would be placed under an Atomic Development Authority, not subject to vetoes, that would in effect internationally license atomic plants based on strategic and geographic criteria. The historian Walter LaFeber notes that this meant that by controlling a majority within the Atomic Development Authority the United States would be able to "control the development of the industrial uses of nuclear energy *within* the Soviet Union." The Soviets predictably rejected Baruch's program, proposing instead the destruction of all extant atomic weapons, the cessation of weapons production, and the outlawry of atomic bombs in principle, all to be followed by discussion of control mechanisms. Baruch responded by insisting that the entire American plan had to be accepted or there would be no agreement at all. Ultimately no agreement was reached, and the international acrimony gave impetus to the August passage of the modified McMahon bill by Congress, prohibiting the exchange of atomic science or technology information altogether.[55]

Reaction to Baruch's alteration of the Acheson-Lilienthal plan was mixed. Some viewed it as drastic, even illegitimate. Walter Lippmann believed making the veto power an issue was a mistake that soured all prospects for an agreement. Niebuhr and the UDA saw things quite differently, viewing Baruch's plan in general and his preclusion of the veto power in particular in an essentially positive light, although they did have several reservations. The national board suggested a U.S. moratorium on atomic weapons production and argued that the United States should promise to destroy its own atomic bomb stockpile within a "stipulated period" of time after an agreement was reached. Finally, in an explicit criticism of one of Baruch's alterations, the UDA declared that fissionable materials should be internationally owned, as the Acheson-Lilienthal plan proposed, instead of just internationally controlled, as Baruch suggested. Nevertheless, despite their reservations, the group characterized Baruch's plan as a "major step forward" in the subordination of "national sovereignty to international collaboration" and, sounding a bit like Wallace, the "first genuine offer to surrender a power of incalculable proportions for the . . . common good."[56]

For Niebuhr in particular such characterizations were unusually optimistic. He had shared Wallace's ambivalence regarding the Truman-Atlee-King declaration back in November 1945, although he approved of the statement's central thrust of moving atomic energy development out of the sole control of the United States and into the hands of an international commission supervised by the UNO. To do so would implicitly acknowledge what was obvious to Niebuhr: that no nation, not even America, was "good enough to be trustee of such an instrument of destruction." Nevertheless, in Niebuhr's view the proposal came too late. By the time of the declaration, he insisted, the Soviets were so mistrustful that they would accept nothing less than the "transmission of the bomb secret to the Security Council," highly unlikely in view of the atmosphere of mutual suspicion that already existed.[57]

In light of such remarks Niebuhr's apparent optimism the following June—as chair of the UDA national board and member of the board's subcommittee drafting an official statement on the Baruch plan—seems especially out of place. The UDA statement insisted that the most important aspect of the Baruch plan was its rejection of the "unanimity principle" on questions of control and development of the atom. The organization was not rejecting the veto in general; indeed, the board explicitly renewed its support of veto power for the five permanent members of the UN Security Council. Yet the UDA insisted that to extend the veto to an international agency charged with supervising atomic energy would be "illogical and probably fatal" to any hopes of establishing effective supervision.[58] It might have been necessary to maintain the Security Council veto to ensure Soviet and U.S. participation in the UNO, but in an Atomic Development Authority the veto was unacceptable if the agency was to be effective.

While it is possible that Niebuhr and his associates actually viewed Baruch's proposal as a truly magnanimous and thus hopeful action on the part of the United States, it is likely that the convoluted logic of the UDA, particularly on the atomic-energy veto issue, derived in part from the relatively recent dispute within the organization over the UN Security Council veto. Otherwise it is hard to understand why the UDA leadership believed that on atomic energy issues any great power would be more inclined to go along with a majority voting against its self-perceived interests than it would be in the Security Council. The nit-picking quality of the distinction hints at the persistence within the board of the earlier divisive debate over the Security Council veto. The UDA dissidents after all had taken up their stand on the issue because of the urgency they felt due to the advent of atomic weapons. Now that the control of atomic energy itself was under consideration it is possible that Niebuhr and his colleagues felt themselves able to compromise, to give the dissidents their due on this more contained topic of foreign policy.

If Niebuhr and the UDA generally favored Baruch's tactics, Wallace had serious misgivings about them—misgivings that were tied to his increasing doubts regarding U.S. policy toward the Soviets in general. In a lengthy letter to Truman in late July Wallace rejected the U.S. plan for its "fatal defect," the central component of which was the separate-stages scheme he had opposed ever since the Truman-Atlee-King declaration the prior fall. The other defective aspects of the Baruch plan, in Wallace's view, included requirements that other nations forswear atomic research for military purposes and disclose all of their fissionable materials resources, while the United States continued to withhold its technological knowledge until satisfied with the operation of international control and inspection mechanisms. In light of the American demands Wallace asked Truman if it was surprising that the Russians did not show any enthusiasm for the American proposal. He questioned how Americans would react if the Russians held an "atomic monopoly" and offered to share information at some "indefinite time in the future," completely at their discretion and then only if the United States promised before the fact not to build any bombs and to disclose full information on its atomic resources. Wallace speculated that the United States would react exactly as the Soviets had, by presenting a counter-proposal "for the record" while turning all available energies toward producing an atomic bomb that would strengthen the American bargaining position.

Wallace concluded that the stages plan in its present form was "not workable." He suggested instead that any agreement had to be worked out as a complete package at the outset. There might be steps in such a package, but their prerequisites and timing had to be stipulated in the initial treaty rather than be subject to any nation's whim. After all, Wallace pointed out to the president, the Russians only held "two cards" in this game, American ignorance of Soviet scientific and technical progress on atomic energy as well as a lack of information regarding Russian supplies of fissionable materials. These cards were not as powerful as the American hand—which included a bomb stockpile, operational manufacturing facilities, long-range bombers, and a global network of air bases—but they were all the Soviets had. And now the United States was demanding that they give up both of their cards right away, while effectively telling them that America would play only after it had seen the Russian hand. The obvious risks of such a policy, Wallace believed, were "deadlock" and an atomic arms race in "deadly earnest."[59]

Along with the idea that all aspects of international control had to be established in advance, Wallace proposed solutions to the atomic energy impasse that paralleled the UDA's reservations regarding the Baruch plan. He asserted, for example, that the United States had to accept an agreement that would commit it to disclosing its atomic information and destroying its bombs at a specified time or in response to specified actions by other nations rather than at its own discretion. The difference between Wallace and the UDA, however, was that where the UDA seemed willing to accept the Baruch plan while offering suggestions for changes, Wallace believed that without the changes the plan was altogether unacceptable. As for the veto issue, Wallace, like Lippmann, found it "completely irrelevant." Veto power, he maintained, existed in effect during the period of negotiating the treaty. Once a treaty along the lines he was suggesting was ratified a veto was meaningless.[60]

Wallace was in no way sure that his alternatives promised success. He was hopeful that the very fact of the Russians' counterproposal indicated they might be willing to negotiate in good faith. But there was no assurance that the Russians would go along with an American policy modified along the lines he (and the UDA) suggested. The Soviets might still choose to "stall until they also have bombs" and could negotiate from a position of greater strength. Nevertheless, Wallace believed that altering American policy in such a manner as to treat the Soviets more as equals than subordinates was the only chance to prevent an arms race. In any case, the United States had nothing to lose by rethinking the logic of its atomic policy. Wallace pointed out to the president that the nation would still retain its technological knowledge and existing facilities during the transition to international control. If any country violated a treaty provision it would be subject to the action deemed appropriate by the remaining signatory nations, including a declaration of war.[61]

Wallace Makes His Case

Beyond the salient issue of international atomic energy control, Wallace used the July letter to Truman as an opportunity to present his critique of the entire scope of U.S.-Soviet relations. In sharp contrast to George F. Kennan's "Long Telegram" of February (of which Wallace was aware, although he had not read it) and its thesis of collective Russian psychopathology, Wallace wrote with sympathy of the Russian historical experience. He recalled over a thousand years of invasions of Russia as well as thirty years of Western animosity toward the Soviet Union. In such a historical context, Wallace argued, American actions since the end of World War II must have seemed particularly threatening to the Soviets. How did they perceive, he wondered, a thirteen billion dollar American military budget, atomic weapons tests in the South Pacific, the continued production of atomic bombs, the manufacture of increasingly advanced long-range bombers capable of delivering those bombs, American plans to arm Latin American nations, and U.S. efforts to secure air bases around the world? Answering his own question, Wallace asserted that to the rest of the world, including the Soviet Union, it would appear America was either preparing to win an inevitable war or was intent on building up such a predominance of force as to intimidate "the rest of mankind." With great prescience Wallace predicted that these policies, rather than gaining America the ordered and peaceful world it desired, would instead result in a "neurotic, fear-ridden, itching-trigger [*sic*] psychology in all the peoples of the world."[62]

Wallace concluded that there were two mutually exclusive American points of view on U.S.-Soviet relations. The first was that it was not possible for the two nations to coexist, making war inevitable. The second was that a war between the United States and Russia would be a global catastrophe, making the avoidance of war imperative. To Wallace the latter perspective was clearly preferable. In line with that preference he made several suggestions to Truman. Above all, he insisted that the U.S. government ought to pursue a policy designed to allay "reasonable" Russian fears and suspicions. At the same time it was necessary to counteract the "irrational fear" of Russia being established within America by "certain individuals and publications." The American people, Wallace believed, had to see that their nation and the Soviet Union could peacefully coexist, and they needed to behave as if they believed in the possibility of that coexistence. The United States was clearly the most powerful nation in the world; for it to continually harp upon the need to strengthen its defenses would make it appear that America was only "paying lip service to peace."[63]

Wallace also spoke publicly on aspects of U.S.-Soviet relations during the summer, primarily on atomic policy and then not too critically of the United States. During the final weeks of congressional consideration of the various atomic-energy bills he continued to articulate a great sense of urgency regarding the need for a viable system of international control. He once more called for international cooperation grounded in spiritual renewal, at one point asserting the need for making Christian morality, in the form of the "Golden Rule," a basis for foreign policy. By defining the Golden Rule as a principle demanding that one take another's viewpoint into account, Wallace gently reiterated his belief that American policy makers ought to consider the Soviet perspective. He also went so far as to call for outlawing atomic weapons altogether, under UNO supervision. For Wallace the atomic era remained a portal to a new age, one of either great human potential or ultimate destruction.[64]

It was on September 12, however, that Wallace finally chose to speak out with the range and force of his July letter in a speech given at Madison Square Garden to a rally of progressive liberals sponsored by ICCASP and the NCPAC. Like NCPAC, ICCASP was founded in 1944 as a means of giving political influence to American artists and scientists. By 1946 it had developed into something of a talent agency, providing movie stars and other celebrities for progressive political drives and public events such as the Madison Square Garden rally. In his speech Wallace touched on many of the issues of international affairs that he had been concerned with for the last several years and, in some cases, decades. He was explicitly critical of both U.S. and Soviet policy. For example, he spoke—to the hissing consternation of the communists and other Soviet sympathizers in the audience—of Russia's "suppression of basic liberties" in Eastern Europe. At the same time, he stated, Americans needed to reject the counsel of those who claimed that Russian communism and the American free enterprise system could not coexist peacefully. He also seemed to depart from his long-held belief in "one world," acknowledging the reality of both American and Soviet spheres of influence, and he repeated his insistence that American leaders should take Russian history into account in formulating national policy. Above all, Wallace asserted, a simple " 'get-tough-with-Russia' policy" would surely fail. With the recent Soviet rejection of the Baruch plan probably in mind, Wallace warned that the "tougher" the United States became the "tougher the Russians will get." [65]

The key for Wallace remained alleviating Soviet fears of the West, convincing the Russians that the United States was not preparing to go to war against them. Once more making cooperation the ultimate goal of international relations, Wallace invoked his old belief that the United States had to practice cooperation if it expected cooperation in return. In this sense it is clear that Wallace had not really let go of his vision of an eventually unified world, for with cooperation would come an easing of tensions, which would engender further cooperation and finally international trust. Ultimately, Wallace predicted, with quintessentially liberal optimism, in an atmosphere of "friendly peaceful competition" the Soviet world and the American world would "gradually become more alike." [66]

The Wallace Controversy

While Wallace was speaking in New York, Secretary of State James Byrnes was in Europe, attending the peace negotiations in Paris and presenting the already hard-line U.S. policy toward the Soviet Union. On September 6 in Stuttgart he gave what his biographer characterizes as a "major get-tough speech" on American policy regarding Germany. In the speech—which must be read in the context of Winston Churchill's influential "Iron Curtain" speech of the previous March— Byrnes announced that the United States and Great Britain intended to merge their zones of occupation in Germany whether or not the Soviet Union was willing to cooperate. Moreover, Byrnes made it quite clear that American occupation forces were to be left in Germany to preempt the possibility of German absorption into Soviet sphere of influence.[67]

The obvious contradiction between the tone and content of Wallace's speech and Byrnes's policy was clear to many, including American journalists who questioned the president about it. Truman's initial response, that Wallace's speech reflected administration policy and that to his mind there was no contradiction between Byrnes's and Wallace's positions, triggered a tremendous public controversy, perhaps the biggest public relations debacle of Truman's presidency. The controversy—both at the time and among historians later—focused on Truman's acknowledgment, when first questioned, that he had read through Wallace's speech before Wallace gave it and had completely approved of it. As the controversy developed, Truman altered his recollection, saying that he only approved of Wallace's right to give the speech. Indeed, after the fact the president claimed only to have glanced at the speech in a brief meeting with Wallace on September 10. In his memoirs Truman actually asserted that he had not read the speech at all, "even in part." Yet, considering the inconsistencies in his own memories of the meeting as well as the questionable reliability that Truman's written recollections demonstrated on other controversial issues, they may not be the best source upon which to assess the historical reality.[68]

In a September 10 diary entry Wallace claimed the president thoroughly read and completely approved of the speech and, to Wallace's mild incredulity, apparently perceived no serious conflict between it and Byrnes's recent policy statements. In an extended discussion of the incident in which they ultimately incline toward Wallace's version of the episode, Wallace biographers Graham White and John Maze suggest that Wallace showed "unusual concern" in getting Truman's approval, which they speculate was an indication he may have been provoking a break with Truman in order to position himself for a run at the presidency on the Democratic ticket in 1948. While this certainly is arguable, it would have been a highly uncharacteristic undertaking for Wallace, and there is no substantial evidence that it was on his mind. Moreover, Wallace's description of thoroughly discussing with Truman a speech he intended to deliver was not actually unusual. There were at least two other instances during the prior year in which Wallace recounted in his diary relatively lengthy, detailed discussions with the president of addresses he was preparing to give. While it is possible that Wallace altered the September 10 diary entry after the fact, it is unlikely that he would have thought to go back and do so in the other two cases. From this we can reasonably infer that Truman read the September 12 speech through with some thoroughness at least and either did not perceive the contradiction with administration policy or, if he did, desired to avoid a confrontation with Wallace. This last possibility is in accord with Wallace's perception of the president as an individual who often expressed complete agreement with two diametrically opposed opinions. Truman, Wallace noted, always seemed "sincere and earnest" and was not at all disturbed by the "different directions in which his mind can go almost instantaneously." [69]

Ultimately, however, the question of how closely Truman read Wallace's speech before its delivery is irrelevant. Whether or not Truman read the speech, by September 12 he certainly must have read through Wallace's letter of July 23 and thus was well aware of the central components of Wallace's thinking on U.S.-Soviet relations. Considering the great similarity of content between the letter and the speech (as well as other expositions of Wallace's thinking, including cabinet discussions in Truman's presence), the speech should only have highlighted the obvious regarding Wallace's views. In light of the course that American policy toward the Soviet Union was taking by late summer 1946, a clear-cut breach between Wallace and the administration was probably bound to occur. In the end Truman seems simply to have bungled his opportunity to control the final break to his own political benefit.

In any case, Byrnes angrily if implicitly insisted on Wallace's resignation by threatening his own. After several days of increasing public embarrassment, Truman asked Wallace to resign. On September 20 Wallace complied, writing to the president that he planned to continue fighting for peace and that he hoped Truman would join him. In a radio address that evening Wallace made clear he had no intention of giving up the struggle for the principles of liberal internationalism that he had so long championed. Once more implying the profound influence the advent of atomic weapons had on his thinking, Wallace reasserted the stark choice he saw before Americans and the rest of humanity, a choice between "life and death for our children and our grandchildren" and perhaps between the "existence and the extinction of man and the world." He insisted that he still believed as he had for years in the principle of "one world" and that there could be no ultimate peace without it. He declared himself opposed to all imperialism, Russian, British, or American, and asserted that the rights of small nations must be taken into account in global affairs. Finally, Wallace concluded by again invoking the Golden Rule, claiming that the degree to which the people of the United States learned to respect the rights of others "as we expect them to respect ours" would determine not just whether all nations eventually would live in one world but whether they would "live at all."[70]

The UDA reacted quickly and strongly to Wallace's ouster, yet in a manner that subtly manifested the nascent rift developing between the group and Wallace. UDA Director James Loeb's personal letter to Wallace, written the day after the latter's resignation, embodied the dilemma of the anticommunist liberals. Loeb made clear his distress at Wallace's ouster from the cabinet and noted how proud he was to have fought hard both for Wallace's confirmation as commerce secretary and alongside Wallace in the full employment campaign. Nevertheless, as he articulated these feelings Loeb also acknowledged his differences with Wallace over aspects of U.S. foreign policy, although he in no sense questioned Wallace's "great personal integrity." Ultimately, Loeb hoped to overcome what he termed a "general confusion in the minds

and hearts" of progressive liberals. Toward this end he expressed the
desire to meet with Wallace and discuss their agreements and differences. He poignantly concluded that he was "earnestly searching
within" himself for answers, trying to develop a balanced understanding
of events.[71]

Much of the sentiment toward Wallace that Loeb articulated was
echoed in the official UDA statement on Wallace's resignation. In
extensively discussed, carefully worded sentences the UDA national
board, like Loeb, acknowledged its strong if qualified support for
Wallace and its sense of the "great loss" that his resignation represented
for American progressives. The statement also was enthusiastic in its
agreement with Wallace's advocacy of one world and a progressive U.S.
foreign economic policy. At the same time the statement implicitly and
explicitly demonstrated the growing areas of disagreement evolving in
liberal internationalist thinking. The board noted, for example, that
Wallace had done a good job of explaining how American policy might
have increased Soviet anxieties but also suggested he had ignored Soviet
policies that raised Western fears. In addition, the UDA statement reasserted the organization's support for the Baruch plan and gently castigated Wallace on some of the specifics of his critique of the plan.[72]

After the UDA board had met and drafted its statement, Loeb once
more wrote Wallace, to inform him of the depth of support he had in
the organization but also with an important proposition connected to
Loeb's own previously expressed hope of meeting with Wallace at some
point. Loeb now suggested that he would like to arrange a meeting
between Wallace and two or three UDA board members, particularly
Niebuhr, who had just returned from Germany. By early October Loeb
was enthusiastic about the possibility, writing that he could think of
nothing "more fruitful" than a meeting between Wallace and Niebuhr,
whom Loeb declared the "two men of greatest personal integrity and
genuine progressivism . . . in American life." With a wholly unintended
irony that in the next two years would reach monumental proportions,
Loeb insisted that a way had to be found in which Wallace and Niebuhr
could reach an accord on American liberalism.[73]

The meeting between Wallace and Niebuhr for which Loeb had
such high expectations never came to pass, however, and it was highly

unlikely that overall agreement, particularly regarding international re-lations, could have been reached between the two men. In part this was due to Niebuhr's response to Wallace's speech and firing, which will be discussed in the next chapter. But the possibility of a meeting of the minds between the two men was unlikely for other, more tran-scendent reasons. By October 1946 much was changing—already had changed—within American political culture as well as within the Amer-ican liberal community. A hard-line policy toward the Soviet Union was in place and was attaining wider and wider acceptance. In addition, the outlines of an image of Wallace as potentially if inadvertently disloyal had been sketched out in the various episodes that had taken place since his removal as Roosevelt's running mate. Moreover, the positions taken by liberals regarding the international control of atomic energy suggest some real division over foreign policy already existed within the liberal community by the time of Wallace's resignation. Liberal attitudes were still in flux when Wallace left the cabinet in September 1946, but not for much longer. The UDA remained supportive of Wallace at the time of his ouster from the cabinet; many of its members and leaders contin-ued to view him as the leading light of American progressive liberalism. Nevertheless, Niebuhr's October response to the Wallace controversy would mark a true hardening of the lines within the liberal community.

8

Hoisting the "Anti-Communist Skull and Bones"

The Liberals Divide

W̲ʜᴇɴ ᴡᴀʟʟᴀᴄᴇ made his speech at Madison Square Garden on September 12, 1946, Niebuhr was in Germany. Niebuhr toured the country for five weeks as a member of a fifteen-person mission, sponsored by the State and War Departments, charged with evaluating the educational system in the American occupation zone. Niebuhr was present when Secretary of State Byrnes spoke in Stuttgart, and his reaction to Wallace's speech arose in part from his perception that the Germans supported Byrnes's hard line. His response to Wallace also issued from what he saw and experienced more generally during his time in Germany. Niebuhr's reaction to Wallace's Madison Square Garden speech precluded any possibility of a meeting such as James Loeb hoped for—in person or of the minds—between the two men. Moreover, Niebuhr's highly visible critique of Wallace's perspective had far-reaching implications for the growing division among American liberals. For one thing, it contributed to the increasingly negative image of Wallace as too tolerant of the Soviets. In addition, it indicated the crystallization of cold war liberalism. In October 1946 what Walter LaFeber called the "Wallace-Niebuhr division" marked the beginning of the final, drawn-out struggle within the American liberal community that ended with Wallace's crushing defeat in the 1948 presidential election.[1] In fall 1946 Niebuhr dramatically and decisively turned against Wallace and the idea of American-Soviet cooperation. By early 1948 many liberals were following his lead.

Niebuhr and "The Fight for Germany"

In late September, as James Loeb was making his tentative efforts to arrange a meeting between Niebuhr and Wallace, Niebuhr wrote a vehement critique of Wallace's speech. The attack was published in the October 21 issue of *Life* magazine as an article entitled "The Fight for Germany." Excerpted in *Time* magazine and eventually reprinted by *Reader's Digest,* with its large, international audience, "The Fight for Germany" was probably the most widely read article of Niebuhr's career.[2] As such it enormously augmented the growing perception of Wallace as soft on the Soviets.

From the outset in the article Niebuhr made clear it was not Wallace's outlook on domestic policy he opposed. Indeed, in the very first sentence Niebuhr insisted that he in fact belonged to Wallace's "school of thought in domestic politics." Rather Niebuhr assailed Wallace's position on U.S.-Soviet relations as expressed in the Madison Square Garden address. Denouncing Wallace's criticism of American policy, Niebuhr declared it dangerous because it would involve the United States in the same "fateful procedure" that led to world war in 1939. Further concessions to the Soviet Union, arising from the "illusions" of the "Wallace attitude," would only increase the likelihood of Soviet success. Not quite accusing Wallace of "appeasement," Niebuhr insisted that Americans ignore Wallace's weak-minded appeals and support the developing U.S. hard line. Thus, as had the Alsop brothers before him in the very same forum, Niebuhr stated his critique of Wallace in the essential terms of cold war liberalism: advocacy of progressive domestic reform policies in conjunction with staunch support for a hard line toward the Soviets, justified by the Munich analog.[3]

The UDA did not initially validate Niebuhr's attack on Wallace, at least not publicly. The November *Bulletin,* for example, summarized "The Fight for Germany" without mentioning Niebuhr's criticism of Wallace. And the same issue prominently touted the UDA's support of Wallace at the time of his firing.[4] Nevertheless, behind the scenes some members were assimilating Niebuhr's assessment. By mid-October, for example, Loeb, although still supportive of Wallace, had become far more critical of his perspective. In response to a letter criticizing

Wallace from the British socialist and Member of Parliament Jennie Lee, Loeb expressed ambivalence. While he insisted that Wallace remained a "fine personality whom I know and love," Loeb nevertheless put much blame on Wallace for the growing division among liberals. Foreshadowing later attacks by himself and other cold war liberals on Wallace as an alleged communist dupe, Loeb declared to Lee that Wallace was "completely naïve," tending to listen to the counsel of the "strangest people."[5]

A central component of Wallace's critique of American policy that Niebuhr attacked in "The Fight for Germany" was the idea that Soviet actions stemmed from reasonable Soviet suspicions of the United States, suspicions derived from American and Western European postwar behavior. While he acknowledged cycles of mutual distrust and admitted the possibility of Western mistakes that might have validated Soviet fears, Niebuhr still argued that the Soviet Union had been "excessively suspicious" during the war, even when receiving massive American aid and even as Roosevelt made "too generous concessions" to Stalin. It was a strange argument for Niebuhr to make, seeming to ignore as it did concurrent wartime policies—such as British and American cooperation with fascists in North Africa and Italy as well as continued hesitation in establishing a full-scale western front—that Niebuhr himself had criticized for potentially undermining Russian trust in the West. Niebuhr's point also ignored the larger context of Soviet–Western European and Soviet-American relations dating back to 1917, which Wallace had explicitly invoked and which might very well have predisposed the Russians to distrust the United States. Niebuhr instead insisted that Soviet fears of the West sprang from the imperatives of Soviet tyranny. Suggesting that he was influenced by the themes of George Kennan's top (but open) secret "Long Telegram" of February, Niebuhr maintained that Soviet suspicions arose from the insecurities of Soviet leaders compelled to demonize the West in order to justify their brutal rule.[6]

Such lacunae lead one to ask what moved Niebuhr in early fall 1946 from the relatively tolerant view he held of the Soviet Union the previous winter to his harsh critique of Wallace's call for moderation toward the Soviets. Clearly his and the UDA's skepticism of Soviet motives and behavior had been building through the year. Nevertheless, one senses in the *Life* article a transitional moment in Niebuhr's outlook, similar to those through which he passed during World War I and in the wake of the Munich crisis of 1938. One possibility is implied by Richard Fox, who notes that while Niebuhr was in Stuttgart experiencing the German reaction to Byrnes's speech he received word that his older brother, Walter, had died suddenly of a heart attack. Niebuhr's relationship with Walter had always been problematic, as the latter's youthful promise devolved over the years into a prodigality from which Niebuhr periodically rescued him. The news of Walter's death impelled Niebuhr into several days of reflection on his father, his father's marked favoritism toward him over Walter during the boys' youth, and Niebuhr's own sense of guilt toward his brother because of that favoritism. Ultimately Niebuhr concluded that because of that guilt as well as his brother's inherent "generosity of spirit," he had generally "erred on the side of leniency rather than severity" with Walter. The implication of Niebuhr's reflections was that greater severity much earlier on might have made a difference in Walter's life. Fox asserts that Niebuhr's conclusion regarding his dealings with Walter "mirrored precisely his thoughts about the Soviets after several weeks in Germany," suggesting that Niebuhr took a lesson from his brother's life and applied it in his interpretation of U.S.-Soviet relations.[7] Yet such a psychological transference, if it did occur in Niebuhr's mind, paralleled the logic of the Munich analog, which Niebuhr long before had fully assimilated into his perspective. That logic of course argued that firmness was more effective in dealing with what could be termed a prodigal nation than were negotiation, compromise, and appeasement, that is, erring on the side of leniency.

It is unlikely, however, that Walter's death alone would have driven Niebuhr to this new, harsh view of Russia. Rather Niebuhr's reflections on Walter's tragic life probably augmented his general reaction to what he saw and heard during his tour of Germany. Suggesting that the old personal dynamic of his ethnicity still informed his social and political outlook, Niebuhr's experience of occupied Germany was itself the driving force behind the marked shift in his commentary on U.S.-Soviet relations during September and October 1946. To correspondents, in fact, Niebuhr wrote that his German tour forced him into a much stronger anti-Soviet position.[8] That assertion was borne out by both the tone and substance of "The Fight for Germany" as well as other articles that Niebuhr wrote upon his return to the United States.

Much that Niebuhr saw in Germany moved him toward a stronger anti-Soviet stance. He recounted widespread tales of Russian machinations and violence in support of German communists, for example. German socialists who resisted Soviet pressures, he insisted, put themselves in "peril of life and liberty." It was not Soviet actions alone that so affected Niebuhr, however. It was also the horrible conditions in which Niebuhr believed the Germans had been placed by both Russian brutality and misguided American policy. "Russian terror," Niebuhr declared, "has cured the Germans of communism," which explained the western Germans' enthusiastic acceptance of American occupation troops, who they viewed as protection against Soviet expansion. Still, if Soviet terror turned the Germans against communism, Western "stupidity," Niebuhr warned, might yet "cure them of attachment to democracy." Western policy undermined the development of a healthy German economy, creating instead an economy of scarcity. Niebuhr wrote of spending a couple of dollars—over six months' wages to a skilled German worker—to purchase candy to pass out to "hungry German children" in the street.[9] To Niebuhr it appeared that the Germans were once more besieged by dreadful social and economic conditions forced upon them by the shortsightedness of Western capitalism.

As he did in the 1920s, Niebuhr in 1946 cast the German people's battle for survival in terms of a universal human struggle against the ravages of modern, urban-industrial society. He again described in desperate and depressing imagery the circumstances in which the German people found themselves after the end of a world war. He wrote of the still pervasive physical effects of war, of abysmally low levels of German industrial production, of severely overcrowded living conditions, and of the "misery of hunger" and its attendant "diseases of malnutrition" from which many Germans suffered. Above all, Niebuhr decried the general economic paralysis preventing Germans from gaining relief from such problems.[10]

Throughout Niebuhr's discussion of postwar Germany there was a tragic tone, sympathetic to the Germans. In Niebuhr's remarks of fall 1946, similar to his earlier discussion of total war, one perceives a strong inclination to forgive the German people, whom he clearly differentiated from the Nazis. It was important, he argued, to preserve a sense of compassion for the "millions" of Germans "unwittingly" complicit in Nazi crimes. Niebuhr insisted that the Germans themselves had loathed Nazism even before they knew of all its horrors and that they fully supported the Allies' punishment of the Nazis, sometimes finding such punishments not harsh enough. Yet he feared that the West, led by the United States, might mete out punishment without discretion, inflicting upon the German people retribution that went beyond righteousness to injustice.[11]

Niebuhr's concerns regarding the dire postwar circumstances of the German people led him not only to his critique of Wallace but also to suggestions for ameliorating those circumstances. This was where American policy had failed, he contended, yet not for the reasons Wallace articulated. It was not a matter of being more tolerant of the Soviets. Rather, the United States needed to recognize that Germany was not going to be reunited because Russia would not allow it, which meant it was time to resurrect western Germany alone. Niebuhr thus called for reestablishing trade between western Germany and the West as well as for what he termed "pump priming" by the United States (foreshadowing the logic of the Marshall Plan): U.S. financial assistance to help Germany rebuild its industrial base.[12]

Niebuhr acknowledged the criticism that communists as well as "honest liberals" would make, that such policies on the part of the United States would undermine the role of the United Nations Organization. To Niebuhr this was a false concern that ignored what to him was obvious: the UNO already was failing because there was no unanimity among the great powers. Niebuhr now rejected the logic of preponderant power he had constructed during the war and with it any real hope for cooperation between America and the Soviet Union. Echoing Kennan's argument for "containment," Niebuhr declared that the United States henceforth had to preserve global peace by a policy of both "firmness and patience" toward the Soviets. Above all the nation could not afford to "yield to Russian pressure point by point." Manifesting the intertwining within his perspective of containment doctrine and the Munich analog, Niebuhr insisted that such surrenders would make war "the more inevitable" for having tried "too desperately to avert it."[13]

Giving up on his always skeptical hope for U.S.-Soviet cooperation implied a greater change in Niebuhr's thought, however, than just the rejection of the principle of preponderant power. It indicated another momentous shift in his thinking, analogous in scope to his acceptance after Munich of the possibility of the relative morality of nations. In the closing paragraphs of "The Fight for Germany" Niebuhr once more pointed out the irony of national behavior, specifically asserting that America was "not really good enough" for this struggle against the Soviet Union. He even suggested that it was this realization that motivated individuals like Wallace. Nevertheless, he argued, such scruples could not form the basis for foreign policy when facing an opponent who exploited trust and compromise. As in 1938 Niebuhr concluded that the United States and the West once again confronted the distinction between "relative justice and tyranny." While he acknowledged that there had once been "more creative elements in Communism than in Nazism," he concluded that something evil had issued from communism despite its original ideals. From Marxism's "illusions" had risen a tyranny and "fanatic fury" that were indistinguishable from the "purer paganism and cynicism" of Nazism.[14]

Having confronted the realization, after 1938, that the nation of his own origins had visited the greatest imaginable evil upon the world, Niebuhr now shifted the locus of global malignancy to another nation. In a way that transference might have rescued Niebuhr's logic of the early 1930s by implying that Germany had simply been one more example, albeit an extreme one, of the inherent immorality of nations. But one senses that this was not the case in Niebuhr's transformation of 1946. In characterizing the Soviet Union as an embodiment of human evil he was not so much demonstrating a larger principle as moving the focus of his vilification from one nation to another. Doing so made it easier for Niebuhr, and for cold war liberals generally, to accept the Germans back into the circle of humanity.

Although the UDA did not wholly support Niebuhr's critique of

Wallace, the organization fully accepted his assessment of American policy regarding Germany. By fall 1946 West German economic recovery became an important concern of the UDA. Indeed, an essential component of that concern was foreshadowed even before Germany's defeat, in spring 1945 when the UDA foreign policy committee released a statement regarding German industrialists and the control of the postwar German economy. The statement was a clear manifestation of the liberal internationalist fear of resurgent fascism as embodied by international cartels. The UDA warned the American public that it would be quite simple for prewar and wartime German industrialists to reestablish their dominance because of the persistence of "international cartel agreements." The UDA hoped that Allied military authorities would see offers of cooperation made by "Nazi industrialists" for what they were: part of a "pre-arranged plan to be followed in case of a German defeat." The statement asserted that in Germany there was not a "single industrialist [alive] who is not Nazi-minded." To return power to such individuals, once the regime that they so crucially supported had been destroyed, would be the ultimate betrayal of the Allied war effort and might lead to another world war.[15]

In October 1946, when the British cabinet recommended to the Council of Foreign Ministers that German heavy industry be socialized under international supervision, the UDA's fear of resurgent fascism led the group wholeheartedly to support the British recommendation. In letters to Secretary of State Byrnes and President Truman the UDA insisted that the British proposal was necessary in establishing a "stable Germany in a peaceful Europe" and preventing the renewal of German militarism. While Americans might validly argue for the merits of a free enterprise economy at home, to Niebuhr and the UDA such an alternative was not viable in war-devastated Europe. If U.S. policy insisted upon complete free enterprise in Germany it would only mean the return to power of the industrialists behind the "Nazi war machine," and that in turn would mean the defeat of all hopes for European democracy at the hands of revitalized European fascism.[16]

Of course, cold war liberal concerns with German economic recovery in fall 1946 also were intertwined with the perceived threat of communist totalitarianism. Indeed, acceptance of the belief that a resurrected western Germany would strengthen western Europe against communist incursion marked the UDA's assimilation of Niebuhr's conceptual transposing of international evil from Germany to the Soviet Union. By late November the UDA's leadership had come to believe that postwar expectations of cooperation between the Soviet Union and the Western democracies had been "too rosily optimistic." While this did not mean that war was now inevitable, the German situation indicated the necessity of preventing the Soviets from establishing a "monolithic, totalitarian" world ruled by Moscow.[17] In the UDA's view failure to revive western Germany would be to allow the Nazi dream of a European empire to come to pass, but as a communist empire ruled by Soviet dictators. The metaphorical transfer of evil was complete.

For the UDA the appropriate course was clear. Beyond the resurrection of German industry under international guidance, Niebuhr and his colleagues also believed that West Germany had to be integrated into a larger European economic community. Implying more residual optimism regarding international organization than Niebuhr maintained alone, the UDA argued for the establishment within the UNO of an "Economic Council for Europe." Prefiguring the Marshall Plan, the group argued for a U.S. loan policy—"pump-priming," as Niebuhr had already termed it—that would promote such federation. The UDA concluded that the recovery of western Germany within an integrated Europe would halt Russian expansion. Once more invoking the logic of containment doctrine (and presaging as well that of the Truman Doctrine), Niebuhr and the UDA declared that by halting Soviet expansion and weakening the strength of "monolithic power blocs operating in all countries as Communist parties," the West might compel Soviet cooperation.[18]

Wallace and Bernard Baruch

As Niebuhr and a still somewhat ambivalent UDA articulated a more antagonistic view of the Soviet Union, Wallace was beginning the process of establishing a role for himself outside government for the first time in more than a dozen years. Having declared upon his resignation his intention of continuing the fight for cooperative internationalism, he chose to do so by returning to journalism. In October 1946 he accepted the editorship of the *New Republic,* a position that would serve as a bully pulpit from which he could battle the forces of cold war intolerance. Yet even before the announcement of his new role Wallace was caught up in yet another controversy. This time it was with the U.S. representative to the UN Atomic Energy Commission, Bernard Baruch, whose atomic policy machinations Wallace had condemned in the months just preceding his ouster from the cabinet. Like earlier episodes, this one in its larger contexts served both to highlight the growing division within American liberalism and to intensify the increasingly negative view that cold war liberals held of Wallace.

Wallace's troubles with Baruch stemmed from the latter's reaction to the publication, at the time of Wallace's firing, of Wallace's July 23 letter to Truman on U.S.-Soviet relations. On September 24 Baruch had sent a lengthy memorandum to the president attacking the criticisms Wallace had made in the letter of Baruch's plan for international control of atomic energy. Baruch's complaints led to an ultimately heated public exchange with Wallace during the first week of October that was powerfully reminiscent in form and tone of the wartime struggle between Wallace and Jesse Jones. As he had with Jones, Wallace made an attempt at reconciliation with Baruch, agreeing to meet with him to discuss their differences. After the meeting Wallace admitted he had erred in criticizing Baruch's proposal for transitional stages. Wallace agreed that, contrary to his earlier criticism, Baruch in fact had proposed that the stages be laid out in the treaty with a timetable in place from the outset of the transition process. Wallace even offered to make a public statement in which he acknowledged this error as well as what he considered other points of accord with Baruch. But in a draft version of the statement, read over the telephone to a Baruch associate, Wallace maintained other criticisms of Baruch's plan, specifically on the issues of whether or not the United States should continue stockpiling atomic weapons during the transition period and how to address Soviet security concerns, particularly as they were manifested in the Russian rejection of the proposed international inspection mechanisms.[19]

Because he was unwilling to make a blanket retraction of all of his criticisms of Baruch's plan, Wallace's hopes for a rapprochement proved unfounded. Baruch responded to Wallace's unpublished draft release with a very public and rather personal attack at a press conference reported in detail at the top of the front page of the *New York Times*. With Manhattan Project director General Leslie Groves as well as the other members of the U.S. atomic energy delegation arrayed dramatically behind him, Baruch insisted to the assembled reporters that at their meeting Wallace had admitted to being misinformed about American atomic policy and had agreed to issue a statement "indicating the mistakes" in his July letter and "expressing agreement with the American position." Then, ignoring the existence of the draft letter Wallace had read over the telephone, Baruch declared that for some reason Wallace had changed his mind about issuing the statement. To cap off his presentation, Baruch released a collection of documents pertinent to the controversy, which included Wallace's July letter, his own September 24 memorandum to Truman, as well as, rather impoliticly, copies of both his and Wallace's draft reconciliation statements. During the course of the press conference Baruch asserted several times that Wallace had done considerable damage to U.S. efforts in ongoing atomic energy negotiations. Wallace's actions, he maintained, were not only "gravely dangerous to the negotiations now under way" but also created "confusion and division" among the American people.[20]

Angered by Baruch's public petulance, Wallace released a statement giving his own version of the controversy. He suggested that Baruch had dealt duplicitously with him throughout, first by trying to coerce him into a blanket retraction of his criticisms, then by publicly lying about Wallace's reneging on such a retraction, and finally by selectively releasing draft statements that were not intended for public scrutiny. Wallace claimed that in neither his September 24 memorandum nor in his attack on Wallace in the *Times* had Baruch grappled with the "serious points of disagreement" existing within the UN Atomic Energy Commission. Baruch, Wallace declared, seemed oblivious to the already existent atomic arms race. Rather than settling the turmoil Baruch's grandstanding had only increased public confusion on the issues. Wallace's barely implicit point was that it was not himself but Baruch who had placed international negotiations and thus global security in

jeopardy. After reiterating what he viewed as his essential points of contention with Baruch, Wallace insisted that the ultimate concern remained not with the procedural issues that Baruch focused upon but
rather with the necessity of overcoming the "absence of attitudes of
mutual trust and confidence between the United States and Russia."
This was a concern that Wallace believed Baruch had completely failed
to address in every forum since presenting his plan back in June.[21]

There was a concurrent controversy over the Baruch plan, related
to the Wallace-Baruch fight, that probably augmented Baruch's anger
toward Wallace and that also illustrated the growing division within liberal ranks. This was an attack on Baruch's atomic energy plan made at a
meeting held in late September in Chicago by a coalition of liberal and
labor organizations—including CIO-PAC, NCPAC, and ICCASP—
known as the Conference of Progressives. In a postconference statement
the group commended the administration for its acknowledgment of
the need for international control of atomic energy but then explicitly
criticized the Baruch plan on the issue of transitional stages, just as
Wallace had. In fact the language of the statement on this point was
a direct paraphrase of the pertinent section of Wallace's July 23 letter
to Truman. Moreover, in the wake of the Wallace-Baruch dispute the
group's leadership retracted its criticism of Baruch just to the extent
that Wallace had retracted his own. And they continued to maintain a
Wallace-like critique of other aspects of Baruch's proposal, particularly
on the issue of the continued U.S. manufacture of atomic bombs and
its potential for undermining U.S.-Soviet trust.[22]

Baruch responded to the group's criticism with a scathing telegram
sent to former interior secretary and current executive chairman of
ICCASP Harold Ickes, CIO president Philip Murray, and former treasury secretary Henry Morgenthau Jr., all of whom spoke at the conference. The turmoil intensified when Ickes broke ranks on the issue, news
of which also made the pages of the *Times*. Having opposed the statement attacking Baruch in a speech at the Chicago meeting, Ickes told
reporters that he was "pretty damn sore" that the executive committee
of the conference had passed it when he was not present. He made clear
he was fully in favor of the U.S. atomic energy plan as presented by
Baruch, and he attacked Soviet atomic-energy proposals, in terms similar to those of Niebuhr and the UDA, as "childish" and unrealistic. In

addition, Ickes—who had an often competitive and tense relationship with Wallace during their years together in Roosevelt's cabinet—declared that he was deeply troubled by the appearance that the statement created of "tieing [*sic*] the conference to the kite of Henry Wallace." Ickes in fact suggested that the passage of the statement had somehow been machinated by Wallace associates.[23] It was a suggestion that prefigured similar attacks made in 1948 regarding alleged communist intrigues within the Progressive Party, of which the Conference of Progressives was a direct precursor.

Despite Wallace's forthright self-defense against Baruch and the backing of many members of the Conference of Progressives, it is unlikely that he was able to salvage more than a moral victory from the entire Baruch episode. By October 1946 Wallace was already facing too many overwhelming factors. One was the prestige Baruch enjoyed from his combined public images as a quintessentially American self-made industrial millionaire and a statesman. Another was that the episode coincided with the publication of Niebuhr's highly critical article in *Life* magazine. A third was public memory of the attacks, however unfair, made on Wallace the year before regarding the issue of sharing atomic energy information. And perhaps the most important factor was the already high level of intolerance toward the Soviets both within and outside of government, along with the associated fear of atomic bombs. In light of such circumstances the controversy between Wallace and Baruch unquestionably hastened the deterioration of Wallace's public image.

The PCA and the ADA

By December, after the dust from his conflict with Baruch had settled, Wallace took up his duties at the *New Republic*. As he did so, the disarray within the American liberal community that Loeb had lamented came to a crucial culmination. Between December 28, 1946, and January 4, 1947, the growing division among liberals was institutionalized in the founding of two new liberal organizations, the popular front Progressive Citizens of America (PCA) and the cold war liberal Americans for Democratic Action (ADA).

The PCA arose out of the evolving cooperation between NCPAC and ICCASP as well as, initially, CIO-PAC. By early 1946 the three groups, especially ICCASP and NCPAC, were pursuing many of the same social, political, and economic goals. Indeed, recognizing their shared aims, in May the three organizations formed a "Coordinating Committee" to mobilize progressive energies for the 1946 campaign season. The leadership of NCPAC and ICCASP decided officially to merge their organizations in November and did so at a two-day conference held in Washington, D.C., on December 28–29, 1946, culminating in the establishment of the PCA. The conference was attended by some three hundred delegates from twenty-one states drawn primarily from the membership of the three groups that formed the coordinating committee back in May. PCA's provenance was clear, its founding principles derived directly from positions taken during the previous year by both the coordinating committee and the Conference of Progressives. PCA bylaws and the group's initial public declarations enunciated all of the standard progressive positions: advocacy of social, economic, and political reforms including full employment; extension of the franchise; an end to racial discrimination; and the safeguarding of the economy from the excesses of monopoly capital. They also vaguely promised to "strive for a just and enduring peace throughout the world."[24]

The new organization's leaders were drawn from the leadership of the groups that lay behind its creation, and no one, including communists, was excluded from membership. The initial leadership cohort included individuals such as the sculptor Jo Davidson and the Broadway public relations lawyer Hannah Dorner of ICCASP, the liberal political organizers C. B. "Beanie" Baldwin and Frank Kingdon of NCPAC, as well as labor leaders such as A. F. Whitney (Brotherhood of Railway Trainmen). It was Wallace, however, speaking on the conference's final day, who was clearly PCA's leader, in spirit if not yet officially. His speech that day, along with his first column written as editor of the *New Republic* and published two weeks earlier, can be viewed as a manifesto for the PCA. In both an appeal for unity and a denial of division among progressives, Wallace contended in his address that the "fundamental progressive faith" was broad enough that it ought not be divided by what he termed "minor issues." Ignoring the increasing tendency of cold war liberals to reject policies aimed at international cooperation, he declared that the essence of American liberalism was a belief in "peace, prosperity, and freedom in one world." In the editorial Wallace made clear that by "one world" he meant the globally shared abundance that he had called for since the first months after American entry into the war.[25]

In both his speech to the PCA and the *New Republic* article Wallace attempted to resolve the issue that lay at the heart of the division within the liberal community—cooperation with communists at home and abroad—by reducing it to simplistic terms. He argued that those individuals who prioritized "hatred of Russia" did not "believe in peace," while those who held the Soviet Union up as a model for the United States did not "believe in freedom." In the domestic context Wallace analogously criticized conservatives who believed that full employment was unattainable in a free, peaceful society and leftists willing to sacrifice freedom "for the sake of jobs and peace." For Wallace the liberal split arose from the efforts of both reactionary anticommunists and communists to lead astray true, global-cooperation-favoring liberals. The danger for American progressives, he insisted, was in getting caught up in a conflict between the "Russian haters and the Russophiles." What he seemed not to realize, or perhaps hoped to transcend, was that by late 1946, while the number of American progressives who could be termed "Russophiles" were few, many were well on the way to becoming "Russian haters."[26]

This oversimplification of the liberal split was intertwined with the popular front outlook of Wallace and his noncommunist liberal colleagues in the PCA. That outlook held that infighting among liberals over the nation's stance toward the Soviet Union was not only unnecessary but in fact was driven by influences outside the liberal community. As Wallace put it in his address to the PCA founding convention, such internecine strife was "engineered by the enemy." And while it is true that Wallace did lay some blame for liberal division at the feet of American communists and fellow travelers, they were not the enemy of which he warned. The real enemy, Wallace suggested, made the communists out as the main threat and manipulated progressives into attacking one another. For Wallace and the popular front liberals of the

PCA, the real enemy of American liberalism, and so of the nation itself, remained big business and its "special pleaders" in journalism and politics. Foreshadowing warnings during the next decade regarding the advent of what would be termed the "military-industrial complex," Wallace maintained that it was large corporations and their supporters in the military that portrayed militarism as the path to peace and prosperity for the United States. In its initial public statement the PCA declared that the U.S. government had "fallen to men of shocking bigotry and striking ignorance." Such men, the document declared, were motivated by the "same stupid arrogance that brought the nation to its knees fifteen years ago." "Spokesmen of monopoly," such men were ready to "sacrifice the welfare of the many to the power of the few." In the view of Wallace and the PCA, in other words, the great danger to American progressivism arose out of the sources of potential domestic fascism that they as well as the cold war liberals had decried since the 1930s. While the cold war liberals focused on communists and the Soviet Union as their new collective enemy, the popular fronters maintained their focus on a potentially resurgent fascist threat.[27]

Connected to Wallace's oversimplification of the liberal divide in December 1946 was an overdrawn optimism regarding the potential for change within the Soviet Union. In the same sense in which Wallace implied that the American Left's willingness to sacrifice freedom for equality was a redeemable flaw, he believed Soviet leaders were slowly becoming democratic. Acknowledging the exaggeration in the Russians' claim that their society was one of complete equality, he nevertheless viewed that claim as a real challenge to the United States. America had to face that challenge squarely, Wallace believed, by overcoming the flaws in its own democracy, by criminalizing racial discrimination and placing reasonable controls upon big business, for example. When Americans fulfilled their nation's ideals then the Russians would be impelled toward greater political freedom in their society.[28] Compromise at home, in other words, would induce cooperation from the Soviet Union internationally.

On January 4, 1947, a week after the PCA founding convention, a second convention met in Washington, D.C., completing the process of institutionalizing the split in American liberalism. Orchestrated by Loeb and the UDA, the one-day meeting establishing the ADA was a smaller affair than the PCA's had been, attended by some 150 invited individuals. That number included most of the leading members of the UDA as well as many prestigious figures associated with American labor and with the New Deal. These included, among others, Niebuhr, Loeb, Alfred Baker Lewis, and Ethel Epstein of the UDA; Walter Reuther of the CIO and David Dubinsky of the International Ladies' Garment Workers' Union; Eleanor Roosevelt and her son Franklin D. Roosevelt Jr. as well as New Deal officials Elmer Davis, Isador Lubin, and Leon Henderson. Also present were economist John Kenneth Galbraith and historian (and UDA member) Arthur M. Schlesinger Jr.[29]

Not surprisingly, there were many similarities between the positions initially articulated by the ADA and those of the PCA. The ADA founders announced their support for the expansion of New Deal social reforms as well as for the protection of civil liberties in a context of economic democracy. In terms that Wallace might have used they insisted on a progressive program that would ensure the political freedom necessary for the attainment of "economic security and greater opportunity for human development." Manifesting the same liberal fear of domestic protofascism that was apparent in Wallace and the PCA's statements, the ADA insisted that this meant preventing "aggregations of economic power" from overwhelming the power of government to "serve the general welfare." And just as Wallace in his speech at the PCA convention had suggested the need for liberals to avoid being influenced by extremists from either end of the political spectrum, an ADA press release asserted that the new organization also "rejected any alliance with totalitarian forces of the Left or Right." There was also apparent agreement in a broad sense over foreign policy. Like the PCA, the ADA made clear their opposition to U.S. policies that had the effect of supporting "fascist or semi-fascist forces" internationally. They also agreed on the need for economic policies that would raise the standard of living around the globe. Initially, the ADA even seemed to open the door to cooperation with the Soviet Union. A foreign policy statement discussed during the conference argued that if the Soviets really were "benevolently concerned" with the workers of the world, then they ought to welcome American policies that supported political and economic democracy in Europe. Yet the door was opened only a crack: the ADA also implied that if the Soviets rejected a U.S. policy that American liberals viewed as progressive, it would prove that Russian policy was only the expression of totalitarianism.[30] For the ADA, American interpretation of American policies was the standard for judging the Soviet Union's behavior.

Despite both the real and apparent similarities between the two groups' initial positions, there were crucial differences from the outset. The founders of the ADA, for example, were much more torn over the question of forming a third party than were the PCA and Wallace, whose statements in December implied the likelihood of such a course of action. At the ADA conference the majority seemed inclined to remain within the confines of the Democratic party. Schlesinger and Eleanor Roosevelt, for example, argued for working within the Democratic party, forgoing any third-party movement. Yet other participants in the meeting, including Loeb, felt that the best way to transform the Democratic Party was to stand outside it, using the promise of ADA support as a lever to move the Democrats in a progressive direction. Steven Gillon asserts that the dilemma over the proper relationship with the Democratic Party dogged the ADA throughout its history.[31]

Liberals, Communists, and the Soviet Union

The third-party issue, however, was not the main source of disagreement between the PCA and the ADA. The fundamental source of division, obvious to all by January 1947, was of course the debate over cooperation with communists and fellow travelers at home and the Soviet Union abroad. The PCA implicitly had taken the popular front stance by not denying membership to communists and by focusing its animosity on protofascism and fascism. The ADA, conversely, built on the legacy of the UDA's founding in 1941, establishing itself as staunchly anticommunist. Still, there was some debate at the ADA founding conference over the issue. If the outcome was foregone it was not clear-cut. The brief allusion in the foreign policy statement to the possibility of U.S.-Soviet cooperation in Europe suggests this. In addition, quite a few of the participants did articulate the long-standing liberal concern with the potential resurgence of fascism, suggesting that they were not focused solely on a communist threat. Indeed, some believed it necessary that the organization live up to its professed opposition to all forms of totalitarianism. In a related sense others worried that the new organization would become too much associated with anticommunism rather than progressive reform, which all believed to be the essence of their new organization. The labor leader Walter Reuther insisted that the new organization had to "stand for something positive" and avoid being characterized only as an anticommunist group. Eleanor Roosevelt also sensed the danger in the manner in which the ADA was thinking itself into existence. Despite the insistence by some present at the meeting that the ADA oppose fascism as strongly as it did communism, Roosevelt believed that the discussion actually indicated that the majority did not "fear fascism as much as . . . communism." In an unintended and ironic validation of the PCA's position, she pointed out that European countries, conversely, feared fascism more. They did not, she asserted, "understand our neglect to fear fascism."[32]

Later in January Loeb sent a long letter to the *New Republic* heralding the formation of the new organization, a letter that unconsciously displayed the ADA position toward communism in all of its complex and at times tortured logic. The establishment of the ADA was both a "counter-attack" against conservatism and a "declaration of independence" from communist influence. That independence, he insisted, was not for purposes of political expediency; that is, this was not about avoiding the "political kiss-of-death" of being associated with communism (although Loeb and the UDA had certainly reacted strongly to that kiss when it was bestowed by the Dies Committee during the war). Nor did the ADA's rejection of the popular front arise from fear of communist seizure of political power in the United States, a mentality Loeb associated with the witch hunters of HUAC. Nor even did the ADA's refusal to admit communists and fellow travelers derive from a rigid "anti-Sovietism," as Loeb predicted that communists and their sympathizers would claim. The ADA's rejection of communists, according to Loeb, expressed rather the "painfully-acquired conviction" of American progressives that they simply could not work with communists.[33]

In a sense Loeb's assertion got at the heart of the matter for the cold war liberals of the ADA. But there was more behind their unwillingness to consort with communists than Loeb's oversimplified explanation suggested. Cold war liberal obstinacy regarding communists dated back to before the founding of the UDA. It dated, in fact, to the disgust American liberals and noncommunist leftists had felt in summer 1939 when many American communists had supported the Nazi-Soviet pact that enabled Germany to begin the war. That disgust only deepened when those same communists swung back to support of the Western Allies after Germany invaded the Soviet Union in 1941. And it was still evident in the UDA's attack on the Win-the-Peace conference in spring 1946. At that time Loeb had written (in another letter to the *New Republic*) that all communists believed, first, that international tensions were caused exclusively by the Western democracies and, second, that "human freedom" was subordinate to "economic security" as a social-political goal. Because of this, he argued, American progressives could not "work *within the same political organizations*" with communists and had to abandon hope for a viable united front. Illuminatingly, Loeb suggested more completely in this earlier letter why this was so. Evoking old American stereotypes of steely eyed, unrelenting political radicals and subversives, he explained that communists were "more active, more consecrated, more zealous" than the liberals who joined them. In comparison most liberals were politically inexperienced and ignorant individuals (the exceptions implicitly being Loeb and his colleagues) who brought little more than a naive, enthusiastic idealism to the political organizations they joined. Foreshadowing ADA political rhetoric of 1948, Loeb implied that the admixture of the hardened communist cadres and the starry-eyed liberal neophytes was one that led inexorably to either the duping or disillusionment of the latter.[34] Cold war liberals such as Loeb, in other words, had long been deeply skeptical of the possibility of liberals and communists working together because they believed that communists could not labor sincerely for the principles of American progressivism and that most liberals lacked the political insight and hardness of will to overcome the wily communists' machinations.

Interestingly, the communist-exclusion issue also had been raised within both the ICCASP and the NCPAC in the weeks before the formation of the PCA but with a very different outcome. In November 1946, for example, ICCASP member Morris Cooke had written chairman Jo Davidson of his belief that the new organization must disassociate itself completely from foreign influence, particularly from "American *Communism* and American *Communists.*" To not do so would expose the new group to conservative Red-baiting. Cooke, like the ADA's founders, believed it possible to oppose communists at home—because of both their ideology and the assumption of Soviet control—while still working for real cooperation with the Soviet Union in international affairs. Similarly, at the last NCPAC steering committee meeting prior to the PCA founding convention, committee member Jerome Udell, after noting his longtime sympathy for the "Russian experiment," called for the proposed PCA bylaws to be altered in such fashion as to declare unequivocally that the organization was not communist and that its members owed their allegiance only to the United States. Udell was opposed by several individuals for a range of reasons that partially prefigured the debate that took place the following month at the founding of the ADA. Some NCPAC steering committee members were explicitly unconcerned about allowing communists to participate in the organization. Others believed that Udell's declaration would weaken progressive support for cooperation with the Soviet Union by attacking an ideology that many associated with that nation. Still others worried that Udell's proposal would only benefit conservatives by creating unnecessary divisions on the Left or by giving the new group an image of standing only for "negative" policies rather than constructive progressive reform.[35] In the end proposals such as Cooke's and Udell's were driven from the field as the founders of the PCA chose to make no anticommunist declarations and to exclude no one from their membership rolls.

The idea that all domestic communists were bound to the dictates of Moscow was raised and dispensed with, if not resolved, in the discussions leading to the formation of the popular front PCA. It became a central assumption, however, of the cold war liberal outlook as it was embodied by the ADA. Yet it belied another component of that outlook, one repeatedly asserted in early 1947: that the rejection of domestic communists did not imply an equivalent animosity toward the Soviet Union. In fact, the cold war liberals' image of American communists as no more than a Soviet fifth column effectively precluded any complete distinction between domestic anticommunism and anti-Sovietism. Some at the initial ADA meeting understood this. Louis Fischer, for example, believed it impossible to "separate the question of communism from Russia." With the logic of Munich implicit, Fischer declared that the United States was engaged in a "clear, ideological war" with the Soviets that had the potential, should America lose it, of turning into a real war. For Fischer and like-minded members of the ADA, the nation's struggle was with the Soviet Union all over the world, not just with American communists, and it was a struggle demanding immediate political and perhaps economic confrontation if military confrontation was to be avoided.[36]

The appearance of balance—that is, an articulated opposition to both fascism and communism in combination with the implication of the possibility of American-Soviet cooperation—in the initial foreign-policy statement of the ADA was false. It was overwhelmed by the absolute rejection of any association with domestic communists. If finding common ground with communists on any issue was impossible and Russia embodied communism, then it followed that there could be no cooperation with Russia. The liberals of the PCA continued to fear fascism and to hope for cooperation with the Soviet Union; this allowed them to associate with communists and sympathizers at home, or at least not to assume the impossibility of doing so. The individuals who met to create the ADA feared communism more than fascism and made anticommunism a touchstone for membership in their organization. In this sense they compelled their own anti-Sovietism. These points may seem obvious, even trite, a half-century after the fact. Yet they are worth stating nonetheless. For this was the historical juncture in which still amorphous if already widely held attitudes began crystallizing into the bedrock assumptions of American cold war political culture. This is when American liberals of both stripes made the crucial choices that underpinned their respective roles in the cold war.

The Popular Front Liberals and the Truman Doctrine

The period immediately following the founding of the PCA and ADA brought a lull in the hostilities between the two factions. But the peace was merely apparent, lasting only until an issue arose over which the two groups could take up the struggle in earnest. President Truman provided just such a focus in an address to Congress on March 12, 1947, proposing $400 million in military and economic aid for the governments of Greece and Turkey. He justified the proposal in terms that became known as the Truman Doctrine, a Manichaean conceptualization of global affairs implying that the repressive right-wing regimes of Greece and Turkey had become the bulwark of democracy on the front line of a new world struggle against communist totalitarianism.

For Wallace and the PCA, Truman's proposal offered a clear example of all they feared from the United States' hard line. Thus in a barrage of attacks on the Truman Doctrine, some of which he made during a speaking tour of England in April, Wallace articulated many of the concerns regarding American policy that he had raised since 1945, along with some new ones. On virtually every point the PCA was in complete agreement. Above all, Wallace and the PCA believed that Truman had trumped up a false crisis in order to frighten the American people into supporting what Wallace described as a "down payment" on eventually limitless expenditures aimed at opposing communist expansion all over the world. He made "unsupported assertions" of imminent danger against a background of "sermonizing and exhortation," all aimed at creating a sense of panic that would ensure congressional and public support for the policy. Truman's policy, Wallace and the PCA contended, created fear and panic when "patience, sympathy and understanding were needed." It initiated a crusade rather than diplomacy and cooperation.[37]

Another great danger, in the popular front view, was that the Truman Doctrine also would initiate dangerous domestic policies as the fear of a ubiquitous communist threat grew. In this regard Wallace and his associates in the PCA once more exhibited the liberal fear of American protofascism. They worried that the hysteria generated by Truman's speech would make far more likely the rise of something like a police state in America. This concern seemed to be borne out only ten days after Truman's speech, when the president issued an executive order creating the Federal Employee Loyalty Program (FELP), which authorized all federal agencies and departments to establish "loyalty boards" to investigate and judge the loyalty of all their employees. The problem was not the desire to rid the government of disloyal persons, which Wallace and many in the PCA viewed as entirely valid. Rather it was that the president had put in place a loyalty program without objective guidelines for determining who was or was not loyal. Just as ambiguous as the Truman Doctrine, Wallace believed, the FELP was a "violation of the fundamental safeguards of Anglo-Saxon justice," made possible by the mood of panic the president had created.[38]

There was another sense, however, in which Wallace and the popular front liberals saw the danger of fascism inherent in the Truman Doctrine. They believed that the specific bill proposed by Truman offered U.S. support to two repressive, militaristic regimes. The Greek government terrorized its own people, and the Turkish government, no less repressive, had refused to join the wartime fight against fascism, rendering it effectively a fascist fellow traveler. With the false representation of Greece and Turkey as bastions of democracy as the context, Wallace and the PCA further worried that the vague, open-ended quality of the Truman Doctrine would lead other reactionary regimes to the American trough. Fascist leaders everywhere could simply "hoist the anticommunist skull and bones" and then demand American aid.[39]

Besides fostering fascism at home and abroad, Wallace and the members of the PCA believed the Truman Doctrine undermined the possibility of a normalization of relations with the Soviet Union in two essential ways. First, it was likely to amplify Soviet fears of the United States. When Truman proclaimed a global struggle between East and West, Wallace and his supporters in the PCA imagined the Soviets would interpret it as a foreshadowing of war. American intervention "on the side of fascism" while testing atomic bombs and conducting war maneuvers around the globe would only amplify Soviet fears, virtually compelling them to arm themselves. Second, Wallace and the PCA argued, support of repressive governments actually benefited communism. Populations being repressed by fascist regimes, popular front logic suggested, were the most likely to undertake communist revolution, meaning that Truman's anticommunist policy could augment the spread of communism rather than deter it. In the end, as America became associated with reaction rather than progressive change, it would become the "most hated nation in the world."[40]

Wallace did not oppose the idea of American foreign aid per se, even foreign aid given for the purpose of preventing the spread of communism. His critique of the Truman Doctrine during spring 1947 was not a frontal assault on all of Truman's aims but rather the presentation of what he viewed as a reasonable alternative. American money, under proper supervision, should fund only "relief supplies" not "military loans," and there should be no support for "undemocratic governments." U.S. dollars were to be used only for butter, not guns, and then only in nations that actually fit American liberal expectations regarding representative government. In addition, Wallace contended, American aid to Greece, or any other nation trying to build or rebuild its economy, should flow through international agencies such as the United Nations. Indeed, one of Wallace and the PCA's strongest criticisms of the Truman Doctrine was that its unilateralism seriously undermined the UN, which for them still embodied the best hope for global cooperation.[41]

Themes from Wallace's past echoed in his discussion of specific sorts of assistance that he deemed appropriate for nations like Greece. At this moment of renewed world crisis, he still believed, America could lead the way into the New Age. He wrote of making loans to Greece only if they were part of "an over-all program of rehabilitation and reconstruction" supervised by American economic planners. In the end what Wallace proposed for Greece was in effect a globalized New Deal in both its agricultural and industrial aspects. In language that could have been drawn from his commentaries on American farmers in the 1920s or on Mexico in the 1930s, Wallace now wrote that Greece needed to learn the "science of fertilizing, crop rotation, and control of animal disease." It needed to obtain modern farm technology and to establish modern industry. Ultimately evoking the image of a Greek Tennessee Valley Authority, Wallace described "dams [that] could be built to develop the power possibilities" of Greek rivers. In 1947 Wallace called for the rebuilding of war-ravaged nations such as Greece in terms similar to those in which he championed the common man during the war. He implied that progress would come to such nations if only they were shown by Americans how to live like Americans.[42] In Wallace's remarkably tenacious vision, America had another chance, if an increasingly slim one, to lead the world to the light.

It was in this context of articulating an alternative to the Truman Doctrine that Wallace's own anticommunism was apparent. For Wallace America's opportunity was not simply the chance to bestow its own largesse upon the needy nations of the world. Rather it lay in showing those nations another path to economic democracy besides communist revolution. With quintessential American logic, Wallace argued that the way to overcome the communist idea was by presenting proof of a better one. The United States had to give the "common man all over the world something better than communism" to turn to and he contended that "democratic planning" could do the trick. There is a poignant irony to such remarks. They exhibit not only Wallace's anticommunism but also his recurrent tendency to envision a global future in essentially American terms. In this sense he served, however inadvertently, as an instrument of American cultural imperialism. The great irony is that Wallace was attacked by his American opponents for serving the cause of communism. It is a paradox that demonstrates, as a recent Wallace biography rightfully notes, just how "rigidly dichotomized" American thinking about international affairs already had become by spring 1947.[43]

Initially, criticism of Wallace's position was relatively muted. The journalist Anne O'Hare McCormick in her regular column warned readers that Wallace's European speeches would undermine U.S. policy in Europe by nurturing foreign suspicions of American motives. More obliquely, correspondent Edwin James held Wallace up as a "lesson for the Russians," proving the reality of free speech in the United States. "No one but an American," James insisted, could criticize his own government's policy while on a foreign tour.[44] In Congress, however, Wallace fared much worse. Some members of the Senate, which was engaged at the time in actual debate of the Greek-Turkish aid bill, called for legal action against Wallace. In comparison to the press, congressional criticism of Wallace was vitriolic. Not surprisingly, Wallace faced especially strong criticism for attacking the Truman Doctrine while traveling outside the United States. Led by Michigan Republican Arthur Vandenberg, a central figure among Truman's bipartisan foreign policy supporters, many senators condemned Wallace as a virtual traitor. Several of Vandenberg's colleagues even called for Wallace's prosecution under the Logan Act of 1799 (which made it a crime for an American citizen to deal with a foreign government regarding a matter in dispute between the two nations or "to defeat the measures" of the U.S. government). Certainly Wallace's public image was not helped by the furor over his trip, which tended to cast him as at least vaguely disloyal. More ironically, congressional anger at his overseas critique of the Truman Doctrine probably helped to pass the legislation.[45]

In a related sense the administration responded to Wallace's speeches in England by effectively cordoning him off from any access to the trappings of American officialdom while he was overseas. "Top Secret" cable traffic between the Department of State and various American embassies and legations in Western Europe repeatedly indicated that the president and his advisors feared the impact of Wallace's critique of the Truman Doctrine upon U.S. foreign relations and that they wanted it clear that Wallace in no way spoke for America. Efforts were made to uncover Comintern machinations in the conception of Wallace's European tour, while official U.S. representatives in the nations he visited were enjoined by the State Department from meeting with or entertaining him, despite the fact that he was a former U.S. vice president and cabinet official.[46]

The Cold War Liberals and the Truman Doctrine

In clear if not stark contrast to Wallace and the PCA, Niebuhr and the ADA came out in support of the Truman Doctrine. There was actually some division within the organization regarding Truman's policy, expressed in discussions at the ADA national meeting in late March, but it was mostly absent from the group's public statements. Much of the dissent—in many cases more ambivalence than outright disagreement—dovetailed with aspects of the Wallace-PCA critique of the Greek-Turkish policy, particularly its condemnation of the reactionary qualities of the Greek and Turkish governments. In this sense liberal responses to the Truman Doctrine did not manifest the complete breach between anticommunist and popular front liberal internationalists that became apparent later in the year. Unlike Wallace and the PCA, however, neither Niebuhr nor the leadership of the ADA saw any serious danger inherent in either the tone or content of Truman's rhetoric.[47]

Nor did they seem particularly worried about the potential damage done to the United Nations by Truman's policy. Niebuhr of course had written off the UN as a viable international force the previous fall. Nothing that occurred in the intervening months had altered that assessment, although he still accepted the idea that the Security Council could act as a bridge between America and the Soviet Union. The ADA, in seeming contrast, asserted that the United States must try to use its power under the auspices of the UN. Despite strong assertions of support for the UN, however, the ADA made no specific proposals for strengthening the organization. Until such time as the UN was able to take over supervision of the situations in Greece and Turkey, the ADA argued that American unilateralism was justified on the basis of America's international responsibilities.[48]

The apparent lack of concern on the part of the cold war liberal internationalists regarding the risks of Truman's policy also derived from what they viewed as the symbolic importance of the Truman Doctrine. Even if flawed, they believed, it promised both to the nation and the world that the United States was finally and irreversibly taking up its international responsibilities. It seemed to sound the death knell of isolationism, and isolationism was, after all, the original foe of the organization from which the ADA had sprung. Niebuhr argued that the Greek-Turkish policy was crucial as a "symbol" of American "determination to remain in Europe," while Wilson Wyatt, invoking Munich, insisted that anyone who argued that America ought not involve itself in global affairs was only reiterating the fateful arguments made "with regard to Hitler in 1940." The anticommunist liberals did acknowledge that the ambiguity of the Truman Doctrine led some critics to charge, as did Wallace and the PCA, that the policy would open the door to American support of reactionary regimes around the world. But they argued that such charges could be refuted simply by choosing the right individuals to administer American support. If those individuals were "men whose genuine faith in democracy is plain and unassailable," the ADA insisted, the flaws in Truman's policy would be neutralized.[49]

Suggesting that a core of shared assumptions still existed between the cold war and popular front liberals, both Niebuhr and the ADA proposed methods for the ultimate defeat of communism that were quite similar to those of Wallace. Niebuhr seemed to view Truman's Greek-Turkish proposal as a stopgap policy. Over the long run he believed that such policies would fail if "economic chaos and political confusion" allowed communism to gain an "ideological victory" in Europe. Foreshadowing the Marshall Plan, Niebuhr speculated that European economic recovery would require some billions of dollars in loans from the United States. Such aid would not be benevolence on America's part, he contended, but rather a means of maintaining full employment within the United States, still a central aim of American progressives. The ADA leadership laid out a more explicit plan for American aid to Greece—ignoring the Turkish aspect of Truman's proposal—with the implication that similar measures could be used elsewhere. Echoing Wallace's call for creating a Greek New Deal, they justified American policy by arguing that the "tranquillity" it would bring to Greece would allow America to "build dams, to plan soil erosion programs, [and] to revive and expand industries" in that country. Both Wallace and the ADA believed that the best preventative to communist expansion was the removal of the economic and political conditions that nurtured communist ideology. But where Wallace and the noncommunist popular fronters of the PCA saw the Truman Doctrine working against such an outcome, the ADA believed that as long as it was administered in proper American progressive liberal fashion, Truman's policy could provide the means for bringing Greece into the democratic, capitalist West.[50]

The Marshall Plan and the Popular Front Fear of Fascism

Following the debate over the Truman Doctrine, the ways in which the anticommunist and popular front liberals responded, respectively, to events occurring between spring 1947 and fall 1948 repeatedly highlighted the fundamental features of the division between them. Moreover, the running debate within the liberal community took place within the context of a larger political culture in which perceptions of both communism and the Soviet Union were fast becoming extremely negative. Thus the liberal internationalists' disagreement contributed to the ongoing delegitimation of Wallace as well as, now, the PCA. The critique presented by Wallace and the popular fronters seemed more and more dissonant within the mainstream of political debate in America for two interconnected reasons. One was that it was portrayed over time in increasingly discreditable terms by its critics, including the ADA. Some historians, however, have suggested that the dissonance of the popular front position resulted from a strident quality that began to appear in the pronouncements of Wallace and his associates by mid-1947, with the implication that such stridency reflected the growing influence of communists in the PCA.[51] Yet the overall logic of the popular front liberal critique of American foreign policy remained essentially the same throughout this period, while an increase in stridency might also have issued from a greater sense of urgency, even desperation, on the part of progressive liberals, without growing communist influence. In the end it seems just as likely that the popular front commentary became more insistent and extreme because of the fundamental shift toward rock-hard, reflexive anticommunism occurring within the general political culture of the nation, with which the anticommunist liberals of the ADA were in complete accord. It was the transformation of perception and discussion within American political culture generally—

as well as the events the transformation both influenced and issued from—that eventually undermined the cognitive validity of the popular front liberal outlook.

The process of transformation was already under way by the time of Secretary of State George Marshall's June announcement of plans for a European Recovery Program (ERP), also known as the Marshall Plan. During the year following Marshall's announcement, the popular front-ers and the anticommunist liberals publicly debated the plan's merits in the context of other developments in foreign and domestic politics, in-cluding, ultimately, Wallace's entry into the presidential campaign of 1948. For cold war liberal internationalists like Niebuhr and the ADA, the Marshall Plan stood as an example of appropriate American policy, one that forswore isolationism without being militaristic; in this sense it was far preferable to the Truman Doctrine. For Wallace and the PCA, however, initial hopeful skepticism turned quickly to cynicism. In their view the ERP became just one more component of an increasingly in-flexible, militaristic, and inherently reactionary policy that was likely to undermine any chance of international cooperation.

Despite his early optimism regarding the Marshall Plan, Wallace soon joined the PCA in attacking it. Together Wallace and the PCA made their attack in what were already familiar terms: damage done the United Nations, general international divisiveness, a sense that Ameri-can foreign policy favored the wrong groups in the international arena, and a fear that the plan would increase the threat of international as well as domestic fascism. Reminiscent of his remarks on the Truman Doc-trine's potential for fomenting Russian adventurism, Wallace cautioned that if the Soviets came to view the ERP as an extension of the Greek-Turkish policy they might take action in Eastern and perhaps Western Europe. "What happened in Hungary," Wallace warned, "may happen elsewhere." In addition, the popular fronters advanced the view that the Marshall Plan, growing out of the Truman Doctrine, also exhibited an insidious misplacement of priorities in postwar U.S. foreign policy, par-ticularly in the case of Germany. The popular front liberals contended that the ERP's assistance would be given not to those nations in Eastern Europe still "living in the rubble created by the . . . Wehrmacht" but rather as incentive to German businessmen. Instead of making Europe whole again with Germany integrated into it, they contended, the Marshall Plan threatened to create a divided Europe with the western portion dominated by a resurrected, potentially fascist West Germany.[52]

Ultimately, Wallace and the PCA's attack on the Marshall Plan expanded into a critique of Truman's policies that asserted that those policies not only threatened to drag the nation into war but also had the potential for militarizing America along fascist lines. Much of what they warned against would later be collectively characterized by President Eisenhower as the "military-industrial complex." They warned of "militarists and bankers" in government who would give Europe over to cartels while turning America into a capitalist police state. Evidence of the latter process they saw in the passage of the antilabor Taft-Hartley Act of 1947 as well as the administration's plans for establishing Universal Military Training (UMT) and resurrecting the military draft with a new Selective Service act. If UMT and a new draft were established, Wallace predicted, Americans and their institutions would be "reduced to gears in the war machine."[53] The federal loyalty investigations and the ongoing activities of HUAC—which by 1948 included the notorious Hollywood hearings—completed the popular front perception of a protofascist domestic threat. In its complexity and coherence it mirrored quite well cold war liberal fears of communist subversion. Yet it was in articulating this fearful image of a fascist America that the popular front liberals probably stepped irretrievably beyond the pale of credibility in American political discourse. For although they only exaggerated the threat from the Right as the cold war liberals exaggerated the one from the Left, by late 1947 many Americans perceived little exaggeration at all in the cold war liberal perspective.[54]

The Marshall Plan and Cold War Liberal Advocacy of Socialism

In part that perception was due to the fact that the cold war liberal commentary, at least on foreign policy, began to dovetail with the administration's positions, above all regarding the Marshall Plan. For

Niebuhr and the ADA, not only did the Marshall Plan not hold out the threats that the popular fronters saw in it, it actually appeared to be a clear step in the right direction for American foreign policy. In fact, the ERP became a watershed issue for Niebuhr and the ADA. They discussed it extensively and in overwhelmingly favorable terms at meetings and in the ADA's public statements, from summer 1947 well into the presidential campaign of 1948. Perhaps most notably, a detailed advocacy of the ERP took up more than a third of the text in the ADA's major foreign policy document of 1947–48, a pamphlet written primarily by Arthur Schlesinger Jr. entitled "Toward Total Peace: A Liberal Foreign Policy for the United States."[55] For Niebuhr and the ADA, the Marshall Plan was both a moral high point for America and a policy they believed they could shape, thus gaining influence in the Truman administration. Richard Pells has described a yearning on the part of liberal intellectuals during these years to be "insiders" and "men of action." He suggests that by publicly and persuasively supporting government policies, they sought to influence the powerful but in so doing suppressed their critical instincts. In this sense high profile advocacy of the Marshall Plan presented a means for the ADA to become a political player in Democratic policy making while pursuing sincerely its members' ideals. As Wilson Wyatt pointed out, the ERP offered a "concrete and significant example" of the role that the group might play in "national life."[56] It quickly became a centerpiece of what could be termed the ADA's foreign policy.

Just as the popular front critique of the Marshall Plan was made in familiar terms, so too was Niebuhr and the ADA's support of the ERP formed in the context of already established positions. They once again stated their belief that European economic recovery was not only good for the United States but also crucial to preventing the communization of Western Europe. Americans had to unite behind the Marshall Plan, the ADA insisted, in order to quickly rescue both Europe and "world peace." This sense of urgency regarding the ERP was augmented by the communist coup that occurred in Czechoslovakia in March 1948, which climaxed with the alleged suicide of democratic Czech foreign minister Jan Masaryk. For the leadership of the ADA Czechoslovakia was a "test case" regarding the survival of democracy in Eastern Europe and possibly the West as well. Thus Masaryk's dramatic and mysterious death convinced the cold war liberals that there was no time to lose in strengthening Western Europe against a communist onslaught. The same sense of urgency underpinned a continued skepticism of the UN. In complete disagreement with Wallace and the PCA, the ADA argued that while the UN still held promise, it had proven for the most part ineffective. Only unscrupulous individuals, the ADA contended, would continue to harp on U.S. evasion of the UN in administering the Marshall Plan at a time when the animosity of the two great powers had rendered the organization incapable of handling such a task. They did not accept the logic that to allow the UN to fulfill its allotted task might actually strengthen its position in international relations.[57]

As with the Truman Doctrine, Niebuhr and the ADA viewed the Marshall Plan as further evidence that the United States was rejecting isolationism and was irreversibly taking up its momentous international responsibilities. Drawing on one of his (and Wallace's) oldest metaphors of national development, Niebuhr suggested that the nation seemed to have "grown up" in the months since the announcement of the Truman Doctrine. Where the latter was a "purely strategic defensive measure," and in that sense a sign of youthful impetuosity, the ERP revealed a more mature understanding on the part of U.S. policy makers of both the "responsibilities of a wealthy nation to a poverty stricken world" as well as the danger inherent when such a nation attempts to isolate itself in such a world. Initially, the ADA too saw the Marshall Plan as different from the Truman Doctrine, at least in the manner in which it was perceived by the American public. As time passed, however, the group reassessed the Truman Doctrine in the light of the Marshall Plan, seeing the former in increasingly positive terms. By the December publication of "Toward Total Peace" the ADA essentially had reversed its original, rather muted criticism of the Greek-Turkish policy, now arguing it was directly descended from Roosevelt's own "quarantine" doctrine of 1937. The only mistake in 1947, they now believed, had been Truman's decision to use the language of crisis in order to overcome an economically recalcitrant Congress. It was that language that led the Soviets, "assisted, wittingly or not, by certain Americans," to establish a propaganda attack on the Truman Doctrine, construing it as an American appeal to aid reactionaries the world over.[58]

In its broadest context the Niebuhr-ADA discussion of the ERP contained new themes as well. For example, while the ADA declared the danger of the "fallacy of assuming that fascism" was dead, by December they were clearly dismissing fascism as a significant threat. They were able to do so for two interconnected reasons. First, their perception of what constituted a fascist threat had greatly narrowed, with that threat now embodied only by certain nations, such as Spain and Argentina, whose regimes seemed to fulfill a focused, traditional definition of fascism. Second, by narrowing their view of fascism and where it could be found Niebuhr and the ADA implicitly dismissed the domestic version of the threat they had so ardently subscribed to not long before. They left Wallace, the PCA, and the communists to argue that the Marshall Plan, in conjunction with UMT and the draft, opened the door to fascism in America. Another new theme also could be glimpsed in the vague remarks recounted above regarding individuals who might criticize either the United States' willingness to bypass the UN or the tendency of the Truman Doctrine to encourage reactionary regimes. This was the beginning, at first muted, of a critique of Wallace and the PCA that increased in both extent and vitriol over the next year, in many ways foreshadowing rhetorical techniques later associated with conservative anticommunism. In Schlesinger's "Toward Total Peace" the ADA asserted that Wallace's beliefs regarding Soviet policy were grounded on the assumption that the Soviets had legitimate misgivings concerning their security. Based on that assumption, the pamphlet claimed, Wallace advocated an American policy aimed at easing Soviet fears by weakening the United States and ceasing resistance to communist expansion. In fact, Wallace had only pointed out that the continued policy of building atomic bombs—as well as the planes in which and the bases from which to deliver them—was likely to cause the Soviets to react by building up their own strength in terms of territory and weapons. And Wallace never called for abandoning resistance to communism; he had in fact articulated a policy of humanitarian and economic aid under the supervision of the United Nations, aimed explicitly at undermining communist expansion. While the ADA advocated similar aid for similar purposes, they failed to acknowledge that for months Wallace and the PCA had been calling for just such a policy.[59]

One other particularly striking new theme emerged in the ADA's discussion of the Marshall Plan. Foreshadowed the year before when the UDA endorsed the British government's proposal for the socialization of German heavy industry, in summer 1947 Niebuhr and the ADA explicitly began to advocate the development of full-fledged socialism throughout Western Europe. Because of the depth of wartime devastation in Europe, the cold war liberals argued that socialism might prove more effective than capitalism at fostering recovery within the context of the ERP. Yet they feared that many Americans might not comprehend the essential differences between the socialism that the cold war liberals championed and the communism they so staunchly opposed. Niebuhr and his associates worried that Americans' devotion to free enterprise would cause them to write off socialism as they did communism.[60] It did not occur to them that many Americans disdained socialism not because of its conflict with free enterprise but rather because of its association with communism, which, however inaccurate, rendered it by this time little better than Nazism. Nor did it occur to the cold war liberals that the extreme quality of this perspective derived in part from the growing anticommunist hysteria to which they themselves contributed.

In the content of their advocacy of socialism in Western Europe one senses the cold war liberals' hope of convincing their fellow Americans that socialism was fundamentally different from communism, that the two ought not be lumped together in determining American policy. In congressional testimony on the ERP, for example, ADA representatives carefully placed socialists among the ranks of "traditionally democratic forces" in Europe. In a somewhat strained historical comparison they asserted that European economies tended much more toward cartels and monopolies than did the American economy. It was strained because it ignored the long-standing critique of American society—including, centrally, an attack on corporate concentration—made by many in their ranks, Niebuhr most notably. The anticommunist liberals were now willing to grant the absolute validity of free enterprise in America in exchange for a U.S. policy allowing socialism to exist in Western Europe.[61]

The cold war liberals' advocacy of European socialism within their discussion of the Marshall Plan has two significant implications. For Niebuhr particularly it suggests the persistence of his old, ambivalent critique of the modern, capitalist West, now formulated in the terms of geopolitics. For him the ERP was bound up in the "geographic and political crystallization" of the great debate of the last century "on how to organize a technical society." America and Russia embodied the two ideological sides of this debate, and both were wrong. In Niebuhr's view, however, there was a way out of this paradox. Invoking the French socialist—and founder of the original "Popular Front"—Léon Blum, Niebuhr embraced the idea of the "third force," meaning the establishment of a true democratic socialism with an explicitly Christian component. The "amalgamation of Christian and socialistic forces," he wrote, would underpin the third force, allowing it to become a viable middle ground between reaction and communism.[62]

Yet to champion socialism was to challenge the free enterprise capitalist values that lay at the center of America's self-image. Thus at the same time he was defending American policy Niebuhr continued to question America's capacity for moral leadership, which is to say that by spring 1948 certain familiar tensions persisted in his commentary. Within these tensions we can discern Niebuhr's continuing evolution away from the absolute construction of the inherent immorality of national behavior he presented in *Moral Man*. It was as if the rapidly accelerating hostility of the cold war gave Niebuhr an increasingly usable foil—the Soviet Union—against which he could, in a relative sense, justify American behavior.

This being the case, it is not surprising that during the first months of 1948 Niebuhr revisited in print his analysis of the relationship between Marxism and Western liberalism, reasserting his central point of the 1930s, that the former was a variant of the latter's essential utopianism. According to Niebuhr it was the combination of political success and the human will to power that had betrayed Marxism in the Soviet

Union. In contrast, the central failings of Western liberalism, especially as embodied by the United States, issued from its exaggerated faith in democracy. Nevertheless, Niebuhr could still conclude that the liberalism of America exhibited a "soft utopianism," in stark contrast to the dogmatic "hard utopianism" of Soviet communism. Yet American utopianism also was prone to dogmatism, perhaps dangerously so, stemming from the manner in which Americans mixed their devotion to democracy with illusions about the equalitarian nature of laissez-faire economics. It was an assumption, Niebuhr contended, that could only have arisen in a nation that, because of its natural endowments, was comparatively free of the injustice that resulted from poverty in other parts of the world. To put it another way, America's will as well as its power derived not from its inherent morality but from its wealth. The United States could attain moral leadership, Niebuhr maintained with typical irony, only as Americans came to understand that their "most cherished political ideals [were] not so much the final norms of politics as the characteristic prejudices of a very privileged nation."[63] Such a realization, however, was not an impossibility. Buried within Niebuhr's spring 1948 ruminations was the implication that, while Soviet communism was doomed by the excesses of ideology, American liberalism might yet transcend those excesses.

The other crucial implication of the Niebuhr-ADA position on socialism and the ERP is one that helps to explain the extremely harsh nature of the attack that they made upon Wallace and the Progressive Party during 1948, that is, it suggests why the cold war liberals, despite their articulated opposition to Red-baiting, were so willing to distort the substance of the popular front liberal commentary and unfairly tar the entire Wallace-PCA enterprise as little more than Moscow-directed subversion. By summer 1947 if the leaders of the ADA wanted to champion socialism—even socialism in Europe—in American policy debates, they faced an extraordinarily difficult struggle. As suggested above, it is unlikely that many Americans by this time differentiated between socialism (or social democracy) and communism. Yet that very differentiation was crucial if the ADA was to gain support for this position. One means of attaining this goal was to attempt the education of the American people and their representatives—literally to explain the differences in content and provenance between socialism and communism. This they attempted in congressional testimony and in various public statements. Another approach, however, was to mark out their opponents in the harshest possible relief; to make it as clear as possible what they themselves were not. In other words, the ADA chose to portray the popular front liberals as either communists or fellow travelers, as dupes or possibly traitors, in order to legitimate their own call for socialism to an administration and electorate that did not much care for such differentiation. It was a strategy that was evident almost from the moment that Wallace declared his candidacy for the presidency.

9

Defeating "Gideon's Army"
The Final Ascendance of Cold War Liberalism

———❖———

ALTHOUGH FOR years Wallace had rejected progressive proposals for the creation of a third party, by the end of 1947 he was convinced that the Democratic party was either lost to progressive liberalism or could only be goaded toward it by the threat of some real competition for liberal votes. By December he was convinced that the Democrats would continue to be a party of "war and depression." Speeches Wallace gave on the road that month manifested his growing sense of urgency and frustration regarding both domestic and foreign affairs. Both the content and tone of these speeches impart the complexity of his logic as well as his passion regarding the issues facing the nation. He spoke of the activities of HUAC and the trampling of American civil liberties, insisting that despite what many believed, the "assault on American freedom" did not come from abroad "but from Americans." And this domestic threat was not from communists or those "who are falsely called Communists" but rather from individuals who hid behind a "mantle of patriotism" while violating others' civil liberties and undermining Americans' "most precious freedoms." Wallace made clear his belief that such methods were little different from the fascism America had fought in World War II. He reiterated his view that the Marshall Plan, like the Truman Doctrine, was dividing the world as the United States backed reactionaries in Europe and "bemoaned the sufferings of unrepentant Germans." In the end, Wallace warned, American policy was going to betray the Allied soldiers "who laid down their lives" in the war, unless American progressives organized themselves and struck back at the reactionary forces that were guiding the nation.[1]

It was for such reasons that Wallace finally decided to go ahead with a third-party candidacy for the presidency. In doing so he initiated the final struggle between the two strains of liberalism that battled for a defining role in American politics and society. It was a struggle characterized by several themes. One was the strategy of distortion developed by the ADA during the campaign of 1948 in its attacks upon Wallace and his popular front associates. By fall that strategy thoroughly destroyed any chance for a reasoned discussion of policy alternatives within the liberal community. In this context a second theme was the persistence with which Wallace and the PCA slipped outside of the American political mainstream, due less to changes in the positions they took than to the narrowing of mainstream political culture itself. Behind these trends, however, one occasionally—and ironically—can discern various concerns and assumptions still shared by all liberals, even as such common ground was increasingly overshadowed by the melodrama of the nation's rapidly growing, obsessive fear of communism. Nevertheless, by the time the struggle between American liberals ended with the election of November 1948, Wallace's public career was over, and his liberal opponents had bound themselves to the conservative imperatives of the emergent cold war political culture.

Wallace's Candidacy and the Beginning of the ADA's Attack

Wallace did not announce his candidacy until December 29, in a speech that rearticulated the whole logical framework that he and the PCA had developed during the prior year. He asserted that American policy since the announcement of the Truman Doctrine had consistently undermined the UNO while supporting virtually fascist regimes, that proposals such as UMT threatened to militarize American society and the American economy, and that the distortions of domestic anticommunism threatened civil liberties at home and peace abroad. Wallace insisted that it was time for progressives to reject the logic of voting "for the lesser of two evils" and vote instead for "peace and security." After once more articulating his hope that the Soviet Union would respond to such behavior and cooperate with America, Wallace dramatically returned to the Old Testament for the imagery that came to characterize his campaign. Reflecting the realization that at best his supporters would be relatively few in number, he recalled "Gideon's Army, small in number, powerful in conviction, ready for action." Invoking the themes of the New Age he had developed over decades, he declared that the success of his modern Gideon's army would "usher in the Century of the Common Man." [2]

The ADA's response was swift. From the start they established a technique of attacking Wallace by associating him in various ways with enemies of liberalism from both the right and the left. For example, in a speech to the organization's first national convention, national chairman Wilson Wyatt linked Wallace's position explicitly with isolation and reaction while implying that Wallace's behavior evoked that of Mussolini and Hitler. Niebuhr, in his speech to the convention, made a more oblique attack that began the process of painting Wallace and the other liberals of the PCA as communist dupes. When in the speech he declared the need to create Léon Blum's third force in America, Niebuhr made clear that only the ADA could embody it. In Niebuhr's view the PCA could not do so because the communists in its ranks eventually would dominate the organization. Any "united front," Niebuhr declared, inevitably became "decreasingly 'united' and increasingly 'front.'" [3]

In the wake of their February convention the ADA quickly began, in James Loeb's words, to "move without delay into the national political arena." Central to this effort was a plan to "take the offensive" against Wallace and the PCA. It was a task that fulfilled the ADA leadership's desire to play a significant role in national politics. But it was important for another reason as well. Loeb contended that Wallace was making too many statements that might lead to the tarring of all liberals, including the ADA, as too far to the left. The efforts of the Dies Committee against the UDA were not that far in the past after all, and the danger must have seemed all the more threatening at a time when the ADA was advocating socialism in Western Europe in its commentary on the Marshall Plan. By attacking Wallace quickly, the ADA would make clear to the American public that Wallace did not speak for all American liberals.[4]

One of the initial strategic proposals for the anti-Wallace campaign was for the production of an extensive pamphlet on Wallace and the PCA that would address all aspects of Wallace's campaign. It would provide source material that local ADA chapters could draw upon in public debates of campaign issues. Schlesinger expressed the hope, one assumes tongue-in-cheek, that the pamphlet might "provoke some red-baiting millionaires into action."[5] The proposal came to fruition in April, and the widely circulated thirty-four-page pamphlet, entitled "Henry A. Wallace: The First Three Months," was the centerpiece of the ADA's early campaign against Wallace. The document took a multifarious approach, smoothly utilizing the techniques of innuendo, quotation out of context, and guilt by association in conjunction with an extensive account of the apparent shifts in Wallace's positions on various issues over time. The finished product portrayed Wallace as inept, indecisive, and insincere.

"The First Three Months" accused Wallace of making tough public statements foisted upon him by communists. They were prepared for him not by speech writers, the pamphlet charged, but rather by the "well disciplined operatives" that surrounded him, a description evoking the image of fanatic, hardened, subversive cadres controlling a naive subject. The pamphlet also asserted that much of Wallace's support came from "Communist-dominated unions and individuals well-known as CP [Communist Party] apologists" and pointed out suspected communists who held important positions in the Wallace campaign. Such statements had several implications. By suggesting that communists and fellow travelers were inserting themselves into crucial roles in the Wallace movement without noting noncommunist liberals in similar positions (New Dealer Rexford Tugwell being the best, but far from only, example), they implied communist domination of both Wallace and the campaign. Also, by drawing so much attention to the role played in the Wallace movement by alleged communists, such remarks implicitly excluded the possibility that progressive liberals might come to the same critical perspective on American politics and foreign policy as the communists without the communists somehow manipulating them into it. It almost goes without saying that innuendoes of this sort made it even less likely that anyone might consider the possibility that an American communist could champion radical reform in the United States without being controlled by the Soviets. In a different form of innuendo, the ADA pamphlet also portentously recounted a July 1945 article—that is, an article published at a time when the UDA ranked among Wallace's staunchest supporters—written by a well-known French communist leader in which he had "generously and . . . significantly" quoted Wallace.[6] Once more the implication was not hard to discern: if a leading French communist could quote from Wallace, then Wallace's ideas must be amenable to communism, which suggested that Wallace could not be that much different from a communist.

"The First Three Months" also quoted Wallace out of context in order to suggest that he actually was not the champion of the progressive ideals that he had so long espoused. For instance, the pamphlet quoted at length from one of Wallace's *New Republic* editorial columns, an essay laying out his position on American labor. The pamphlet quoted him as writing that

> If a strike takes place in one of the little handful of industries which are essential to the continued life of the nation, the industry should be taken over and operated by the government until a settlement can be reached. . . .[7]

If this was what Wallace in fact had written, it might have suggested that he was prepared to sacrifice the "common man" fairly quickly to the needs of the state, substantiating the ADA's overarching portrayal of Wallace as too amenable to totalitarianism. But there was much more to the paragraph. Some of it was elided from the interior of the passage without indication, while the truncation of the paragraph, which was indicated by ellipsis, greatly altered the passage's meaning. What Wallace wrote was far more complex than what the ADA published. After a lengthy and detailed discussion of various methods of mediating labor-management disputes, Wallace actually concluded:

> If, *in spite of everything that can be done in the way of fact-finding, conciliation and voluntary arbitration,* a strike takes place in one of the little handful of industries which are essential to the continued life of the nation, that industry should be taken over and operated by the government until a settlement can be reached. *During this period of operation there should be no profits to the owners, in order to avoid the situation we have seen in the past where the government has simply acted as a stooge for the employers, who have hidden behind the pressure created by public indignation against the strikers and let the government drive a harder bargain with the workers than is fair or just. When the government acts, let it act truly as the representative of all the people.*[8]

Wallace in fact had made crystal clear his belief that government take-overs of essential industries ought to take place only as a last resort and only under circumstances in which the workers' interests were fully protected.

The suggestion that Wallace really was not the champion of the common man he had long been portrayed as was tied to another central theme of "The First Three Months." The pamphlet contended that Wallace so frequently and starkly shifted his stance on issues—including issues of principle—and either exaggerated or lied in his public statements so often, that he simply could not be trusted. As evidence the pamphlet discussed several episodes in which Wallace allegedly either contradicted himself or behaved in some other manner that belied a position he had taken earlier. In each case, however, the stories were told in fragmented fashion—again quoting Wallace incompletely or out of context—and with a great deal of unsubstantiated innuendo. In recounting the statements Wallace made regarding the Czech coup, for example, "The First Three Months" made much of the fact that Wallace had publicly first suggested that the communist takeover was a response to an attempt by the American ambassador to stage a "rightist coup" in Prague. According to the pamphlet, when confronted with the fact that the ambassador had not yet arrived in Czechoslovakia at the time the coup started, Wallace explained that he believed that the ambassador's public declaration of hope that Czechoslovakia would participate in the ERP was "clearly a provocative statement" as far as the Soviets were concerned. Wallace later backed off a bit, insisting that when he attributed responsibility for the coup to the U.S. ambassador he should have qualified his remarks "to some degree." Yet he still asserted that in the crisis conditions existing in Czechoslovakia at the time, the invitation from the U.S. ambassador for the Czechs to partake in the ERP must have troubled the Russians. The ADA pamphlet at this point did not address the logic of Wallace's explanation of his remarks. Instead, immediately following its last quotation of Wallace on the matter, it ominously and starkly stated the tragic fact of Jan Masaryk's death as if Wallace's comments were somehow retroactively responsible for it.[9] "The First Three Months" also failed to address the fact that Wallace's take on the sources of the Czech crisis fit quite well with his earlier assessment of the crisis in Hungary in 1946, an assessment in which he clearly had stated his belief that if the Soviets perceived no change in American policy (from the Truman Doctrine), what had happened in Hungary was likely to happen elsewhere.

The ADA tract greatly overdrew the implication that Wallace's clarification of his remarks on the Czech crisis was somehow evidence of either his insincerity or the extent to which he was being manipulated by communists. Wallace had perhaps spoken too soon and simplistically about events in Czechoslovakia, but his clarification was relatively minor and quite consistent with his long-standing perspective on U.S.-Soviet relations. Certainly it was no more of a shift than any politician might make on almost any issue under analogous circumstances. It is possible that Wallace, because he had for so long presented himself as an incorruptible champion of matters of principle, was more vulnerable than others to this sort of niggling attack when he did shift ground. It is also true that the Czech coup was another example of the increasing divide between Wallace and the popular front liberals' perspective on international affairs and that of more mainstream liberals and conservatives. Nevertheless, on this issue and others as well, the ADA pamphlet drew far more damning implications from such shifts than were warranted.[10]

The Progressive Party and the
Question of Communist Control

Throughout the spring and early summer Wallace traveled across the nation speaking to large and enthusiastic crowds, technically as an independent candidate, although he was universally considered the candidate of a third party embodied by the PCA. In mid-May Wallace engaged in a brief and somewhat sensational open correspondence with Josef Stalin on the possibility of the United States and the Soviet Union attempting to negotiate their differences in a calm fashion. The exchange, somewhat surprisingly, elicited relatively little criticism at the time, either in the press or from the ADA. In terms of content there was nothing particularly striking about Wallace's letter, in which he articulated various well-established themes in the course of proposing specific actions aimed at reducing tensions between the two nations. Perhaps more surprising was Stalin's moderate, even conciliatory response, which was broadcast on Moscow radio. Stalin was extremely complimentary of Wallace—which probably did the latter little good in terms of American politics—effectively characterizing the letter as an act of true statesmanship. Stalin concluded by asserting that he considered Wallace's proposals a valid basis for agreement and for the development of "international cooperation" between the Russians and Americans.[11]

When the ADA did criticize the exchange between Wallace and Stalin that fall, it did so in rather oblique and contradictory fashion. First, the ADA asserted that Wallace's effort was an indication of his arrogance, of his belief that he could resolve the cold war single-handedly. Second, the group insisted that a close reading of Stalin's response showed that the Soviet leader ignored several of the steps Wallace believed had to be taken in order to end the cold war. In other words, the ADA dismissed Wallace's diplomacy both because it was personal and unofficial and because the Soviet leader had not immediately and explicitly acknowledged every component of the American's proposal (which, if it was illegitimate to begin with, was an inherently irrelevant criticism).[12] In one sense it was another niggling criticism of Wallace.

In another, however, it suggests the extent to which the ADA had assimilated what had become a quite narrow American definition of diplomacy as far as the Soviet Union was concerned. Any Soviet response that was less than complete acceptance of an American position was deemed unworthy of discussion and further proof of the Russians' intransigence.

Because of the exchange, Wallace received some predictable criticism in the press. Yet it was not as extensive as one might have expected. This was likely due to the perceived context of the Wallace-Stalin correspondence, a contemporaneous and confusing exchange of diplomatic notes between the U.S. and Soviet governments in which the White House appeared—in the U.S. press—to renege upon an invitation to negotiations it had extended to the Soviets. In a manner strangely reminiscent of the controversy over Wallace's Madison Square Garden speech in September 1946, Truman once more seemed to fumble national affairs.[13] Criticism of Wallace was perhaps minimized because his action seemed reasonable, even statesmanlike, in comparison.

Two months after the Wallace-Stalin exchange, on July 23, more than 3,200 popular front delegates met in Philadelphia for the founding convention of the Progressive Party. During the three-day meeting they nominated Wallace and progressive Democratic Idaho senator Glen Taylor, respectively, as the new party's presidential and vice presidential candidates. An actor prior to the Depression and senator only since 1944, over a period of many months Taylor had established a record of supporting Wallace's positions on most issues. He decided to stand with Wallace after a series of actions by the president convinced him that Truman's foreign policy was inherently imperialistic and, as such, was rapidly leading the nation toward war with the Soviet Union.[14] On the evening of July 24, 1948, in front of a crowd of 32,000 at Shibe Park baseball stadium and with Taylor alongside him, Wallace accepted the nomination as presidential candidate of the party he had virtually created. In his acceptance speech he rearticulated well-established positions, in several instances more boldly than ever before. He clearly differentiated himself and the Progressives from the Truman administration—and, by implication, the cold war liberals—on economic and foreign policy issues. The speech set the tone for the entire convention, a tone of challenge to the fundamental assumptions of American cold war political culture.

Wallace's remarks regarding the actual policies he would undertake if elected followed the logic of his established critique. He came very close to proposing the socialization of certain key components of the economy (as the new party would actually propose in its platform, discussed below). In language that resonated with that of the Populists of the 1890s, and in the name of establishing "progressive capitalism," Wallace proclaimed his commitment to using the democratic government to control and, if necessary, "to remove from private hands the power of huge corporate monopolies and international big business." Foreshadowing a dramatic campaign trip through the American South during the subsequent weeks, Wallace also pledged himself and the new party to the cause of racial equality, promising to "fight the murderers" who impeded legislation that could end segregation and bring equality to African Americans. In foreign affairs Wallace assured his fellow Progressives that he would pursue peaceful negotiations with the Soviets while also taking action to strengthen the UNO. Above all, he gave his word to turn the "power and prestige" of America to helping the world's common people instead of their "exploiters and rulers." [15]

The Progressive Party convention was portrayed from the start by much of the mainstream press as little more than a set piece of political theater staged by the communists who allegedly controlled the PCA. In this context the greatest drama surrounded the writing of the new party's platform. Yet while the platform's creation and its ultimate content were clearly influenced by individuals who were either communists or sympathetic to communism, characterizing that influence with terms such as "domination" or "control" would be a great exaggeration. The platform committee of the Progressive Party was chaired by the New Deal social planner and "Brain Truster" Rexford G. Tugwell. Wallace intentionally distanced himself from the platform-writing process and thus had only an indirect influence on the document's specific content. Nevertheless, and not surprisingly, the platform often reflected positions he had established as his own over time. Indeed, in many areas the Progressive Party platform simply reiterated themes that Wallace and the PCA had been stressing for months and in some cases years. In the realm of foreign affairs, for instance, the platform renewed the call for strengthening the role of the UNO. Nevertheless, the platform's assertion that the revitalization of the organization could be attained by "restoring the unity of the Great Powers" attests to the degree to which the popular fronters had lost touch with mainstream political realities, in both domestic and international contexts.[16]

The document also extensively exhibited the popular front liberal concern with resurgent fascism in both domestic and global terms. In the platform's first paragraphs the Progressives asserted that the "root cause" of the crisis facing America was "big business" and that the growth of private power to the point where it dominated the state was "in its essence . . . fascism." The platform decried "invisible government" and programs of "monopoly profits through war preparations . . . and suppression of dissent." It insisted that the Truman administration financed and armed "corrupt fascist governments" around the world, and the Marshall Plan was again described as an attempt to rebuild Nazi Germany and subjugate the European economy to that of the United States.[17]

In similar fashion the platform's policy proposals issued from the popular fronters' established critique of Truman administration policies and the antifascist paradigm. The Progressive Party demanded the repeal of the peacetime draft and rejection of Universal Military Training. Upholding workers' rights to organize, bargain collectively, and strike, they demanded the repeal of the Taft-Hartley Act and the full restoration of collective bargaining guarantees enacted during the New Deal. Only such actions, they declared, could keep business from using government to establish a "dictatorship over labor." In addition, the platform insisted upon the repudiation of the Truman Doctrine and an end to military and economic support of "reactionary and fascist" regimes. It also called once again for the repudiation of the Marshall Plan, claiming that the essentials for dealing with Germany were "denazification and democratization, punishment of war criminals, . . . decartelization, . . . [and] reparations to the victims of Nazi aggression."[18]

In one category of domestic policy the Progressive Party platform starkly illustrated how far out of touch the popular fronters were with mainstream American political culture. In a platform section entitled

"Abundance" the Progressives moved farther toward socialism, if not communism, than either they or Wallace ever had before. In the name of breaking "monopoly's grip" on the economy, they called for public ownership of the "largest banks, the railroads, the merchant marine, the electric power and gas industry" as well as industries primarily dependent on government funding or purchases, such as the aircraft industry. This socialistic transfer of ownership, however, would be buttressed by antimonopoly laws whose descriptions evoked quintessentially American calls for reform dating back to the Populist era. They included better enforced antitrust laws, the abolition of discriminatory freight rates, and the repeal of laws protecting railroads from antitrust prosecution.[19]

Ironically, the Progressive Party platform writers seemed more sensitive to the socialist implications of this plank of their platform than did the cold war liberals of the ADA. One platform committee member asserted the necessity of making clear that the new party's proposals regarding the economy were "not identical with socialism." With strained logic he argued that the plans for public ownership did not imply centralized planning. Moreover, he insisted that by eliminating monopoly in certain sectors of the economy, the Progressives' policies actually would aid "private enterprise" in others. The ADA, in notable contrast, never even raised this issue, either at the time of the Progressives' convention or in extensive attacks on Wallace and the new party during the fall. Indeed, in a widely disseminated anti–Wallace/Progressive Party blast of October, the ADA strained credulity by declaring that on domestic policy the new party's platform was "merely an imitation," if a somewhat amplified one, of the Democratic party program.[20]

Why did the anticommunist liberals not criticize the popular fronters' call for socializing large parts of the U.S. economy? Several explanations come to mind. It is likely, for instance, that they felt themselves vulnerable in light of their own stand on the Marshall Plan, discussed earlier. In a related sense it is also probable that Niebuhr and the ADA did not criticize the Progressives on this issue simply because they agreed with the popular fronters. The division between the two groups, after all, had never been over domestic reform. Indeed, it may be that by summer 1948 the cold war liberals of the ADA in effect had become "closet socialists," at least regarding domestic policy. Niebuhr, it should be remembered, always condemned the Soviet Union's corruption of Marxism, not Marxism's essential analysis or original intent. And as late as February 1948 he was still willing to characterize himself publicly as a socialist, if a "quite heretical" one. Nevertheless, by summer, the ADA was apparently unwilling to call for socialism within the United States. This was evidenced in the rather moderate platform proposals—other than the one on civil rights—that the group made to the Democratic Party in early July. With the exception of the civil rights issue, the ADA called for little from the Democratic Party on domestic policy besides restoration and maintenance of the New Deal. On the question of regulating monopoly, the area most directly connected to the Progressives' socialization proposals, the ADA simply insisted that U.S. antitrust laws had "not been strong enough" and needed to be "strengthened at once." [21] Yet, when the Progressives only a month later went so much further toward socialism on the same question, the ADA not only did not criticize them, they actually downplayed the Progressive proposals as only slightly amplified versions of Democratic platform planks. And this was at a time when the ADA was stridently attacking the Progressives in the most extreme terms on foreign policy. In other words, regarding domestic reform the ADA was prepared to make only moderate demands of what it regarded as an essentially conservative regime but one it hoped to influence. The ADA was willing to attack the popular fronters in the most vitriolic, exaggerated fashion in defense of that regime's foreign policy, in part to maintain that influence, but it would not attack the popular fronters on issues of domestic reform with which it was in accord, even when the popular fronters' demands went far beyond the mainstream. To avoid criticizing the Progressives on those issues was a way of supporting their position without actually appearing to do so. The cold war liberals thus let the Progressives give voice to aims that the two groups shared but that the anticommunists feared to articulate.

In any case, the section of the Progressive Party platform that engendered the most criticism was that regarding U.S.-Soviet relations. The greatest controversy arose regarding the so-called Vermont amendment. Offered by several delegates from Vermont during the final platform session on July 25, it was a brief and rather straightforward statement of principle that declared that "although we are critical of the present foreign policy of the United States, it is not our intention to give blanket endorsement to the foreign policy of any nation." It was clearly meant as a corrective to what some delegates perceived in the draft platform as an endorsement of Soviet policy implied by the document's extensive critique of American policy. But, as one of them later noted, the authors of the amendment were unaware upon their arrival at the convention hall that the platform committee itself was already addressing this very issue, by accepting a different amendment, one much broader in scope. The broader-scope, more complex Schuman amendment (named for its author, the Williams College political scientist Frederick L. Schuman) included a passage on culpability for international tensions, asserting that "responsibility for ending the tragic prospect of war is a joint responsibility of the Soviet Union and the United States," an implicit way of saying what the Vermont amendment stated directly. It was adopted by the convention delegates with little discussion or fanfare, before the Vermont amendment was presented.[22] The Vermont amendment, in other words, was redundant from the moment of its proposal.

The fact of the Vermont amendment's redundancy was absent from virtually all press accounts of the episode. In some cases this may have been because members of the press were working from pre-Schuman amendment drafts of the platform, just as were many of the delegates. But many of the press accounts also explicitly denied the fact that, despite its redundancy, the Vermont amendment was still debated at length—for some twenty minutes—and quite openly at the platform session. This process included the action of the session's (allegedly communist) chair who, upon realizing that the Vermont amendment was not strongly supported, called explicitly and repeatedly for speakers who were in favor of it in order to make sure that the minority position had a fair hearing. Several years later, one of the amendment's authors stated plainly that after this open discussion, in a voice vote on the amendment it was clear that the "No's outweighed the Yes's." Nevertheless, the *New York Times* reported that the "Communists and Fellow Travelers['] . . . complete control" of the convention was proven by the "shouting down" of the amendment, while the *Louisville*

Courier-Journal insisted portentously that the "hard inner core of control in the Progressive party" clearly showed where "its heart lies" when the time came to "push through the party's platform declaration on foreign policy." Such reportage suggests the accuracy of the popular fronters' expectation that, as Taylor put it, "they will Red-smear us no matter what we say or do."[23]

The question of communist influence within the Progressive Party was at the same time the great issue and nonissue of the convention and fall campaign. It was the great issue because so much was made of it at the time by the new party's critics, with such destructive consequences. It was the great nonissue, however, because it was truly a red herring. There is virtually no doubt that many communists and communist sympathizers appeared in the party's ranks as well as its leadership. Yet a persuasive case proving their domination of the convention and the party has never been made, while much belies it.[24] Certainly the extraordinarily open nature of debate at the convention does much to obliterate the accusations of communist staging. In addition, the view that popular front liberals were continually manipulated, duped, by communists denies the obvious intelligence and political perspicacity of many of these individuals, despite the ADA's tendency to describe them as naive. They were well aware of those with whom they associated. Tugwell, for example, realized that the party contained individuals with whom he did "not at all agree" and who he supposed were communists. Nevertheless, having done political battle with them over the platform, he concluded that the document was a fair one, representing "something of what each group . . . wanted," attained through compromise, not domination.[25] In addition, the fact that Wallace had championed most of the positions laid out in the platform long before there was any question of his being manipulated by communists further undermines the assumption of a controlling communist influence at the convention.

Indeed, the long-standing advocacy by both anticommunist and popular front liberals of many of the positions eventually taken by the new party actually suggests an organic conjunction of aims between the communists and the liberals in the Progressive Party, that is to say, the reality of a "popular front." The ADA itself implicitly acknowledged this in several contexts, albeit most of them in the domestic realm. The glaring lack of an ADA critique of the Progressives' proposal for socializing important components of the U.S. economy was one. The explicit and seemingly anomalous ADA admiration for Wallace's courageous antisegregationist campaign appearances in the South—that is, within the context of a nascent civil rights movement in which communists had been at the forefront since the 1930s—is a second example. Fundamental accord with the PCA regarding U.S. policy toward Spain and Palestine suggests that there was even room for agreement on some aspects of international relations.[26] If it was possible that communists could share Progressives' aims on some issues, why could they not do so on others? It may very well have been the case that some individuals within the new party took their stand against the Vermont amendment, for example, because they were communists toeing Moscow's line. It is clear, however, that opposition to the amendment also came from non-communists who in no sense advocated reflexive support of the Soviet Union but instead saw the amendment as either redundant or too much of a surrender to Red-baiting. Is it not also possible that an American communist could oppose the amendment for the same reasons, either in addition to or exclusive of any desire to follow the dictates of Moscow? Why could the cold war liberals not imagine an "American communist," influenced by a Russian model, perhaps, but acting within an essentially American cultural context, not under the control of malignant Russian puppeteers? The answer of course is that, because of their own experiences, they viewed communists by definition as individuals who subordinated their will to that of Moscow (a view that ironically evoked nineteenth-century assumptions regarding Catholics and Jews that no one in the ADA would have tolerated in 1948). It was virtually impossible for them even to consider the (somewhat naive) prospect raised by Wallace, that there might be "as much variation among Communists as among Democrats and Republicans." In the view of the cold war liberals, to be a communist was to serve the Soviet Union.[27]

If there was one aspect of this issue toward which Wallace and the Progressives clearly occupied a weak position, it was in their expectations regarding the Soviet Union. Wallace, for example, often not only oversimplified the nature of Soviet communism vis-à-vis American capitalism but also was probably too hopeful of the likelihood of full Soviet cooperation in international affairs. In part this arose from the nature of Wallace's optimistic political rhetoric, which itself derived from his style of editorial writing: the clear-cut, brief presentation of simple object lessons. Nevertheless, the Soviet regime was clearly far more brutal and dictatorial than Wallace and the Progressives seemed willing to acknowledge. Yet even on this issue the cold war liberals greatly overdrew their critique. In accusing Wallace of appeasing the Soviets they unfairly misrepresented his actual views. They ignored, for instance, his repeated calls for U.S. support of UN-administered humanitarian aid explicitly for the purpose of undermining the spread of communism by alleviating the conditions in which it thrived. Moreover, it is in no way clear that a more moderate approach to the Soviets—which is all that Wallace ever called for—might not have brought about changes in the Soviet system decades sooner than they finally came about. After all, both Kennan and Niebuhr argued at length that Stalin intentionally portrayed the United States to the Soviet people as a warmongering imminent threat in order to frighten them into submission and allegiance. That of course implied that if America acted in a less threatening manner, a suggestion that Wallace had raised repeatedly beginning with his July 1945 letter to Truman, then Stalin's grip on power might have been weakened.

In any case, it is clear that Wallace and the popular fronters never called for any actual compromise of American security. Yet many of their critics not only accused them of just that but did so in a fashion that made it ultimately impossible to discern just what the popular fronters really did advocate. In this sense a whole range of at least arguably reasonable positions regarding American foreign policy were eliminated from public discussion. This is not to say that all that the popular fronters advocated was valid or cogent but rather that it ought to have remained within the framework of debate—to be rejected perhaps, but on the basis of real substance instead of sensationalized misrepresentation. Yet the popular fronters' positions were ultimately rejected not because of their actual content but because of the oversimplified and demonized fashion in which they were represented by political opponents, centrally including Niebuhr and the ADA.

The cold war liberals' contribution to this outcome—their choice to cast their lot with the most conservative imperatives of the cold war in order to maintain influence—was replete with ironies. For one thing the ADA's demonizing of Wallace and the Progressive Party echoed the split on the Left that Niebuhr had so strongly condemned in German politics of the interwar era for enabling the Nazis to attain power. The final irony was that by painting all that the Progressives proposed in broad strokes and thus helping render it taboo, the anticommunist liberals surrendered the moral and political leverage that inhered in some of the popular front's arguments, leverage that the anticommunist liberals might have used not only to help moderate the eventual tensions of the cold war but to compel a far more progressive domestic policy as well.

The "Guru Letters" and Berlin

Besides the attacks made by the ADA, Wallace's problems were amplified by his treatment in the mainstream press. Indeed, despite his own journalistic background, Wallace had long seemed to suffer from the manner in which he was portrayed in the press. Curtis MacDougall, in his history of the Progressive campaign of 1948, suggests that this situation stemmed at least in part from Wallace's awkwardness, his inability to establish the sort of cordial relations with reporters that, say, Franklin Roosevelt always seemed to manage. MacDougall also argues that Wallace's image suffered because he was never willing to take seriously the need to prepare for press conferences by preparing answers for questions that were likely to be asked. He tended to respond in an off-the-cuff fashion, which frequently landed him in trouble.[28] To whatever extent this was true in the larger context of his career, it is certain that Wallace's ineptitude in dealing with the press cost him dearly at the Progressive Party convention in 1948, in a brief episode in which his spiritualism also came back to haunt him, so to speak.

On the afternoon of the convention's first day, July 23, Wallace held a press conference attended by nearly four hundred individuals, most of whom were reporters. Midway through the conference a reporter asked, "Mr. Wallace, do you repudiate the 'Guru Letters'?" He was referring to the collection of letters that Wallace allegedly wrote to his theosophical associate Nicholas Roerich during the mid-1930s, discussed in chapter 2. The letters, copies of which had been making their way around Washington for years, had become public knowledge during the first half of 1948 thanks to the conservative columnist Westbrook Pegler, who not only published excerpts from the letters but "interpreted" several passages in the most damaging way possible. Wallace had ignored their publication, while Pegler had been trying to get Wallace to own up to their authenticity. Now Wallace was confronted with the correspondence in a seemingly inescapable context. His handling of the confrontation was almost grotesque in its awkwardness.[29]

One can only imagine Wallace's extreme discomfort at being confronted on such a personal and sensitive subject, even if he anticipated such questioning. Perhaps he fleetingly recalled controversies from the past, when he had spoken unconventionally in public regarding spiritual issues. Or perhaps he feared that if he acknowledged his spiritualistic activities to the smallest degree, then the full range of those activities might somehow come to light. In any case, a tense exchange ensued, characterized by Wallace's repeated refusals to respond to the question, repeated by several reporters, including Pegler. Even when relatively sympathetic journalists queried him Wallace still responded in a stilted fashion. The profoundly uncomfortable moment finally passed when someone asked an unrelated question.[30]

Hostile newspapers, not surprisingly, had a field day over the exchange, poking merciless fun at Wallace. Even sympathetic columnists berated Wallace for not responding to the query.[31] To a degree they were being unfair, since questions of such a personal nature—that is, regarding what were essentially religious beliefs—were generally not asked of public figures in that era. On this point one only has to recall, for example, the manner in which reporters avoided addressing Franklin Roosevelt's paralysis throughout his White House years. But Roosevelt always had enjoyed a much warmer relationship with the press than did Wallace. And as MacDougall suggests, whatever warmth of feeling for Wallace may still have resided within the American press corps was dissipated by the Guru Letters debacle on July 23.

Despite its awkwardness, however, it is doubtful that the Guru Letters episode did as much damage to Wallace's image and campaign as did another, larger crisis of the cold war itself that cast a shadow over the Progressives' convention in Philadelphia: the ongoing U.S.-Soviet confrontation over Berlin. Reacting to the U.S. decision to introduce a new West German currency, on June 23 the Soviets cut off all surface traffic to West Berlin, effectively rendering it a Western island in a Soviet sea. The administration's response was a dramatic "air-lift" into the city that lasted 320 days. To most Americans, the "Berlin crisis" seemed to validate the sense of conflict and crisis that Truman—with the frequent if not always intentional support of the ADA—had nurtured since March 1946. In the context of international disputes over atomic energy, political crises in Western and Eastern Europe, domestic loyalty investigations and spy trials, as well as a presidential election in which a major candidate was being tarred as a puppet of the communists, the Soviet action at Berlin appeared to presage a new world war. The airlift thus seemed a heroic American effort to avoid such an outcome while still defending the West Berliners from communism.

Wallace's response to the crisis and the airlift clearly flowed from the political logic that he and the popular fronters had long articulated. He insisted that the crisis in Berlin was a creation of the administration and its bipartisan supporters, who needed a "permanent crisis" upon which to base their demands for continued "spending for war preparation." When he spoke at length about Berlin in his nomination acceptance speech at the Progressive Party convention, his remarks were jarring. Wallace argued that the crisis need not have happened—indeed, that it did not "happen" but rather "*was caused.*" The Berlin crisis was the logical outcome of the "get tough" policy of the Truman administration and its militarization of American society. The insistence on maintaining prosperity by preparing for war risked a peace that was not only fragile, Wallace contended, but unjust. For it aimed at resurrecting the same German nation that just a few short years before had been the great and evil enemy of the United States, while the Soviet Union, which had been America's great ally, was transformed into an enemy.[32]

It is certainly possible to characterize Wallace's remarks regarding the Berlin crisis as excessively strident. To the extent that this was the case, his stridency can be attributed to his real fear that war was imminent as well as to a profound anger arising from his belief that it did not have to be so. It is also possible that the dramatic tenor of his remarks was a response to the ostracizing and demonizing that he and the popular fronters had been subjected to for so long. The further they were isolated from the mainstream of American political culture, the more extreme their critique of that culture became. Yet to a great extent the increasing stridency of the popular front critique was relative, which is to say, in many of its aspects the popular front response to events differed little by summer 1948 from what it had been all along. It was the context that changed. For many Americans the Soviet blockade of Berlin in June 1948 seemed to prove the logic of the Truman Doctrine as well as the Munich analog, just as the North Korean invasion of South Korea seemed to do two years later. For Wallace and the Progressives to persist in criticizing American policy toward the Russians no longer made sense in the context of events as most Americans, even many once sympathetic to the popular front perspective, understood them.[33]

One great irony was that Niebuhr agreed with Wallace regarding Berlin, at least in the sense that Berlin itself was not worth going to war over. Because Berlin was always vulnerable to Russian pressure, he allowed that it perhaps "should have been abandoned" when the four-power control of Germany had first broken down. But this was the furthest extent of Niebuhr's agreement with Wallace. In fact, for Niebuhr the crisis over Berlin embodied in microcosm virtually the entire cold war. For one thing, Niebuhr believed that the key issue was the potential "loss of prestige," which he considered a substantive risk. Foreshadowing the later U.S. cold war obsession with "credibility," he argued that an American loss of international prestige would have immediate repercussions in international affairs. Invoking the logic of Munich as well as the assumption of a monolithic global communism controlled by Moscow, Niebuhr argued that if the United States abandoned Berlin then "Russian pressure" would surely increase in other areas. Ultimately invoking containment doctrine as well, Niebuhr concluded that the only way to maintain the global peace, meager though it might be, was by a "political and strategic program, designed to hold back the Russian ideological and military power" until Western Europe had regained enough strength to no longer be threatened by it.[34] For Niebuhr Berlin was worth the risk of war because of its symbolic value.

Not surprisingly, the ADA directly attacked Wallace's position regarding Berlin. In their view, his criticism of Truman's airlift was treacherous and came at just the moment when Germany's "democratic leaders . . . were once again rallying their exhausted forces against the threat of dictatorship."[35] In other words—and with an irony that is at once tragic and comical—Germany's old capital was now the Sudetenland in a new Munich crisis. The nation that only a few years earlier the ADA condemned for its brutality had transformed into a helpless democratic victim of a new and equally brutal onslaught. It was an interpretation that highlighted an essential point of division between the cold war and popular front liberals. Not only was it the case that the cold war liberals perceived virtually no chance for cooperation with the Soviets while the popular fronters still held out hope; the anticommunist liberals also had forgiven Germany its decade of moral transgression and turned it into the sympathetic focus of the struggle defined by the Truman Doctrine. Wallace and the Progressives, in contrast, were unwilling to forgive and forget so quickly or easily. By this time, however, and despite its inherent cogency and historical validity, the popular front logic failed. The Berlin airlift marked in substance and symbol the fact of the cold war's existence, with all of its implications in terms of American political and strategic thinking. The time during which moderating alternatives might have been seriously considered had passed. It was no longer possible to speak in terms of complex and shared responsibility for international tensions. Wallace and the Progressives' main argument against Truman's policy at Berlin—that the American hard line precipitated the crisis—was no longer politically viable. The same could be said for Wallace's candidacy.

Anticlimax: Fall Campaign and Election

Wallace nevertheless undertook a full cross-country campaign in the wake of the Progressive Party convention. Throughout the speeches he gave ran the same themes he had championed since leaving the Truman administration two years before. Perhaps most memorable, and certainly most courageous, was Wallace's series of racially integrated rallies in the American South. Across the region he spoke before integrated crowds and stayed in African-American homes. It was a campaign virtually without precedent, and Wallace suffered for it, literally and in political terms. In some instances he was actually driven from a platform without getting to deliver a speech as he became the focus of a powerful southern conflation of segregationism and anticommunism.[36]

Interestingly, the ADA expressed much admiration for Wallace's antisegregation campaign swing through the South in 1948, despite the fact that communists had been in the vanguard of the battle for civil rights in the region since the 1930s. In a second anti-Wallace pamphlet, "Henry A. Wallace: The Last Seven Months of His Presidential Campaign," the ADA's approval of Wallace's southern campaign stood out in bold relief from the harsh criticism that made up the rest of the document. There were some oblique criticisms, but the overall tone of the ADA's reportage on the southern campaign was laudatory, expressing respect for Wallace's calmness in the face of violence and his willingness to bring the "conversation" in the South around to the previously "non-controversial topic of Jim Crow."[37]

The ADA's willingness to praise Wallace's campaign in the South probably stemmed from several interconnected sources. For one thing, the issue of civil rights had become the area in which the ADA felt it could claim real success in influencing the Democratic Party during summer 1948. At the Democratic convention the group believed itself instrumental in forcing the party hierarchy to accept a strong civil rights plank in the party's platform. The meaning of that success was heightened for the members of the ADA by its contrast with their abject failure to compel the party to reject Harry Truman's renomination. The civil rights issue became the focus of the cold war liberals' desire to be "players" in the upper echelons of American politics. Loeb boasted to one of his colleagues that the ADA's "victorious fight on the civil rights issue" at the Democratic convention would "be recorded in the history books."[38] With so much of their collective self-esteem attached to the civil rights issue it is not far-fetched to think that the ADA would support anyone who fought for it. Moreover, the ADA lauded Wallace in this effort just as it forewent criticizing the new party's platform planks calling for the socialization of major industries. In both cases the ADA was supporting, either explicitly or implicitly, blows the popular fronters struck for domestic reform goals long-shared by all American progressives.

Its measured praise for Wallace's southern campaign notwithstanding, the ADA's attack on Wallace and the new party began in earnest even before the Progressives' convention commenced, with Loeb's appearance before the new party's platform committee on July 22. The committee held two full days of open hearings, during which some seventy-five organizations and individuals spoke, offering up a wide range of suggestions for the platform's content. Loeb's "testimony" was extraordinarily harsh, hardly aimed at the constructive improvement of the platform. He condemned the new party on fundamental issues, above all its unwillingness to denounce communism and its stand on the Marshall Plan, which by this time had become a bellwether issue for the ADA. He also restated his organization's belief that the Progressives were orchestrating "deliberate and consistent" opposition to progressive Democratic congressional candidates, thus following a "well-known Communist tactic" of treating the "anti-totalitarian progressive as the major enemy." Loeb's denunciation of the Progressives was virtually absolute, essentially a rationale for disbanding the organization. Loeb himself recognized this, noting that if the Progressives accepted the ADA's proposals, the new party would in effect "be destroyed," since it would be renouncing the essential reasons for its existence. In fact, he anticipated that the new party would reject his counsel, once more proving itself "an instrument of Soviet policy."[39]

Despite his own admission that both the tone and content of his remarks were extreme, Loeb expressed surprise to several acquaintances that the committee refrained from questioning him when he finished speaking. Loeb and the ADA also seemed shocked that, immediately following Loeb's testimony, committee chairman Tugwell had responded with a sharply worded rebuttal, characterizing Loeb's remarks as "unscrupulous and demagogic" as well as "insincere, hypocritical and immaterial." A description of the episode in "The Last Seven Months" implied that the Progressives did not question Loeb because they could not counter the truth of his remarks.[40] What the pamphlet failed to acknowledge was that the ADA had released Loeb's statement hours before he actually appeared before the committee, which allowed Tugwell the time to write, release, and read his own response to Loeb's remarks. Nor did it acknowledge what Tugwell pointed out centrally in his response: that Loeb's statement could only in the most strained manner be construed as constructive testimony. He was proposing, after all and in the clearest language, that the Progressives disavow their quintessential positions and, by so doing, disband themselves. In view of that one can only wonder what questions Loeb expected them to ask. In the end Loeb's statement to the Progressive Party platform committee and the response he received simply reflected the fact that, by late July, the popular fronters and the cold war liberals had attained a virtually diametric opposition. There was really nothing left for them to discuss.

Its profound misgivings notwithstanding, at the end of August the ADA formally endorsed Harry Truman for the presidency. Having done so, the cold war liberals continued their assault on Wallace and the Progressive Party with increasing virulence through late summer and autumn, stressing already familiar themes. Their campaign culminated in October with the release of two ADA documents, "The Last Seven Months" and "An Appeal to the Liberals of America." With the exception of its section on Wallace's campaign in the South, "The Last Seven Months" carried on very much in the style and content of its predecessor, "The First Three Months." It once again made use of portentous innuendo, as in a passage suggesting that Tugwell was really much more supportive of the ERP than he let on during the platform committee hearings. The explanation for Tugwell's alleged reticence on this crucial issue, according to "The Last Seven Months," was that it was just another in a series of popular front liberal "capitulations to the more rugged and purposeful men around Wallace."[41] In the ADA's construction liberals such as Tugwell and Wallace were well-meaning but naive and lacking in will; they were thus always overborne by the tough, jungle-savvy communists who surrounded them in their popular front organizations.

Like the ADA tract of the spring, "The Last Seven Months" also distorted the historical record relative to the Progressive Party. This was evident, for instance, in the tract's account of the debate of the Vermont amendment during the last session of the new party's convention. The drafting, submission, debate, and inclusion of the Schuman amendment were glossed over. The Vermont amendment was then portrayed in the ADA pamphlet as a heroic attempt by a lone Vermont delegate to strengthen the Schuman amendment's allegedly weak acknowledgment of joint U.S.-Soviet responsibility for international tensions. The pamphlet, in other words, ignored the fact that the Vermont amendment was an entirely separate entity with essentially the same aim as part of Schuman's amendment and that it was presented in total ignorance of either the Schuman amendment's existence or its prior inclusion in the platform. With now characteristic portentousness, "The Last Seven Months" concluded that Tugwell, once more in response to the dictates of the new party's "iron-fisted" communist controllers, had declared the Vermont amendment unnecessary and so "the Vermonter was effectively silenced." [42] It is true, of course, that the ADA's description of the episode differed little from many mainstream press accounts published in July. But the journalists at least had the excuse of not knowing at the time of the inclusion of the Schuman amendment in the platform. By the time the ADA published "The Last Seven Months" that information had long been available.

By early September the ADA's leadership had decided more was needed than lengthy pamphlets and brief press releases if they hoped to stop the damage they feared Wallace's campaign was doing to the Democrats. Moreover, some in the organization were concerned that the ADA would lose its recently attained political prestige—would not be able to "keep its name in the papers nationally," as national board secretary Joseph Rauh put it—unless new strategies were undertaken. [43] Also they continued to worry about the longer-term harm to liberalism arising from what they considered the new party's shameless usurpation of FDR's liberal legacy. So in addition to the production of "The Last Seven Months," the ADA decided to issue a document that would fall somewhere in between the formats of the exposé pamphlet and the quick response press release. Niebuhr himself was chosen to draft a document that would be "An Appeal to the Liberals of America." The plan was for a statement of two or three pages at most, to which would be appended the signatures of "as many prominent liberals and New Dealers" as could be persuaded.[44] Niebuhr's hurriedly written draft was narrowly focused and harsh, harping on the image of communists controlling the Progressive Party and insistent not only that Wallace's candidacy had been "inspired" by them but that "notorious followers of the party line" held all the "levers of power" within the organization. Invoking the Munich analog in his attack, Niebuhr asserted that Wallace's greatest transgression was in suggesting that his "policy of yielding to Russian pressure" was somehow an extension of FDR's foreign policy.[45]

The final document, released in mid-October, was only marginally more measured in its language than Niebuhr's draft, if far more comprehensive in scope. Sent out to potential signers under a cover letter articulating the ADA's fear that the Progressives undermined the liberal cause, the "Appeal" was an enumeration of the various sins that the ADA believed Wallace and his associates committed. The document accused the new party of attempting to wreck the "liberal-labor coalition" of the New Deal, while calling itself "Progressive" and acting in "the name of the ideals" of FDR. Implicitly claiming Roosevelt's legacy for themselves, the ADA insisted that the Progressive Party in fact represented a break from America's democratic tradition as well as a "corruption of liberalism." They contended that the fundamental difference between Roosevelt and the new party was the latter's "theory of collaboration with Communists." The "Appeal" also insisted that the essence of Roosevelt's foreign policy was far different from that of the Progressives. Invoking the logic of the Truman Doctrine, the broadside asserted that the Progressives' foreign policy betrayed "free people throughout the world" at a time when the great issue was "between those who believe in human freedom and those who do not." Mincing no words, the appeal declared that in this struggle the Progressive Party had "lined up unashamedly with the forces of Soviet totalitarianism." And for any who still missed the point, the document concluded that a "vote for the Progressive Party" was a vote "for the destruction of the anti-totalitarians of Europe."[46] There was no nuance, no complexity, not even the innuendo of "The Last Seven Months." In the "Appeal to Liberals" the Manichaean construction of the global cold war was brought home. Wallace and his associates were no longer political opponents with whom to debate; they were the enemy, to be opposed at all costs and destroyed.

There of course is no way of knowing the actual extent to which the ADA's campaign against Wallace helped Truman. But considering the relatively narrow margin of Truman's surprise victory in 1948, it seems reasonable to speculate that the ADA's efforts against Wallace at least swung a crucial if small number of liberal votes. Nevertheless, despite having endorsed Truman, virtually no one in the ADA expected him to win in November. Indeed, literally on the eve of the election the group's leaders were busy planning the first moves of a strategy aimed at regaining the presidency from the Republicans in 1952.[47] Yet even if Truman's victory was a surprise for the ADA, by the end of October the Progressive Party's cause truly was lost in all senses. As far as Wallace and the Progressive Party's prospects were concerned, the actual election of 1948 was quite anticlimactic.

Receiving slightly more than a million votes, only some 2.4 percent of the total popular vote nationally, Wallace failed even to attain the numbers that might have promised future influence for himself and the Progressives in mainstream liberal councils. In addition, the more politically viable aspects of Wallace's platform had been co-opted by Truman, partly in response to pressure orchestrated by the ADA. So Wallace and the Progressives were left only with the more politically radical of their positions to champion. As a result, at no time after 1948 did the popular fronters attain any influential voice in American politics or foreign affairs.

Wallace's reputation was shattered at the end of a campaign that in a sense began with his speech at Madison Square Garden in September 1946. It was a campaign that embodied virtually all of the causes he had battled for at least since attaining the vice presidency in 1941 and in some cases for decades. In the arena of domestic affairs Wallace ended his public career fighting for much of what the ADA and other American progressives would continue to champion over the next several decades, although with inconsistent success. As Wallace quickly faded from the public scene after November 1948, with him went any real possibility of high profile public criticism of the American hard line toward the Soviet Union as well as of its underlying logic. Indeed, having helped to drive the popular fronters from the stage of mainstream politics by tarring them as communists and dupes, during the next decade the anticommunist liberals of the ADA ironically found themselves defending against attacks on their own loyalty made by the ideological successors of Martin Dies.[48]

In the end it is not really a question of who "won" within the liberal community by 1948. In the terms of their shared critique of American society, neither the cold war nor the popular front liberals really attained anything that could be called victory. Because of their detestation of communism, their desire to attain influence in mainstream American politics, and their own definition of what was possible in those politics, Niebuhr and his colleagues in the ADA ultimately and ironically acted to the benefit of conservative ideals rather than their own. And in so doing they set the pattern for later liberals, who would operate within a constrained range of politically viable actions that almost always validated conservative political agendas. When one considers that the original, essential quest of Niebuhr and his associates had not been to fight communism but rather to create a modern society that preserved the general welfare while also maintaining the individual's sense of self, one perceives the final irony of 1948. This was that in helping to destroy Wallace and the Progressives, the cold war liberals may also have destroyed their greatest potential allies in such a quest.

Epilogue

"Things Have Changed Greatly"

THE HALF decade following the Progressive Party's shattering 1948 electoral defeat was filled with developments that greatly heightened cold war tensions, domestically and internationally. By the early 1950s the United States had experienced high-profile espionage trials, the announcement of the Soviet Union's explosion of an atom bomb, the "fall" of China to communism, the rise of Joe McCarthy and communist "witch-hunting," and the start of the Korean War. In this context three events took place in 1952 that can be viewed together as bringing a degree of closure to the conflict between the two factions within American liberalism as well as to the roles played by Reinhold Niebuhr and Henry Wallace within that conflict. The first event was the publication of *The Irony of American History,* the last of Niebuhr's best-known books. The other two events were part of Wallace's career. The first was the September 1952 publication in the nationally distributed Sunday newspaper magazine *This Week* of an article by Wallace entitled "Where I Was Wrong," in which he seemed to retract his late-1940s critique of American cold war policy. The second was the ongoing recording (begun in 1951) of Wallace's reminiscences upon his life and career as part of the Columbia University Oral History Collection.[1] The concurrence of these undertakings as well as their substance marked a culmination of several crucial themes in the lives and thinking of these two men and the political culture in which they centrally figured. As such, they offer an opportunity for closing this study by returning to its original foci in the context of drawing conclusions regarding its larger themes.

Niebuhr and *The Irony of American History*

Like Niebuhr's other books that are recognized as milestones in his career as a cultural and political philosopher, *The Irony of American History* can be viewed as both a restatement and culmination of central Niebuhrian themes that had evolved over years and even decades. In *Irony* Niebuhr returned to his critiques of American liberal complacency and of social-science perspectives on reform as well as to his defense of the open society of the West. In this sense *Irony* arose directly from Niebuhr's early critical commentary on modern urban-industrial civilization. As Richard Fox has noted, *Irony* was both a "sharp attack on communism" and a "vindication of pragmatic democracy." The transcendent if implicit conclusion of *Irony*, however, was the idea, present in Niebuhr's thinking since Munich, that one nation (such as the United States) might be so much more moral, in a relative sense, than another nation (the Soviet Union, for example) as to render the difference virtually absolute. Yet in order to reach such a conclusion Niebuhr wrote a book characterized, as several historians have noted, by oversimplification of terms, of concepts, and, especially, of history.[2]

Such reductionism is apparent literally from the book's first words, in which Niebuhr declared that "everybody" understood the "obvious meaning" of the global struggle in which America was engaged. Combining the black-and-white simplicity of the Truman Doctrine with his own long-standing critique of liberal culture articulated with such irony in *The Children of Light and the Children of Darkness,* Niebuhr insisted that the United States was "defending freedom against tyranny . . . trying to preserve justice against a system which has, demonically, distilled injustice and cruelty out of its original promise of a higher justice." Despite extensive restatements of his earlier, ironically complex critique of the complacency-engendering effects of America's wealth upon national attitudes, *Irony* was dominated from the outset by clear-cut cold war polarities. Occasional nuance notwithstanding, Niebuhr represented communism as an absolute unvarying evil. Moreover, in its international context he saw communism as implicitly monolithic and dominated by Russia. "In every instance," Niebuhr insisted, this "demonic religio-political creed" transformed the partial flaws of liberalism into "consistent and totally harmful ones." Less than a decade after the fall of the Third Reich and the end of the Holocaust, Niebuhr contended that the United States faced a "vast . . . movement which generates more extravagant forms of political injustice and cruelty . . . than . . . *ever known in human history.*"[3]

Niebuhr's discussion of various aspects of the cold war itself was also simplistic, displaying a tendentious casualness toward the facts of history and the logic of international affairs. Such laxity was apparent, for example, when he attempted to explain the resentment that many less-developed nations felt toward the United States, which often drove them into the Soviet Union's calculating embrace. Although Niebuhr could write of the cold war as an "international class war," he seemed oblivious to the historical and socio-economic implications not only of colonialism but of modern international industrialism as well. Thus he could claim that it was Americans' propensity for trumpeting their prosperity, as a means of proving American cultural superiority, that engendered Third World resentment. This explanation, of course, ignored the fact that Western prosperity—of which American material wealth, according to his own analysis, was only a concentrated version—was partially grounded upon the historical exploitation of colonial labor dating back centuries.[4]

Niebuhr's explanation of the cold war in *Irony* was also marked by oversimplified historical/geographical analogy. Thus he utilized the term "feudalism" to represent virtually any nonindustrial political economy, no matter how far distant it was in time and space from actual European feudalism. For instance, he characterized the Middle East as a "decadent Mohammedan feudal order" that was in the process of disintegration. In a related point he drew a comparison between the inevitable decline of global communism and the historical waning of Islam, seemingly unaware that by the latter he was actually referring to the political decline of the Ottoman empire and ignoring the actual persistence and growth of Islamic culture throughout the twentieth century. Such cultural and historical obtuseness also was manifested in the ease with which Niebuhr characterized the entire complex range of Asian societies in broad, patronizing strokes. All Asian nations Niebuhr dismissed (as did many Americans of his era, including Wallace) as "sleeping-waking cultures in which the drama of human history is not taken seriously" or as the "dying sleeping cultures of the Orient."[5]

Even in discussing domestic affairs, Niebuhr's historical perspective in *Irony* was extraordinarily narrow. He wrote, for example, of the "fluidity of the American class structure" as an explanation for the lack of "social resentments" in the United States, while virtually ignoring the issue of race. A similarly narrow outlook emerged in his uncharacteristically strong praise of the New Deal as an example of the "pragmatic" qualities of American politics (as he put it, a "triumph of 'common sense'"). In speaking of the long-term results of New Deal labor policy, he contended that a framework of "equilibrated power" (between labor and management) had been established by the late 1930s, apparently forgetting his and his colleagues' own harsh condemnation only five years earlier of the passage of the powerfully antilabor Taft-Hartley Act, which undermined key components of the New Deal's protective labor legislation.[6]

The reductionist framework of *Irony* allowed Niebuhr to revisit many of the older themes of his commentary and to introduce a few new ones, fashioning all of them into a context for his essential contention: despite its flaws the United States had muddled through rather admirably as a democracy and a haven for individual freedom. Central among the old themes was Niebuhr's critique of the modern scientific-technological mentality that he had critically associated for so long with individuals such as John Dewey and Henry Wallace. Among other things, Niebuhr wrote, the modern confidence in "human power over historical destiny" had paved the way for Marxism (which was, he once more pointed out, little more than a utopian corruption of liberalism). In addition, and perhaps most ironically from Niebuhr's perspective, the scientific era not only had produced great benefits for humanity but also had issued in global and atomic war. Indeed, Niebuhr believed, the ironic cultural dominance of science ultimately lay more heavily upon America than any other nation. Not only had technological superiority made the United States the most powerful nation in the world, it also had bound the nation inextricably, through the interests and responsibilities derived from power, to the affairs of the other nations of the world. Accepting fully the fundamental assumptions of geo-politics—which had direct implications for his cold war commentary—Niebuhr insisted that the scientific and technological knowledge that made America supremely strong made it supremely vulnerable as well.[7]

At the height of his career—more than two decades beyond the years in Detroit, when he had felt so inferior to doctors, scientists, and businessmen—Niebuhr was able to argue that the "'scientific' approach" so beloved by liberal reformers of all sorts had failed. Idealist hopes, both liberal and communist, that social reform would issue automatically from increased education and "scientifically perfected social institutions" had proved pretentious at best. In the case of communism, Niebuhr added, such hopes ultimately had engendered great evil. And while liberal ideology perhaps had not spawned the tyranny associated with communism, it had led in the case of the United States to long-term, globally irresponsible pacifism and isolationism. Even though World War II had been a corrective to such "idealistic" irresponsibility, Niebuhr still saw residual danger in the continuing advocacy of plans for world government on the part of liberals like Wallace. Along with the denunciation of atomic weapons, Niebuhr viewed such plans as nothing other than the "old pacifist escape" from the dilemma of war.[8]

In any case, the scientific outlook from which Niebuhr believed such "illusions" as isolationism, pacifism, and proposals for world government derived had found the tensions of the cold war intractable. The all-encompassing global struggle was not simply the result of statesmen failing to take the advice of social scientists. No, the hopes of the liberal idealists had proven false for far more complex reasons, notably the failure of the scientific perspective to "discover that integral, self-transcendent center of personality," which even in 1952 remained an important normative in Niebuhr's evaluation of society. Indeed, he argued, "scientific culture" tended to "obscure the mystery" of the individual's "freedom and uniqueness." Science was oblivious to the importance of personality and the connections between individual and community.[9]

Yet despite the baleful influence of the idealistic, overly scientific aspects of Western and particularly American culture that Niebuhr had criticized for more than a quarter of a century, in *Irony* he once again defended America as the epitome of the open society he had championed in the wake of the Munich crisis. Amidst all his ironic reflections on American politics and culture, Niebuhr throughout the book repeatedly asserted, with only the mildest countervailing criticism, the moral superiority of American society, despite its many flaws. It was a superiority highlighted by juxtaposition with the tyranny built upon the foundation of Marxism's more distilled, dogmatic idealism. America, Niebuhr insisted, had achieved a reasonable level of social justice because rampant individualism actually had been moderated by pragmatic "collective action." Americans had not, fortunately, lived up to their own hyper-individualistic dogma.[10] Where Russian communism's social consciousness had hardened into a demonic religious-political movement, American liberalism, its ideological pretensions notwithstanding, had established political institutions that protected citizens against the abuse of power. "Common sense," Niebuhr declared, had triumphed over the laissez-faire ideology of businessmen and the speculations of social scientists. In the same vein, he contended, America had "learned the lesson of history tolerably well . . . , saved by a certain grace inherent in common sense" rather than reliance on "abstract theories."[11]

In the book's final pages Niebuhr returned to the multifaceted question of irony in the human condition, concluding with a final attack on Russian communism as well as an unambiguous assertion of what could be termed the "outsider's perspective" in cultural criticism. Into the "monstrous evils" of communism—still clearly, if implicitly, monolithic—were piled idealistic error upon error. Communism "transmuted religious truths . . . into political slogans" and in so doing became a foe of formidable global proportions. Incapable of assimilating irony, communism was thus equally incapable of the self-correction Niebuhr saw inherent in American culture. American democracy, conversely if not always intentionally, nurtured irony and thus self-criticism. Returning once more to his post-Munich insights regarding the open society, Niebuhr again implied the sense of cultural place he had attained in the course of his career as the detached outsider, widely respected for his ironic perspective. "Knowledge of irony," he wrote, "is usually reserved for observers," that is, for outsiders rather than "participants." Yet participants with a sufficient "degree of transcendence over the vicissitudes of their nations" could at times bring the outsider's perspective to the mainstream, as Niebuhr certainly had. Such sensitive, transcendent individuals, Niebuhr declared, could articulate the communal self-criticism that would illuminate the ironic situation in which they and their fellow citizens were involved and thus bring the irony to the surface for all to see. By doing so, Niebuhr believed, such individuals—among whom he surely included himself—might lead their compatriots to "abate the pretensions and dissolve the irony." [12] A society like America, in other words, by nurturing individuals such as Niebuhr nurtured as well the capacity for the very self-criticism that over time might help it transcend its flaws.

Wallace's "Recantation"

In *The Irony of American History* Niebuhr reaffirmed and elaborated the central themes he had developed over the previous two decades. He meshed his skeptical critique of his nation's culture, politics, and foreign policy with an appreciation of what he viewed as America's ironic successes. In the process he fashioned a place for himself, if not at the core of mainstream culture then at least at a privileged critical vantage point from which to observe it. He was, in other words, as close to being a cultural insider as an individual of his background and intellectual inclinations was likely to get.

For Wallace the situation by 1952 was quite different. After four years of ostracism and vilification, he had come to question some of the assumptions he had articulated during the campaign of 1948, to the point of publishing, in the form of the article "Where I Was Wrong," something of a recantation of his cold war stance. Yet when read closely, and particularly when read in the context of his concurrently recorded oral history interviews, "Where I Was Wrong" turns out to be at most a partial recantation of Wallace's cold war critique and one confined to a rather narrow range of issues. Indeed, by augmenting a reading of

Wallace's article with a reading of pertinent portions of the oral history, one can see just how much of Wallace's postwar vision remained intact.

To a great extent the article, published at the height of the McCarthyite witch-hunt, was dominated by a tone of public confession (rather than, say, quiet personal reflection) common during the McCarthy era. In this context the piece reflected a fundamental change in Wallace's view of Stalin and the Soviet Union. The time for accommodation in U.S.-Soviet relations—even the time for talking about accommodation—he now insisted was past. Indeed, the central "error" that Wallace acknowledged was in having expected the Soviets to have "had more sense than to do what they have been doing during the past few years." He had been cured, he now declared, of his overly optimistic expectations regarding Soviet behavior. While in no sense renouncing his "stand for peace" of the late 1940s, Wallace agreed with the cold war liberals that the Soviet Union was, or had become, wholly expansionist.[13]

Wallace also appeared to have come around to the cold war liberal perspective regarding other aspects of global communism. For instance, like Niebuhr, Wallace now declared Russian communism "utterly evil" while implying that Chinese communism was possibly salvageable. Through a simplistic, nationalistic cultural lens similar to Niebuhr's, Wallace described China as a "dragon . . . stirred out of its sleep," likely to turn on the Soviets when it realized that there was no point in trading "feudalism" for "Russian communism." In addition, Wallace suggested an explanation of Asian resentment toward the West that was similar to Niebuhr's. Asia, he contended, was a region of farmers and agricultural workers earning below-subsistence incomes in the face of magnificent Western wealth. That circumstance seemed, for the moment, to reinforce the appeal of Russian propaganda to the peoples of Asia. Yet despite his assumption that Asian resentments would eventually turn as much against Moscow as against the West, Wallace also had come to accept the cold war liberal construction of a Moscow-dominated, monolithic global communism. He spoke, for example, of the Soviet Union, "through Mao Tse-tung," having "millions of Chinese workers at its disposal to be impressed into the Chinese army."[14]

In explaining his change of heart, Wallace suggested various reasons for his "mistaken" perceptions of the immediate postwar years. Prior to 1949, he asserted, he was convinced that the Soviets "really wanted and needed peace." After that year, however, he became increasingly "disgusted with Soviet methods," ultimately deciding that Russian leaders wanted the cold war to persist, even at the risk of military hostilities. Wallace's growing skepticism and disgust regarding the Soviets after 1949 arose from several factors. He was shocked, for instance, by revelations regarding Russia's atomic spies as well as testimony by American ex-communists regarding Soviet espionage in the West. But Wallace felt that his "greatest mistake" of the late 1940s lay in not denouncing the communist coup in Czechoslovakia in February 1948. While he still believed that much of his analysis at the time was sound, he now agreed that the communists who took power in Czechoslovakia were "ruthless" and "Russian-trained," rather than patriotic members of an indigenous Czech movement. Wallace also acknowledged being deceived by the Soviets during his vice presidential visit in 1944 to Soviet Asia. He had been led to believe that in Siberia the Soviet Union was building a productive society grounded in economic democracy. (He was careful to point out, however, that not only was there no way he might have seen through the Russian ruse but that other Western visitors, such as the Republican internationalist Wendell Willkie, were fooled as well.) Finally, Wallace acknowledged that time had brought him to a "new understanding" of the Korean situation. As it had for many Americans, whether dedicated or wavering cold warriors, Korea helped convince Wallace of the Soviet Union's malignant global intentions. "Russia," Wallace declared, was "still on the march," and all that remained to be seen was whether it would conquer all of Asia.[15]

Nevertheless, for an article that generally was read as a comprehensive recantation, aspects of Wallace's late-1940s critique of American policy still remained intact within "Where I Was Wrong."[16] For instance, Wallace—still very much the agricultural scientist with an appreciation of technological expertise—argued with ambivalent approval that "in their totalitarian way" the Soviets had brought the "full power of science to bear" in all areas of production. Foreshadowing American cultural anxieties of the late 1950s and early 1960s, Wallace even implied the possibility of the Soviet Union eventually surpassing the United States in its scientific and technological supremacy. In addition, Wallace still held to his critique of Western colonialism and rearticulated his call for better global efforts on behalf of the "common man." In this vein he fully maintained his late 1940s advocacy of the UNO, insisting that its agencies, instead of direct U.S. interventions, be the mechanism for aiding the common man worldwide.[17]

To the extent that "Where I Was Wrong" actually repudiated Wallace's cold war critique, there are indications that he was moving toward it for some time prior to September 1952. As early as 1950 he had begun to give up his once-powerful resistance to the pressures of Red-baiting. In his speech to the Progressive Party convention in February 1950, for instance, Wallace called upon the party finally to adopt the Vermont resolution (with its explicit refusal to endorse the foreign policy of any nation), rejected at the July 1948 convention, in order to demonstrate to the nation that the Progressives were not "apologists for Russia and Communism." In another address the following year he explicitly attacked the communists who, he contended, had "spoiled" the Progressives' campaign in 1948 "in their fanatical way."[18]

The most significant foreshadowing of the 1952 article, however, was Wallace's break in summer 1950 with the Progressive Party over its stand on the Korean War. Like many Americans, including cold war liberals such as Niebuhr, Wallace viewed the North Korean invasion very much as a Soviet action, with the North Koreans and Chinese acting as little more than Russian puppets. Breaking with the Progressive Party's leadership, Wallace pronounced the American-led UN effort to repel the North Koreans a "just war." On July 15, 1950, Wallace released a statement that unconditionally supported the U.S.-UN effort and declared his belief that the Soviets could have prevented the North Korean attack and stopped the war whenever they wished. It was a view that stood in stark contrast to his position on the Berlin crisis of 1948, during which, despite the Soviet Union's direct and explicit action, he had placed much blame upon the United States. To this extent Wallace had finally been won over by the logic of the cold war liberals. In August 1950, when the Progressives formally refused to support the American position, he resigned from the party. In response to criticism from a long-time Progressive colleague that his resignation would destroy the party, Wallace argued that the Progressives were toeing the Soviet line and so destroying themselves.[19]

Even though Wallace's 1952 recantation was only partial, and even though he still maintained many aspects of his internationalist vision of the 1940s, the question remains why he repudiated as much of his earlier stance as he did. Several factors probably contributed to Wallace's altered perspective. Above all, perhaps, was the stark reality of the cold war, both at home and abroad. This is to say that to some extent Wallace's perspective was likely altered by a context analogous to that which made his 1948 stand on Berlin seem incongruous, if not treasonable, to many Americans. In 1948, while most Americans viewed the Soviet blockade of Berlin as tantamount to a military attack, Wallace saw a chance for accommodation with the Soviets, including resolution of the Berlin crisis, if only the United States were more understanding of the Soviet perspective. By the early 1950s, however, the cold war was so deeply entrenched that its existence altered the range of viable alternatives even for Wallace. Most Americans now saw no possibility of accommodation with the Soviets, only the possibility of minimizing Soviet transgressions. It was within this new, narrower reality that Wallace construed not only the events of 1952 but those of earlier years as well. Thus he revised his interpretation of the Czechoslovakian coup, now viewing it as a ruthless example of Soviet expansionism. And that episode in turn became part of the context for interpreting the North Korean invasion of South Korea. In addition, in Korea the fact of American military involvement triggered Wallace's always staunch patriotism. As he put it in his July 1950 statement on the UN action, "when my country is at war and the United Nations sanctions that war, I am on the side of my country and the United Nations."[20]

An additional factor driving Wallace's recantation can be characterized loosely as the domestic impact of the cold war. Wallace was unquestionably affected by the experience of being driven from the political mainstream and subjected to over four years of vilification in American public discourse. Between 1949 and 1953 Wallace spent a vast amount of time attempting to correct or refute real and perceived slights and slanders upon his career and character. Time and again old canards were raised and new attacks were launched, many of them with complex origins dating back to the bureaucratic conflicts of the war years. For example, Wallace was condemned, in closed hearings of the House Committee on Un-American Activities, in connection with wartime uranium shipments to the Soviet Union. The materials in question actually had nothing to do with atomic weapons, yet when the substance of the hearings made its way, inaccurately, into the press, it became an occasion for resurrecting the false 1945 accusation that Wallace had advocated, in a Truman cabinet meeting, "giving the bomb" to the Soviets. In another case, when a Siberian labor camp survivor mentioned in a memoir how Wallace and his entourage had been deceived by the Soviets during his tour of the region in 1944, the media turned the story into a tale of Wallace selling out the prisoners by ignoring their plight and advocating aid to their brutal keepers.[21] Ultimately, in a poignantly ironic cold war moment that went unremarked at the time, Wallace even found himself making common cause with several of his detractors of the 1940s, including Truman, General Leslie Groves, and journalist Joseph Alsop, when they joined Wallace as foci of various HUAC investigations.[22] In light of such travails, it seems reasonable to conclude that at some point Wallace—like so many other Americans hounded by various components of the McCarthy-era witch-hunt apparatus—felt compelled to back down from at least some aspects of his cold war critique.

Having said this, it is important to reiterate that one must be careful upon reading "Where I Was Wrong" not to see more of a reversal in Wallace's perspective than was really there. The corrective to such a misreading, as I have suggested, is the Columbia oral history, recorded during the years bracketing the publication of the article. Wallace's taped reminiscences make clear that he still held to many of the positions he articulated in the 1940s (and in some cases long before). To be sure, much of the repudiation contained in "Where I Was Wrong" is validated, both in tone and content, in the oral history. Here, too, for example, Wallace spoke of his increasing disillusionment regarding accommodation with the Soviets as he became aware after 1948 of the brutal realities of Russian control of Czechoslovakia. And he recounted the process by which he reached the conclusion that by early 1949 the

Soviets had decided the cold war worked to their advantage, which meant to Wallace that a U.S. policy of reason and compromise could no longer be effective. Nevertheless, in the end Wallace evoked an image of lost opportunity, very much in line with his 1940s critique of American policy. The last chance for U.S.-Soviet accommodation, he suggested, may have been his exchange of open letters with Josef Stalin in the spring of 1948. "But today [1951] is not May 1948," he said, "and things have changed greatly since then." He was still convinced that there had been a possibility immediately after the war to build "one world of peace." Now, in the early 1950s, he speculated, such a possibility might still remain, but he was certain it was "not nearly as great" as it had been only a few years—and an entire era, one might add—before.[23]

This sense of lost opportunities—which in effect validated rather than repudiated his reasoning of the 1940s—was a central theme in Wallace's oral history, lending an air of both despair and chastened hope to his reminiscences. Such qualities were apparent when he expressed thorough disillusionment with all three American political parties, declaring that he had seen enough of their "undesirable elements" and was now "very glad to leave all three of them alone." Despair and hope were also evident in Wallace's fear that the United States was failing to "furnish constructive leadership to the common men of the world," of whom he still saw himself a champion. By failing in this capacity, Wallace warned, America and Western Europe were leaving the door open to the Russians, who had proven so adept (as Niebuhr too had noted) at appealing to the misery of the oppressed. If the United States and Western Europe continued to reject his proposals for "one world," including UN-administered aid, he warned, "the most extraordinary barbarities" could result. And with unaccustomed cynicism he suggested that such barbarities were likely to come at the hand of his beloved "common man."[24]

Along with such observations, however, Wallace reiterated many of his old convictions and hopes, if somewhat less optimistically. He continued to believe in the liberal dream that an educated, informed populace would eventually do the right thing. And he made clear that the "long-time welfare of all mankind" remained his ultimate concern as an

American. Wallace also still believed that the universe and God were progressive. The purpose of life was improving life, which meant making it more abundant for all, which to him was simply a "progressive matter." But Wallace had come to understand that there could be no progress without "danger of retrogression." One had to act even in the face of tragic consequences. Sounding uncannily like a young Reinhold Niebuhr at Yale in the 1910s, Wallace insisted that "genuine creative advance is only possible when man as a moral being steps in with the fiat, 'I will.'" In this context he even addressed for the first time in many years, if somewhat obliquely, his spirituality. Wallace asserted that anyone who seriously asked the question "What is the chief end of man?" had to be "a mystic." But the crucial question, he qualified, was whether hopes for human welfare could be "brought into action here on Earth."[25]

Above all, Wallace still held to his dream of "one world" that Niebuhr so remorselessly derided. He continued to call for economic democracy in combination with political democracy, a global New Deal for the common man, and, eventually, world government. In this context Wallace also persisted in his characteristic cultural imperialism, if in a more subdued form. Thus for Wallace in the early 1950s, as in the 1940s, the United States had to lead the way toward globally shared abundance, albeit in support of the UN rather than in its place. This meant altering U.S. policy toward Third World nations, no longer dealing with dictatorial elites while abandoning the masses to the communists. To attain "one world," Wallace contended, America must furnish effective leadership to the common people of the world, to compete at that fundamental level with the Soviet Union. Evoking his speeches and writings of the war years, he insisted that in Asia, the Middle East, and elsewhere, the United States must have a "big program for advancing the living standards of the people."[26]

At the same time, and perhaps reflecting a more chastened state of mind, Wallace emphasized that his call for such policies was not grounded upon an idealized view of the common man. Despite the great pride he felt regarding his 1942 "Century of the Common Man" speech, Wallace now realized, in light of events since 1948, that the common man was "nothing sacred." He was only a "potentiality and a very great force" whose energy could be turned to many purposes, good and evil. Wallace still believed this to be the century of the common man, but he also believed it remained to be seen whether it would be "blessed or cursed." [27] For Wallace the answer to that question still hung in the balance, more precariously than ever. Yet he remained certain that it was an answer to which America still held the key.

Conclusions: The Ironies of American Liberal Internationalism in the Postwar Era

In examining the outcome of the conflict between the two factions of liberals lined up behind Niebuhr and Wallace, one can observe—in good Niebuhrian fashion—a complex of ironies. Some of these ironies touched only one side of the divide, others were shared in some sense by both. For example, Niebuhr, Wallace, and many of their respective associates, for all their differences, shared an inherently, if implicitly, nationalistic outlook. Despite their rivalry, they all assumed during the 1940s that the United States was essentially a benevolent, righteous, and culturally superior nation that ought to lead the world. Although Wallace and his colleagues began to question aspects of that perspective, it remained for the Vietnam War generation to do so in a comprehensive fashion.

In an irony of a different sort, liberals on both sides of the split ultimately were "captured" by the logic of cold war liberalism in ways they would never have imagined. This can most easily be seen in Wallace's case in view of his 1952 "recantation." It can also be said of his 1948 supporters who recanted, particularly as they too departed the Progressive Party by the early 1950s, leaving it finally to the communists who allegedly had controlled it from the outset. Yet this idea of being captured by the logic of cold war liberalism applies to the anticommunist liberals as well. To the extent that Niebuhr became an apologist for "pragmatic" American politics and policy, his social thought was unquestionably shaped—and distorted—by the preoccupations of the cold war. This effect can be glimpsed in *The Irony of American History*, and it was commented upon before that by the sociologist David Riesman in a 1951 exchange of letters with Niebuhr. In the exchange Riesman asserted, very much to Niebuhr's irritation, that in Niebuhr's writings the individual who recognized the concept of "original sin" fared much better than "the hopeful, utopian and trusting liberal."[28] Riesman implied, in other words, that Niebuhr's efforts at attaining an objective, "realistic" perspective might in fact be morally weighted.

The ADA was "captured" by the cold war as well, in several senses. Remaining at the margins of Democratic party affairs, it never attained the influence in American politics that its founders had hoped its 1948 campaign efforts would win for it. Having by 1948 already surrendered on most issues to moderate and conservative imperatives, the organization found it virtually impossible, until the 1960s, to bring much pressure to bear for progressive domestic reform in the face of cold war fears that it had helped to generate. In addition, by 1950 the ADA itself faced public attack as part of an "international conspiracy to socialize America."[29] And some ADA members were captured by their own logic in another, perhaps more insidious sense. They came to view the struggle between "freedom" and "totalitarianism" in increasingly rigid, even arrogant, cultural-geographical terms. Thus Schlesinger could write in 1951 that the West, although not perfectly free, was the only place where the aspiration for freedom had not been "totally extinguished." He could not see the condescension and insensitivity in this assertion not only toward the nonaligned nations but toward those who yearned and fought for freedom from within totalitarian countries as well. He could not imagine that aspirations for freedom might even be stronger in such places.[30]

A further shared irony in the Wallace-Niebuhr divide, a more personal one, lay in the parallel shift in both Niebuhr's and Wallace's public stature during the course of their careers. Niebuhr had established himself as one of a handful of prominent commentators on national and international affairs and in this sense had transformed himself into an insider. But while he continued to write at a rate that most academics would envy, *Irony* was his last great book. By the end of the decade (in part because of poor health) he had become more a gray-haired political elder than a shaper of opinion. Wallace, meanwhile, returned on a small scale to his earliest loves, the land and plant and animal breeding. On a small farm in upstate New York he spent the rest of his life experimenting with strains of strawberries and chickens. Yet the location of the farm, so far from the Midwest of his youth and prepolitical careers, served to underline how far removed he was from the old sense of place that had formed him, how much of an outsider—in every sense—he had become. His public appearances were infrequent, and he never attained anything like Niebuhr's respected status within the liberal community. For the most part he passed the remainder of his life as a figure of ridicule, disdain, and pity, when he was thought of at all. Would his public reputation have revived had he lived longer into the Vietnam era than he did? (Wallace died in 1965 of amyotrophic lateral sclerosis.) One can only speculate.

The irony in this dual shift—Niebuhr moving from relative outsider to relative insider while the general trajectory of Wallace's career was just the reverse—lay in the fact that Niebuhr, whose critique was grounded in his sense of being on the outside looking in, attained mainstream credibility. But the irony also lay in the role that Wallace's hugely overdrawn association with communism played in the shift. In reality, both men's commentaries on international relations grew out of their complementary assessments early in the century of essentially the same phenomena: the social effects of the advent of modern urban-industrial culture. As we have seen, both Niebuhr and Wallace sought what could be termed communitarian solutions to the alienation that arose from the conditions of modern existence. In Niebuhr's case this search had drawn explicitly on the Marxist tenets that were erroneously associated with Wallace by the late 1940s. Whatever Wallace was envisioning for America in the 1920s and 1930s and for the world in the 1940s, it was neither communism nor socialism. Indeed, it was an alternative to communism and socialism that he sought. This may explain why Wallace and many of the progressive liberals who supported him by the mid-1940s never really embraced communism as well as why they were not nearly as fearful of it as the cold war liberals. What Wallace created, in his amalgam of experimentalism, spiritualism, and "cooperation," was something of an American analog for the radical ideologies that had come out of nineteenth-century Europe. It was not the first time that such a phenomenon had occurred in the American heartland.

Not surprisingly, considering his own extraordinarily ironic bent, Niebuhr's ideological evolution seems particularly shot through with ironies. For example, his long-standing denunciation of mechanistic, moralistic idealism was itself firmly grounded by the 1940s upon two ideal constructs. First, his concept of the "open society," which he saw embodied by the West, was an inherently idealistic assessment of the very culture whose spiritual and social failings he had spent several decades attacking. Second, the Munich analog, which Niebuhr had assimilated rapidly and thoroughly after 1938, was an idealistic construct in the sense that it transformed the specifics of a historical episode into a transcendent principle of politics and policy making. The Munich analog, elevated to a high level of abstraction, enabled Niebuhr and others to direct a powerful yet ahistorical attack against Wallace and the popular front liberals for urging greater understanding of the Soviet perspective. Indeed, it was Wallace, the alleged idealist, who repeatedly and vainly attempted to assert a specific historical context upon the increasingly tense international atmosphere of the immediate postwar years.

This complex of ironies illuminates some fundamental features of American political culture of the last half century. It suggests that in their approach to international affairs Americans and their leaders have been more easily swayed by simple, pseudoscientific constructions—of the very sort for which Niebuhr criticized John Dewey, the social scientists, and Wallace—than by presentations insistent upon the complexities of history and morality. To put it another way, one is left wondering if Niebuhr's ominous warnings not to expect too much were somehow transformed into imperatives to expect nothing at all. Did Niebuhr's powerful criticism of the calls for global cooperation made by Wallace and others augment reflexive hard-line policies, in that sense doing more damage by what they precluded than good by what they fostered? Did Niebuhr's thoroughgoing skepticism of ameliorative ideologies, insistent on its own sophistication, become a shield for a simplistic, mechanical assertion of American power in the years following World War II? Or did Niebuhr's logic prevail because it seemed to support the age-old and equally simplistic American image of a wholly independent, unentangled nation, while visions such as Wallace's—often simplistic in their own ways—promised nothing but entanglement and complicated decisions? American political leaders accepted the logic—or what they took to be the logic—of Niebuhr and the cold war liberals: that communists could not be negotiated with, only opposed; that force or the threat of force was always to be used in place of negotiations with powerful nations whose ideologies differed from America's. As this distilled version of Niebuhr's logic rose to dominance, the possibility of nuanced diplomacy was set aside for decades. This, too, was ironic, in light of the actual complexity of much of Niebuhr's commentary.

In the end, ironically it is Niebuhr—the German-American outsider—who stands as a proxy of sorts for the American experience of these years. For as he observed the events of the mid- and late 1940s, decades of analogs, including that of Munich, informed his perspective as they did the perspectives of most Americans. For Niebuhr the risks of the popular front liberal outlook were analogous to those of, say, the Protestant liberal perspective in the 1920s regarding social reform as well as to Western liberal delusions in the 1930s regarding the rise of fascism. He had seen it all before. So it is not surprising that in attacking Henry Wallace in 1946 he used the same logic he had earlier in his critiques of the Social-Gospel and social-science reformers as well as of isolationists and pacifists. Wallace and the popular fronters became subject to the dismissive assumption, implicit and explicit in Niebuhr's reasoning, that they were incapable of addressing or even comprehending the threat that Niebuhr and like-minded liberals believed communism and the Soviet Union posed the United States by the late 1940s. To those Americans who accepted Niebuhr's logic after 1946, Wallace appeared too concerned with the harsh vicissitudes of Russian history, and American insensitivity to those vicissitudes, to act forcefully in the face of perceived Soviet aggressiveness. He appeared too willing to place the "open society" of the West at risk once again.

If a thinker as sensitive and serious as Reinhold Niebuhr could be so overwhelmed by old reflexes and assumptions, then we are left with a difficult and not especially hopeful question: How can public discourse be kept truly open to a full range of options and vigorous self-criticism, which ultimately is what renders it truly vital? How can a democratic society, even in fearful times, shape its policies while remaining open to perspectives that may not at a given moment appear to be viable—and might in fact never be so—but that nevertheless merit considered attention? This is what Wallace and the popular front liberals implicitly stood for: keeping the discussion as wide open as possible. The final irony, perhaps, is that Niebuhr and most of the cold war liberals would have claimed that they stood for the same thing. But their fears, which were finally their nation's fears, led them to bring down their popular front colleagues and in so doing tragically narrow the scope of public debate.

Notes

Abbreviations Used in the Notes

ADA	Papers of Americans for Democratic Action
CBBUI	C. B. Baldwin Papers, University of Iowa
CC	*Christianity and Crisis*
CCY	*Christian Century*
CIO-PAC	CIO Political Action Committee
CS	*Christianity and Society*
FDRL	Franklin D. Roosevelt Library
HAW	Henry A. Wallace
HAW-COHC	Henry A. Wallace Columbia Oral History Interview
HAWD	Henry A. Wallace Diary
HAWI	Henry A. Wallace Papers, University of Iowa
HAWI-Speeches	Wallace Speech Collection, University of Iowa
HAW-LC	Henry A. Wallace Papers, Library of Congress
HAWR	Henry A. Wallace Papers, Roosevelt Library
HAW-UCB	Wallace Speeches at the UC Berkeley
NA	National Archives
NR	*New Republic*
NYT	*New York Times*
PCA	Progressive Citizens of America
PPUI	Papers of the Progressive Party, University of Iowa
RN	Reinhold Niebuhr
RN Papers	Reinhold Niebuhr Papers, Library of Congress
RG	Record Group (National Archives collections)
RR	*Radical Religion*
WF	*Wallaces' Farmer*
WT	*World Tomorrow*

PREFACE

1. Lillian Hellman, *Scoundrel Time,* 86.

2. RN, "The Fight for Germany," *Life,* 21 October 1946, 65–68, 70, 72.

3. Although it would be incorrect to argue that Niebuhr had a direct influence on the formulation of U.S. foreign policy in 1946, Paul Merkley makes clear that from 1941 on—beginning with his championing of the Lend-Lease bill—Niebuhr was well known to the Roosevelt administration, serving it in an advisory capacity on various foreign-policy-related issues. Paul Merkley, *Reinhold Niebuhr: A Political Account,* 189–90.

4. RN, "Fight for Germany," 65.

5. Niebuhr himself had attested to this in 1944, as Wallace was in the midst of his losing battle to retain the Democratic vice presidential nomination that year. As chairman of the Union for Democratic Action, Niebuhr sent a telegram of support to Wallace decrying FDR's declaration of his own candidacy without naming Wallace (or anyone else) as his running mate. Niebuhr insisted that if the coming electoral campaign was to "have meaning for the future" it had to be "fought on behalf of Roosevelt and Wallace." RN to HAW, July 1944, ADA, ser. 1. See below, chap. 7.

6. See below, chap. 7.

7. RN, "Fight for Germany," 65–66. See below, chap. 8.

8. Walter LaFeber, *America, Russia, and the Cold War: 1945–1966,* 258.

9. Wallace, Niebuhr, and others were liberals by virtue of their support—to varying degrees and for diverse reasons—of the sort of domestic social reforms that, by the late 1930s, were embodied in the institutions created by the New Deal. Such reforms, conceived in what was known as the "progressive tradition," were implicitly related to nineteenth-century American liberalism by an overarching belief in the preservation of individual liberties. By the early twentieth century, however, this had come to mean the use of government for the protection of individual opportunity as it was threatened in various ways by large-scale modern industrial civilization.

10. One partial exception to this assertion was the ongoing critique presented by journalist Walter Lippmann.

11. Richard M. Freeland suggests something like this in *The Truman Doctrine and the Origins of McCarthyism: Foreign Policy, Domestic Politics, and Internal Security, 1946–1948.* Also see Robert Griffith, "American Politics and the Origins of McCarthyism," in *The Specter: Original Essays on the Cold War and the Origins of McCarthyism,* ed. Robert Griffith and Athan Theoharis (New York: New Viewpoints, 1974).

12. By "conservative," I mean ideological and political resistance domestically to the extension of federal power, particularly in the form of the welfare state, coupled with staunch anticommunism at home and abroad. Such a definition necessarily evades the consideration of domestic conservatives, such as Robert A. Taft, who remained "isolationists" or "unilateralists" during the cold war era. In view of the fact that the roots of "isolationism" were not wholly or even essentially conservative, this seems a reasonable evasion.

13. On the ways in which the strategic assumptions of the cold war actually increased the likelihood of (possibly nuclear) war between the United States and the Soviet Union, see Richard Ned Lebow and Janice Gross Stein, *We All Lost the Cold War* (Princeton: Princeton University Press, 1994).

14. John Lewis Gaddis, "The Tragedy of Cold War History," *Diplomatic History* 17 (Winter 1993): 1–16. Gaddis greatly, if implicitly, extended the logic of his attack upon the revisionists in *We Now Know: Rethinking Cold War History* (New York: Oxford University Press, 1997). For an extended critique of that book, see Mark L. Kleinman, "Revision of 'Revisionism' or Return to Orthodoxy?" *Peace and Change* 23 (July 1998): 386–98.

15. Examples of this new historiography are Harvey Klehr, John Earl Haynes, and Fridrikh Igorevich Firsov, *The Secret World of American Communism* (New Haven: Yale University Press, 1995); Richard Gid Powers, *Not without Honor: The History of American Anticommunism* (New York: Free Press, 1995); and Klehr and Ronald Radosh, *Looking for Spies in All the Wrong Places: The Amerasia Spy Case: Prelude to McCarthyism* (Chapel Hill: University of North Carolina Press, 1996). For representative critiques, see Robert Shaffer, "A Not-So-Secret Agenda," *Reviews in American History* 24 (1996): 500–506; Richard M. Fried, "Crying Wolf: American Anticommunism," *Reviews in American History* 24 (1996): 681–85; and Michael E. Parrish and Joseph W. Esherick, "Looking for Spys in All the Wrong Places," *Reviews in American History* 25 (1997): 174–85.

CHAPTER 1

1. By the term *internationalism* I mean the belief arising around the turn of the twentieth century, grounded in interconnected assumptions ranging from the economic to the cultural, that the United States both needed and was obligated to be fully and centrally involved in international affairs.

2. Niebuhr is often mentioned in this capacity. See, for example, Lawrence S. Wittner, "Pursuing the 'National Interest': The Illusion of Realism," 282–87; and Kenneth W. Thompson, "Moral Reasoning in American Thought on War and

Peace," 386–99. Michael Joseph Smith calls Niebuhr "perhaps the most important figure in American realism," in *Realist Thought from Weber to Kissinger*, 17–18.

3. See, for example, Richard Hofstadter, *The Age of Reform: From Bryan to FDR*, and "Cuba, the Philippines, and Manifest Destiny," in Hofstadter, *The Paranoid Style in American Politics and Other Essays* (New York: Alfred A. Knopf, 1965), as well as T. J. Jackson Lears, *No Place of Grace: Antimodernism and the Transformation of American Culture, 1880–1920*.

4. The major exceptions to this statement would be the works of William Appleman Williams and other historians who rely on concepts such as the "Open Door" or economic imperatives to explain the sources of American foreign policy. By asserting the primacy of maintaining foreign markets for American production (in Williams's case, this included agricultural production, during the latter half of the nineteenth century) as a driving factor in the formulation of policy, they have implied the importance of America's transformation into a modern industrial nation, since it was the surplus of America's increasing industrial output that allegedly required overseas outlets. See, for example, Williams, *The Tragedy of American Diplomacy*, and *The Roots of Modern American Empire: A Study of the Growth and Shaping of Social Consciousness in a Marketplace Society* (New York: Random House, 1969); also see Walter LaFeber, *The New Empire: An Interpretation of American Expansion, 1860–1898* (Ithaca: Cornell University Press, 1963), as well as Emily S. Rosenberg, *Spreading the American Dream: American Economic and Cultural Expansion, 1890–1945* (New York: Hill and Wang, 1982).

5. Pells, *Radical Visions and American Dreams: Culture and Social Thought in the Depression Years*. Lears also develops this theme in *No Place of Grace*, focusing on the decades surrounding the turn of the twentieth century.

6. Croly, *The Promise of American Life* (New York, 1949), 414; cited in Pells, *Radical Visions*, 6. Examples of such perspectives can be seen in Mumford, "The City"; Brooks, "The Literary Life"; and Stearns, "The Intellectual Life," all in Stearns, ed., *Civilization in the United States* (London: Jonathan Cape, 1922). See Pells, *Radical Visions*, 7, 24–28. On Wallace's notion of "cooperation," see below, chap. 2. On the southern Agrarians, see Paul K. Conkin, *The Southern Agrarians*.

7. The eminent Swedish economist Gunnar Myrdal, in his highly acclaimed 1944 study of race in America, quoted Wallace at length in his role as champion of the "common man." Myrdal, *An American Dilemma: The Negro Problem and American Democracy* (New York: Harper and Brothers, 1944), 11. Similarly, in a discussion of the connections between American domestic and international liberalism, the historian Alonzo Hamby characterized Wallace as the "one great advocate of the liberal cause." Hamby, "Sixty Million Jobs and the People's Revolution: The Liberals, the New Deal, and World War II," 594. George Gallup, "'Mac' and

'Ike' Our Top Heroes," *NYT,* 18 June 1946. Gallup's polling data had Wallace ranked as the seventh most admired man in the nation.

8. Cordell Hull, *The Memoirs of Cordell Hull,* vol. 1, 209; John Morton Blum, *Years of Crisis: 1928–1938,* vol. 1 of *From the Morgenthau Diaries,* 282, 39; Harold L. Ickes, *The Inside Struggle: 1936–1939,* vol. 2 of *The Secret Diary of Harold L. Ickes,* 394; Will Alexander and Samuel Bledsoe, quoted in Graham White and John Maze, *Henry A. Wallace: His Search for a New World Order,* ix–x. Also see Gardner Jackson to Milo [Perkins], 4 June 1948, and subsequent dates, Gardner Jackson Papers, FDRL.

9. See HAW to Enrique de Lozada, 16 June 1942, and attached documents (includes letters to brother and son), HAWR.

10. Will Riley to Charles Beard, 31 December 1932; Riley to Louis Murphy, 6 December 1934; Riley to HAW, 22 April 1933, Will Riley Papers, University of Iowa Libraries, Special Collections.

11. Schlesinger, *The Coming of the New Deal,* vol. 2 of *The Age of Roosevelt,* 33; White and Maze, *Henry A. Wallace,* 307. Schlesinger probably was also borrowing from well-known left-wing journalist Dwight Macdonald's exaggerated 1947 portrait of Wallace, *Henry Wallace: The Man and the Myth,* in which Macdonald described Wallace at length—relying heavily upon quotation out of context and upon recounting only portions of anecdotes—as a "man divided against himself" (128–45).

12. See Richard J. Walton, *Henry Wallace, Harry Truman, and the Cold War,* as an example of this interpretation.

13. The first volume of Edward L. and Frederick H. Schapsmeier's biography of Wallace, *Henry A. Wallace of Iowa: The Agrarian Years, 1910–1940,* is an example of sidestepping the issue of Wallace's spiritualism. They make only two specific, and brief, mentions of Wallace's non-mainstream spiritual propensities in the entire book (137, 274).

14. Norman D. Markowitz, *The Rise and Fall of the People's Century: Henry A. Wallace and American Liberalism, 1941–1948,* 333–42. Markowitz did not, however, address the wider range of Wallace's spiritual relationships, probably because they predated the chronological focus of his study. J. Samuel Walker also discussed Wallace's relationship with Roerich but was apparently unaware of the wider range of Wallace's spiritualistic activities. Walker, *Henry A. Wallace and American Foreign Policy,* 50–60. In an article for the popular history magazine *American Heritage* which also focused on Wallace's relationship with Roerich, Walker and Charles Errico briefly alluded to the greater extent of Wallace's "quest for spiritual satisfaction." But since their intent was to bring the somewhat sensational story of Wallace and Roerich to the popular press, they did not go into any detail regarding Wallace's

other spiritual relationships. See their "The New Deal and the Guru," 93. Theodore A. Wilson briefly outlined the range of Wallace's spiritualistic pursuits during the 1920s and their influence on his commentary in "Henry Agard Wallace and the Progressive Faith," 45.

15. See Mark L. Kleinman, "Searching for the 'Inner Light': The Development of Henry A. Wallace's Experimental Spiritualism," *Annals of Iowa* 53 (Summer 1994): 195–218; and White and Maze, *Henry A. Wallace*. In 1983 Stow Persons suggested that Wallace's "religious migration" was "not without lasting effects on his thinking about public matters." See Persons, "Comment" on Richard S. Kirkendall's "The Mind of a Farm Leader," in *Annals of Iowa* 47 (Fall 1983): 158.

16. White and Maze, *Henry A. Wallace*, 5–6.

17. The extraordinary closeness between Uncle Henry and his grandson Henry A. Wallace, as well as the impact it had on the latter's intellectual growth, is discussed by the Schapsmeiers in *Henry A. Wallace of Iowa*, 2, 17–18; by Russell Lord in *The Wallaces of Iowa*, 10–12; and by White and Maze in *Henry A. Wallace*, 6. It was also noted in a 1947 preelection campaign profile of Wallace entitled "Wallace the Farmer," by Kenneth Stewart (*PM* [magazine], 26 October 1947, 8).

18. Wallace, *Statesmanship and Religion*, 45–47.

19. Lord, *The Wallaces of Iowa*, 2–5; HAW to Marie A. Peterson, 25 January 1937, RG 16, box 2635, NA.

20. Schapsmeier and Schapsmeier, *Henry A. Wallace of Iowa*, 5–6, 17–18.

21. Ibid., 11–12.

22. Richard Wightman Fox, *Reinhold Niebuhr: A Biography*, 2–5.

23. Ibid., 3. It is an interesting coincidence, in light of the present comparison of Wallace and Niebuhr, that Gustav Niebuhr's father owned and ran a large farm that had been "held by his family since the thirteenth century." Although Gustav would work for a short time on a farm in Illinois before training for the ministry, this lengthy heritage seems to have had little impact on the course of his career and less, if any, on Reinhold's.

24. Ibid., 3–5.

25. Ibid., 5–6. This was in clear contrast to H. Richard Niebuhr, Reinhold's younger brother, who also became a renowned theologian. Richard would prove to be much more reserved, in both personality and theological doctrine.

26. Ibid., 4–5.

27. Ibid., 10–12, 18–21.

28. Ibid., 24–25.

29. Fox implies something like this, explaining that Niebuhr's financial needs during the 1920s led him to accept a position writing unsigned editorials for the *Christian Century* but did not eclipse his "desire for recognition." That desire

Niebuhr satisfied by submitting signed articles for which he was not paid. Fox furthermore argues that Niebuhr's output in the *Century* allowed him to create the "loyal audience" that eventually subscribed to the various journals that Niebuhr himself subsequently edited (73). In this vein it is illuminating that in an "Intellectual Autobiography" that Niebuhr wrote in 1956 for inclusion in a collection of essays by others about his thought, the critiques of his philosophy that he was most concerned with were those of "historians and political scientists," members of the disciplines he considered "most critical of the illusions of our culture," the illusions that he himself was exposing. In addition, in the same essay he similarly noted that it might have been his "dominant political interests" that led him to "engage in this analysis of man's collective life." Charles W. Kegley, ed., *Reinhold Niebuhr: His Religious, Social, and Political Thought*, 13, 17.

    30. George F. Kennan, *Memoirs, 1925–1950* (Boston: Little, Brown, 1967), 9–12; Ronald Steel, *Walter Lippmann and the American Century*, 55–56, 84–85, 186, 192, 195–96.

CHAPTER 2

    1. Malcolm O. Sillars asserts that Henry A. Wallace, during his tenure as editor of *Wallaces' Farmer*, "wrote at least 60 percent of the editorials and approved the remainder." Sillars, "Henry A. Wallace's Editorials on Agricultural Discontent, 1921–1928," 132. On Wallace's use of a dictaphone, see Russell Lord, Introduction, *Democracy Reborn*, by HAW, 8–9.

    2. HAW-COHC, 78. The articles Wallace wrote about his western travels in 1909 have been collected and edited by Richard Lowitt and Judith Fabry in *Henry A. Wallace's Irrigation Frontier: On the Trail of the Corn Belt Farmer, 1909* (Norman: University of Oklahoma Press, 1991). On p. 10 they discuss Wallace's other contributions to *Wallaces' Farmer* prior to taking over its editorship. An example of the sort of byline pieces Wallace wrote prior to 1921 can be seen in HAW, "Studying Agricultural Europe," *WF*, 9 May 1913.

    3. HAW-COHC, 47–48.

    4. Ibid., 48–49.

    5. Ibid., 49–50, emphasis original.

    6. White and Maze, *Henry A. Wallace*, 8; William James, *The Varieties of Religious Experience* (New York: Mentor Books, New American Library, 1958), 292–328.

    7. Specific examples of Wallace's writing on these topics number in the hundreds. A cursory reading of virtually any issue of *Wallaces' Farmer* published during Wallace's tenure as editor will bear out such assertions concerning his continual

participation in agricultural science. See Schapsmeier and Schapsmeier, *Henry A. Wallace of Iowa*, 16–29; and White and Maze, *Henry A. Wallace*, 11–14.

8. Schapsmeier and Schapsmeier, *Henry A. Wallace of Iowa*, 27–28.

9. This point really cannot be overstressed. There are literally hundreds of letters a year during most of the 1920s between Wallace and various correspondents concerning corn crossbreeding research.

10. See, for example, HAW to Schwarzebrunner (Yugoslavia), 18 October 1929; HAW to Baross (Hungary), 18 October 1929; H. L. Parker (France) to HAW, 18 February 1930; HAW to Ellinger (France), 24 February 1930; HAW to Zerner (Germany), 27 March 1930, HAWI. Wallace also studied weather and natural phenomena prediction and tracked the results of a wide range of research, some of which verged upon—and at times drifted into—the realm of pseudo-science. See Kleinman, "Searching for the 'Inner Light,'" 197–99.

11. Schapsmeier and Schapsmeier, *Henry Wallace of Iowa*, 24; Lord, *The Wallaces of Iowa*, 8; HAW, "Human Pedigrees," *WF,* 9 February 1923, 205. By the end of the decade, even though he had advised the readers of *Wallaces' Farmer* that there was little reason to go back beyond their great-grandparents in creating a family genealogy table, Wallace himself had compiled information on collateral lines of his own family dating back at least to "the early eighteen hundreds" and possibly as far back as 1710. HAW to Mrs. Donald K. Moore, 27 February and 4 April 1929, HAWI.

12. HAW, "Ebbing Tide of Farm Population," *WF,* 28 March 1924, 497.

13. The term "wisdom religion" is taken from a prominent Theosophist, William Quan Judge, with whose writings Wallace was familiar. See Judge, *Echoes from the Orient: A Broad Outline of Theosophical Doctrines,* as well as *William Quan Judge, 1851–1896: The Life of a Theosophical Pioneer and Some of His Outstanding Articles.* For a full discussion of the nature and extent of Wallace's spiritualism, see Kleinman, "Searching for the 'Inner Light,'" 195–218.

14. Bruce F. Campbell, *Ancient Wisdom Revived: A History of the Theosophical Movement,* 27.

15. Ibid., 29. See also Judge, *Echoes,* 1, 16–19.

16. Campbell, *Ancient Wisdom Revived,* 166–67; George Russell, *The Candle of Vision,* 10–11. Russell described his spiritual awakening and outlined his beliefs in *Candle of Vision.* See esp. chap. 1, "Retrospect." That Wallace had read this volume of Russell's work is evident in HAW to Charles O. Roos, 24 November 1931, HAWI.

17. HAW-COHC, 82; Russell, *Candle of Vision,* 170; Russell, *Cooperation and Nationality,* 6–7; Russell, *Candle of Vision,* 173–74.

18. HAW, "Odds and Ends," *WF,* 6 September 1930, 1419; HAW to G. W.

Russell, 22 December 1930, HAWI; HAW to Mark Hyde, 14 July 1930; also HAW to Hyde, 24 December 1930, HAWI.

19. See Kleinman, "Searching for the 'Inner Light,'" 203–17.

20. "In the Foreground: Tradition Rich Author of Northern Ways," *Swedish Tribune-News*, 11 January 1922, translated by Even L. Moberg, 2 September 1953; "Juanita Roos: Author-Composer" (no journal title or date [circa 1945]); "Indian Policies Look Far Ahead" (no journal title or date [circa early 1930s]), Johan Oscar Roos (1827–1896) and Family Papers, 1856–1975, Minnesota Historical Society.

21. HAW to Juanita Roos, 23 November 1931; Russell to HAW, 6 November 1931, HAWI.

22. HAW and William L. Brown, *Corn and Its Early Fathers*, 118–19. On Wallace's agreement with Carver's philosophy, see Schapsmeier and Schapsmeier, *Henry A. Wallace of Iowa*, 18–19, as well as "I.S.C. and Simpson Knew George Washington Carver as a Struggling Student," *Des Moines Register*, 17 January 1943, and HAW to Carver, 22 October 1932, HAWI.

23. Juanita Roos to HAW, 22 October 1931; Charles Roos to HAW, [30 December 1931], HAWI.

24. Campbell, *Ancient Wisdom Revived*, 159.

25. See bottom of 14 October 1931 form letter from Dower for handwritten Wallace note stating his desire to "know the next step" (in response to the last line of a Dower letter: "*If you would know the next step write now*" [emphasis original]). Also see HAW to Roos, 28 November 1931; Dower to HAW, 8 April 1932; Dower to Charles Roos, 1 June 1932; Dower to HAW, 28 October 1932, HAWI.

26. Dower to HAW, 11 March 1932, HAWI.

27. Dower to HAW, 1 July 1932; Dower to HAW, 9 September 1932; Charles Roos to HAW, [Summer 1932?]; HAW to Russell, 22 October 1931, HAWI; "Odds and Ends," *WF*, 7 August 1925, 1011; HAW to Charles Roos, 31 December 1931, HAWI.

28. HAW to Dr. J. F. Corbett, 14 October 1931, HAWI.

29. The Wallace-Roerich relationship and the controversies that arose from it are discussed in Kleinman, "Searching for the 'Inner Light,'" 207–13; White and Maze, *Henry A. Wallace*; Torbjörn Sirevag, *The Eclipse of the New Deal and the Fall of Vice-President Wallace, 1944*, 510–20; Markowitz, *Rise and Fall*, 333–42; and below, chap. 2. J. Samuel Walker also discussed Wallace's spiritualism and his association with Roerich in *Henry A. Wallace and American Foreign Policy*, 50–60. Although he accepted the Guru Letters as authentic, Walker was apparently unaware of the larger, primarily theosophical context of Wallace's activities.

30. Roerich, *Realm of Light*, 4–5, 18–20.

31. See below, chap. 4.

32. Markowitz, *Rise and Fall* 336–38; Sirevag, *Eclipse of the New Deal,* 512–13.

33. The Pegler columns appeared daily in the *Los Angeles Examiner,* among other places, 9–12 March 1948. In fact, some of the letters did begin with "Dear Guru," which is the origin of their collective sobriquet, the Guru Letters.

34. See, for example, HAW to Roerich, 29 October 1933, item 121; fragmentary note in Wallace's handwriting, item 80, Guru Letters folder, Samuel Rosenman Collection, FDRL. That Wallace on occasion discussed his spiritual concerns with an interested Roosevelt has been speculated upon and is demonstrated in at least one letter from Wallace to the president. In the letter Wallace referred to a spiritually oriented reading that Roosevelt recommended to him; in turn Wallace urged Roosevelt, in language he also used in his letters to Roerich, to "be the 'flaming one,' the one with ever-upward-surging spirit to lead us into the time when the children of men can sing again." HAW to FDR, 28 October 1933, item 94, Guru Letters. Also see Sirevag, *Eclipse of the New Deal,* 520–26.

35. HAW to Madam and Professor Roerich, 1 September 1933, item 148; HAW to "M" (a code for Roerich), n.d., item 130; HAW to "Prof. R.," n.d., item 103; HAW to "M," January 1933(?), item 53, Guru Letters folder.

36. Items 2, 4, and 5, Guru Letters. There is a two-page "code word sheet" in the Guru Letters folder of the Rosenman papers, indicating to whom the various sobriquets in the letters applied.

37. Roerich, *Realm of Light,* 13.

38. Markowitz, *Rise and Fall,* 341.

39. HAW to Johndro, 19 January 1931; Charles Roos to HAW, 18 February 1932, HAWI.

40. HAW to Charles Roos, 22 January 1932; HAW to Charles Roos, [4 February 1932], HAWI.

41. HAW to Johndro, 22 October 1931; HAW to Johndro, 24 October 1931, HAWI, emphasis original.

42. HAW to Charles Roos, 7 April 1932, HAWI.

43. HAW to Charles Steiner, 31 March 1931, HAWI; HAW, "Odds and Ends," *WF,* 12 July 1929, 995.

44. HAW, "Odds and Ends," *WF,* 12 July 1929, 995.

45. HAW, "A Utopia of Extinction," *WF,* 6 June 1924, 843.

46. HAW, "The Last of the Individualists," *WF,* 3 October 1924, 1289.

47. HAW, "City People and the Future of Farming," *WF,* 11 November 1925, 1618.

48. HAW, "Building without Bitterness," *WF,* 24 October 1924, 1388.

49. HAW, "The Wages of Imperialism," *WF,* 16 May 1926, 722; "The Menace

of Imperialism," *WF*, 10 June 1927, 835. As extraordinarily well read as he was, it is likely that by the mid-1920s Wallace had either read or otherwise become familiar with Lenin's thesis construing imperialism as the ultimate development of capitalist civilization. Lenin's pamphlet, *Imperialism, the Highest Stage of Capitalism*, had appeared in Western-language translations as early as 1920. Wallace himself referred to Lenin in 1934, comparing him in a narrow sense to John Calvin, the prophet Amos, and Protestant reformer John Knox. See HAW, *Statesmanship and Religion*, 104.

50. HAW, "The Menace of Imperialism," *WF*, 835; "Danger Ahead," *WF*, 19 January 1923, 76.

51. The devil theory was strengthened in the 1930s by the impact of the Nye Committee investigations of munitions manufacturing and war profiteering. The committee's report established an image in the public mind of calculation, conspiracy, and callousness on the part of certain American and international corporations. See Geoffrey S. Smith, "Isolationism, the Devil, and the Advent of the Second World War: Variations on a Theme," 60–62.

52. Warren I. Cohen discusses the members of this group, including Beard, and the development of their collective critique in *The American Revisionists: The Lessons of Intervention in World War I*. Beard's increasingly critical view of American foreign policy during the decade after the war is examined in Thomas C. Kennedy, *Charles A. Beard and American Foreign Policy*, chap. 4.

53. Beard and Beard, *The Rise of American Civilization*, in which see vol. 2, *The Industrial Era*, 704–705, 710. For evidence of the Beards' influence on Wallace, see HAW, "The Great Experiment," *WF*, 4 July 1924, 942. On the basis of his reading of the Beards' 1927 work (aspects of which he had probably seen earlier in magazines such as the *New Republic*), Wallace invited Charles Beard to participate in an agricultural conference in May 1927. HAW to Beard, 27 May 1927, HAWI. Wallace noted that Beard's acceptance of the invitation brought "joy to my heart," since it was clear to him that Beard understood the "magnitude of the forces with which we are coping." HAW to Beard, 3 June 1927, HAWI.

54. HAW, "Getting Rid of War," *WF*, 22 February 1924, 293. Wallace discussed other nations that had chosen the path of commercial imperialism and had thus gone to war to maintain their empires. He wrote, for instance, of French misadventures in Morocco in "The Cost of Imperialism," *WF*, 17 July 1925, 942.

55. HAW, "The Empire of the United States," *WF*, 7 April 1922, 454. Already, Wallace pointed out by way of example, "several prominent Americans," including Franklin D. Roosevelt, had formed a company for the purpose of investing "the German marks which are held in the United States in German property." This, Wallace suggested, was just "another straw indicating the direction of the wind."

Without "consciously willing it," Americans were creating the need for a "new type of American diplomacy." HAW, "Investing in Germany," *WF*, 13 October 1922, 1189.

56. To substantiate this assertion, the Beards quoted a 1925 speech given by Curtis Wilbur, then secretary of the navy. After calculating the vast extent of American overseas loans and investments, in combination with annual business revenues, Wilbur insisted that such "vast interests must be considered when we talk of defending the flag." The Beards concluded that this speech "tersely and neatly [characterized] the new situation." *Rise of American Civilization*, 2:705.

57. HAW, "Armistice Day," *WF*, 7 November 1924, 1440; "The Most Hated Nation," *WF*, 6 October 1922, 1157.

58. HAW, "Liberty Enlightening the World," *WF*, 23 July 1926, 987. Wallace articulated similar critiques of U.S. policy in Mexico and Nicaragua. See HAW, "Asking for War," *WF*, 21 January 1927, 84; "Arbitration with Mexico," *WF*, 15 April 1927, 580.

59. Quoted in Wallace's editorial "A Word of Prophecy," *WF*, 17 August 1923, 1102.

60. HAW, "Toward a Philosophy of Co-Operation," *WF*, 8 February 1924, 208–9.

61. Thorstein Veblen, *The Theory of the Leisure Class: An Economic Study of Institutions*, 238–40; *The Theory of Business Enterprise*, 10–19, 20–23, 38–48. On Wallace's early acquaintance with Veblen and his work, and its impact on Wallace's thinking, see Lord, *The Wallaces of Iowa*, 189; Markowitz, *Rise and Fall*, 12–14; and Schapsmeier and Schapsmeier, *Henry A. Wallace of Iowa*, 32–35. Also see HAW, "Odds and Ends," *WF*, 30 August 1929, 1167.

62. HAW, "Toward a Philosophy of Co-Operation," 208–9; "Whosoever Would Be Chief among You," *WF*, 2 May 1924, 694.

63. HAW, "Toward a Philosophy of Co-Operation," 209; Veblen, *Leisure Class*, 15–16. In 1914 Veblen would examine the concept more fully throughout history in *The Instinct of Workmanship and the State of the Industrial Arts*.

64. HAW, "A Word of Prophecy," 1102; "Toward a Philosophy of Co-Operation," 209.

65. HAW, "Capper-Volstead Bill in Danger," *WF*, 12 August 1921, 1040. In this editorial Wallace was trying to undermine the credibility of an attempt by several U.S. senators to weaken an agricultural cooperation bill by adding a provision that would subject cooperative associations to antimonopoly laws. Wallace felt that since cooperatives' policy decisions would be made "more or less publicly," unlike those of many profit-oriented corporations, there was no need for such a provision.

Any unfair price increases made by cooperatives would be known before the fact and thus be subject to an already extant "provision against unjust prices."

66. HAW, "Toward a Philosophy of Co-Operation," 209.

67. Ibid. Also see "The Burden of Being Civilized," *WF*, 16 July 1926, 966, in which Wallace wrote that the growth of population along with the increased complexity of business and social organizations had rendered "the old human habits, once valuable, positively dangerous."

68. The Schapsmeiers suggest that McNary-Haugen not only represented the disaffection of a portion of the agrarian population during the twenties but also was a precursor of New Deal "social justice" legislation in "embryonic form." Schapsmeier and Schapsmeier, *Henry A. Wallace of Iowa*, 95.

69. HAW, "'The Poison of Socialism,'" *WF*, 3 April 1925, 501.

70. HAW, "Anarchy versus Socialism," *WF*, 4 November 1927, 1429.

71. HAW, "Odds and Ends," *WF*, 28 March 1931, 437; "A New Farmer for a New Age," *WF*, 30 October 1925, 1420; "The Coming Battle for the Farm," *WF*, 4 September 1925, 1123. Also see HAW, "Where Are We Going?" *WF*, 6 March 1925, 334. In Russell's view rural cooperation promised an opportunity for the agricultural community to gain a greater degree of control over not only its produce but its life as well. By directing their affairs locally, from field to market, country dwellers would obtain a greater—and more just—share of the rewards. Instead of living at the mercy of middlemen who reaped the larger part of the profit from agricultural production, farm communities would become self-sufficient, marketing their own product, and so improve the quality of rural life. Russell was explicitly not advocating state involvement (and in this he differed from much of what Wallace ultimately proposed) but rather "self-help," at both the individual and community levels. As Russell portrayed it, the cooperative movement would promote greater social cohesion, bringing an end to the breakdown of rural culture. In Ireland he envisioned planned, prosperous, self-sufficient cooperative communities eventually forming the "foundation of a new social order in Ireland," of a new "Irish civilization." Russell, *Cooperation and Nationality*, 21–23, 63–66.

72. HAW, "A Word of Prophecy," 1102; "Two Jobs," *WF*, 15 June 1928, 894.

73. HAW, "Odds and Ends," *WF*, 23 April 1926, 623. Also see HAW, "The Farmer and the Laborer," *WF*, 19 August 1921, 1065; and "Labor and Farm Relief," *WF*, 2 September 1927, 1114.

74. HAW, "Odds and Ends," *WF*, 2 March 1928, 335. At a dinner celebrating the twentieth anniversary of Teddy Roosevelt's Country Life Commission, of which Uncle Henry had been a member, Wallace noted that "there were numerous millionaires present." The meeting indicated to him an increased "interest on the

part of a few really intelligent, wealthy men" in agriculture's problems as well as "the problem of where our civilization is drifting." Ibid.

75. HAW, "Odds and Ends," *WF,* 10 December 1932, 641; "Prejudice," *WF,* 14 June 1930, 1104.

76. HAW, "Morality in Economics," *WF,* 4 November 1921, 1341.

77. HAW to Charles Roos, 31 December 1931, HAWI.

78. HAW, "Fighting in the War of 1931," *WF,* 12 September 1931, 1010; "Neighbors to People of Every Land," *WF,* 9 July 1932, 372.

CHAPTER 3

1. RN to Samuel Press, 2 March 1914, RN Papers. Richard Fox, who quotes the same letter, devotes an entire chapter of his biography of Niebuhr to Niebuhr's sense of not belonging at Yale. Fox, *Reinhold Niebuhr,* 24–25, 28.

2. RN, *Leaves from the Notebook of a Tamed Cynic.*

3. RN, "The Validity and Certainty of Religious Knowledge" (B.D. thesis, Yale Divinity School, 1914), RN Papers.

4. William James, *A Pluralistic Universe,* 60, 260–62, 311–12.

5. RN, "The Validity and Certainty of Religious Knowledge," 28.

6. See Fox, *Reinhold Niebuhr,* esp. chap. 2.

7. RN, *Leaves,* 1919, 24. (In all citations from *Leaves* the page reference is preceded by the year in which Niebuhr made the diary entry.)

8. Ibid., 1926, 98. Niebuhr's apparently extremely confirmed bachelorhood did not end for another five years, in the third year of his tenure at Union Theological Seminary. In 1931 he married a visiting English theology student, Ursula Keppel-Compton, who Fox notes "took much of the initiative" in the courtship. Fox, *Reinhold Niebuhr,* 124–32.

9. RN to Samuel Press, 2 March [1914], RN Papers. The tension in Niebuhr over his German-American background has been well noted by Kevin Michael Shanley in his unpublished doctoral dissertation. Arguing against the interpretation that Niebuhr had disavowed his German roots, Shanley contends that Niebuhr was in fact proud of his heritage, if sometimes torn by it. Shanley, however, does not see Niebuhr's angst over his ethnicity in the larger complex of personal doubts that Fox suggests and in which I am attempting to place it. Shanley, "Reinhold Niebuhr and Relations between Germany and America (1916–1956)" (Ph.D. diss., State University of New York at Albany, 1984), vi, 45–48.

10. RN, *Leaves,* 1916, 8.

11. RN, "The Failure of German-Americanism," *Atlantic Monthly,* July 1916, 13–18.

12. Ibid., 14–15. Niebuhr's comparison of German-Americans with the Irish was indeed odd, considering that it was made in the wake of Progressive Era attempts to reform urban political corruption, with which Irish-Americans were notoriously associated in the public mind.

13. RN, *Leaves*, 1918, 14.

14. RN, "The Present Day Task of the Sunday School," in *Young Reinhold Niebuhr*, ed. William G. Chrystal (New York: Pilgrim Press, 1977), 89–90.

15. RN, "Love of Country," *Evangelical Herald*, 18 April 1918, 2, emphasis added.

16. Ibid.

17. On contemporary definitions of "personality" as a sense of individual connection, rather than of self-sacrifice to the collectivity, see Albert C. Knudson, *The Philosophy of Personalism;* Ralph T. Flewelling, *Personalism and the Problems of Philosophy;* as well as "Personalism," *Encyclopedic Dictionary of Religion*, 1979. Also see Donald Meyer, *The Protestant Search for Political Realism, 1919–1941*, 21.

18. RN, "Tyrant Servants," in *Young Reinhold Niebuhr*, 168; "Is Western Civilization Dying?" *CCY*, 20 May 1926, 652. In words that Wallace would have easily understood, Niebuhr wrote that he was "convinced that the impersonal relationships of a city are not conducive to the highest morality." Living in the urban world tended to detach the individual from "his social group," creating isolation of spirit if not of body. In such a condition, Niebuhr held, "it is not easy to maintain the highest form of virtue." "Tyrant Servants," 168. Also see RN, *Does Civilization Need Religion?* 24–25.

19. RN, *Leaves*, 1925, 78–79.

20. RN, "Tyrant Servants," 169–70.

21. Unsigned editorial, "Henry Ford and Industrial Autocracy," *CCY*, 4 November 1926, 1354.

22. RN, "The Nation's Crime against the Individual," *Atlantic Monthly*, November 1916, 609, 611.

23. Ibid., 609–10.

24. Ibid., 610.

25. Ibid., 610–13.

26. Ibid., 613.

27. Ibid., 613–14; "Tyrant Servants," 170.

28. RN, "America and Europe," in *Young Reinhold Niebuhr*, 141, 144; "Germany and Modern Civilization," *Atlantic Monthly*, June 1925, 844.

29. RN, "Is Europe on the Way to Peace?" in *Young Reinhold Niebuhr*, 159. The Dawes Plan in fact was named after Chicago banker, and later vice president of the United States, Charles G. Dawes, the plan's principal architect. See also RN,

"The American Empire," *CCY,* 25 June 1925, 820–21, on the need for the United States to ground its foreign policy in a moral and spiritual rather than simply business ethic, as well as "Puritanism and Prosperity," *Atlantic Monthly,* June 1926, 721, for an example of Niebuhr taking the United States to task for its insensitivity to European perceptions of American economic policy in the 1920s.

30. See RN, "Wanted: A Christian Morality," *CCY,* 15 February 1923, 201; as well as *Does Civilization Need Religion?* 47–48. As noted earlier, this construction culminated in Niebuhr's infamous attack on progressive liberalism, *Moral Man and Immoral Society: A Study in Ethics and Politics,* xi, 8–9. Also see Michael Joseph Smith, *Realist Thought from Weber to Kissinger,* 106–7.

31. RN, "The Nation's Crime," 613; *Leaves,* 1919, 23. On Niebuhr's tentative hopefulness regarding international relations during the early 1920s, see "America and Europe," 143; "A Trip through the Ruhr," in *Young Reinhold Niebuhr,* 127; "The Despair of Europe," ibid., 132–36 (esp. 134); and "The Dawn in Europe," ibid., 151–53.

32. RN, "The Will to Peace," *CCY,* 6 May 1926, 574.

33. RN, "Germany and Modern Civilization," *Atlantic Monthly,* June 1925, 843.

34. Ibid., 843, 848.

35. Ibid., 846–47.

36. Ibid., 847; RN, "Is Protestantism Self-Deceived?" *CCY,* 25 December 1924, 1661–62. That he had read (probably in German) and been affected greatly by Weber's thesis about Protestantism and the genesis of modern capitalism is clear in several other articles and reviews that Niebuhr wrote that were concerned in whole or in part with Weber's famous book *The Protestant Ethic and the Spirit of Capitalism.* See, for example, RN, "European and American Reform" and "Puritanism and Prosperity" (both already cited), as well as "Capitalism—A Protestant Offspring," *CCY,* 7 May 1925, 600–601; and "How Civilization Defeated Christianity," *CCY,* 15 July 1926, 895–96.

37. RN, "Berlin Notes," in *Young Reinhold Niebuhr,* 1924, 154.

38. RN, "The German Klan," *CCY,* 16 October 1924, 1330–31.

39. RN, "Germany in Despair," in *Young Reinhold Niebuhr,* 1923, 128, 130–31.

40. RN, "Henry Ford and Industrial Autocracy," 1355, emphasis added.

41. RN, "The Church and the Industrial Crisis," *Biblical World,* November 1920, 590.

42. RN, "European and American Reform," 1110. Also see "The German Church and the Social Gospel," *CCY,* 29 October 1925, 1334.

43. Niebuhr's skeptical construction regarding the unlikelihood of individual

morality transferring to the group, which was present in nascent form in his Yale thesis, made it essentially impossible for Niebuhr to ever embrace the Social Gospel wholeheartedly. For this reason interpretations that have portrayed Niebuhr's intellectual development from the 1920s to 1930s as a more or less clear-cut shift from the Social Gospel to Marxism are greatly overdrawn. The most cogent example of such an interpretation of Niebuhr is Paul Merkley's otherwise extraordinarily insightful *Reinhold Niebuhr: A Political Account* (Montreal: McGill-Queen's University Press, 1975). Also see Meyer, *Protestant Search,* 222–23.

44. RN, *Leaves,* 1925, 74–75.

45. Walter Rauschenbusch, *Christianity and the Social Crisis,* 351–53, 357, 151.

46. RN, "Puritanism and Prosperity," 722–24, emphasis added.

47. Rauschenbusch, 151, 194–95. Rauschenbusch advocated the new social "sciences," including "political economy and sociology," insisting that they could work as guides in understanding these laws and in taking action for social reconstruction. Ibid., 209. RN, "Shall We Proclaim the Truth or Search for It?" *CCY,* 12 March 1925, 345; "Religious Imagination and the Scientific Method," in *Proceedings of the National Conference of Social Work, at the Fifty-Fifth Annual Session, Memphis, Tennessee, 2–9 May 1928* (Chicago: University of Chicago Press, 1928), 54–56.

48. Rauschenbusch, *Christianity and the Social Crisis,* 177.

49. RN, *Leaves,* 1920, 32.

50. RN, "Is Protestantism Self-Deceived?" 1661; "Protestantism in Germany," *CCY,* 4 October 1923, 1258–59.

51. RN, *Does Civilization Need Religion?* 4, 6–7.

52. Ibid., 49–50.

CHAPTER 4

1. For a full discussion of *Moral Man and Immoral Society,* see Fox, *Reinhold Niebuhr,* 136–47.

2. HAW to Frank O. Lowden, 6 January 1931; HAW to Adolph S. Ochs, 1 June 1931; HAW to Senator William E. Borah, 13 June 1931; HAW to Benson Y. Landis, 26 January 1934, HAWI.

3. John Maynard Keynes, *The Economic Consequences of the Peace.* Wallace implied in a 1930 editorial that he had read Keynes's work some time before. HAW, *WF,* 19 April 1930, 789. HAW, "Odds and Ends," *WF,* 23 May 1931, 681. (Also see HAW to Rev. William A. Crawford-Frost, 18 September 1931, and HAW to Dr. Robert Wallace, 30 November 1931, HAWI.) HAW, "Odds and Ends," *WF,*

23 May 1931, 681; HAW to Richard Brugger, 26 May 1931, HAWI; HAW, "French Fight Easy Money," *WF*, 19 March 1932, 158–59; HAW to Hon. Lloyd Thurston, 11 January 1932, HAWI. Also see HAW, "War Hate Still Drags Us Down," *WF*, 1 August 1931, 886.

4. HAW to Roy Manley, 11 November 1930, HAWI. Also see HAW, "Canceling Foreign War Debts," *WF*, 27 December 1930, 1976; HAW to Clifford Gregory, 18 December 1931; HAW to P. H. Breen, 27 July 1932, HAWI.

5. HAW, "Foreign Trade and the Depression," *WF*, 31 January 1931, 130–31; "World-Wide Depression and Revolution," *WF*, 20 September 1930, 1511; HAW to N. E. Lindskoog, 29 January 1931, HAWI; HAW, "Tariff Insanity Is World-Wide," *WF*, 9 May 1931, 632; *New Frontiers*, 79; HAW to FDR, 26 August 1932, and HAW to L. R. Combs, 31 January 1933, HAWI.

6. On the Soviet Union as an agricultural experiment, see HAW, "Collective Farming in Russia," *WF*, 19 April 1930, 788; HAW to Mattie Howard, 20 March 1931, HAWI; HAW, "Keep Your Eye on Russia," *WF*, 24 May 1930, 1000; "Big Wheat Farming in Russia," *WF*, 10 May 1930, 916. On potential U.S.-Soviet agricultural competition, see HAW, "Odds and Ends," *WF*, 18 April 1931, 541; and "Odds and Ends," *WF*, 6 September 1930, 1419. For the economic reasoning behind Wallace's opposition to loaning money to the Soviets, see HAW to FDR, 29 September 1933; HAW to Hull, 29 September 1933; HAW to Dante Pierce, 21 October 1933; and HAW to Frank C. Walker, 28 October 1933, HAWI; J. Samuel Walker, *Henry A. Wallace and American Foreign Policy*, 39–40.

7. RN, "Let Liberal Churches Stop Fooling Themselves," *CCY*, 25 March 1931, 402; "Economic Perils to World Peace," *WT*, May 1931, 154.

8. RN, "Economic Perils," 155. Also see RN, "Awkward Imperialists," *Atlantic Monthly*, May 1930, 671.

9. To Niebuhr, the German debt was shocking in its amount and draconian in its effects. He insisted that the "idea that any nation" would "suffer economic servitude" for sixty years over a war fought from 1914 to 1918 was "so fantastic" as to raise a question about "the sanity of statesmen." RN, "Economic Perils," 155.

10. RN, "Germany Wrestles with Her Debts," *CCY*, 30 July 1930, 935–36; "Economic Perils," 155–56.

11. HAW, "Foreign Trade and the Depression," 130–31; HAW to P. H. Breen, 27 July 1932, HAWI. Also see HAW to Hon. Lloyd Thurston, 11 January 1932, HAWI.

12. HAW to L. Housel, 28 December 1931, HAWI.

13. RN, "Awkward Imperialists," 670–71. Also see RN, "Perils of American Power," *Atlantic Monthly*, January 1932, 90–91.

14. RN, "Awkward Imperialists," 671–72, 674.

15. John D. Hicks, *Republican Ascendancy, 1921–1933*, 149–52; RN, "Awkward Imperialists," 674–75.

16. RN, "The Spiritual Life of Modern Man," *Alumni Bulletin of the Union Theological Seminary*, June–July 1930, 155; *Reflections on the End of an Era*, 70–74; "Revival of Feudalism," *Harper's Magazine*, March 1935, 484.

17. RN, "Spiritual Life of Modern Man," 155; "Perils of American Power," 92.

18. HAW to Lowden, 16 January 1932, HAWI; HAW, *Statesmanship and Religion*, 5–7; *New Frontiers*, 41, 69–70.

19. HAW to Thomas T. Kerl, 4 December 1931; HAW to Clark M. Eichelberger, 21 April 1932, HAWI. Also see HAW to Dan W. Turner (governor of Iowa), 21 February 1931, HAWI; and HAW, "To Buy Gunpowder or Pork?" *WF*, 6 February 1932, 57.

20. HAW, *America Must Choose*, 1.

21. Ibid., 10–11, 15–16.

22. Ibid., 11–12; *New Frontiers*, 87–88.

23. HAW, *America Must Choose*, 14, 19.

24. HAW, "The Rules of the Game," *Survey Graphic*, July 1934, 317. Also see HAW, "The Tyranny of Greed," *Collier's*, 6 October 1934, 38. HAW, "Spiritual Forces and the State," *Forum and Century*, June 1934, 355; "We Are More Than Economic Men," *Scribner's*, December 1934, 324. Also see HAW, "In Search of New Frontiers" (speech delivered at the Biennial Convention of the National Federation of Business and Professional Women's Clubs, 18 July 1935), *Vital Speeches of the Day*, 29 July 1935, 706.

25. HAW, "The Rules of the Game," 317–18.

26. Pells, *Radical Visions and American Dreams*, 72. See George Soule, *A Planned Society* (Gloucester, Mass.: Peter Smith, 1965); and Stuart Chase, *A New Deal* (New York: Macmillan, 1932).

27. RN, "After Capitalism—What?" *WT*, 1 March 1933, 203; *Reflections*, 29.

28. RN, *Reflections*, 29.

29. Ibid., 51–52.

30. Ibid., 52.

31. Ibid., 56–57. This chapter of *Reflections* is entitled "The Significance of Fascism."

32. Ibid., 58–59.; RN, "Revival of Feudalism," 483.

33. Fox, *Reinhold Niebuhr*, 121–24, 134–36; RN, "Radical Religion," *RR*, Autumn 1935, 3. Louis H. Tietje insists that Niebuhr was never a Marxist "in any coherent sense of the term." He justifies this assertion by arguing that Niebuhr at no time demonstrated more than a "minimal grasp" of the fundamentals of "Marxist theory." Tietje, "Was Reinhold Niebuhr Ever a Marxist?" 357–58. In

fact, Niebuhr was clearly fluent in what might be called a "lay interpretation" of Marxism and was influenced by Marxist thought to a degree that was common in left-liberal critiques of capitalism. In this sense, Niebuhr was intellectually at least as much a Marxist as were many avowed Marxists.

34. RN, "Religion as a Source of Radicalism," *CCY,* 11 April 1934, 493; *Reflections,* 127–28.

35. RN, *Reflections,* 193; "Radicalism and Religion," *WT,* October 1931, 326; "The Religion of Communism," *Atlantic Monthly,* April 1931, 462–63.

36. RN, *Reflections,* 93–94; "Radicalism and Religion," 326–27.

37. RN, *Reflections,* 93–94; "Radicalism and Religion," 326–27; "Our Machine Made Culture," *Christendom,* Autumn 1935, 188–89. Niebuhr also referred to a "socialist analysis" that was not "doctrinaire" and implied that this was how he perceived his own commentary. RN, "Why German Socialism Crashed," *CCY,* 5 April 1933, 451.

38. RN, "Germany—A Prophecy of Western Civilization," *CCY,* 2 March 1932, 287–88.

39. RN, "Our Romantic Radicals," *CCY,* 10 April 1935, 474–76. Also see RN, "The Revolutionary Moment," *American Socialist Quarterly,* June 1935, 8–13.

40. RN, "The Religion of Communism," 464; *Moral Man,* 187.

41. RN, "The Religion of Communism," 464–65.

42. RN, "The Land of Extremes," *CCY,* 15 October 1930, 1242; "The Church in Russia," *CCY,* 24 September 1930, 1145–46. Also see RN, "Russia Makes the Machine Its God," *CCY,* 10 September 1930, 1081.

43. Bruce Kuklick suggests substantial differences between the Pragmatisms of Dewey and James, growing out of the former's "Hegalianism" and the latter's "naturalistic" psychology. See Kuklick, *Churchmen and Philosophers: From Jonathan Edwards to John Dewey,* 234–35.

44. Fox, *Reinhold Niebuhr,* 136–37. Daniel F. Rice suggests that Fox's criticism of Niebuhr is overdrawn. See Rice, *Reinhold Niebuhr and John Dewey: An American Odyssey,* 17–19.

45. John Dewey, *Philosophy and Civilization,* 318–19; RN, *Moral Man,* xiv. Also see RN, "The Pathos of Liberalism," *The Nation,* 11 September 1935, 303.

46. Dewey, *Philosophy and Civilization,* 326.

47. Ibid., 321–22.

48. Westbrook, *John Dewey and American Democracy,* 524. For a thorough and well-reasoned account of the entire pseudodebate between Niebuhr and Dewey during the thirties, demonstrating both the complexity of, as well as the strong affinities between, the two men's commentaries, see Westbrook, 523–32. Also see Rice, *Reinhold Niebuhr and John Dewey,* throughout.

49. Dewey, "Intelligence and Power," 306.

50. Nevertheless, if Niebuhr's overly harsh critique of Dewey was in fact something of an unconscious defense of the prophetic Protestantism that Niebuhr believed he was championing, then Dewey's perception of the disagreement was not altogether inaccurate.

51. For Dewey's version of personality, however, religion was not a prerequisite. In fact, he argued that formal religion might even be a hindrance to its attainment. Dewey, *A Common Faith*, 14–15. Also see Kuklick, *Churchmen and Philosophers*, 251–52. Westbrook argues that the differences between the two men were ultimately "differences of emphasis," though crucial nevertheless to the "development of liberal-democratic thought." Westbrook, *John Dewey and American Democracy*, 524. Rice notes that years later Niebuhr actually admitted that he had been too severe in his criticism of Dewey. Rice, *Reinhold Niebuhr and John Dewey*, xvii.

52. HAW, "The Farmer and Social Discipline," *Journal of Farm Economics* 16 (January 1934): 10.

53. Ibid., 22–23.

54. Ibid.; HAW to Louis L. Horsch, 15 August 1935, HAWI.

55. Richard S. Kirkendall, *Social Scientists and Farm Politics in the Age of Roosevelt*, 24–29; Schlesinger, *Coming of the New Deal*, 36–38, 70–73; William E. Leuchtenburg, *Franklin D. Roosevelt and the New Deal, 1932–1940*, 48, 72–73, 77–78; HAW to Robert W. Rogers, 17 May 1946, RG 40, NA.

56. HAW, *New Frontiers*, 255. Rexford G. Tugwell, Wallace's Assistant Secretary, put it more bluntly, acknowledging that the crop reduction would pay farmers "to be social-minded," in that sense "harnessing a selfish motive for the social good." Quoted in Schlesinger, *Coming of the New Deal*, 72. HAW, *New Frontiers*, 257–59, 264–66. Also see HAW, "The Farmer and Social Discipline," 2–8; and "The Rules of the Game," 320.

57. HAW, "American Agriculture and World Markets," *Foreign Affairs* 12 (January 1934): 223; *America Must Choose*, 20; HAW to E. G. Brockway, 9 May 1931, and HAW to Henry Morgenthau Jr., 3 September 1932, HAWI; HAW, "Farm with Your Neighbor" (speech given over NBC network from Washington, D.C., 24 September 1933), HAW-UCB. Also see HAW, "Emergencies and Fundamentals" (speech given in Muncie, Indiana, 14 November 1933), HAW-UCB.

58. Leuchtenburg, *Franklin D. Roosevelt*, 198–204. Leuchtenburg asserts that Hull "won the backing" of Wallace in 1934, with the latter's "enormously influential" *America Must Choose* carrying the day in the public debate.

59. See HAW, "The Roerich Pact," *Bulletin of the Pan-American Union*, May 1935, 359–60; "Pan-American Art and Science Pact Is Signed," *Washington Post*, 16 April 1935 (in Wallace scrapbook, HAW-LC).

60. HAW to Hull, 31 August 1933; Hull to HAW, 29 September 1933, HAWI. HAW's address to the members of the Pan-American Union, 15 April 1935, in "The Roerich Pact," 361; HAW to FDR, [Summer(?) 1933], HAWI.

61. HAW's address, in "The Roerich Pact," 362.

62. HAW to Dr. J. F. Corbett, 14 October 1931, HAWI.

63. "Unity of purpose" was part of the title of an unpublished speech that Wallace gave before the Agricultural History Society, 27 December 1934. HAW, "Unity of Purpose As an Historical Force," MS, HAWI; "In Search of New Frontiers," 705–6.

64. HAW, "In Search of New Frontiers," 707; *Statesmanship and Religion,* 121; *New Frontiers,* 253–54.

65. HAW, "Spiritual Forces," 352, 354; *Statesmanship and Religion,* 124–26; *New Frontiers,* 254.

66. Fox, *Reinhold Niebuhr,* 155–57; RN, "Why I Leave the F.O.R.," *CCY,* 3 January 1934, 17–18. On Niebuhr's evolution away from pacifism during the 1930s, see Meyer, *Protestant Search for Political Realism,* 356–61.

67. RN, "Why I Leave," 17; *Moral Man,* 171–72, 233, 240–44. Also see RN, "What Chance Has Gandhi?" *CCY,* 14 October 1931, 1274; "Professor Niebuhr Replies," *CCY,* 31 January 1934, 155; and "Militant Pacifism," *The Nation,* 19 December 1934, 718.

68. RN, *Interpretation of Christian Ethics,* 68–69.

69. RN, "Peace Lessons from the Orient," *Christian Advocate,* 19 May 1932, 523.

70. Ibid., 523–24.

71. RN, *Reflections,* 246–47; "Pacifism and Sanctions" (a symposium by Niebuhr and J. N. Sayre), *RR,* Winter 1935, 29. Also see "Ex Cathedra," *WT,* 21 December 1932, 578.

72. RN, "Pacifism and Sanctions," 27–28.

73. HAW, *Statesmanship and Religion,* 75, 131; *New Frontiers,* 273; RN, *Interpretation of Christian Ethics,* 129–30.

CHAPTER 5

1. HAW, *Whose Constitution? An Inquiry into the General Welfare,* 128–31, 135–37. Also see HAW, "America's Choice: As Mr. Wallace Now Sees It," *United States News* 18 May 1936, 18 (photocopy in scrapbook, HAW-LC), as well as "The Creditor Position of the United States," article written for the *London Daily Telegraph* and for release to the American press, MS, 8 February 1937, 5, HAW-UCB.

2. HAW, *Whose Constitution?* 265–67, 307; also see HAW, "Constitution

Day, 17 September 1937," MS, HAWI. Wallace defined the "general welfare" in various ways over the years: above all, he viewed it as a "common sense" manner of determining political and economic mechanisms that would allow every American to work at the same time both for his or her own ends and for those of the larger community, as well as a "steady, balanced increase" in the production and distribution of goods in ways that would not "destroy the initiative on which the incentive for wealth production is based." HAW to [Lynn W.] Eley, 23 June 1951, HAWI; *Whose Constitution?* 308–9; HAW, *Paths to Plenty,* viii–ix.

3. HAW, *Whose Constitution?* 309–10.

4. RN, "Pawns for Fascism—Our Lower Middle Class," *American Scholar,* Spring 1937, 146–47, emphasis original.

5. RN, "Catholicism and Anarchism in Spain," in *Love and Justice: Selections from the Shorter Writings of Reinhold Niebuhr,* 74–75 (originally published in *RR,* Spring 1937); "Unhappy Spain," *RR,* Summer 1937, 3. Also see RN, "Catholicism and Communism," *RR,* Winter 1936, 4–5.

6. RN, "The Failure of Sanctions," *RR,* Autumn 1936, 5; "Brief Notes," *RR,* Spring 1937, 7; also see "Which Way, Great Britain?" *Current History,* November 1936, 38.

7. RN, "Japan and the Christian Conscience," *CCY,* 11 November 1937, 1391; "America and the War in China," *CCY,* 29 September 1937, 1195; "The War in China," *RR,* Autumn 1937, 2.

8. HAW, *Paths to Plenty,* 80; HAW to FDR, 22 March 1938, HAWI. Also see HAW, "Constitution Day"; and HAW to Riley, [April 1939], HAWI.

9. HAW to General Hugh S. Johnson, 22 September 1938, HAWI.

10. HAW, "Inter-American Culture," *Think,* October 1939, 6.

11. Ibid., 36.

12. HAW, *The American Choice.* On the title, see Curtis Hitchcock to HAW, 27 August 1940, HAWI.

13. Thorstein Veblen, *Imperial Germany and the Industrial Revolution* (New York: The Viking Press, 1939); HAW, *American Choice,* 39–42.

14. HAW, *American Choice,* 36–37.

15. Ibid., 135–36.

16. Ibid., 138–39, 31–33, 36–37; HAW to FDR, 29 December 1940, HAWI. Also see Schapsmeier and Schapsmeier, *Henry A. Wallace of Iowa,* 39; HAWD, 21 April 1942; and HAW to James Parton, 28 February 1941, HAWI.

17. HAW, *American Choice,* 101, 143.

18. Robert Dallek, *Franklin D. Roosevelt and American Foreign Policy, 1932–1945,* 233–36; HAW to George S. Messersmith, 11 July 1940, HAWI.

19. Schapsmeier and Schapsmeier, *Henry A. Wallace of Iowa,* 40–42.

20. HAW to Hull, 16 December 1940, HAWI.

21. Dallek, *Franklin D. Roosevelt and American Foreign Policy,* 175–76; HAW to Hull, 16 December 1940. Wallace also elaborated on his earlier ideas for Mexican-U.S. intercultural exchange, from improving Spanish-language studies in the United States to the creation of university exchange programs. See HAW to Sumner Welles, 26 December 1940; Nelson Rockefeller to HAW, 31 January 1941, HAWI. HAW to FDR, 26 December 1940; HAW to FDR, 30 December 1940, HAWI.

22. HAW to Hull, 16 December 1940, HAWI.

23. RN, "Peace and the Liberal Illusion," *The Nation,* 28 January 1939, 117; "The International Situation," *RR,* Winter 1937, 2. Also see RN, "Mr. Niebuhr's Rebuttal," *The Nation,* 11 February 1939, 187.

24. RN, "Peace and the Liberal Illusion," 117. For Niebuhr's dictum on democracy, see *The Children of Light and the Children of Darkness,* xiii. Also see below, chap. 6.

25. RN, "Ten Years That Shook My World," *CCY,* 26 April 1939, 542.

26. Ibid.

27. RN, "Peace and the Liberal Illusion," 117–18.

28. Ibid., 118; RN, "The Hitler-Stalin Pact," *RR,* Fall 1939, 2; RN, "The Church in Germany," *The Intercollegian and Far Horizons,* February 1937, 93. For Wallace's linkage of the Nazis with Satan, see HAW, "Price of Free World Victory: The Century of the Common Man" (speech delivered to the Free World Association, New York City, 8 May 1942), in *Vital Speeches of the Day* 8 (1 June 1942): 483–85.

29. Niebuhr still believed in late 1938 that, for all of its flaws, Marxism's historical dialectic was "probably a more accurate description of historical processes than the simpler idea of progress implicit in liberal religion." RN, "The Return to Primitive Religion," *Christendom,* Winter 1938, 6.

30. Shanley asserts that the Nazis' success in Germany was the "source of much consternation and embarrassment" to Niebuhr, proving again Niebuhr's great "sensitivity" regarding his "German heritage." Shanley, "Reinhold Niebuhr and Relations," 149.

31. RN, "The War against the West," review of Aurel Kolnai, *The War against the West,* in *RR,* Winter 1938, 37–38; "Germans and Nazis," *Spectator,* 22 September 1939, 401; "The War against the West," 38. Also see RN, "Synthetic Barbarism," in *Christianity and Power Politics,* 117–30 (originally published in *New Statesman and Nation,* 9 September 1939).

32. RN, "The War against the West," 38; "Leaves from the Notebook of a War-Bound American, September 18, 1939," *CCY,* 15 November 1939, 1405; also see RN, "The International Situation," *RR,* Winter 1940 [1939], 2.

33. RN, *The Irony of American History* (New York: Charles Scribner's Sons, 1952). See below, epilogue.

34. RN, "What Is at Stake?" *CC*, 19 May 1941, 1; "Editorial Notes," *CS*, Winter 1940, 9.

35. RN, "The Crisis," *CC*, 10 February 1941, 1; "What Is at Stake?" 1. Niebuhr attributed the phrase "open society," as he used it here, to the philosopher Henri Bergson.

36. RN, "The Crisis," 1; "What Is at Stake?" 1.

37. RN, "The Christian Faith and the World Crisis," *CC*, 10 February 1941, 6.

38. See Christopher Lasch, *The New Radicalism in America, 1889–1963: The Intellectual as Social Type*, 300–301. Also see Rice, *Reinhold Niebuhr and John Dewey*, 17–18; and Daniel Day Williams, "Niebuhr and Liberalism," in Kegley, ed., *Reinhold Niebuhr*, 271.

39. RN, "Russia and Karl Marx," *The Nation*, 7 May 1938, 530; "Ten Years," 543.

40. RN, "Ten Years," 543. Also see RN, "Ideology and Pretense," in *Christianity and Power Politics*, 114–15. RN, "Fellow Travellers," *RR*, Winter 1940 [1939], 7–8.

41. RN, "The Hitler-Stalin Pact," 1; "New Allies, Old Issues," *The Nation*, 19 July 1941, 51.

42. See Schlesinger's essay in Lloyd C. Gardner, Schlesinger, and Hans J. Morgenthau, *The Origins of the Cold War* (Waltham, Mass.: Ginn and Co., 1970), 50–55; RN, "Hitler-Stalin Pact," 2; "New Allies," 51.

43. RN to Kenneth Leslie, 9 May 1940, RN Papers.

44. See HAW to Irving Kluger, 6 February 1941; "Wallace," interview by Edward Stuntz, 2 March 1941, wire-service photostat, HAWI; and HAW, "Day of the New World," *NYT Magazine*, 11 October 1942, 3, 27.

45. HAW, "Second Chance" (speech to the Foreign Policy Association, New York City, 8 April 1941), in *Democracy Reborn*, 177.

46. RN, "America and the Enslaved Nations," *CC*, 6 October 1941, 1.

47. RN, "Pacifism and America First," *CC*, 16 June 1941, 2–5; "American Doldrums," *CC*, 22 September 1941, 1–2.

48. RN, "Pacifism and America First," *CC*, 16 June 1941, 2–5; "American Doldrums," *CC*, 22 September 1941, 1–2.

49. RN, "The War Situation," *CS*, Winter 1940, 3; *NYT*, 31 January 1941, sec. 1, p. 5; U.S. Congress, Senate Committee on Foreign Relations, *To Promote the Defense of the United States*, S. 275, pt. 1, 171. Also see Fox, *Reinhold Niebuhr*, 199; and Merkley, *Reinhold Niebuhr: A Political Account*, 149. RN, "The Lend-Lease Bill," *CC*, 10 February 1941, 2.

50. RN, "American Response to the World Crisis," *CS*, Spring 1941, 4; "Union

for Democratic Action," *CS,* Summer 1941, 6; *NYT,* 29 April 1941, 9. Niebuhr's central importance to the establishment and vitality of the UDA is asserted by both Fox and Merkley. Fox, *Reinhold Niebuhr,* 200; Merkley, *Reinhold Niebuhr: A Political Account,* 153–55.

51. Fox, 197, 200; Merkley, 149, 154.

52. Fox, 200; Merkley, 154; UDA, "A Program for Americans," [April 1941], ADA, ser. 1; see below, chap. 8.

53. Fox, 201. RN, *The Nature and Destiny of Man: A Christian Interpretation:* vol. 1, *Human Nature;* vol. 2, *Human Destiny.*

54. Fox, 203; RN, *Nature and Destiny* 1:4, 22, 24; 2:304 n. 4, 318.

55. RN, *Nature and Destiny* 1:50–52, 35; 2:111.

56. Ibid., 1:15, 57, 58, 66, 67–68.

57. Ibid., 2:111, 248–49; Fox, 214.

58. RN, "Repeal the Neutrality Act," *CC,* 20 October 1941, 1; "America's Last Chance," *CC,* 14 July 1941, 1–2. Also see *NYT,* 11 May 1941, 19.

59. Geoffrey S. Smith, "Isolationism," 73, 75–76. Also see Smith, *To Save a Nation: American Countersubversives, the New Deal, and the Coming of World War II,* 69.

60. UDA press release, May 24, [1941]; RN, "America First and Domestic Reaction" and "The Enemy within the Gates," UDA Research Letter, October 1941, 5; and RN (as chairman of the UDA) to Henry Noble McCracken and Robert M. Hutchins, 13 September 1941, ADA Papers.

61. Geoffrey Smith, "Isolationism," 60–62; RN, "The Enemy within the Gates," 5–6.

62. RN, "We Are at War," *CC,* 29 December 1941, 2.

63. RN, "The Unity of History," *CC,* 4 May 1942, 1–2.

CHAPTER 6

1. *UDA Bulletin,* December 1941.

2. HAW to Josephus Daniels, 3 May 1943, HAWR; HAW, "We Are All Americans," MS (speech delivered in New York City at a rally celebrating "I Am an American Day," broadcast over CBS network, 16 May 1943), Hopkins Papers, FDRL. Also see HAW, "General Statement Summarizing Impressions of His Trip through the South American Republics, Released through the Embassy at Bogota," 24 April 1943, HAWI.

3. See Sirevag, *Eclipse of the New Deal,* 98, and throughout.

4. Ibid., 114–20.

5. HAW, "The Price of Free World Victory," 482–83; also see HAW, "Foundations of the Peace," *Atlantic Monthly,* January 1942, 40. For evidence of Wallace's ongoing interest in dietary experimentation, see Robert S. Harris to HAW, [early March 1941]; Harris to HAW, 17 March 1941; HAW to Professor [Major] John G. Glover, 21 March 1941; HAW to Glover, 28 March 1941, HAWI.

6. Sirevag, *Eclipse of the New Deal,* 444–45.

7. "Dr. Niebuhr Backs Use of U.S. Convoys," *NYT,* 11 May 1941; "Why Appeasers in the State Dept., Mr. President?" *UDA Bulletin,* August 1941; Loeb to UDA members, 8 December 1941, ADA, ser. 1.

8. "A Congress to Win the War," *NR,* 18 May 1942, 683–711.

9. Ibid., 698, 707.

10. "Dies Charges 'Plot' to Smear Congress," *NYT,* 24 June 1942, p. 10.

11. "Dies Committee Smears UDA as 'Red,'" *UDA Bulletin,* June 1942; "Kingdon Asks Dies' Hearing," *NYT,* 26 June 1942, 5; [Michael Straight], "An Outrageous Smear," unpublished typescript, ADA, ser. 1. The June *Bulletin* article drew directly on the logic of Straight's unpublished editorial. See Bruce Bliven to Loeb, 19 May 1942, ADA, ser. 1.

12. See, for example, "Martin Dies and His Committee on 'Un-Americanism': A Special Supplement," *The Nation,* 3 October 1942; "Kingdon Asks Dies' Hearing"; "Dies Committee Smears UDA"; *What's Doing in the UDA,* 3 August 1942, throughout.

13. RN, "A Reply to Martin Dies" (radio address, March 11, 1943), PPUI.

14. Ibid.

15. RN, "The End of a Total War," *CS,* Autumn 1944, 3.

16. RN, "The Bombing of Germany," *CS,* Summer 1943, 3.

17. RN, "Judgment and Forgiveness," *CS,* Summer 1944, 9–10.

18. HAW, "Price of Free World Victory," 483–85. The Schapsmeiers imply Wallace's advocacy of measures of total war in *Prophet in Politics: Henry A. Wallace and the War Years, 1940–1965,* 30–32.

19. Robert A. Divine, *Second Chance: The Triumph of Internationalism in America during World War II,* 29–34.

20. HAW, "Second Chance," in *Democracy Reborn,* 176.

21. HAW, "Unity of the Future," draft MS, 26 February 1942 (date on cover letter, HAW to Julian P. Fromer), HAWI.

22. HAW, "Free World Victory," 483–84; "New Paths to Freedom," *This Week Magazine,* 27 December 1942, 2.

23. For examples of Wallace's cultural imperialism, see HAW, "Address of the Honorable Henry A. Wallace, Vice President of the United States, broadcast from the National Broadcasting Studio, Seattle, Washington, sponsored by the Insti-

tute of Pacific Relations," 9 July 1944, HAWI-Speeches; *Our Job in the Pacific,* 17, 8–9, 11; and "Chengtu Speech," [1944].

24. Alvin Hansen to HAW, 6 May 1941; HAW to Hansen, 13 May 1942, HAWR; HAW to FDR, 5 February 1943, HAWI. Also see HAW, "How We Can Meet War Debts—and Live Better," *PM's Daily Picture Magazine,* 18 January 1943. Markowitz, *Rise and Fall,* 97; HAW, "Full Employment" (draft typescript of speech dated 5 January 1944, delivered to CIO-PAC on 15 January 1944), HAWI-Speeches. Also see HAW, "The Danger of American Fascism," *NYT,* 9 April 1944, reprinted in HAW, *Democracy Reborn.*

25. CIO-PAC, "Program of the CIO Political Action Committee," [1944], 2–5, CBBUI, box 16; and "All Men Are Neighbors," [1944], CBBUI, box 15.

26. RN, "The Enemy within the Gates," 5–6; "American Public Opinion on Foreign Policy," typescript, March 1944, 2, ADA, ser. 1.

27. RN, "Leaves from the Notebook," 1406; "Chastisement unto Repentance or Death," *CS,* Spring 1942, 3–4.

28. RN, "Chastisement unto Repentance or Death," 3–4. In making this analogy between early national U.S. history and the circumstances of international relations during World War II, Niebuhr, Wallace, and other internationalists of the 1940s were perpetuating a discourse begun earlier in the century by American internationalists. See Steigerwald, *Wilsonian Idealism in America,* 52–55.

29. RN, "The Aftermath," *CS,* Fall 1941, 2.

30. RN, "Repeal the Neutrality Act," 1. Also see RN, "The Unity of History," 1.

31. RN, "The Unity of History," 1–2.

32. HAW, "World Organization," in *Democracy Reborn,* 200–201.

33. Ibid.

34. RN, "Plans for World Reorganization," *CC,* 19 October 1942, 6, 4. Also see RN, "Plans for World Organization," *CS,* Summer 1942, 6.

35. RN, "Plans . . . Reorganization," 3.

36. RN, "Editorials," *CS,* Spring 1943, 7, 9.

37. RN, "The Perils of Our Foreign Policy," *CS,* Spring 1943, 18–19; "Common Counsel for United Nations," *CC,* 5 October 1942, 1–2

38. RN, "The Possibility of a Durable Peace," *CS,* Summer 1943, 9–10; also see RN, "World War III Ahead?" *The Nation,* 25 March 1944, 356–58, as well as Niebuhr's review of Paul Hutchinson, *From Victory to Peace,* in *CS,* Winter 1943, 36–37. Niebuhr's critique of the Federal Council of Churches' "Six Pillars of Peace" gives a sense of his views on world constitution proposals. See RN, "A New Report on Just and Durable Peace," *CC,* 22 March 1943, 6–7; "Six Pillars of

Peace," *CC,* 31 May 1943, 5–6, 28 June 1943, 6–8, 12 July 1943, 6–7; "International Ideals and Realities," *CS,* Summer 1944, 3–4; "Factors of Cohesion," *Spectator,* 18 June 1943, 562.

39. *A Program for Americans* (New York: Union for Democratic Action, [ca. April 1941]), 6; RN to Louis Fischer, 28 September 1942, ADA, ser. 1; Eduard Heimann, *Liberty through Power: A Study of the United Nations* (New York: Union for Democratic Action Educational Fund Inc., March 1943).

40. "Democratic Objectives for World Order," typescript, 25 March [1944], ADA, ser. 1.

41. RN, "American Public Opinion on Foreign Policy."

42. "The International Situation Today: Union for Democratic Action and Committee for a Democratic Foreign Policy Conference Report," typescript labeled "Not for Publication in Whole or in Part," March 1944, ADA, ser. 1.

43. "The International Situation Today."

44. HAW to Elmer McClain, ca. June 1944; HAW to Edwin S. Smith, 13 November 1944, HAWR; also see HAW, *Soviet-Asia Mission,* 241–42, 245–46.

45. HAW, "Practical Religion in the World of Tomorrow," typescript, 8 March 1943, HAWI, 11–12; *Soviet-Asia Mission,* 246 (emphasis original), 240.

46. CIO-PAC, "Program of the CIO Political Action Committee," 2.

47. CIO-PAC, "All Men Are Neighbors," emphasis original.

48. RN, "Russia and the Western World," *CS,* Summer 1942, 7; "The Anglo-Russian Pact," *CC,* 29 June 1942, 2–3.

49. RN, "New Allies, Old Issues," *The Nation,* 19 July 1941, 50; "Russia's Partnership in War and Peace," *CC,* 23 February 1942, 3.

50. RN, "Russia's Partnership," 2–3; "Russia and the Western World," 7–8.

51. See, for example, RN, "Editorials," *CS,* Spring 1943; "Russia and the West," *The Nation,* 16 January 1943, 82–83.

52. RN, "Russia and the West," 83; "The Perils of Our Foreign Policy," 20.

53. RN, "Russia and the West," 124–25.

54. Ibid., 82–83; "Power Politics and Justice," *CS,* Winter 1943, 6–7; "Nationalism and the Possibilites of Internationalism," *CS,* Autumn 1943, 6.

55. RN, *The Children of Light and the Children of Darkness,* 32–33, 57–58.

56. Ibid., 10–16.

57. Ibid., 132–33, 182.

58. Ibid., 4–5, 122–23.

59. Ibid., 153–56, 158.

60. Ibid., 168–69, 179.

61. Ibid., 187–89.

CHAPTER 7

1. "A Congress to Win the War and the Peace," *NR*, 8 May 1944, 643–53.
2. Ibid., 643, 652.
3. Ibid., 644.
4. Ibid., 644–45.
5. Ibid., 645.
6. Loeb to Robert Hannegan, 13 July 1944, ADA, ser. 1. On Wallace's popularity among Democrats, see Markowitz, *Rise and Fall*, 104; and Gallup, "The Gallup Poll," *Washington Post*, 19 March 1943; RN to HAW, July 1994, ADA, ser. 1; Sirevag, *Eclipse of the New Deal*, 149–50; Loeb to Claire Sifton, 18 July 1944, ADA, ser. 1.
7. Loeb to Claire Sifton, 24 July 1944; Loeb to HAW, 15 November 1944, ADA, ser. 1.
8. HAW, "Full Employment"; also see "Henry Wallace's Charter for Postwar Prosperity: Text of Henry A. Wallace's prepared statement before the Senate Commerce Committee, January 25, 1945," HAWI-Speeches. HAW, *Sixty Million Jobs*, 151–53, 6–7; Markowitz, *Rise and Fall*, 142–46.
9. HAW, *Sixty Million Jobs*, 133–34.
10. [UDA], "An Economic Roadmap for the Reconversion and Postwar Years," typescript, [ca. May–August 1945], ADA, ser. 1.
11. RN, "The Coming Domestic Battle," *CS*, Spring 1945, 8.
12. See copy of the invitation, HAWI; Loeb to HAW, 11 January 1945, ADA, ser. 1. According to Loeb's letter, the dinner was attended by more than five hundred people. RN to "Wallace Sponsor," 17 February 1945; "Union for Democratic Action Announces Rally for Henry A. Wallace and Full Post-War Employment," press release, 17 February 1945, ADA, ser. 1.
13. Markowitz, *Rise and Fall*, 129–35, 143–46; Sirevag, *Eclipse of the New Deal*, 165–71; "Director, Washington Office" to Leo Goodman et al., 8 March 1945; "Full Employment Campaign Materials," n.d.; Loeb to Paul Sifton, 26 March 1945, ADA, ser. 1; UDA, "What Happened to the Full Employment Bill: A Story of Appeasement," *UDA Congressional Newsletter*, 15 December 1945.
14. UDA, *From the Garden of Eden to Dumbarton Oaks* (New York: Union for Democratic Action, [Spring 1945]), ADA, ser. 1.
15. Mortimer Hays to Edward Stettinius, 28 February 1945, ADA, ser. 1.
16. UDA, *From the Garden of Eden*.
17. RN, "Dumbarton Oaks," *CS*, Winter 1944, 3–6. Also see RN, "Is This 'Peace in Our Time'?" *The Nation*, 7 April 1945, 382–84.
18. UDA, *From the Garden of Eden*.

19. "Excerpts from the Speech of Mortimer Hays, Chairman, Foreign Policy Committee, Union for Democratic Action," [ca. May 1945], ADA, ser. 1.

20. Ibid.; UDA, "Big Three Asked to Break Vicious Circle of Distrust," statement, [June 1945], ADA, ser. 1.

21. UDA, "Big Three Asked to Break."

22. Ibid.; Lippmann, quoted in Divine, *Second Chance*, 290–91.

23. UDA, Foreign Policy Committee, "A Statement on the Argentine Hoax and Certain Proposals for Salvaging the Good Neighbor Policy," 13 June 1945, 5, ADA, ser. 1.

24. Ibid., 6–8.

25. RN, "The Atomic Bomb," *CS*, Fall 1945, 1, 3–4.

26. Ibid. For Niebuhr's later recantation of his criticism of the U.S. decision to drop the bomb, see Fox, *Reinhold Niebuhr*, 224–25; James B. Conant to RN, 6 March 1946; RN to Conant, 12 March 1946, RN Papers, box 3. RN, "The Atomic Bomb" [different article, same title], *CS*, Winter 1945, 4.

27. UDA, National Board, "Foreign Policy Statement," *UDA Bulletin*, November 1945.

28. Anthony W. Smith, "Statement on World Organization," 9 February 1946; Loeb to RN, 14 January 1946, ADA, ser. 1.

29. Smith, "Statement on World Organization," 2; Lewis to RN, 17 January 1946, ADA, ser. 1.

30. Ethel S. Epstein, "Statement on Foreign Policy," typescript, [ca. late January–February 1946], ADA, ser. 1.

31. Loeb to RN, 14 January 1946; RN to Loeb, [ca. 15 January] 1946; "Statement Prepared by Dr. Hans Simons," 14 February 1946, ADA, ser. 1.; RN, "The Atomic Bomb," Winter 1945, 4; "The Myth of World Government," *The Nation*, 16 March 1946, 312–14.

32. UDA, National Board of Directors, "The Foreign Policy of the Union for Democratic Action," [ca. 5 June 1946], ADA, ser. 1.

33. Ibid.

34. HAWD, 21 March 1946; Associated Press, "Wallace Says U.S. Forces Should Quit Iceland Base," *NYT*, 22 March 1946, 4.

35. Joseph Alsop and Stewart Alsop, "The Tragedy of Liberalism," *Life*, 20 May 1946, 68–70, 72, 74, 76.

36. Steven M. Gillon, *Politics and Vision: The ADA and American Liberalism, 1947–1985*, 11; Curtis D. MacDougall, *The Components of the Decision*, 104–5; Alsop and Alsop, "Tragedy of Liberalism," 68.

37. [Loeb and Niebuhr], "Draft of Statement to Be Submitted to the UDA Board," typescript [5 April 1946], ADA; Loeb, "Mustn't Say the Naughty Word!"

UDA Bulletin, June 1946. Also see Loeb, "Progressives and Communists," *NR,* 13 May 1946, 699.

38. HAWD, 7 and 17 August 1945; HAW, "The Significance of the Atomic Age," unpublished typescript, dated 15 October 1945, 1, HAWD.

39. HAW, "Significance of the Atomic Age," 2; UDA, press release, 9 August 1945, ADA, ser. 1.

40. HAW to Truman, 17 October 1945; HAW to Truman, 9 November 1945; HAWD, 13 December 1945; "Atomic Energy: A Statement by Honorable Henry A. Wallace, Secretary of Commerce, before the Special Committee on Atomic Energy, United States Senate," 31 January 1946, 7–8, HAWI-Speeches.

41. HAW, "Atomic Energy: A Statement," 9; Paul S. Boyer, *By the Bomb's Early Light: American Thought and Culture at the Dawn of the Atomic Age.*

42. HAW, "Significance of the Atomic Age," 2–3.

43. UDA, *Congressional Newsletter,* 15 October and 1 November 1945; *UDA Bulletin,* February 1946. Also see UDA, "Union for Democratic Action Opposes May-Johnson Bill," release and statement, 21 October 1945, ADA, ser. 1.

44. Boyer, *By the Bomb's Early Light,* 52.

45. UDA, *Congressional Newsletter,* 1 March, 1 April, 2 July, and 16 July 1946.

46. Boyer, *By the Bomb's Early Light,* 52; HAWD, 27 February 1946; Mac-Dougall, *Components of the Decision,* 112; Frank Kingdon to Truman, telegram, 2 March 1946; and Kingdon to Truman, 15 March 1946, CBBUI, box 1.

47. Boyer, *By the Bomb's Early Light,* 52, quoting Alice Kimball Smith, *A Peril and a Hope: The Scientists' Movement in America, 1945–47;* UDA, *Congressional Newsletter,* 3 August and 16 August 1946.

48. HAW, "Atomic Energy: A Statement," 4–6.

49. HAWD, 21 September 1945; Dean Acheson, *Present at the Creation: My Years in the State Department,* 174–75; White and Maze, *Henry A. Wallace,* 219–20. Also see Wallace's diary entry for 18 September 1945.

50. Felix Belair, "Plea to Give Soviet Atom Secret Stirs Debate in Cabinet," *NYT,* 22 September 1945. The *Daily Mirror* editorial is quoted in White and Maze, *Henry A. Wallace,* 220.

51. HAWD, 23 September 1945; HAW to Truman, 24 September 1945. Also see HAW, *The Price of Vision: The Diary of Henry A. Wallace, 1942–1946,* 485n.

52. HAWD, November 16, 1945; "Peaceful Atomic Abundance: An Address by Henry A. Wallace, Secretary of Commerce, before a Mass Meeting Arranged by the Independent Citizens' Committee of the Arts, Sciences and Professions, Inc.," 4 December 1945, HAWI-Speeches.

53. HAW, "Peaceful Atomic Abundance," 1–3, 4, 6, 7.

54. LaFeber, *America, Russia, and the Cold War,* 41.

55. Ibid., 41–42, emphasis original.

56. Steel, *Walter Lippmann,* 434; UDA, National Board of Directors, "The Foreign Policy of the Union for Democratic Action"; UDA, National Board of Directors, "Baruch Atomic Energy Plan Supported," press release, typescript, [June 1946], ADA, ser. 1; "Atomic Energy—That's Dynamite," *UDA Bulletin,* June 1946.

57. RN, "The Atomic Bomb," Winter 1945, 3–4.

58. "Atomic Energy—That's Dynamite"; UDA, "Baruch Atomic Energy Plan Supported."

59. HAW to Truman, 23 July 1946, in HAWD, September 1946.

60. Ibid.

61. Ibid.

62. Ibid. For evidence of Wallace's awareness of Kennan's telegram, see King Fleming to HAW, 16 April 1946, in HAWD, same date.

63. HAW to Truman, 23 July 1946, HAWD.

64. HAW, "Statement by Henry A. Wallace, Secretary of Commerce, on the 'You and the Atom' Program, Columbia Broadcasting System," release, typescript, 31 July 1946, HAWD. Also see "An Address by Henry A. Wallace, Secretary of Commerce," before the Institute on World Control of Atomic Energy, 15 July 1946, HAWI-Speeches.

65. MacDougall, *Components of the Decision,* 112; HAW, "Text of Speech Delivered by Secretary of Commerce Henry Wallace at the Independent Voters Madison Square Garden Rally, Thursday, September 12th, under the Auspices of the Independent Citizens' Committee of the Arts, Sciences and Professions and the National Citizens' Political Action Committee, As Delivered," typescript, in HAWD.

66. HAW, "Text of Speech."

67. David Robertson, *Sly and Able: A Political Biography of James F. Byrnes,* 478–79; "Text of Byrnes's Speech," *New York Herald Tribune,* 7 September 1946.

68. Harry S. Truman, *Off the Record: The Private Papers of Harry S. Truman,* 94–95; David McCullough, *Truman,* 514; Truman, *Year of Decisions,* 557. For examples of the unreliability of Truman's written recollections, see Barton J. Bernstein, "Understanding the Atomic Bomb and the Japanese Surrender: Missed Opportunities, Little-Known Near Disasters, and Modern Memory," *Diplomatic History* 19 (Spring 1995); Gar Alperovitz et al., *The Decision to Use the Atomic Bomb and the Architecture of an American Myth* (New York: Knopf, 1995); Robert J. Lifton and Greg Mitchell, *Hiroshima in America: Fifty Years of Denial* (New York: G. P. Putnam's Sons, 1995).

69. HAWD, 10 September 1946; White and Maze, *Henry A. Wallace,* 225;

HAWD, 15 October 1945, 15 March, 22 March, and 24 July 1946; White and Maze, *Henry A. Wallace*, 232.

70. HAWD, 20 September 1946. For details of the public controversy, see Markowitz, *Rise and Fall*, 186–93; White and Maze, *Henry A. Wallace*, 231–40; McCullough, *Truman*, 513–18. HAW, text of radio address, 20 September 1946, CBBUI.

71. Loeb to HAW, 21 September 1946, ADA, ser. 1.

72. Loeb to UDA members, 26 September 1946; Loeb to HAW, 27 September 1946; "Union for Democratic Action Statement on Henry Wallace," typescript, [24 September 1946], ADA, ser. 1. Also see "Remarks of Dr. James Loeb, Jr., National Director of the Union for Democratic Action," transcript of remarks delivered on radio station WMCA, 29 September 1946, ADA, ser. 7.

73. Loeb to HAW, 27 September 1946; and Loeb to HAW, 2 October 1946, ADA, ser. 1.

CHAPTER 8

1. Fox, *Reinhold Niebuhr*, 227–28; RN to Ursula Niebuhr, 6 September 1946, RN Papers; LaFeber, *America, Russia, and the Cold War*, 258.

2. RN, "The Fight for Germany," 65–68, 70, 72; Fox, *Reinhold Neibuhr*, 229.

3. RN, "Fight for Germany," 65–66.

4. RN, "Niebuhr Reports on Germany" and "Praise for Statement on Wallace Policy," *UDA Bulletin*, November 1946, 1.

5. Lee to Loeb, 19 September 1946; Loeb to Lee, 11 October 1946, ADA, ser. 2; Loeb to HAW, 23 October 1946, ADA, ser. 1.

6. RN, "Fight for Germany," 66.

7. Fox, *Reinhold Niebuhr*, 228. Also see RN to Ursula Niebuhr, 6 September 1946, RN Papers.

8. RN to Hans Stroh, 1 October 1946; and RN to Joseph M. Jones, 30 September 1946, RN Papers.

9. RN, "Will Germany Go Communist?" *The Nation*, 5 October 1946, 371–72; "Fight for Germany," 65, 67–68; "A Report on Germany," *CC*, 14 October 1946, 6; "Mr. Wallace's Errors," *CC*, 28 October 1946, 1; RN to Ursula Niebuhr, 3 September 1946, RN Papers.

10. RN, "Report on Germany," 6; "Will Germany Go Communist?" 372.

11. RN, "The Plight of Germany," *CS*, Spring 1945, 7; "Report on Germany," 6.

12. RN, "Fight for Germany," 70; "Mr. Wallace's Errors," 1.

13. RN, "Fight for Germany, 70; "Mr. Wallace's Errors," 2.

14. RN, "Fight for Germany," 72.

15. UDA, "Statement Sent to Secretary of War Stimson, April 10, 1945, by Mortimer Hays, Chairman of Union for Democratic Action's Foreign Policy Committee," ADA, ser. 1.

16. RN to Byrnes, 23 October 1946, ADA, ser. 1; RN to Truman, 22 November 1946, ADA, ser. 7. Both letters were signed by Niebuhr in his capacity as chairman of the UDA, with the letter to Truman explicitly written "on behalf of" a large group of American liberal internationalists whose names appeared below his signature. Also see UDA, "For Immediate Release," 28 October 1946; "Group Urges Reich Plants Be Socialized," *Washington Post*, 25 November 1946; and "A Memorandum on the German Problem in the Light of Soviet Policy," 23 November 1946, ADA, ser. 1.

17. UDA, "Memorandum on the German Problem," 1.

18. Ibid.

19. "Statement by Baruch on Controversy with Wallace and Texts of Exchanges between Them," *NYT*, 3 October 1946; [HAW], "Letter Proposed to Mr. Bernard M. Baruch by Telephone Call to Mr. Ferdinand Eberstadt at Approximately 4:30 P.M. on October 2, 1946," RG 40, file 104251, NA.

20. "Baruch Accuses Wallace of Errors in Atom Letter and Balking at Retraction," *NYT*, 3 October 1946; "Statement by Baruch on Controversy with Wallace."

21. "Statement of Mr. Henry A. Wallace in Reply to Mr. Bernard M. Baruch on Atomic Energy, October 3, 1946," RG 40, file 104251, NA, 1–4.

22. CIO-PAC, "Report of Conference of Progressives, Hotel Continental, Chicago, Sept. 28–29, 1946," PPUI, box 39; "Summary Release of Conference of Progressives, September 28–29," CBBUI, box 4; [Coordinating Committee, Conference of Progressives], "For Release: Upon Receipt," press release and transcript of press conference, 15 October 1946, CBBUI, box 4.

23. [Coordinating Committee, Conference of Progressives], "For Release: Upon Receipt"; Thomas J. Hamilton, "Ickes Challenges Liberals on Atom," *NYT*, 8 October 1946.

24. PCA, "Statement for Release" and the "Final Call and Program, Conference of Progressives," 22–29 September 1946, CBBUI, box 4; MacDougall, *Components of the Decision*, 113–14; Gillon, *Politics and Vision*, 16; PCA, "By-Laws, Progressive Citizens of America," December 27, 1946, and "Program for Progressives," December 29, 1946, CBBUI, box 5.

25. MacDougall, *Components of the Decision*, 113–14; Gillon, *Politics and Vision*, 16; HAW, "Unity for Progress," 29 December 1946, CBBUI; and HAW, "Jobs Peace Freedom," *NR*, 16 December 1946, 786.

26. HAW, "Unity for Progress"; "Jobs Peace Freedom," 786.

27. HAW, "Unity for Progress"; "Jobs Peace Freedom," 788; PCA, "Program for Progressives."

28. HAW, "Jobs Peace Freedom," 789.

29. ADA, "For Immediate Release: Committee of the Whole," 4 January 1947, ADA, ser. 2; Gillon, *Politics and Vision*, 16–19.

30. "For Immediate Release" (begins with words "More than 150 leaders"), 4 January 1947; "Domestic Policy," [1947]; "Foreign Policy," [1947], ADA, ser. 2.

31. HAW, "Unity for Progress"; "Jobs Peace Freedom," 789; UDA, "[Minutes of the] UDA Conference January 4, 1947," ADA, ser. 2; Gillon, *Politics and Vision*, 19–20.

32. UDA, "[Minutes of the] UDA Conference January 4, 1947."

33. Loeb to *New Republic*, release, 23 January 1947, ADA, ser. 2.

34. Loeb, "Progressives and Communists," *NR*, 13 May 1946, 699, emphasis original.

35. Morris Cooke to Jo Davidson, 21 November 1946; Cooke to Davidson, 26 November 1946; Cooke to Philadelphia Chapter of ICCASP, 24 December 1946, Jo Davidson Papers, FDRL, emphasis original; NPAC, "Minutes of Meeting of Steering Committee of National Citizens Political Action Committee," 3 December 1946, CBBUI, box 19.

36. UDA, "[Minutes of the] UDA Conference January 4, 1947."

37. HAW, "The Fight for Peace Begins," *NR*, 24 March 1947, 12; "Text of Address by Henry A. Wallace," 13 March 1947, HAWI-Speeches; "The State Department's Case," *NR*, 7 April 1947, 12; "Speech Delivered at the Central Hall, Westminster," England, 11 April 1947; and "Speech Delivered at King's Hall, Belle Vue, Manchester," England, 12 April 1947, HAWI-Speeches; PCA, "Statement on President Truman's Message to Congress on Greece and Turkey," 12 March 1947, CBBUI, box 22; "Brief Filed with Senate Foreign Relations Committee," 31 March 1947, CBBUI, box 21; HAW, "Back to the United Nations," speech, typescript, 31 March 1947, HAWI-Speeches.

38. HAW, "A Bad Case of Fever," *NR*, 14 April 1947, 12–13.

39. HAW, "Text of Address by Henry A. Wallace"; "The Fight for Peace Begins," 12–13; "The State Department's Case," 12; "The Way to Help Greece," *NR*, 17 March 1947, 12–13; and "The Truman Doctrine—or a Strong UN," *NR*, 31 March 1947, 13; ibid., 12; "Back to the United Nations." Also see HAW,

"Speech Delivered at the Central Hall, Westminster." PCA, "Statement on President Truman's Message to Congress on Greece and Turkey," and "Brief Filed with Senate Foreign Relations Committee."

40. HAW, "The Way to Help Greece," 13; "Text of Address by Henry A. Wallace"; "The Fight for Peace Begins," 13; PCA, "Statement on President Truman's Message to Congress on Greece and Turkey"; "Brief Filed with Senate Foreign Relations Committee."

41. HAW, "The Truman Doctrine—or a Strong UN," 12; "Back to the United Nations"; "The State Department's Case," 13; PCA, "Statement on President Truman's Message to Congress on Greece and Turkey"; "Brief Filed with Senate Foreign Relations Committee." Also see [PCA], "Suggestions Made on Foreign Policy Statement," 22 March 1947, CBBUI, box 20.

42. HAW, "The Way to Help Greece," 12–13; "Text of Address by Henry A. Wallace."

43. HAW, "Text of Address by Henry A. Wallace"; "Speech Delivered at the Central Hall, Westminster"; "Broadcast in the B. B. C. Home Service," 13 April 1947, HAWI-Speeches; White and Maze, *Henry A. Wallace*, 248–49.

44. Anne O'Hare McCormick, "Abroad: On Watering the Weeds of Suspicion," *NYT*, 14 April 1947; Edwin L. James, "Wallace Tour Proof We Have Free Speech," *NYT*, 13 April 1947.

45. "Wallace Disowns Third Party Aim; Vandenberg Prods Truman on Him," "Wallace Prosecution Asked as Congress Furor Mounts," both in *NYT*, 13 April 1947; "Speed on Mid-East Bill Likely as a Repudiation of Wallace," *NYT*, 16 April 1947.

46. Douglas to Secretary of State, telegram, "secret," 2 April 1947; Acheson [acting secretary] to Douglas, telegram, "secret," 4 April 1947; Hickerson to Wailes, memorandum, 5 April 1947; Caffery to Secretary of State, telegram, "top secret," 3 April 1947; Acheson to American Embassy, Paris, telegram, "top secret," 14 April 1947; Caffery to Secretary of State, telegram, "top secret," 13 April 1947; Acheson to American Legation, Stockholm, telegram, "secret," 11 April 1947; Acheson to American Legation, Bern, telegram, "top secret," 18 April 1947, NA, RG 59, decimal file 1945–49, box 16.

47. RN, "European Impressions," *CC*, 12 May 1947, 2; [ADA], release of speech by Wilson Wyatt, 8 April 1947, ADA Papers, ser. 2. On debate and division within the ADA over the Truman Doctrine, see Gillon, *Politics and Vision*, 26–29.

48. [RN], "Notes on Foreign Policy," 27 May 1947, ADA, ser. 1; release of speech by Wilson Wyatt.

49. RN, "American Power and European Health," *CC*, 9 June 1947, 1; release of speech by Wilson Wyatt; [ADA], "Text of Statement by Wilson W. Wyatt,

National Chairman of Americans for Democratic Action, and Leon Henderson, Chairman of the Executive Committee, Americans for Democratic Action, on Appointments to Greek Aid Commission," 19 April 1947, ADA, ser. 2.

50. [RN], "Notes on Foreign Policy"; release of speech by Wilson Wyatt.

51. For example, White and Maze, *Henry A. Wallace,* p. 253.

52. [PCA], "Foreign Policy," 28 June 1947, CBBUI, box 21; HAW, "What We Must Do Now," *NR,* 14 July 1947, 13; HAW, "The UN—Our Hope," *NR,* 21 July 1947, 12; HAW, "Bevin Muddies the Waters," *NR,* 30 June 1947, 11; [PCA], "Short Draft of Foreign Policy Statement," 30 September 1947; and PCA, "Statement on Foreign Policy," 4 October 1947, CBBUI, box 21.

53. HAW, "The Wallace Plan vs. the (Hoover) (Dulles) Marshall Plan, Testimony by Henry A. Wallace before the House Committee on Foreign Affairs," 24 February 1948, 4, 12, 8–9, 15–16, 21–23, HAWI; "Speech by Henry A. Wallace," 18 May 1948; and "Statement of Henry A. Wallace to Armed Services Committee, U.S. Senate," 30 March 1948, HAWI-Speeches; HAW, "Universal Military Training," *NR,* 1 December 1947, 12–14.

54. The Wallace-PCA decision to attack UMT and the draft was grounded in their very understanding of the Marshall Plan's dynamic in U.S. political culture: that many Americans genuinely appreciated the humanitarianism of the ERP. One of the best ways for outflanking the ERP in public debate, the popular fronters believed, was to use the issue of universal military training to demonstrate the "true character of our present negative national policies." Such a tactic would provide the "clearest distinction" between Wallace and the PCA on the one side and the "Administration and Republicans" on the other. LCFjr [Lew Frank] to Wallace *inter alios,* 26 November 1947, CBBUI, box 10.

55. ADA, "Toward Total Peace: A Liberal Foreign Policy for the United States" (Washington, D.C.: ADA, [1947]). Published in early December 1947, "Toward Total Peace" was written primarily by Schlesinger as chair of an ADA committee charged with the task of producing a foreign policy statement. See ADA, ser. 2, and "Abridged Proceedings of National Board Meeting of Americans for Democratic Action," vol. 2, 21 September 1947, ADA, ser. 2.

56. ADA, "Toward Total Peace," 42. Also see RN, "The Marshall Plan," *CC,* 13 October 1947, 2; and "Address of Wilson W. Wyatt, National Chairman of American for Democratic Action, Opening ADA's First National Convention," 20 February 1948, ADA, ser. 4, box 1; Richard H. Pells, *The Liberal Mind in a Conservative Age: American Intellectuals in the 1940s and 1950s,* 26; "Address of Wilson W. Wyatt." Also see Mary Sperling McAuliffe, *Crisis on the Left: Cold War Politics and American Liberals, 1947–1954,* 32.

57. RN, "The Marshall Plan," 2; ADA, "Toward Total Peace," 6, 10–12; Loeb

to "All ADA Chapters," 22 March 1948, ADA, ser. 2; RN, "Amid Encircling Gloom," *CC,* 12 April 1948, 41.

58. RN, "America's Wealth and the World's Poverty," *CS,* Autumn 1947, 3; "Progress toward Maturity," *CS,* Winter 1947, 8; "Statement of Americans for Democratic Action on the Marshall Plan," 16 July 1947, ADA, ser. 2; ADA, "Toward Total Peace," 26, emphasis original.

59. ADA, "Toward Total Peace," 22–23, 16–17. The ADA came out explicitly in favor of restoring the draft by spring 1948, although they were more hesitant regarding the UMT. Loeb to "All ADA Chapters"; ADA, "Statement on Foreign Policy," 11 April 1948, ADA, ser. 2.

60. ADA, "Toward Total Peace," 15, 38; RN, "America's Wealth and the World's Poverty," 4.

61. At the ADA convention in February 1948 Niebuhr was still willing to characterize himself as at least a "heretical socialist," by which he meant that he ascribed to what he considered the original humanitarianism of Marxism but rejected the transformation of Marxism into a "vexatious tyranny." "Address by Reinhold Niebuhr to the First National Convention of Americans for Democratic Action," 21 February 1948, ADA, ser. 4. "Statement of Paul A. Porter, for Americans for Democratic Action before the Senate Foreign Relations Committee on the European Recovery Program," 24 January 1948; "Statement of David D. Lloyd, for Americans for Democratic Action before the House Foreign Affairs Committee on the European Recovery Program," 4 February 1948, ADA, ser. 2.

62. "Address by Reinhold Niebuhr"; RN, "The 'Third Force' in Europe," *CS,* Spring 1948, 3.

63. RN, "The Sickness of American Culture," *The Nation,* 6 March 1948, 267–68; "Two Forms of Tyranny," *CC,* 2 February 1948, 4–5; "America's Wealth and the World's Poverty," 4.

CHAPTER 9

1. HAW, "Full Text of Henry A. Wallace's Speech Announcing His Independent Candidacy for President" (New York: National Wallace for President Committee, [January 1948]); "Address of Henry A. Wallace," delivered at Buffalo, N.Y., 11 December 1947, HAWI-Speeches.

2. MacDougall claims Wallace decided to run at a meeting held on 2 December 1947. MacDougall, *Components of the Decision,* 224. HAW, "Full Text of Henry A. Wallace's Speech."

3. "Address of Wilson W. Wyatt"; "Address By Reinhold Niebuhr"; Memo-

randum from ADA National Political Committee to ADA chapters, 3 January 1948, ADA, ser. 2.

4. Loeb to ADA Executive Committee, 16 March 1948, ADA, ser. 2.

5. Ibid.; Schlesinger to Libby [Elizabeth Donahue], 27 April 1948, ADA, ser. 7.

6. ADA, "Henry A. Wallace: The First Three Months" (Washington, D.C.: Americans for Democratic Action Publicity Department, [1948]), 1–3.

7. ADA, "The First Three Months," 31, ellipsis original.

8. HAW, "Where We Stand on Labor," *NR*, 30 December 1946, 911, emphasis added for contrast.

9. ADA, "The First Three Months," 8–9.

10. This was a tendency that "The First Three Months" shared with political commentator Dwight Macdonald, in his book *Henry A. Wallace: The Man and the Myth*. Macdonald's logic and approach to attacking Wallace were quite similar, if far more extensive, than those of the ADA pamphlet. In fact, it is likely that the writers of the ADA pamphlet drew on Macdonald's critique, which they were aware of at least as early as February 1948, when Macdonald and Loeb corresponded regarding the possibility of the ADA either advertising the book to its membership or reviewing it in an issue of the *ADA World*. Macdonald to Loeb, 28 February 1948; and Loeb to Macdonald, 9 March 1948, ADA, ser. 2.

11. HAW, "An Open Letter to Premier Stalin," 17 May 1948; "The Text of Stalin's Reply," *NYT*, 18 May 1948, typescript copy, PPUI, box 35.

12. ADA, "Henry A. Wallace: The Last Seven Months of His Presidential Campaign" (Washington, D.C.: Americans for Democratic Action Publications Department, [1948]), 13.

13. Chicago Council of American-Soviet Friendship, "Exchange of Notes Between the U.S.A. and the U.S.S.R.: The Soviet Union Responds to U.S. Bid for Peace," *Report on the News*, 12 May 1948, PPUI, box 35; MacDougall, *Components of the Decision*, 351–52; Markowitz, *Rise and Fall*, 274; also see Warren Moscow, "Wallace Presents Peace Bid to Stalin," *NYT*, 12 May 1948.

14. MacDougall, *Components of the Decision*, 306–9.

15. HAW, "Acceptance Speech by Henry A. Wallace," 24 July 1948, CBBUI, box 13.

16. Progressive Party Platform Committee, "Peace, Freedom, and Abundance: The Platform of the Progressive Party Adopted at the Founding Convention, Philadelphia, July 23–25, 1948," PPUI, box 9.

17. Ibid.

18. Ibid.

19. Ibid.

20. [Paul Sweezy?], "Notes for PCA Program," [June 1948?], PPUI, box 44; [ADA], "An Appeal to the Liberals of America," October 1948, ADA, ser. 2.

21. "Address by Reinhold Niebuhr"; "Platform Proposed by Americans for Democratic Action to the Democratic National Convention, 1948," ADA, ser. 4. In the name of maintaining their self-styled nonpartisanship, the ADA actually submitted the same platform proposals to the Republican National Convention in June. See untitled ADA release, 17 June 1948, ADA, ser. 2.

22. MacDougall, *Components of the Decision*, 563–71; James Hayford to MacDougall, 12 August 1952, PPUI, box 32.

23. MacDougall relates at length and verbatim the entire debate of the Vermont amendment. MacDougall, *The Decision and the Organization*, 572–78. The newspaper reports are quoted by MacDougall on p. 571.

24. Most of the literature addressing the question of communist influence upon the Progressive Party suggests that such influence was limited. Joseph R. Starobin even suggests that, contrary to the common belief that Wallace was manipulated by the communists, it was Wallace who did the manipulating, creating a "discreet liaison in which the Communists would do the work" that his own liberal associates could not or would not do. Starobin, *American Communism in Crisis, 1943–1957*, 155, 170–71, 182–84. Also see Markowitz, *Rise and Fall*, 253–56; McAuliffe, *Crisis on the Left*, 38–39; and MacDougall, *Components of the Decision*, 274–75. Guenter Lewy asserts a dominant role for the communists in the Progressive Party but provides no documentation whatsoever to substantiate his claims; nor does he contend directly with the several historians whose documented analyses disagree with his. Lewy, *The Cause That Failed: Communism in American Political Life* (New York: Oxford University Press, 1990), 216.

25. Tugwell to Peter Kortner, 8 October 1948; and Tugwell, "Open Reply to Mr. Borgese," 20 August 1948, Rexford G. Tugwell Papers, FDRL. Also see Frederick L. Schuman, "Notes and Comments on Philadelphia, July 23–25, 1948: The Founding Convention of the Progressive Party," PPUI, box 4.

26. ADA, "The Last Seven Months," 19–21; ADA, "Wallace Statement," 11 April 1948; Loeb to Harold Eskew, 7 October 1948. ADA, "Statement on Spain," 11 April 1948, ADA, ser. 2; ADA, "Platform Proposed."

27. Wallace was quoted by the ADA in "The Last Seven Months" (11). The ADA presented the quotation as an example of how far-fetched or naive Wallace's thinking could be.

28. MacDougall, *Decision and the Organization*, 494–95.

29. Ibid., 497–504.

30. Ibid., 495–98.

31. Ibid., 498–99.

32. HAW, "Statement on the Berlin Crisis," 23 July 1948, HAWI-Speeches; "Acceptance Speech," 24 July 1948, CBBUI, box 13, emphasis original.

33. White and Maze, in *Henry A. Wallace*, 269, suggest something like this when they assert that it was the Berlin blockade that "finally ensured public rejection" of Wallace's "approach to foreign policy."

34. RN, "The Battle of Berlin," *CS*, Autumn 1948, 5.

35. ADA, "The Last Seven Months," 12.

36. HAW-COHC, 5123; White and Maze, *Henry A. Wallace*, 277–80.

37. ADA, "The Last Seven Months," 19–21; also see Loeb to Eskew, 7 October 1948, ADA, ser 2.

38. Gillon, *Politics and Vision*, 44–50; Loeb to David C. Williams, 2 August 1948, ADA, ser. 2.

39. MacDougall, *Decision and the Organization*, 547–48; ADA, "Testimony of James Loeb, Jr., National Executive Secretary of Americans for Democratic Action," release, 22 July 1948, Rexford G. Tugwell Papers, FDRL. Also see Loeb to Eskew, 7 October 1948.

40. Loeb to Williams, 2 August 1948; and Loeb to Robert H. Ellis, 4 August 1948, ADA, ser. 2; ADA, "The Last Seven Months," 6.

41. ADA, "The Last Seven Months," 6.

42. Ibid., 7, 8.

43. Joseph Rauh Jr. to Loeb, 3 September 1948, ADA, ser. 2.

44. Loeb to Niebuhr, 17 September 1948; and Loeb to Leon Henderson, memorandum, 21 September 1948, ADA, ser. 2.

45. [RN], "An Appeal to American Liberals and Progressives, (Draft)," [19 September 1948], ADA, ser. 2.

46. [ADA] to "Dear So-and-So," draft cover letter, 7 October 1948, ADA, ser. 2; RN, "An Appeal."

47. See Schlesinger to Loeb, Rauh, and James A. Wechsler, 1 November 1948, memorandum regarding "Post-Election Problems of ADA"; and [ADA], "American Liberals in Politics," [late October–early November 1948], ADA, ser 2.

48. See, for example, Gillon, *Politics and Vision*, 77–82.

EPILOGUE

1. RN, *The Irony of American History* (New York: Charles Scribner's Sons, 1952); HAW, "Where I Was Wrong," *This Week Magazine*, 7 September 1952, 7, 29, 30; "The Reminiscences of Henry Agard Wallace," *NYT* Oral History Program and the Columbia University Oral History Collection. The recording of Wallace's reminiscences was done in several episodes from 1951 to 1953.

2. Fox, *Reinhold Niebuhr*, 244. For examples of historians' criticism of *Irony*'s oversimplification, see Fox, 247; and Richard Reinitz, *Irony and Consciousness: American Historiography and Reinhold Niebuhr's Vision*, 93–94, 109.

3. RN, *Irony*, 1, 57, 3, 15, 22, 65, emphasis added.

4. Ibid., 110. On p. 112, Niebuhr did briefly acknowledge the class implications of imperialism and colonialism but in such a manner as to implicitly deny any American culpability for exploitation of the Third World.

5. Ibid., 114, 128, 120.

6. Ibid., 99–100, 103, 101.

7. Ibid., 4, 45, 65, 74.

8. Ibid., 19, 37–40.

9. Ibid., 18, 8, 9. Also see p. 62.

10. Ibid., 10–11. Also see pp. 90–92.

11. Ibid., 22, 34, 75. Also p. 89.

12. Ibid., 165, 170, 153–54.

13. The confessional tone of the article, suggested by its title, was augmented by the "witch-hunt" style caption above the title on the opening page. It characterized Wallace's remarks as the "startling admissions" of a former "Russian apologist." HAW, "Where I Was Wrong," 30, 7.

14. Ibid., 30.

15. Ibid., 7, 29.

16. Numerous letters, both critical and complementary, received by Wallace in the wake of the publication of "Where I Was Wrong" indicate that readers generally viewed it as a full-scale, rather than partial, recantation of his anti–cold war stance of the late 1940s. See HAWI, microfilm reel 48.

17. HAW, "Where I Was Wrong," 29, 30.

18. "Text of Address by Henry A. Wallace, Second National Convention of The Progressive Party," 24 February 1950, Anna Eleanor Roosevelt Papers, FDRL; HAW, "March of the Common Man: Constructive or Destructive?" (address to the Community Church of Boston, 21 January 1951), Louis H. Bean Papers, FDRL.

19. HAW-COHC, 5145–47; White and Maze, *Henry A. Wallace*, 287–91. Also see HAW to Tugwell, 31 July 1950, Tugwell Papers, FDRL. For Niebuhr's view that the North Korean invasion was a Soviet "venture," see RN to Will Scarlett, [June] 1950, RN Papers. For his general approval of the U.S.-UN military effort as well as his belief in Soviet machinations in Asia, see RN, "The World Council and the Peace Issue," *CC*, 7 August 1950, 107–8; "Editorial Notes," *CC*, 16 October 1950, 130; and "New Light on the Old Struggle," *CS*, Fall 1950, 3–4.

20. Quoted in White and Maze, *Henry A. Wallace*, 289.

21. Regarding the uranium shipments, see "Testimony of Henry A. Wallace

before the House Committee on Un-American Activities," 25 January 1950, HAWI-Speeches. Microfilm reel 48 of HAWI contains literally dozens of letters and documents regarding these cases and others that Wallace battled in 1951 alone. See, for example, HAW to Henry Hazlitt, 13 March, 3 April, 10 April, and 30 April 1951; HAW to *Catholic Digest,* 21 July 1951; HAW to Truman, 19 September 1951; HAW to DeWitt Wallace, 19 June 1951; HAW to Hon. Pat McCarran, 6 June 1951, HAWI, reel 48. In one case, a book author actually lumped Wallace in a sentence with Aaron Burr and Klaus Fuchs, a sentence the publisher saw fit to remove after Wallace's protest. See HAW to William Henry Chamberlain, 22 July 1951; Chamberlain to HAW, 26 July 1951; HAW to Henry Regnery Co., 22 July, 4 August, and 13 September 1951; Henry Regnery to HAW, 31 July and 7 September 1951, HAWI, reel 48.

22. HAW to Leslie Groves, 7 March, 20 March, and 22 June 1951; and Groves to HAW, 3 July 1951; HAW to Joseph Alsop, 20 October 1951 and 23 August 1952; Alsop to HAW, 30 June, 31 July, and 20 August 1952, HAWI, reel 48.

23. HAW-COHC, 5135, 5138–39.

24. Ibid., 5158, 5172–73.

25. Ibid., 5177, 5180, 5179, 5184.

26. Ibid., 5187–88, 5189–90.

27. Ibid., 5174.

28. RN to David Riesman, 26 June and 30 June 1951; Riesman to RN, 30 June 1951, RN Papers.

29. Gillon, *Politics and Vision,* 56, 77–78.

30. Schlesinger, "Draft of Open Letter to Pandit Nehru," [10 September 1951], RN Papers.

Selected Bibliography

PRIMARY SOURCES

Manuscript Collections

National Archives
    Papers of the Secretary of Agriculture, Record Group 16
    Papers of the Secretary of Commerce, Record Group 40
    Papers of the Department of State, Record Group 59

Franklin D. Roosevelt Library
    Paul Appleby Papers
    Louis H. Bean Papers
    Adolph A. Berle Papers
    Mordecai Ezekiel Papers
    Harry L. Hopkins Papers
    Gardner Jackson Papers
    Gardiner Means Papers
    Henry Morgenthau Jr. Papers
    Anna Eleanor Roosevelt Papers
    Franklin D. Roosevelt Papers
    Samuel Rosenman Papers
    Alexander Sachs Papers
    Rexford G. Tugwell Papers
    Henry A. Wallace Papers as Vice President

State Historical Society of Wisconsin
    Papers of Americans for Democratic Action
    Papers of James Loeb

Library of Congress Manuscript Collections
    Vannevar Bush Papers
    Raymond Clapper Papers
    Tom Connally Papers
    Jo Davidson Papers
    Elmer Davis Papers

Felix Frankfurter Papers
Harold L. Ickes Papers
Jesse H. Jones Papers
Reinhold Niebuhr Papers
Joseph L. Rauh Jr. Papers
Henry A. Wallace Papers
William Allen White Papers
University of Iowa Libraries, Department of Special Collections
C. B. Baldwin Papers
Dante M. Pierce Papers
Papers of the Progressive Party
Daniel F. Riley Papers
Will Riley Papers
Fred Stover Papers
Henry A. Wallace Papers

Kirby Page Papers, Southern California School of Theology
Johan Oscar Roos (1827–1896) and Family Papers, 1856–1975, Minnesota
    Historical Society
Speeches of Henry A. Wallace, 1933–1940. University of California, Berkeley.
Eleanor Roosevelt Oral History Transcripts: Interviews with James I. Loeb and
    Joseph L. Rauh
"The Diary of Henry A. Wallace, January 18, 1935–September 19, 1946."
    Iowa City: University of Iowa, 1977.
"The Reminiscences of Henry Agard Wallace." 1963. Oral History Collection,
    Columbia University

Other Primary Sources

The journalistic output of both Niebuhr and Wallace was prodigious (during his editorship of *Wallaces' Farmer* from 1921 to 1933 alone, for example, Wallace either wrote or supervised the writing of somewhere in excess of six thousand editorial columns). In light of this I have chosen not to list either man's article bibliography, hoping that citations in the footnotes will suffice for curious readers.

Acheson, Dean. *Present at the Creation: My Years in the State Department.* New
    York: W. W. Norton, 1969.
Beard, Charles, and Mary Beard. *The Rise of American Civilization.* 1927. Single
    volume ed. New York: Macmillan, 1930.
Bergson, Henri. *Creative Evolution.* Translated by Arthur Mitchell. New York:
    Random House, 1944; Westport, Conn.: Greenwood Press, 1975.
Byrnes, James F. *All in One Lifetime.* New York: Harper and Brothers, 1958.
Dewey, John. *A Common Faith.* New Haven: Yale University Press, 1934.
———. "Intelligence and Power." *New Republic,* 25 April 1934, 306–7.
———. *Philosophy and Civilization.* New York: Minton, Balch, 1931.
Flewelling, Ralph T. *Personalism and the Problems of Philosophy.* New York: Methodist Book Concern, 1915.
Flynn, John T. *The Roosevelt Myth.* New York: Devin-Adair, 1948.
Forrestal, James. *The Forrestal Diaries.* New York: Viking, 1951.

Hayek, Friedrich A. *The Road to Serfdom.* Chicago: University of Chicago Press, 1944.

Hellman, Lillian. *Scoundrel Time.* Boston: Little, Brown, 1976.

Hull, Cordell. *The Memoirs of Cordell Hull.* 2 vols. New York: Macmillan, 1948.

Ickes, Harold L. *The First Thousand Days: 1933–1936.* Vol. 1 of *The Secret Diary of Harold L. Ickes.* New York: Simon and Schuster, 1953.

———. *The Inside Struggle: 1936–1939.* Vol. 2 of *The Secret Diary of Harold L. Ickes.* New York: Simon and Schuster, 1954.

———. *The Lowering Clouds: 1939–1941.* Vol. 3 of *The Secret Diary of Harold L. Ickes.* New York: Simon and Schuster, 1954.

James, William. *A Pluralistic Universe.* London: Longmans, Green, 1909.

Johndro, L. Edward. *The Earth in the Heavens: Ruling Degrees of Cities, How to Find Them.* 1929. New York: Samuel Weiser, 1973.

———. *The Stars: How and Where They Influence.* San Bernardino, Calif.: Doherty Publishing Co., 1929.

Judge, William Quan. *Echoes from the Orient: A Broad Outline of Theosophical Doctrines.* 1890. Point Loma, Calif.: Aryan Theosophical Press, 1921.

———. *William Quan Judge, 1851–1896: The Life of a Theosophical Pioneer and Some of His Outstanding Articles.* Compiled by Sven Eek and Boris de Zirkoff. Wheaton, Ill.: Theosophical Publishing House, 1969.

Keynes, John Maynard. *The Economic Consequences of the Peace.* New York: Harcourt, Brace and Howe, 1920.

Knudson, Albert C. *The Philosophy of Personalism.* New York: Abingdon Press, 1927; New York: Kraus Reprint, 1969.

Macdonald, Dwight. *Henry Wallace: The Man and the Myth.* New York: Vanguard, 1947.

Millis, Walter, ed., with E. S. Duffield. *The Forrestal Diaries.* New York: Viking, 1951.

Niebuhr, Reinhold. *Beyond Tragedy.* New York: Charles Scribner's Sons, 1937; Salem, N.H.: Ayer, 1984.

———. *The Children of Light and the Children of Darkness: A Vindication of Democracy and a Critique of Its Traditional Defense.* New York: Charles Scribner's Sons, 1944.

———. *Christianity and Power Politics.* New York: Charles Scribner's Sons, 1940.

———. *The Contribution of Religion to Social Work.* New York: Columbia University Press, 1932; New York: AMS Press, 1971.

———. *Does Civilization Need Religion? A Study of the Social Resources and Limitations of Religion in Modern Life.* New York: Macmillan, 1927.

———. *The Essential Reinhold Niebuhr: Selected Essays and Addresses.* Edited by Robert McAfee Brown. New Haven: Yale University Press, 1986.

———. *An Interpretation of Christian Ethics.* New York: Harper and Brothers, 1935.

———. *The Irony of American History.* New York: Charles Scribner's Sons, 1952.

———. *Leaves from the Notebook of a Tamed Cynic.* 1929. New York: Richard R. Smith, 1930.

———. *Love and Justice: Selections from the Shorter Writings of Reinhold Niebuhr.* Edited by D. B. Robertson. Philadelphia: Westminster Press, 1957.

———. *Moral Man and Immoral Society: A Study in Ethics and Politics.* New York: Charles Scribner's Sons, 1932.

———. *The Nature and Destiny of Man: A Christian Interpretation.* Vol. 1, *Human Nature;* vol. 2, *Human Destiny.* New York: Charles Scribner's Sons, 1943.

———. *Reflections on the End of an Era.* 1934. New York: Charles Scribner's Sons, 1936.

———. *Reinhold Niebuhr on Politics: His Political Philosophy and Its Application to Our Age as Expressed in His Writings.* Edited by Harry R. Davis and Robert C. Good. New York: Charles Scribner's Sons, 1960.

———. *Young Reinhold Niebuhr: His Early Writings, 1911–1931.* Edited by William G. Chrystal. St. Louis: Eden Publishing House, 1977.

Norris, George W. *Fighting Liberal: The Autobiography of George W. Norris.* New York: Macmillan, 1945.

Rauschenbusch, Walter. *Christianity and the Social Crisis.* New York: Macmillan, 1907; Harper Torchbooks, 1964.

Roerich, Nicholas. *Realm of Light.* New York: Roerich Museum Press, 1931.

Russell, George "Æ." *The Candle of Vision.* London: Macmillan, 1920.

———. *Cooperation and Nationality.* 1912. Chicago: Cooperative League, 1940.

Stimson, Henry L., and McGeorge Bundy. *On Active Service in Peace and War.* New York: Harper and Brothers, 1947, 1948.

Truman, Harry S. *Off the Record: The Private Papers of Harry S. Truman.* Edited by Robert H. Ferrell. New York: Harper and Row, 1980.

———. *Year of Decisions.* Vol. 1 of *Memoirs by Harry S. Truman.* New York: Doubleday, 1955.

———. *Years of Trial and Hope.* Vol. 2 of *Memoirs by Harry S. Truman.* New York: Doubleday, 1956.

Tugwell, Rexford G. *A Chronicle of Jeopardy: 1945–55.* Chicago: University of Chicago Press, 1955.

U.S. Congress. Senate. Committee on Foreign Relations. *To Promote the Defense of the United States.* 77th Cong., 1st sess., 1941. S. 275, part 1.

Veblen, Thorstein. *The Engineers and the Price System.* New York: B. W. Huebsch, 1921.

———. *The Instinct of Workmanship and the State of the Industrial Arts.* New York: Macmillan, 1914; New York: Augustus M. Kelley, 1964.

———. *The Theory of Business Enterprise.* New York: Charles Scribner's Sons, 1904; New York: New American Library, Mentor Books, 1958.

———. *The Theory of the Leisure Class: An Economic Study of Institutions.* New York: Macmillan, 1899; New York: Random House, Modern Library, 1934.

Wallace, Henry A. *America Must Choose: The Advantages and Disadvantages of Nationalism, of World Trade, and of a Planned Middle Course.* World Affairs Pamphlets, no. 3. New York: Foreign Policy Association, and Boston: World Peace Foundation, 1934.

———. *The American Choice.* New York: Reynal and Hitchcock, 1940.

———. *The Century of the Common Man.* Edited by Russell Lord. New York: Reynal and Hitchcock, [1943].

———. *Democracy Reborn.* Edited by Russell Lord. New York: Reynal and Hitchcock, [1944]; Da Capo Press, 1973.

———. *New Frontiers.* New York: Reynal and Hitchcock, 1934.

———. *Our Job in the Pacific.* New York: American Council Institute of Pacific Relations, 1944.

———. *Paths to Plenty.* Washington, D.C.: National Home Library Foundation, 1938.

———. *The Price of Freedom.* Washington, D.C.: National Home Library Foundation, 1940.

———. *The Price of Vision: The Diary of Henry A. Wallace, 1942–1946.* Edited by John M. Blum. Boston: Houghton Mifflin, 1973.

———. *Sixty Million Jobs.* New York: Reynal and Hitchcock; Simon and Schuster, 1945.

———. *Soviet-Asia Mission.* With the collaboration of Andrew J. Steiger. New York: Reynal and Hitchcock, 1946.

———. *Statesmanship and Religion.* London: Williams and Norgate, 1934.

———. *Technology, Corporations, and the General Welfare.* Chapel Hill: University of North Carolina Press, 1937.

———. *Whose Constitution? An Inquiry into the General Welfare.* New York: Reynal and Hitchcock, 1936; Westport, Conn.: Greenwood Press, 1971.

Wallace, Henry A., and William L. Brown. *Corn and Its Early Fathers.* [East Lansing]: Michigan State University Press, 1956.

Weber, Max. *From Max Weber: Essays in Sociology.* Translated and edited by H. H. Gerth and C. Wright Mills. New York: Oxford University Press, 1946.

SECONDARY SOURCES

Adler, Les K., and Thomas G. Paterson. "Red Fascism: The Merger of Nazi Germany and Soviet Russia in the American Image of Totalitarianism, 1930's–1950's." *American Historical Review* 75 (1970): 1046–64.

Almond, Gabriel A. *The American People and Foreign Policy.* 1950. New York: Praeger, 1960.

Anderson, Clifford B. "The Metamorphosis of American Agrarian Idealism in the 1920's and 1930's." *Agricultural History* 35 (1961): 182–88.

Bingham, June. *Courage to Change.* New York, 1961.

Blum, John Morton. *Years of Crisis: 1928–1938.* Vol. 1 of *From the Morgenthau Diaries.* Boston: Houghton Mifflin, 1959.

———. *Years of Urgency: 1938–1941.* Vol. 2 of *From the Morgenthau Diaries.* Boston: Houghton Mifflin, 1965.

———. *Years of War: 1941–1945.* Vol. 3 of *From the Morgenthau Diaries.* Boston: Houghton Mifflin, 1967.

Boyer, Paul. *By the Bomb's Early Light: American Thought and Culture at the Dawn of the Atomic Age.* New York: Pantheon Books, 1985.

Burns, James MacGregor. *Roosevelt: The Lion and the Fox.* New York: Harcourt, Brace and World, 1956.

———. *Roosevelt: The Soldier of Freedom.* New York: Harcourt Brace Jovanovich, 1970.

Campbell, Bruce F. *Ancient Wisdom Revived: A History of the Theosophical Movement.* Berkeley: University of California Press, 1980.

Coffey, John W. *Political Realism in American Thought.* Lewisburg, Pa.: Bucknell University Press, 1977.

Cohen, Warren I. *The American Revisionists: The Lessons of Intervention in World War I.* Chicago: University of Chicago Press, 1967.

Conkin, Paul K. *The Southern Agrarians.* Knoxville: University of Tennessee Press, 1988.

Dallek, Robert. *The American Style of Foreign Policy: Cultural Politics and Foreign Affairs.* New York: Alfred A. Knopf, 1983.

———. *Franklin D. Roosevelt and American Foreign Policy, 1932–1945.* New York: Oxford University Press, 1979.

Diggins, John P. *The American Left in the Twentieth Century.* New York: Harcourt Brace Jovanovich, 1973.

———. *The Rise and Fall of the American Left.* New York: W. W. Norton, 1992.

Divine, Robert A. *Second Chance: The Triumph of Internationalism in America during World War II.* New York: Atheneum, 1967.

Ekirch, Arthur, Jr. "Charles A. Beard and Reinhold Niebuhr: Contrasting Conceptions of National Interest in American Foreign Policy." *Mid-America* 59 (April–July 1977): 103–16.

Fairlie, Henry. *The Spoiled Child of the Western World: The Miscarriage of the American Idea in Our Time.* Garden City, N.J.: Doubleday, 1976.

Ferrell, Robert H. *American Diplomacy in the Great Depression: Hoover-Stimson Foreign Policy, 1929–1933.* New York: W. W. Norton, 1957.

Fitz-Simons, Daniel Whitford. "Henry A. Wallace: Diplomat, Ideologue, and Administrator, 1940–1945." Ph.D. diss., St. John's University, 1977.

Foster, James Caldwell. *The Union Politic: The CIO Political Action Committee.* Columbia: University of Missouri Press, 1975.

Fox, Richard Wightman. *Reinhold Niebuhr: A Biography.* San Francisco: Harper and Row, 1985.

———. "Reinhold Niebuhr: Self-Made Intellectual." *Library of Congress Quarterly* 40 (1983): 48–55.

———. "Reinhold Niebuhr and the Emergence of Liberal Realism, 1930–1945." *Review of Politics* 38 (April 1976): 244–65.

———. "Who Can but Prophesy? The Life of Reinhold Niebuhr." *Wilson Quarterly* 8 (Autumn 1984): 82–93.

Freeland, Richard M. *The Truman Doctrine and the Origins of McCarthyism: Foreign Policy, Domestic Politics, and Internal Security, 1946–1948.* 1970. New York: New York University Press, 1985.

Gaddis, John Lewis. *The United States and the Origins of the Cold War, 1941–1947.* New York: Columbia University Press, 1972.

Gilbert, Martin. *The Roots of Appeasement.* New York: New American Library, Plume Books, 1966.

Gillon, Steven M. *Politics and Vision: The ADA and American Liberalism, 1947–1985.* New York: Oxford University Press, 1987.

Graebner, William. *The Age of Doubt: American Thought and Culture in the 1940s.* Boston: Twayne Publishers, 1991.

Hamby, Alonzo. "Henry A. Wallace, the Liberals, and Soviet-American Relations." *Review of Politics* 30 (1968): 153–69.

———. "Sixty Million Jobs and the People's Revolution: The Liberals, the New Deal, and World War II." *Historian* 30 (1968): 578–98.

Harries, Richard, ed. *Reinhold Niebuhr and the Issues of Our Time.* Grand Rapids, Mich.: William B. Eerdmans, 1986.

Hartz, Louis. *The Liberal Tradition in America: An Interpretation of American Political Thought since the Revolution.* New York: Harcourt Brace Jovanovich, 1955.

Hays, Samuel P. *The Response to Industrialism, 1885–1914.* Chicago: University of Chicago Press, 1957.

Hicks, John D. *Republican Ascendancy, 1921–1933.* New York: Harper and Row, 1960; Harper Torchbooks, 1963.

Hofstadter, Richard. *The Age of Reform: From Bryan to F. D. R.* New York: Vintage Books, 1955.

Hunt, Michael H. *Ideology and U.S. Foreign Policy.* New Haven: Yale University Press, 1987.

Kegley, Charles W., ed. *Reinhold Niebuhr: His Religious, Social, and Political Thought.* 2d ed. New York: Pilgrim Press, 1984.

Kennan, George F. *American Diplomacy, 1900–1950.* Chicago: University of Chicago Press, 1951.

Kennedy, Thomas C. *Charles A. Beard and American Foreign Policy.* Gainesville: University of Florida Presses, 1975.

Kirkendall, Richard S. "Henry A. Wallace's Turn toward the New Deal, 1921–1924." *Annals of Iowa* 49 (Winter/Spring 1988): 221–39.

———. "The Mind of a Farm Leader." *Annals of Iowa* 47 (Fall 1983): 138–53.

———. *Social Scientists and Farm Politics in the Age of Roosevelt.* Columbia: University of Missouri Press, 1966.

Kirschner, Don S. "Henry A. Wallace as Farm Editor." *American Quarterly* 17 (1965): 187–202.

Kuklick, Bruce. *Churchmen and Philosophers: From Jonathan Edwards to John Dewey.* New Haven: Yale University Press, 1985.

LaFeber, Walter. *America, Russia, and the Cold War: 1945–1966.* New York: John Wiley and Sons, 1967.

Lasch, Christopher. *The New Radicalism in America, 1889–1963: The Intellectual as Social Type.* New York: Alfred A. Knopf, 1965.

Layton, Edwin. "Veblen and the Engineers." *American Quarterly* 14 (1962): 64–72.

Lears, T. J. Jackson. *No Place of Grace: Antimodernism and the Transformation of American Culture, 1880–1920.* New York: Pantheon Books, 1981.

Leuchtenburg, William E. *Franklin D. Roosevelt and the New Deal, 1932–1940.* New York: Harper and Row, 1963; Harper Colophon Books, 1963.

———. *The Perils of Prosperity, 1914–1932.* Chicago: University of Chicago Press, 1958.

Lord, Russell. *The Wallaces of Iowa.* Boston: Houghton Mifflin, 1947.

Lowitt, Richard, and Judith Fabry, eds. *Henry A. Wallace's Irrigation Frontier: On the Trail of the Cornbelt Farmer, 1909.* Norman: University of Oklahoma Press, 1991.

McAuliffe, Mary Sperling. *Crisis on the Left: Cold War Politics and American Liberals, 1947–1954.* Amherst: University of Massachusetts Press, 1978.

McCullough, David. *Truman.* New York: Simon and Schuster, 1992.

MacDougall, Curtis D. *The Components of the Decision.* Vol. 1 of *Gideon's Army.* New York: Marzani and Munsell, 1965.

———. *The Decision and the Organization.* Vol. 2 of *Gideon's Army.* New York: Marzani and Munsell, 1965.

———. *The Campaign and the Vote.* Vol. 3 of *Gideon's Army.* New York: Marzani and Munsell, 1965.

Maddux, Thomas R. "Red Fascism, Brown Bolshevism: The American Image of Totalitarianism in the 1930s." *Historian* 40 (1977): 85–103.

Markowitz, Norman D. *The Rise and Fall of the People's Century: Henry A. Wallace and American Liberalism, 1941–1948.* New York: Free Press, 1973.

May, Henry F. *The End of American Innocence: A Study of the First Years of Our Own Time, 1912–1917.* New York: Oxford University Press, 1959.

Merkley, Paul. *Reinhold Niebuhr: A Political Account.* Montreal: McGill-Queen's University Press, 1975.

Meyer, Donald. *The Protestant Search for Political Realism, 1919–1941.* 2d ed. Middletown, Conn.: Wesleyan University Press, 1988.

Namorato, Michael V. *Rexford G. Tugwell: A Biography.* New York: Praeger, 1988.

Noble, David W. *The End of American History: Democracy, Capitalism, and the Metaphor of Two Worlds in Anglo-American Historical Writing, 1880–1980.* Minneapolis: University of Minnesota Press, 1985.

Pells, Richard H. *The Liberal Mind in a Conservative Age: American Intellectuals in the 1940s and 1950s.* New York: Harper and Row, 1985.

———. *Radical Visions and American Dreams: Culture and Social Thought in the Depression Years.* New York: Harper and Row, 1973.

Pierce, Robert Clayton. "Liberals and the Cold War: Union for Democratic Action and Americans for Democratic Action, 1940–1949." Ph.D. diss., University of Wisconsin, Madison, 1979.

Radosh, Ronald, and Leonard P. Liggio. "Henry A. Wallace and the Open Door." In *Cold War Critics,* edited by Thomas G. Paterson. Chicago: Quadrangle Books, 1971.

Reinitz, Richard. *Irony and Consciousness: American Historiography and Reinhold Niebuhr's Vision.* Lewisburg, Pa.: Bucknell University Press, 1980.

Ribuffo, Leo. "Fascists, Nazis and American Minds: Perceptions and Preconceptions." *American Quarterly* 26 (1974): 417–32.

Rice, Daniel F. *Reinhold Niebuhr and John Dewey: An American Odyssey.* Albany: State University of New York Press, 1993.

Robertson, D. B. *Reinhold Niebuhr's Works: A Bibliography.* New York: University Press of America, 1983.

Robertson, David. *Sly and Able: A Political Biography of James F. Byrnes.* New York: W. W. Norton, 1994.

Rosenof, Theodore. *Patterns of Political Economy in America: The Failure to Develop a Democratic Left Synthesis, 1933–1950.* New York: Garland, 1983.

Ross, Irwin. *The Loneliest Campaign: The Truman Victory of 1948.* New York: New American Library, 1968.

Rouse, Joseph. *Knowledge and Power: Toward a Political Philosophy of Science.* Ithaca: Cornell University Press, 1987.

Schapsmeier, Edward L., and Frederick H. Schapsmeier. "Henry A. Wallace: New Deal Philosopher." *Historian* 32 (1970): 177–90.

———. *Henry A. Wallace of Iowa: The Agrarian Years, 1910–1940.* Ames: Iowa State University Press, 1968.

———. *Prophet in Politics: Henry A. Wallace and the War Years, 1940–1965.* Ames: Iowa State University Press, 1970.

———. "Religion and Reform: A Case Study of Henry A. Wallace and Ezra Taft Benson." *Journal of Church and State* 21 (1979): 525–35.

———. "The Wallaces and Their Farm Paper: A Story of Agrarian Leadership." *Journalism Quarterly* 44 (1967): 289–96.

Schaub, Thomas Hill. *American Fiction in the Cold War.* Madison: University of Wisconsin Press, 1991.

Schlesinger, Arthur M., Jr. *The Crisis of the Old Order.* Vol. 1 of *The Age of Roosevelt.* Boston: Houghton Mifflin, 1957.

———. *The Coming of the New Deal.* Vol. 2 of *The Age of Roosevelt.* Boston: Houghton Mifflin, 1959.

———. *The Politics of Upheaval.* Vol. 3 of *The Age of Roosevelt.* Boston: Houghton Mifflin, 1960.

———. *The Vital Center: The Politics of Freedom.* Boston: Houghton Mifflin, 1949.

Shanley, Kevin Michael. "Reinhold Niebuhr and Relations between Germany and America (1916–1956)." Ph.D. diss., State University of New York at Albany, 1984.

Sherwin, Martin J. *A World Destroyed: The Atomic Bomb and the Grand Alliance.* New York: Vintage Books, 1977.

Shi, David E. *The Simple Life: Plain Living and High Thinking in American Culture.* New York: Oxford University Press, 1985.

Sillars, Malcolm O. "Henry A. Wallace's Editorials on Agricultural Discontent, 1921–1928." *Agricultural History* 26 (1952).

Sirevag, Torbjörn. *The Eclipse of the New Deal and the Fall of Vice-President Wallace, 1944.* New York: Garland, 1985.

Smith, Geoffrey S. "Isolationism, the Devil, and the Advent of the Second World War: Variations on a Theme." *International History Review* 4 (1982): 55–89.

———. *To Save a Nation: American Countersubversives, the New Deal, and the Coming of World War II.* New York: Basic Books, 1973.

Smith, Michael Joseph. *Realist Thought from Weber to Kissinger.* Baton Rouge: Louisiana State University Press, 1986.

Smith, Ruth Lynette. "The Individual and Society in Reinhold Niebuhr and Karl Marx." Ph.D. diss., Boston University, 1982.

Starobin, Joseph R. *American Communism in Crisis, 1943–1957.* Cambridge: Harvard University Press, 1972.

Steel, Ronald. *Walter Lippmann and the American Century.* New York: Vintage Books, 1981.

Steigerwald, David. *Wilsonian Idealism in America.* Ithaca: Cornell University Press, 1994.

Stone, Ronald H. *Christian Realism and Peacemaking: U.S. Foreign Policy.* Decatur, Ga.: Abingdon Press, 1988.

———. *Reinhold Niebuhr: Prophet to Politicians.* New York: University Press of America, 1981.

Swain, Bruce M. "Henry A. Wallace and the 'Guru Letters': A Case of Successful Stonewalling." *Mid-America* 69 (1987): 5–19.

Thompson, Kenneth W. "Moral Reasoning in American Thought on War and Peace." *Review of Politics* 39 (1977): 386–99.

Tietje, Louis H. "Was Reinhold Niebuhr Ever a Marxist?" Ph.D. diss., Union Theological Seminary, 1984.

Toulouse, Mark G. *The Transformation of John Foster Dulles: From Prophet of Realism to Priest of Nationalism.* Macon, Ga.: Mercer University Press, 1985.

Walker, J. Samuel. *Henry A. Wallace and American Foreign Policy.* Westport, Conn.: Greenwood Press, 1976.

Walker, J. Samuel, and Charles J. Errico. "The New Deal and the Guru." *American Heritage,* March 1989, 92–99.

Walton, Richard J. *Henry Wallace, Harry Truman, and the Cold War.* New York: Viking, 1976.

Weiler, Richard Michael. "Statesmanship, Religion, and the General Welfare: The Rhetoric of Henry A. Wallace." Ph.D. diss., University of Pittsburgh, 1980.

West, Cornel. *The American Evasion of Philosophy: A Genealogy of Pragmatism.* Madison: University of Wisconsin Press, 1989.

West, Elliot. "The Roots of Conflict: Soviet Images in the American Press, 1941–1947." In *Essays on American Foreign Policy,* edited by Margaret F. Morris and Sandra L. Myres. The Walter Prescott Webb Memorial Lectures, no. 8. Austin: University of Texas Press, 1974.

Westbrook, Robert B. *John Dewey and American Democracy.* Ithaca: Cornell University Press, 1991.

White, Ronald C., Jr., and C. Howard Hopkins. *The Social Gospel: Religion and Reform in Changing America.* Philadelphia: Temple University Press, 1976.

White, Graham, and John Maze. *Henry A. Wallace: His Search for a New World Order.* Chapel Hill: University of North Carolina Press, 1995.

Wiebe, Robert H. *The Search for Order, 1877–1920.* New York: Hill and Wang, 1967.

Williams, William Appleman. *The Tragedy of American Diplomacy.* Revised ed. New York: Dell, 1962.

Wilson, Theodore A. "Henry Agard Wallace and the Progressive Faith." In *Three Progressives from Iowa: Gilbert N. Haugen, Herbert C. Hoover, Henry A. Wallace,* edited by John N. Schact. Iowa City: Center for the Study of the Recent History of the United States, 1980.

Wittner, Lawrence S. "Pursuing the 'National Interest': The Illusion of Realism." *Reviews in American History* 13 (June 1985): 282–87.

Index

357

360 *Index*

Dubinsky, David, 181, 231
Dukakis, Michael, x
Dumbarton Oaks plan, 157, 182–85.
See also United Nations

"Economic Council for Europe": UDA
argument for, 223
Economic Defense Board, 145
economic imperatives: foreign policy
and, 306 n.4
economic nationalism, 63–66, 81
economy: effect of war on, 63–65, 180;
effect on working class, 70–71; fascism and, 138–39; Progressive Party
platform on, 265–66; UN and, 185;
U.S., 113; Wallace's theory, 43–44.
See also Germany: economy; global
economy
Eden Theological Seminary, 17
Edinburgh University, 135
education: Dewey on, 99–100
Eisenhower, Dwight, xiii, 246
employment. *See* full employment
Employment Act of 1946, 182
Epstein, Ethel S., 189, 190, 231
espionage, xiv, 291
Ethiopia, 109
Europe: occupation policy, 185; unrest
in, 116–17; U.S. role in revitalization
of, 180; Wallace on, 295
European Recovery Program (ERP). *See*
Marshall Plan
Evangelical Herald, 68
experiential knowledge, 52, 99, 100

factories: Niebuhr's criticism of, 59–60
farmers: cooperation among, 103–4. *See
also* agriculture; rural society
Farrell-Peron regime, 187
fascism: ADA on, 249; capitalism and,
123–25; economy and, 138–39; in
Germany, 93, 109; liberals' fear of,
233; Niebuhr on, 82–83, 93–94, 96,
112, 114–15, 123–25, 128, 136,
138–39, 151, 172, 249; popular front
liberals on, 230, 238–39, 244–46,
264; threat of, 138–39, 144, 158,

168, 222, 249; UDA on, 137–40,
144, 148–51, 158, 187–88; Wallace
on, 91, 106, 168. *See also* Nazism
Federal Employee Loyalty Program
(FELP), 238
Fellowship of Reconciliation, 107
feudalism: Niebuhr's perception of, 285
"Fight for Germany, The" (Niebuhr), x,
216–23
Fischer, Louis, 236
Ford, Henry, 60, 86–87
foreign policy, xiv; on atomic energy,
201–7; economic imperatives and,
306 n.4; toward Germany, 210, 219,
220, 221–23, 245–46; liberal split
over, 214–15; Niebuhr on, 116, 132–
33, 159, 304 n.2; progressive liberals
on, 182, 264, 269–70, 280; UDA on,
165, 182–85, 191, 221–23; Wallace
on, 7, 237–41, 245–46; on war
debts, 41–42. *See also* Marshall Plan;
Truman Doctrine
Forrestal, James, 200–202
Fox, Richard, 54, 99, 136, 218, 284
France: failure to support League of
Nations sanctions, 109–10; State Department cooperation with, 147, 149;
treatment of Germany, 79; war debts,
80
Franco, Francisco, 114
freedom of expression, 129
full employment: UDA on, 158, 177,
180–82; Wallace on, 156–57, 178–
82

Gaddis, John Lewis, xiv
Galbraith, John Kenneth, 231
Gallup polls, 306–7 n.7
genealogy: Wallace on, 310 n.11
General Assembly, 182
general welfare: Wallace's definition of,
113, 114, 324–25 n.2
genetic equality: Wallace on, 119
geopolitics, 170, 251, 287
German American Bund, 138
German-Americans: Niebuhr on, 54–
56, 57, 317 n.12

buhr, 213, 216; on split within UDA, 190; on third-party movement, 232; on Wallace and Progressives, 177–78, 216–17, 256, 277–78; on Wallace's resignation as secretary of commerce, 212–14
Logan Act, 241
London Conference, 64–65
Long, Huey, 96, 106
"Long Telegram," 217
Louisville Courier-Journal, 268
loyalty investigations, 238, 246
Lubin, Isador, 231
"Lublin Pole" government, Poland, 187
Luce, Henry, x
Ludendorff, Eric von, 68

MacDonald, Dwight, 307 n.11, 342 n.10
MacDougall, Curtis, 271–73
Manchuria, 109
Manhattan Project, 196, 225
Markowitz, Norman D., 12
Marshall, George, 245
Marshall Plan, 220, 223, 243, 245; Niebuhr and ADA on, 245–53; Wallace and Progressives on, 245–46, 264, 340 n.54
Marxism: religion and, 94–97, 126; science and, 95; in Soviet Union, 97–98. *See also* Niebuhr, Reinhold: on Marxism
Masaryk, Jan, 247–48, 260
May-Johnson bill, 196, 197, 198
McCarthy, Joseph, xii
McCarthy era, 290, 294
McCormick, Anne O'Hare, 240
McMahon Act, 197, 198, 199, 203
McNary-Haugen bill, 45–46, 315 n.68
Mexico: cultural interchange with U.S., 326 n.21; U.S. oil companies in, 122; Wallace on, 122–23, 145
Middle East, 285
military: bases in Iceland, 192–93; control of atomic energy, 195–99; Wallace on dangers of, 230
military-industrial complex, 230, 246
Monroe Doctrine, 85

morality: individuality and, 159–60; personality and, 72; of total war, 152–53; urbanization and, 317 n.18; of U.S., 84–86, 159. *See also* human nature; Niebuhr, Reinhold: on morality; religion
Moral Man and Immoral Society (Niebuhr), 62, 77, 99, 101, 108, 128, 184
Morgenthau, Henry, Jr., 10, 226
Mumford, Lewis, 7, 95–96
Munich, xi, xiv, 125, 187; Niebuhr and, 21, 123–25, 162–63, 218, 280, 288, 300
Murray, Philip, 181, 226
Myrdal, Gunnar, 306 n.7
mysticism: Wallace and, 24–25

Nation, The, 75, 77
National Citizens Political Action Committee (NCPAC), 198, 209, 226. *See also* Conference of Progressives; Progressive Citizens of America
nationalism: economic, 63–66, 81; German, 61–62, 63; individuality and, 61–63; Niebuhr on, 61–63, 70, 77; Soviet, 172; U.S., 166–67, 172; Wallace on, 89, 113, 116–17. *See also* imperialism
"Nation's Crime Against the Individual, The" (Niebuhr), 61
Native American culture, 29, 31
Nature and Destiny of Man, The (Niebuhr), 135–37
Nazi Party, 68–69, 109; claim on Czechoslovakia, 117
Nazism: Niebuhr on, 125–31, 170, 221, 326 n.30; postwar fear of, 222; Wallace and Progressives on, 119, 120, 132, 153, 264
Nazi-Soviet pact, 234
NCPAC. *See* National Citizens Political Action Committee
neutrality: Niebuhr on, 115–16
Neutrality Act of 1939, 137–38
New Age, 87–89, 105, 121, 154, 239–40; atomic era and, 196–97; World War II and, 161